PIONEER MOTHER MONUMENTS

PIONEER MOTHER MONUMENTS

Constructing Cultural Memory

CYNTHIA CULVER PRESCOTT

UNIVERSITY OF OKLAHOMA PRESS : NORMAN

Earlier versions of parts of chapters 2 and 4 appeared in "The All-American Eternal Family: Sacred and Secular Values in Western Pioneer Monuments," in *We Are What We Remember: The American Past through Commemoration*, edited by Jeffrey Lee Meriwether and Laura Mattoon D'Amore, 334–58 (Cambridge: Cambridge Scholars Publishing, 2012). Published with the permission of Cambridge Scholars Publishing.

Portions of chapters 2, 3, and 4 were previously published in "Representing the Ideal American Family: Avard Tennyson Fairbanks and the Transformation of the Western Pioneer Monument," *Pacific Historical Review* 85, no. 1 (February 2016): 110–42. Reprinted with the permission of the University of California Press.

Some material from chapters 5 and 7 has previously appeared in "Pioneer Mothers for the New Millennium," in *Excavating Memory: Sites of Remembering and Forgetting*, edited by Maria Theresia Starzmann and John R. Roby (Gainesville: University Press of Florida, 2016). Reprinted with permission of the University Press of Florida.

LIBRARY OF CONGRESS CATALOGING-IN-PUBLICATION DATA

Names: Prescott, Cynthia Culver, 1975– author.
Title: Pioneer mother monuments : constructing cultural memory / Cynthia Culver Prescott.
Description: First edition. | Norman, OK : University of Oklahoma Press, [2019] | Includes bibliographical references and index.
Identifiers: LCCN 2018025085 | ISBN 978-0-8061-6197-6 (hardcover : alk. paper)
Subjects: LCSH: Women pioneers—Monuments—West (U.S.) | Frontier and pioneer life in art. | Nationalism and collective memory—United States. | National characteristics, American. | Sex role—United States—History. | Whites—Race identity—United States. | United States—Race relations.
Classification: LCC E21 .P74 2019 | DDC 305.800973—dc23
LC record available at https://lccn.loc.gov/2018025085

The paper in this book meets the guidelines for permanence and durability of the Committee on Production Guidelines for Book Longevity of the Council on Library Resources, Inc. ∞

1 2 3 4 5 6 7 8 9 10

CONTENTS

ILLUSTRATIONS

COLOR PLATES

FIGURES

MAPS

PREFACE

When I tell people that I am a historian, they often remark that history is boring. But when I say that I research and teach about the American West, their expressions quickly turn to excitement. "Ooh, I love the Old West," they tell me. For many, the West conjures images of dusty mining towns or cowboys on the open range. Enter John Wayne in a cowboy hat. Or, for my millennial students, HBO's *Deadwood*. If women appear at all, they are nameless saloon girls or prostitutes. Those who grew up watching *Little House on the Prairie* on television in the 1970s, or playing the *Oregon Trail* computer game in the 1980s, might think of covered wagons, women, and children. But even Melissa Gilbert's spunky television character bears only a limited resemblance to the imagery depicted in prominent pioneer mother monuments erected over the past 125 years—let alone the realities of frontier life. And whether any women appear in popular memory of the Old West, we remember the West as a wild land settled by white, English-speaking Americans. Spanish-speaking and African American settlers, Asian and European immigrants rarely appear. And indigenous peoples appear only as "savages" to be defeated or displaced.

Reading Laura Ingalls Wilder's classic *Little House* series as a child sparked in me a lifelong fascination with frontier life. Reading those books with my mother might have even launched me on my future career as a historian of gender in the American West. Rereading *Little House on the Prairie* now with my daughter, I notice elements of Wilder's stories that I glossed over as a child: The Ingalls family's fear of indigenous peoples, and young Laura's determination to see a "papoose," just as she viewed baby animals running wild on the prairie. The Ingalls' eagerness to squat on Native lands, where Pa can pull himself up by his bootstraps seemingly unaided by federal policies displacing indigenous peoples and supporting western settlement and railroad construction. Wilder's construction of Ma Ingalls as a longsuffering pioneer mother, and Ma's determination to bring white civilization to wild western lands. Laura's resistance to being constrained under a wide-brimmed sunbonnet designed to protect her femininity and whiteness. The *Little House* books contain wonderful stories with engaging characters, yet they also reveal the roles of race and gender within popular memory of the American West.

While introducing my daughter to the wonders of frontier life through the pages of Wilder's best-known novel for children, I have also been savoring Pamela Smith Hill's rich annotation of Wilder's autobiography, *Pioneer Girl*.[1] Reading these two overlapping narratives of Anglo-American western settlement by one of America's best-loved authors, I find myself in a moral quandary. I want my daughter to understand that the "savage" Indians that both fascinated and repulsed the Ingalls family were not wild animals but people—people who, like several of her friends, happen to have browner skin than she does. How do I explain to a seven-year-old the racism that enabled the theft of Native lands, let alone the legacy of inequality that persists in our community on the Great Plains and throughout the United States? And how do I explain the creative license that Laura Ingalls Wilder and her daughter and editor, Rose Wilder Lane, took with Laura's memories? Or how Laura's memory of events—at least as recorded in *Pioneer Girl* and the *Little House* books—diverged from historical reality? Of course, what I accept as historical reality was itself reconstructed by historians based on other contemporary primary sources that were each biased in their own ways. How do we unpack our deep history of racism and sexism while maintaining historical empathy for our (literal and figurative) ancestors? How do we separate myth from reality without destroying a beloved story?

The same themes of white civilization, Indian savagery, and maternalism that I wrestle with in Wilder's stories also surround us in public monuments erected throughout the American West and across the United States. Although many of us regularly encounter these statues and other images of frontier life, rarely do we take the time to really *see* them. Yet, examining the many pioneer-themed monuments erected since the supposed closing of the frontier in the 1890s reveals how artists, donors, and residents chose to remember—and forget—the American West.

In this book, I seek to do just such an examination, based on a close reading of some 200 public monuments erected in the American West (and East) since 1890, including 185 that I label as pioneer monuments. Unfortunately, publishing images of all 200 monuments within these pages is not possible. So I invite you to visit my website, Pioneer Monuments in the American West, www.pioneermonuments.net, to learn more about each sculpture included in this study, as well as about commemoration within particular regions. The website features multiple color images of most of the monuments as well as interactive features, including a map that allows you to watch the monuments appearing across the American landscape over time, and a search feature to identify the pioneer monument nearest you. I encourage you to peruse the website alongside this book, which traces change over time in these monuments to reveal how Americans have used frontier memory to meet their own needs and the needs of a changing society over the past 125 years.

ACKNOWLEDGMENTS

Stephen Aron planted the seeds of this project when he encouraged me to incorporate pioneer monuments and material culture sources into my doctoral dissertation on white settlers in Oregon's Willamette Valley. My colleague Kimberly Porter watered those seeds by repeatedly asking me what I was doing with those pioneer monuments. Thank you to Steve for starting me down this path, and to Kim for nudging me along. With their encouragement, I set out to write a history of what I call the Pioneer Mother movement. But as I traveled the western United States in search of pioneer woman monuments from the 1920s and 1930s, people that I met along the way kept pointing me toward other, more recent statues. Thanks to Steve also for persuading me that these less-known postwar monuments and the seeming disappearance of enormous statues from the 1920s were in fact crucial parts of this story. Out of that realization grew this book.

Thank you to the many people who have encouraged my research and challenged my thinking about this project over the past decade, including Einar Kvaran, Lawrence Culver, Katherine Jellison, and Jim Mochoruk. Thanks also to those who have critiqued my writing, including Susan Rugh and the University of North Dakota (UND) History Workshop, as well as Nathan Rees, Rebecca Weaver-Hightower, and David Culver for reading complete drafts of this manuscript. I am also grateful to the writing group members who provided invaluable feedback on my work: Nikki Berg Burin, Hans Broedel, William Caraher, Caroline Campbell, Chris Basgier, Yee Han Chu, David Haeslin, Patrick Henry, Sheila Liming, and Elizabeth Scharf. Special thanks to Michael Lansing, who has encouraged and challenged me throughout this project, providing invaluable editorial guidance.

Many individuals and institutions have my gratitude for making this research possible, including Ann Barton and Blagg-Huey Library Special Collections at Texas Woman's University; Oregon Historical Society

Research Library; Oregon State Archives; Texas State Archives; Oklahoma Historical Society Research Center; Kansas Historical Society State Archives and Library; Smithsonian Institution Archives of American Art; Portland (Oregon) Art Museum; Brown County (Minnesota) Historical Society Archives; L. Tom Perry Special Collections, Brigham Young University; Church of Jesus Christ of Latter-day Saints Church History Library; J. Willard Marriott Library, University of Utah; City of Portland Archive and Records Center; McCracken Research Library, Buffalo Bill Center of the West; Missouri Valley Special Collections, Kansas City Public Library; Special Collections and University Archives, Wichita State University Libraries; Saskia Kesners, Colorado Springs Fine Arts Center; James McGough, Cyrus E. Dallin Museum; Anne Woodhouse, Missouri History Museum Library and Research Center; Julie Dunn-Morton, St. Louis Mercantile Library at University of Missouri–St. Louis; John Mead, Lovett Library, Pampa, Texas; John Konzal, the State Historical Society of Missouri; Robin T. Dettre, Inventories of American Painting and Sculpture, Smithsonian American Art Museum; Dave Aamodt, National Frontier Trails Museum; Dawn Botsford, UND Office of Ceremonies and University Events; Leah Witherow, Colorado Springs Pioneers Museum; Steven Sitz, Liberal Memorial Library, Liberal, Kansas; and Greg Wysk, State Historical Society of North Dakota Archives. Thanks also to all those who directed me to relevant (and seemingly irrelevant) monuments, or who posted images of monuments to Waymarking.com, Wikipedia, or other sites.

I am grateful to UND's Senate Scholarly Activities Committee, the UND Fine Arts and Humanities Scholarship Initiative, Cynthia and Frank Schulte, and the UND Department of History for financial support.

Thanks to those who provided photography for this book and the accompanying website: Alexis Sayer; Pamela Riney-Kehrberg; Ann Reed; Aimee (Duchsherer) Williams; Pamela Pierce; Joy and Alma Richie; Juti Winchester; Angela Harrison-Urlacher; Lisa Allen; Michael Lansing; David and Anna Prescott; and David, Virginia, Tim, and Kathleen Culver.

And finally, special thanks to my unofficial research assistants and beloved family members: Mom, Dad, David, Anna, Tim, Kathleen, Matt, Grace, Cecilia, Tim, Sarah, and Emily.

PIONEER MOTHER MONUMENTS

INTRODUCTION
Monuments and Public Memory

Upon his death in 1876, Yankee-born California settler, philanthropist, and recluse James Lick bequeathed $100,000 (at least $2.8 million in 2015 dollars) to erect a monument in downtown San Francisco celebrating the arrival of white American culture to post-gold-rush California. Sculptor Frank Happersberger modeled the 800-ton sculpture (plate A) after the elaborate monuments placed in Paris in the late nineteenth century. It combined sculptural portraits of famous white men with female allegories depicting Anglo-American civilization around a phallic stone pillar. Read together, the various sculptural elements told a story that would have been familiar to its viewers of social Darwinist progression from wild Indians to uncouth frontiersmen to civilized white society. Although newspapers across the United States eagerly followed the monument's creation in the 1890s, the *James Lick Pioneer Monument* would elicit little public attention for the next 125 years, except when external events thrust it into the spotlight.

In 1906, two decades after the Lick monument's completion, a mighty earthquake shook San Francisco Bay. Fires sparked by that earthquake destroyed most of the city but left James Lick's monument unscathed. The sight of Lick's pioneer monument towering over the smoldering rubble inspired society matron Ella Sterling Mighels to envision a new San Francisco pioneer monument, one that would strip away much of the Lick monument's retelling of California's supposed discovery and economic development by white men in favor of a domestic scene of an Anglo-American woman holding church at her knee. Through negotiation with artists, donors, and other powerful men, Mighels's image would become the first public statue of an image more familiar to most Americans today: a Pioneer Mother.

By the 1920s, white Americans had grown confident in their displacement of indigenous peoples but increasingly anxious about changing gender and sexual norms. They turned to Pioneer Mother monuments to shore up what they considered traditional values. Remarkably similar statues of white women in sunbonnets striding westward appeared throughout the United States in the 1920s and 1930s (see plates B, C, and D). Deviations from the accepted pioneer imagery (such as plate E) sparked public protest. Monuments to Pioneer Mothers—sometimes accompanied by their husband or children—would continue to be erected in cities and smaller towns for decades to come.

For most of the twentieth century, San Franciscans largely forgot James Lick's monument. Like many of the 185 pioneer monuments erected in the United States since the late 1880s, its urban location declined, and most people walked by the statue without paying it any attention. But when the city proposed, in the early 1990s, to move the statue to accommodate the construction of a new city library, public controversy erupted. Preservationists opposed its relocation and called for protective maintenance. Others wanted it removed altogether. Civil rights protestors who associated the monument with cultural humiliation and genocide splashed gallons of red paint on it. The San Francisco Art Commission compromised by installing a brass plaque explaining the impact of white settlement on California's Native population, but interested groups, ranging from Native rights groups to the Roman Catholic archdiocese, disagreed on what that interpretive sign should say. In recent years, progressive voices in communities across the United States have called for similar reinterpretation of other existing statues, pushing for new public monuments to tell more inclusive stories (plate F). But at the same time, conservative groups and communities seeking to attract heritage tourism have erected new statues (plate G) that closely resemble the Pioneer Mother monuments of the 1920s.

I begin with analysis of the *James Lick Pioneer Monument*, as it was produced and received across time, because it encapsulates the arc of this book, which explores the ways in which pioneer monuments were erected, forgotten, and rediscovered from the late 1880s to the present. For more than 125 years, American frontier commemoration has changed in response to western race relations, shifting gender norms, and religious and regional identity. But through it all, I argue, pioneer monuments used gendered imagery to enshrine white settlers on the landscape. *Pioneer Mother Monuments* is the first book to delve into this long and complex history of remembering, forgetting, and rediscovering iconic white pioneers. It demonstrates that for more than a century, many different American communities have used statues of pioneer mothers and pioneer families to express local pride as well as national identity. By comparing some 200 western monuments (185 explicitly honoring pioneers) erected in the United States from the 1880s to the present, this book reveals how Americans used public art to embrace frontier mythology and grapple with modern life, and the extent to which historical memory of the frontier remains central to American national identity. Examining these monuments and their unique place in cultural memory and public debate helps us understand the persistence of American settler colonialism, determine the fate of these monuments in a changing society, and begin to imagine a way forward toward a more inclusive society.

WESTERN HISTORY AND MYTHOLOGY

Few Americans today pay any attention to the 185 pioneer monuments scattered across the U.S. landscape. But most would immediately recognize the sunbonneted Pioneer Mother depicted in many of them. And nearly all Americans embrace—at least to some degree—the myths of American exceptionalism and individualism enshrined in these pioneer monuments.

Part of this book's contribution lies in its reconsideration of the mythical frontier narrative and how that narrative is literally enshrined across U.S. towns and highways. Frontier narratives are foundational to American national identity and to the field of U.S. western history. Three years after the U.S. Census Bureau declared the closing of the frontier in 1890, historian Frederick Jackson Turner spoke at a special meeting of the recently incorporated American Historical Association at the World's Columbian Exposition in Chicago, Illinois. In "The Significance of the Frontier in American History," Turner argued that the nation's frontier past had profoundly shaped American society.[1] Although few today agree with his assumption (widespread at the time) that westward expansion represented social progress from savagery to civilization, or with his argument that the frontier was the basis of American character and democracy, Turner's "frontier thesis" dominated western history for the next century. Beginning in the mid-1980s, scholars dubbing themselves New Western historians challenged this Turnerian model of western history. They analyzed the West as a distinct geographic region, rather than a frontier process repeated in different places at different times. Patricia Nelson Limerick and others argued that western history is better understood as a story of conflict and conquest than of national progress.[2] But the American public—schooled in a Turnerian understanding of U.S. history and inundated with frontier imagery in popular culture—tends to dismiss the key insights of New Western history as so much political correctness. In *Pioneer Mother Monuments*, I examine how popular memory that was formed by Turner's valorization of the frontier shaped pioneer commemoration throughout the twentieth century, and how late twentieth-century challenges to Turner's framework influenced public memory of westward expansion and its place in American national identity.

Popular portrayals of the Old West have shifted over the past century to meet changing American cultural needs. Yet certain key elements remain fairly consistent from late nineteenth-century dime novels to early twenty-first-century television shows. We imagine the West to be a land of adventure, like in a John Wayne movie, where masculine cowboys battle the barren environment or uncivilized Indians. Or perhaps we envision pioneers chopping down trees to build a log cabin and carve out a better life for their families as in *Little House on the Prairie.* Either way, we lionize these independent white men for succeeding against adversity in a manner not so dissimilar from Turner's westward march of Euro-American civilization.[3]

Pioneer Mother Monuments also engages scholars' hesitancy to view western history through the lens of settler colonialism. Emphasizing comparisons among different settler societies, settler colonial studies examines the process by which foreign people migrate into a region and displace indigenous populations. Following Patrick Wolfe, scholars using a settler colonialism framework analyze settlement not as a temporary stage that a nation goes through but as a persistent and ongoing structure. Western historians are generally willing to acknowledge connections between the U.S. and Canadian Wests rooted in colonialism, and perhaps similar historical links to Australia, New Zealand, and South Africa. But western scholars—not to mention the American public—are far more resistant to claims that settler colonialism is ongoing.[4] We forget that the so-called free land that lured white settlers westward was stolen from Native peoples. And we ignore the persistence of indigenous peoples in the face of attempted eradication.[5] We embrace the myths, but choose to erase the inconvenient truths, of our settler colonial heritage. I argue that these habits of mind motivated the erection of pioneer monuments and continue to underpin Americans' embrace and neglect of those public statues.

MONUMENTS AND PUBLIC MEMORY

Pioneer Mother Monuments builds on work connecting historical knowledge and public mythology in the creation of public historical monuments. "The impulse behind the public monument," explains art historian Kirk Savage, "was an impulse to mold history into its rightful pattern."[6] The choice of subjects for such monuments, and how those subjects are depicted, reveals more about the people who erected the monuments than it does about the historic figures or events they sought to memorialize.[7] The iconography chosen for sculptures of important individuals and composite characters convey a particular view of that individual, event, or experience. Yet popular reception of these works often departs—at times radically—from the sculptor's intent. Marianne Hirsch and Valerie Smith argue that "cultural memory" is produced through "acts of performance, representation and interpretation."[8] Thus comparing the erectors' intent to the populace's changing reactions to public monuments is important. Tracing changing depictions of the past in these commemorative statues, as well as popular reaction to artists' interpretations, provides a valuable window into the American public's understanding of their history and themselves.

In recent decades scholars like Michael Kammen and Kirk Savage have paved the way for *Pioneer Mother Monuments* by examining the ways in which monument building reflected contemporary concerns about politics, race, and gender in various regions and periods.[9] Many scholars agree that the late nineteenth and early twentieth centuries were a golden age of American memorialization. In response to the "cultural amnesia" produced by the modern cycle of intentional destruction and reconstruction of the built environment, communities throughout the United States created what sociologist Paul Connerton called a "topography of remembering."[10] Communities throughout the United States erected monuments and historical markers to their white forefathers. While some honored military or government leaders, many of these monuments celebrated a category of people, such as World War I doughboys or Civil War veterans. Soldier monuments could even be ordered from stock catalogs.[11]

As Savage has documented, this process of memorialization was particularly pronounced in the nation's capital. Celebratory monuments to great men proliferated in the late nineteenth century.[12] After 1900 they were eclipsed by the National Mall, which was remade from a park of tree-lined meandering paths into its modern more formal open space dominated by the Ulysses S. Grant and Abraham Lincoln memorials. Meanwhile, many more monuments to military leaders (including both Union and Confederate soldiers) and other prominent individuals were erected throughout the District of Columbia and in the neighboring states of Maryland and Virginia. These prominent projects inspired interest nationwide in commemorating national and regional history by erecting monumental sculpture.

Perhaps the largest body of scholarship on American monuments focuses on portrayals of race relations in monuments to the Old South erected in the decades following the Civil War. Kirk Savage, Cynthia Mills, Pamela Simpson, and others have written about the erection of Confederate monuments in the decades following the War between the States, arguing that artists used gendered depictions of white women embodying the values of the Old South to juxtapose their moral rightness against uncivilized black slaves.[13] Race is depicted explicitly in these works, as it is in studies of commemoration in South Africa, because the history of these places has long been framed around a racial binary.[14] While monuments to the Confederate "lost cause" have received significant scholarly attention, researchers have been far less quick to engage with race and gender issues in public monuments in the more ethnically diverse American West.

Because the body of literature on Confederate commemoration is so rich, and because it explicitly raises questions of race, gender, and regional identity, it serves as a valuable comparison for this study of western pioneer monuments. Scholars and the wider public have largely ignored the numerous monuments commemorating white westward migration and settlement erected across the country following the closing of the frontier in the 1890s. And even less scholarly and public attention has focused on monuments to white settlers erected in response to more recent social change since World War II. *Pioneer Mother Monuments* addresses this need by tracing changing portrayals of white settlement in pioneer monuments erected from the 1880s to the present, with particular attention to monuments erected since 1945.

This study is also spurred by recent public debate over monuments and memorialization. Interest in building new monuments declined across the United States at midcentury, only to resurge in recent decades. Since Maya Lin's controversial Vietnam Veterans Memorial was completed in 1982, monuments to Korean War and World War II veterans, civil rights leader Martin Luther King Jr., and President Franklin Delano Roosevelt have all taken their place on the National Mall and adjacent Tidal Basin in Washington, D.C. Maya Lin's stark yet contemplative wall of veterans' names has had a profound influence on memorial conception and design. As Savage argues, "National memorials are now expected to be spaces of experience, journeys of emotional discovery, rather than exemplary objects to be imitated."[15] The 2011 King monument challenges its viewers to find hope amid despair. In contrast, the 2004 World War II Memorial declares the moral rightness of U.S. involvement in that conflict, celebrating battles won, rather than remembering lives lost. Amid this new wave of memorialization—and as part of a broader challenge to the continued use of Confederate imagery—Americans have begun to reexamine old monuments to the Old South. Many now argue that early twentieth-century southern monuments are inherently racist and should be removed or reinterpreted. As Americans in the North and South debate the future of Confederate monuments, we would do well to learn from the unstudied history of pioneer monuments in the American West, which likewise reinforce white cultural dominance and tell stories that are central to our national identity.

The legacy of race-based slavery remains central to popular memory of southern history. In contrast, Americans remember the Old West as a place where rugged masculinity was acted out, and we celebrate the settlement of supposedly untamed lands. Of course, in popular memory, those manly men were always white, and—in Hollywood films as in real life—they often acted out their masculinity through their dominance of Native peoples.[16] White settlers' success in displacing indigenous peoples made it easy for Americans to imagine the West as a white man's land. This focus on Anglo-Americans (meaning U.S.-born, English-speaking whites, not necessarily of Anglo-Saxon descent) ignores the West's richer ethnic diversity, encouraging white Americans to forget the presence not only of Native Americans, but also of Latino, Asian, and African Americans. Western women appear in these narratives not as actors but as tropes: lowly Indian squaw drudges versus white Pioneer Mothers embodying white civilization. Like the Afrikaner *volksmoeder* in South Africa, the American Pioneer Mother icon is paradoxical.[17] The symbol of (white) motherhood played a powerful role in American national identity. Yet it was precisely white women's gender containment—within a sunbonnet, within a family, and within the domestic sphere—that made it possible for pioneer mothers to play such an important role in nation building.

Many Americans, and particularly those residing in northern states, have begun to recognize that Confederate monuments are problematic because they enshrine the legacy of slavery and racism on the American landscape. But most Americans continue to celebrate narratives depicting colonial and nineteenth-century westward expansion, which are central not only to western regional but to U.S. national identity. While a desire to remember early settlers' hard work and determination is understandable, we generally resist interrogating the core beliefs in individualism and American exceptionalism that underpin these stories and serve as foundational national myths. Pioneer commemoration ignores the conquest of indigenous peoples, the meeting of diverse cultures in the region, and women as agents rather than just symbols of white civilization. Western communities erected pioneer monuments to claim their own place within the project of national expansion, and to grapple with collective guilt over the conquest of indigenous peoples.[18] Through analysis of some 200 statues erected by a range of communities across 125 years, this book demonstrates that statues of Pioneer Mothers and pioneer families became a common language used to express local pride and national identity. Studying public monuments to white pioneers and Pioneer Mothers brings gender into conversation with the burgeoning field of settler colonialism and reveals the intersections of race, gender, sexuality, and regional identity in public memory.

WESTERN PIONEER MONUMENTS

Despite persistent public interest in western historical memory, relatively little popular or scholarly attention has been paid to western pioneer *monuments.* Scholars have long recognized the intimate connection between western mythology and western art.[19] But existing studies of western monuments concentrate almost exclusively on prominent sculptures erected during the first three decades of the twentieth century, a time when communities commemorated women as the embodiment of closely held cultural values. Many of these works focus on the erection of a single monument.[20] Paul Scolari's survey of pioneer monuments revealed that between 1890 and 1930, Americans defined western history through two characters, the Indian and the pioneer.[21] But like other scholars working on western statuary, Scolari closely analyzed only a few specific works, without fully unpacking relationships among those sculptures. In contrast, *Pioneer Mother Monuments* provides a close reading of 185 monuments commemorating white settlers—many of them women—and their dispossession of Native peoples, contextualized through a variety of archival sources. Art historian Annette Stott argued convincingly that nineteenth-century images of what she called Prairie Madonnas—True Women whose covered wagons simultaneously maintained their domesticity and formed their improvised halos—were replaced in the early twentieth century by new, stronger images of active Pioneer Women striding westward in sturdy boots and sunbonnets.[22] Yet, my close examination of western monuments erected to rural women in the 1920s and 1930s, alongside popular culture of that period, reveals that this transition was more complex than Stott's formal analysis of western painting and sculpture suggests. This study examines westerners' motivations for erecting those statues, how artists represented frontier people in the statues, and how those monuments have been received—or ignored—by their communities ever since.

This book contributes to the existing literature by focusing on underanalyzed monuments, emphasizing the uses of gender and family ideology in commemoration. It contributes to social and cultural history as well as art history by modeling ways to read public art (formal analysis) in conjunction with archival materials (social history methods). My examination of changing depictions of pioneer men, women, and families in public monuments highlights both changing artistic styles and shifting cultural norms. Formal analysis of public monuments alongside contemporaneous fine art and popular imagery reveals the extent to which commemoration lagged behind artistic innovation throughout the long twentieth century. Reading this study's comprehensive sample of pioneer-themed statues against artists' and donors' statements and newspaper coverage of popular reception over time uncovers the complex interplay among these different groups in erecting and accepting or rejecting public monuments.

Pioneer Mother Monuments brings these western-themed monumental sculptures into conversation with one another, tracing changing representations of white settlers in public monuments from the 1880s to the present. Building on the existing studies of pioneer monuments from the 1890s to the 1930s, I use monumental sculpture to explore how Americans throughout the twentieth century grappled with modernity by repeatedly reimagining nineteenth-century frontier women and families. I explore how artists' perspectives and community identities produced subtle yet important distinctions in monument designs that simultaneously celebrated their foremothers' sacrifices and instructed future generations on proper behavior. As anthropologist Michael Rowlands argues, some monuments "work," while others spark condemnation.[23] Following Barbara Berglund, I argue that westerners' social ordering through pioneer imagery helped to make those pioneer images central to U.S. national identity and to make those westerners more American.[24] Assessing public reception of the monuments erected over a century from their creation to today uncovers how Americans from Massachusetts to California, and from Alaska to Florida, used western mythology to enshrine particular notions of gender and white civilization, to define American nationhood, and to grapple with social change.

This study breaks new ground by integrating previously unstudied postwar monuments into a longer and more complex history of frontier commemoration. Informed by anthropologists' and sociologists' explorations of "the work of memory," I examine how and why western communities chose to remember—or forget—their past in different ways.[25] I argue that communities throughout the American West and as far east as Massachusetts embraced pioneer monuments as a means to claim their own place within a national narrative of westward expansion. Just as there has been a recent burst in monument construction on the National Mall, I show that a second age of memorialization is also occurring in many communities in the American West. I argue that Native activism and New Western history scholarship inspired a few communities to reexamine the values portrayed in their pioneer monuments. And a handful of new monuments use more inclusive imagery or even critique earlier monuments' portrayals of racial and gender relations. But far more pioneer monuments (like the recent World War II Memorial) have simply borrowed iconography from monuments erected nearly a century earlier. Like monuments erected in the 1920s and 1930s, most monuments erected since the 1980s reassure local residents that old values will persist amid rapid population growth, increasing ethnic diversity, and changing gender norms. Following Hirsch and Smith, I argue that these monuments "perform important cultural memory work in constituting and consolidating group identities."[26] By connecting local history to a national story of manifest destiny, they offer westerners a sense of belonging to something bigger than themselves.

Uniting a formal study of multiple monuments with archival evidence left by artists, donors, and the popular press reveals changing depictions of gender, race, and religion in public statuary. Reading the statues against their sculptors' statements and personal biographies, donors' guidelines, and press coverage of the statues uncovers limited contestation amid broad agreement about the shape that pioneer commemoration should take. Tracing changing treatments of the statues in local newspapers and promotional materials exposes the extent to which Americans forgot or chose to reinterpret previously popular monuments. But reading the two hundred statues in this study together reveals a broader arc of U.S. national identity. Similar to sociologist Erving Goffman's "pictorial pattern analysis" of gender display in advertising, my analysis identifies common ways in which individuals and communities have positioned themselves in relation to shared narratives of westward expansion.[27] I demonstrate that artists, donors, and viewers made the female body a site of not only frontier memory but also national determination. While depictions of gender, family, race, and religion changed over time, all two hundred of these statues expressed those varied cultural ideals in relation to a shared frontier history. And, again as in Goffman, exceptions—or incidents of public controversy—sometimes prove the rule. These monuments hold white settlers—and particularly pioneer mothers—up as the embodiment of national ideals of freedom, democracy, and individualism. They offer white nuclear families as symbols of the American nation. And they define Americanism as the embodiment of westward expansion, even as they exclude and erase indigenes and other peoples of color.

In recent years, individuals in both the North and the South have challenged commemorations of the lost cause as being inherently racist, and cities such as New Orleans have gone so far as to remove statues of Confederate leaders. But Americans have been far more hesitant to critique pioneer commemoration because it is so central to U.S. national identity. Some pay lip service to inclusivity, while others dismiss multiculturalism as mere political correctness. Regardless, we resist applying the insights of settler colonial studies to American pioneer narratives because to do so would call into question foundational myths of Jeffersonian agrarianism and American exceptionalism, and lay bare white conquest of Native lands and peoples.

This study demonstrates that for the past century, Americans have embraced a particular gendered and racialized image of westward expansion. Erecting a bronze statue of a pioneer woman or family celebrates frontier women's persistence in the face of adversity. Yet it also effectively erases a much more problematic and contested history of indigenous depopulation and removal (some would argue genocide), as well as complex and highly problematic histories of immigration and environmental transformation—all core elements of U.S. history that many Americans would prefer to forget. Instead, we hold fast to images of self-made men and self-sacrificing white Pioneer Mothers, while ignoring the real costs their achievements exacted on the landscape and peoples of color. I argue that, by the late twentieth century, pioneer narratives became so embedded in American popular culture—ranging from public art to television shows and sports team mascots—that different communities were able to adapt those shared narratives to their own purposes.

Pioneer monuments became a space in which different groups enacted their anxieties and desires; those different groups' needs and uses of the monuments changed over time. The monuments memorialize early settlers in a given location, yet how artists and donors choose to depict those early settlers instructs future generations in particular cultural values. Through these public sculptures, the creators and sponsors identify perceived problems in contemporary society and suggest better ways to live in the future. Most of these sculptures were backward looking, seeking to promote traditional values they felt were under attack, but a few critiqued past cultural norms. Once erected, however, these pioneer monuments became pieces of public art, open to reinterpretation and put to multiple uses by diverse groups of Americans.

While most public monuments honor famous individuals, pioneer monuments commemorated supposedly universal frontier men and, especially, frontier women. Focusing on portrayals of women and familial relationships in these monuments illuminates how communities used public art to construct shared cultural norms. Depictions of white women and families over 125 years of pioneer monuments further reveals how Americans used gendered imagery and nostalgic portrayals of the family unit to erase persistent ethnic and racial inequality from their collective memory. If, as postcolonial studies scholars Fredric Jameson and Anne McClintock insist, the family always stands in for the nation, then monuments celebrating frontier families contend that the United States is founded on middle-class white families and teach Americans to accept their assigned place within the nation's social hierarchy.[28]

This study's close reading of two hundred western monuments, combined with various archival sources, teaches at least six important lessons about how monuments operate in society: First, a monument's design shapes its meaning and how it is viewed by public audiences. Pioneer monument designs both reflected and helped reinforce changing gender and family ideals from the 1880s to the present. Second, the monument's context influences its meaning. The statue's physical and social setting shape how it is perceived. Third, individuals' reasons for viewing a monument shapes their interpretation of that statue. A tourist who has traveled a significant distance to view a monument will see it differently than someone who passes by the same sculpture every day. Fourth, viewers use—and sometimes abuse—public statues to fulfill their own purposes. Several of the monuments examined in this book have been defaced, stolen, or severely damaged by individuals seeking to make a political point or to profit from its theft. Fifth, viewers' cultural identities affect their perceptions of the monument. Native Americans, African Americans, and recent immigrants are all likely to interpret monuments to white settlers differently than are descendants of those settlers. Members of the Church of Jesus Christ of Latter-day Saints (Mormons) are likely to find special resonance in monuments to Mormon handcart pioneers. Sixth, statues tend to garner attention when they are erected, but that attention dwindles over time unless something happens to attract public notice again. All too often, we pass by public monuments without really *seeing* them. This study demonstrates the importance for all of us to see these pioneer statues anew.

Pioneer Mother Monuments is divided into seven chapters in rough chronological order. In the first two chapters, I trace the development between 1890 and 1940 of a monolithic image of western womanhood: a young sunbonneted woman carrying white civilization to the supposedly savage frontier. I analyze well-known 1920s monuments, like Bryant Baker's *Pioneer Woman* in Ponca City, Oklahoma, and August Leimbach's twelve identical *Madonna of the Trail* monuments, erected from coast to coast by the Daughters of the American Revolution (DAR), as well as lesser-known statues commissioned throughout the Midwest and West during that period. Pioneer monuments erected from the 1890s through 1920 were explicitly designed to celebrate the triumph of Euro-American civilization. In chapter 1 I examine narratives of civilization and savagery portrayed in these early monuments and explore the influence of public reception on pioneer monument design. In the next chapter, I analyze statues erected from the mid-1920s to the start of World War II, revealing that gender anxieties amid the Jazz Age and the Great Depression inspired a shift away from Pioneer Women in favor of less forceful Prairie Madonna images.

The next two chapters focus primarily on pioneer commemoration after World War II, exploring differing attitudes toward pioneer monuments in different locations. Focusing on gender and family norms and religion, chapters 3 and 4 explore how these postwar pioneer monuments both reflected and reinforced changing American family ideals. In chapter 3 I argue that after World War II, westerners grappled with modernity by erecting new forms of pioneer monuments. Depression-era tributes to conservative maternalism (chapter 2) yielded to celebrations of the white middle-class nuclear family (chapter 3). But the generational tensions and avant-garde art movements of the 1960s encouraged some westerners to explore new possibilities for pioneer memorialization.

Chapter 4 reexamines themes of civilization and changing family norms discussed in earlier chapters through the lens of religion. Revisiting the eras discussed in the first three chapters, in chapter 4 I argue that shifting portrayals of Mormon families in pioneer monuments highlight Latter-day Saints' efforts to assimilate into the broader American society while remaining true to LDS doctrine and cultural values.

The final three chapters, which are organized more thematically, assess the status of pioneer commemoration in recent decades in various locations. I argue that, beginning in the early 1990s, multiculturalism and New Western history encouraged some western communities to question the dominant iconography of pioneer monuments and to neglect or "forget" prominent sculptures in their midst.[29] At the same time, smaller and more conservative communities actively embraced their frontier pasts, rediscovering old statues or erecting new ones, and ushering in a second golden age of pioneer memorialization. Chapter 5 demonstrates that clashing cultural values amid the late twentieth-century culture wars produced very different pioneer commemoration in disparate locations. In chapter 6, I examine pioneer monuments as a means to historicize bland suburbs and attract heritage tourism. And chapter 7 explores the various ways in which westerners chose to remember, forget, or reinvent their pioneer statuary at the dawn of the new millennium.

Since the 1890s, Americans have claimed their place within a national story of westward expansion and responded to local social change by erecting pioneer monuments. For the past century, they have done so by copying or creatively adapting standard images of swashbuckling white pioneer men and sunbonneted white pioneer women. How and why did Americans embrace such uniform pioneer imagery? What does that uniformity mean, and in what ways has it been challenged? Just how racist are these statues? If they are racist, how should we respond? Before we can answer these questions, we must understand how these remarkably similar monuments came to be. We begin, in chapter 1, with a look at how late nineteenth-century ideas about white supremacy, manifest destiny, and proper gender roles coalesced into a standard iconography centered on a sainted generic Pioneer Mother.

CHAPTER 1

ENSHRINING WHITE CIVILIZATION IN EARLY PIONEER MONUMENTS, 1890–1920

In 1905, white women leaders of the suffrage movement gathered in Portland, Oregon, to dedicate Alice Cooper's statue of *Sacajawea* (more accurately spelled Sacagawea; see plate H), in honor of the Shoshone guide for the Lewis and Clark expedition and to commemorate "the pioneer mother of Old Oregon." But Anglo-American men and women throughout the West soon came to challenge the idea that an image of the famed Shoshone guide could rightfully commemorate the sacrifices of white settlers. This female sculptor's depiction of a Native woman soon yielded public attention to male sculptors' celebrations of generic Pioneer Mothers as symbols of rural nostalgia, white domination, and traditional gender roles. Between 1905 and 1930, the racial dynamics of proper pioneer monuments became set in stone (and bronze) through conversations and sometimes heated confrontations among donors, artists, and public audiences. By the late 1920s, western pioneer monuments would abandon images of indigenous peoples and famous individuals, instead coalescing around a monolithic image of a sunbonneted Pioneer Mother, which would be replicated in communities throughout the American West.

Monumental sculptures like Cooper's *Sacajawea* were selected for creation and display through partnerships between government agencies and private donors, and many such monuments appear to have enjoyed widespread popular support. But, as scholars of monuments to the Confederate lost cause have clearly shown, early twentieth-century public monuments were erected to endorse the political and social agendas of their often wealthy backers.[1] Historical accuracy was less important than promoting the donors' imagined versions of the past. Focusing on negotiations surrounding the design and erection of pioneer monuments highlights how commemorative statuary was collectively curated by sculptors, heritage organizations, and large and small donors to display history lessons on the American landscape. Examining how these monuments portrayed western settlement reveals how Americans chose to remember Anglo-American westward migration—and to forget the damaging effects of settler colonialism on nonwhite peoples. In this chapter and the chapters that follow, I explore how the erection and public reception of these monuments worked together to shape American memory of the frontier.

As early settlers grew elderly in the decades following the supposed closing of the frontier in 1890, organizations and private individuals throughout the western United States built monuments to honor their pioneer forefathers and mothers. As early as 1883, W. Lair Hill urged "some capable hand" in the Oregon Pioneer Association "to gather up the scattered materials and erect a monument to the pioneer mothers of Oregon."[2] This impulse to memorialize early pioneers was similar in many ways to current calls to remember the sacrifices of World War II veterans—the so-called greatest generation—before that generation passes by, creating what Pierre Nora calls *lieux de mémoire* (sites of memory).[3] At the turn of the twentieth century, the first generation of white settlers in Oregon celebrated their success in transforming the landscape, economy, and society from the rough living conditions and cultural mixing that were characteristic of frontier life. By the 1890s, orderly farmsteads produced goods for the market economy. Portland gradually shed its Stumptown moniker to become a modern, progressive city. Like those who valorize the greatest generation, early settlers and their descendants sought to commemorate those who had laid the foundation for that settled society, and to create lasting monuments to what they viewed as those early settlers' tremendous achievement.[4]

Wealthy donors and voluntary associations across the western United States similarly sought to memorialize their own founding fathers by erecting monuments to early white settlers sculpted by famous artists. Pioneer monument building paralleled and drew inspiration from fin de siècle monument building elsewhere in the United States and Europe. Colossal Beaux-Arts monuments were commonplace in late nineteenth-century France, as what Sergiusz Michalski calls "statuomania" inspired the erection of many statues of questionable artistic taste honoring minor celebrities.[5] In the United States, the massive Abraham Lincoln and Ulysses S. Grant memorials came to anchor the National Mall in Washington, D.C., shortly after World War I. Meanwhile, southern whites grappled with the profound economic and social changes wrought by the Civil War, Reconstruction, and the rise of the New South by clinging to the race-based power structure of the Old South. Segregation laws and monuments to Confederate leaders and soldiers reinforced this racial divide by commemorating the lost cause.[6]

Contemporaneous western monuments to early white settlers consistently labeled those settlers as "pioneers," indicating that they had carved a path for others to follow. Monument erectors believed those pioneers to be the vanguard of white civilization in the West. As Gail Bederman argued, Americans at the turn of the twentieth century used the term *civilization* in various ways to legitimize different claims to power. But in the context of frontier memory, this term was consistently used to evoke the imagined cultural superiority of the Western world (meaning Europe and European settler societies such as the United States). Adapting Charles Darwin's theory of evolution to human societies, late nineteenth-century Euro-Americans identified civilization as a specific stage in human racial evolution that followed the more primitive stages of barbarism and savagery. Pronounced gender differentiation—in which manly men worked to protect and provide for delicate, spiritual women—was among the traits that they believed distinguished civilized white culture.[7] Late nineteenth- and early twentieth-century pioneer monuments consistently celebrated the arrival of this so-called white civilization (in the form of manly pioneers and saintly Pioneer Mothers) to the allegedly untouched western wilderness and supposedly savage (uncivilized) indigenous peoples. But artists and donors often disagreed about the proper way to represent the civilized white men and women who settled in the Far West, and at times those disagreements boiled over into public controversy, providing a valuable window into turn-of-the-century thinking about race, gender, and regional identity.

Even as settlers celebrated their success in carrying white civilization to savage lands and peoples, they remained insecure about their place within that society. At the turn of the twentieth century, white Americans in the Northeast, Southeast, Midwest, and Far West were all anxious about dramatic changes to their society. The second industrial revolution was transforming the United States from a young nation of yeoman farmers to a global industrial power. Industrialization lured native born and

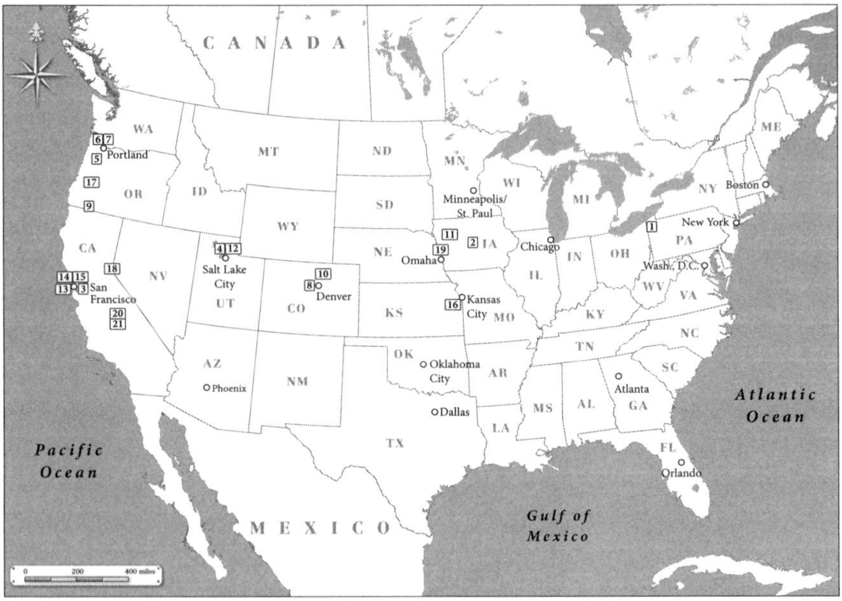

MAP 1. Pioneer Monuments Erected prior to 1920. Map by Gerry Krieg. Numbers on the map correspond with a chronological listing of monuments in the appendix.

immigrant alike to rapidly growing cities. And industrialization, urbanization, and the end of the frontier era all threatened to emasculate middle-class white men who no longer provided for their families through land ownership and subsistence farming. Aging western settlers joined eastern urbanites in embracing tales of masculine adventures in the Wild West as an antidote to their growing anxiety.

Nonetheless, while southern monuments hearkened back to an earlier era of civility and clear racial divisions, western settlers had little interest in returning to the hardships of frontier life. Instead, they sought to commemorate early white settlers to demonstrate how far they had come from an era of trade and conflict with indigenous peoples and the struggle for mere survival. By erecting massive bronze monuments sculpted by famous artists, growing communities declared themselves to be cosmopolitan centers on par with Paris or New York. At the same time, white westerners sought to justify settler colonialism. White southerners worked hard to keep African Americans in place as a meek, impoverished labor force. But white westerners believed the proper place for Native peoples was in the past. Thus, the myth of the "disappearing Indian"—a widespread

American belief that Indians were a primitive people who would necessarily disappear in the face of white civilization—bore particular power in regions seeking to separate themselves both from indigenous peoples and from their own less-refined frontier pasts.

Across the country, Philip Deloria and others have argued, white Americans reinforced their cultural dominance by commemorating the passing of what they termed "noble savages."[8] At the same time, they assumed aspects of indigenous culture to stave off neurasthenia (nervous exhaustion, a condition thought to result from overcivilization) and become better middle-class urban men and women. Urbane easterners joined fraternal organizations such as the Improved Order of the Red Men and sent their sons to Boy Scouts and their daughters to Camp Fire Girls, where they donned Indian-inspired garb and performed primitive tasks in the wilderness. Western men told tall tales about the early days on the frontier, when they wore buckskin clothing and hunted wild game like the indigenous men whose lands they had settled. But playing Indian was more dangerous for western women, who sought to distance themselves from the flexible gender roles typical of frontier life. Like their counterparts in the South championing the Confederate lost cause, western women embraced maternalism and narratives of womanly sacrifice to shore up their gender and racial identity.

Like Cooper's *Sacajawea* statue, pioneer monuments drew on these racial narratives of civilization and savagery. Most of the earliest monuments depicted specific famous men as well as a broader class of white settlers. Several featured both white settlers and the noble savages they had displaced. But amid rising xenophobia and anxieties about changing gender norms, wealthy donors embraced increasingly similar images of generic white settlers they called pioneers. By the late 1920s, varied images of Native guides and chiefs, wealthy businessmen, starving cannibals, and buckskin-clad frontier settlers gave way to remarkably similar statues of a sunbonneted Pioneer Mother, who selflessly carried the supposed blessings of white civilization to unsettled frontiers, armed only with a Bible or a rifle. In this chapter, I examine the various forms that pioneer monuments took prior to 1920 and explore why those diverse images were abandoned in favor of an iconic Pioneer Mother in the 1920s. In so doing, I reveal the processes by which prominent individuals and various groups negotiated their ideas about the past and about contemporary racial and gender relations, as well as how those ideas came to be enshrined in western places.

THE MARCH OF WHITE CIVILIZATION

The first western pioneer monuments were erected in the years immediately following the 1890 Wounded Knee massacre. While historians now recognize that deadly event as an anticlimax to decades of U.S. military efforts to force Native peoples onto reservations, in the 1890s, western settlers worried about possible future Indian attacks and feared a loss of economic opportunity as the frontier's promise of free land ended. Yet they also sought to demonstrate their sophistication as a newly settled postfrontier society and their cultural superiority to the indigenous peoples they had displaced. Portraying an inevitable progression from Indian savagery to white civilization justified white settlers' displacement of Native peoples and absolved white guilt.[9] Just as southern elites mourned the passing of the Old South through memorialization, from the late 1880s to World War I, western settlers expressed their diverse anxieties and yearnings through public monuments that celebrated the arrival of white American civilization in the Old West.

The earliest pioneer monuments borrowed stylistically from European and southeastern U.S. monuments to tell distinctly western stories celebrating white settlers. Like several Confederate monuments erected in the late nineteenth century, San Francisco's 1894 *James Lick Pioneer Monument* (plate A) was modeled after grandiose European Beaux-Arts commemorative statues of the era, featuring realist sculptures of famous men—sometimes combined with allegorical figures—mounted on large stone bases. But where French monuments commemorated both major and minor political figures, and late nineteenth-century Confederate monuments generally celebrated a military hero or common soldier atop a tall pillar, several prominent early western pioneer monuments combined portraits of prominent men with allegorical sculptural elements around large central columns. Although they explicitly honored specific famous individuals, western monuments such as San Francisco's James Lick monument and Salt Lake City's Brigham Young monument (discussed in chapter 4) were labeled by donors and contemporary viewers as pioneer monuments, indicating that those famous individuals were intended to represent a broader class of white settlers. Like the art and architecture among which

Cyrus Dallin's portrait of Brigham Young (which later topped Salt Lake City's monument) was displayed at Chicago's 1893 World's Columbian Exposition, these pioneer monuments emphasized the superiority of Euro-American culture.[10] And like historian Frederick Jackson Turner's famous lecture at that 1893 world's fair declaring the "Significance of the Frontier in American History," white Americans defined western history as an evolution from Indian savagery to white civilization. Erecting colossal pioneer monuments proclaimed their young western cities to be cosmopolitan centers on par with Paris and Rome, and western American civilization to be equal to that of western Europe. Those monuments also declared white dominance over disappearing Indian savages.

San Francisco–based artist Frank Happersberger sculpted that city's *James Lick Pioneer Monument* to enshrine a history of Anglo dominance on the California landscape. Yankee-born James Lick had worked as a carpenter and piano builder in South America, earning a small fortune, which he then multiplied by investing in San Francisco real estate during the California gold rush. This eccentric millionaire refused to leave his fortune to his illegitimate son, choosing instead to support his philanthropic interests and to inscribe physical tributes to his own success on the San Francisco landscape.[11] Lick bequeathed a stunning $100,000 ($2.8 million in 2015 dollars) to the city of San Francisco to fund bronze "statuary emblematic of the significant epochs in California history" since the Spanish mission era.[12] The resulting monument was erected in front of San Francisco's city hall. Although that 1897 city hall was soon destroyed by the fire that followed the city's enormous 1906 earthquake, Lick's forty-seven-foot-tall, 800-ton monument stubbornly survived, towering over the destroyed city and becoming not only a postfrontier lieux de mémoire but also a symbol of the city's determination to rebuild.

San Francisco's Lick monument features a massive stone column and bronze sculptural elements that commemorate prominent men who had helped to establish Anglo-American California. Together, those bronze sculptures and reliefs construct a whitewashed narrative of California history typical of that era. Anglos chose to emphasize the godly influence of kindly Spanish padres (which conveniently skirted their undesirable Catholicism) and the romance of elite Spanish landowners. This story of the region's Spanish fantasy past was told and retold throughout California at the turn of the twentieth century, through novels such as Helen

Hunt Jackson's *Ramona*, historical pageants, and Los Angeles's wildly popular *Mission Play*.[13] These stories enabled Anglos to ignore the plight of indigenous Californians, who were decimated by Euro-American contact and settlement, and to forget that most Spanish-speaking peoples in California during the Spanish and particularly Mexican periods were of mixed racial heritage, rather than the genteel and lily white Spaniards depicted in stories like *Ramona*. In an era of Chinese exclusion, the Spanish fantasy past also erased the ethnic diversity of gold-rush California. Frank Happersberger's version of California history began with its discovery by Europeans, followed by the Spanish-led conquest and conversion of its indigenous peoples. He focused on Yankee-led economic expansion during the Mexican period, which was soon replaced with even greater wealth and an Anglo population explosion during the gold rush. That rough-and-tumble frontier period in turn gave way to more refined Anglo civilization in the late nineteenth century, culminating in the business accomplishments of the monument's donor.

In keeping with late nineteenth-century European and American memorial sculpting traditions, the Lick monument combines female allegorical figures symbolizing abstract ideals and a historical tableaux with portraits honoring specific men, including James Lick himself. Happersberger's design—which was chosen from among twenty-eight competitive entries—was markedly similar to a Beaux-Arts monument to a minor French politician, *Léon Gambetta Monument*, by sculptor Jean-Paul Aubé and architect Louis-Charles Boileau, which was placed in the courtyard of Paris's Louvre Palace in 1888 at the height of French statuomania.[14] Like the Aubé piece, the Lick monument placed a bronze allegorical figure atop its central spire. But where Aubé used martial figures and symbols of political ideals to commemorate Gambetta's military and political leadership, Happersberger followed the Statue of Liberty, given by France to the United States in 1886, and many monuments to the Confederate lost cause, embodying the core values of his monument in a female figure. Modeled after the Roman goddess Minerva, Eureka—accompanied by the grizzly bear that since the 1846 Bear Flag Revolt had been a widely recognized symbol of California—tops the phallic central granite column.

Stone plinths at the base of that column likewise combine female allegories embodying the blessings of Euro-American civilization with male

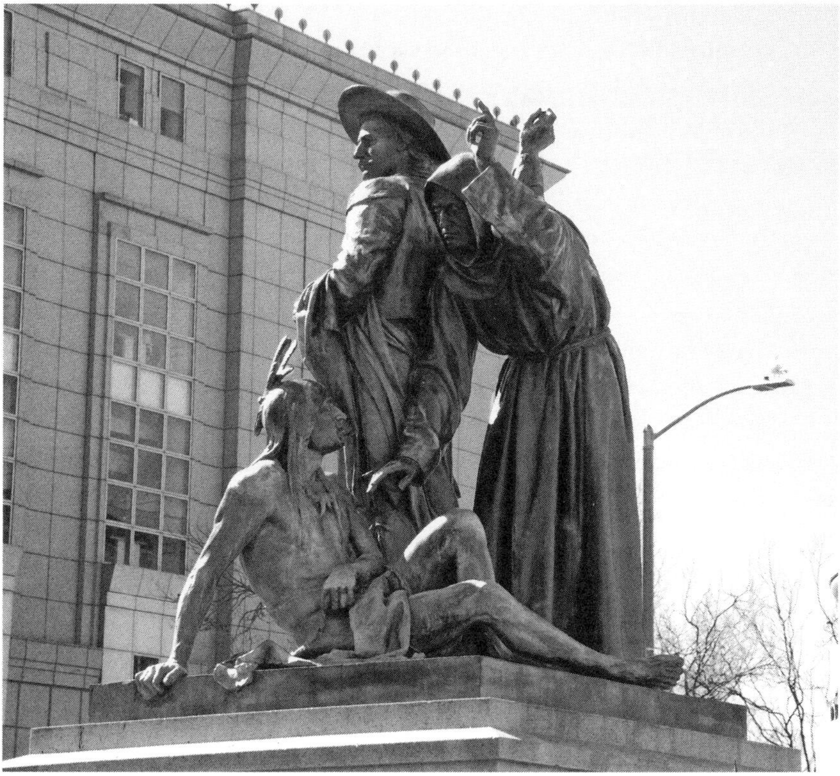

FIGURE 1.1. Frank Happersberger, *Early Days.* Detail of *James Lick Pioneer Monument,* San Francisco, California, 1894. Photograph by Lisa Allen. This portion of the Lick monument (plate A) became controversial in the late twentieth century for its depiction of California race relations.

historical figures. *Early Days* (figure 1.1) depicts a Franciscan missionary leaning over a prone Indian man whom he seeks to convert—together portraying the region's Spanish colonial period (1769–1821) and the decimation of indigenous populations—and a Californio vaquero (cowboy) from the vast ranches of the Mexican era (1821–1848). A trio of Anglo-American miners representing the 1849 gold rush conveniently omits the presence of Chinese, Mexican, and Indian miners. Alto relief plaques surrounding the central pedestal depict Californio vaqueros lassoing a bull; a white trapper trading with Indians; Anglo-Americans crossing the Sierra Nevada range by covered wagon; and an American homesteading family. The pillar also displays two key dates: 1848 for the discovery of gold and the end of the Mexican-American War with the signing of the Treaty of Guadalupe Hidalgo, under which the United States claimed California, and 1850 for California statehood.

The granite pillar is encircled by portrait medallions of white men—each identified by name—that Happersberger credited with collectively founding California. The individuals thus honored represent two common forms of what Lorenzo Veracini calls settler colonial "screen memory": marking initial colonial exploration and nostalgic narratives of settler pasts.[15] Happersberger's selection and ordering of the famous men in his honor roll reveal a great deal about how he and many Anglo-Californians of his generation conceived California history. Happersberger began his narrative with Sir Francis Drake claiming the region for England in 1579, and Franciscan missionary Father Junípero Serra establishing the Spanish missionary system that brought Christianity and white settlement to California in 1769. Rather than celebrate the wealthy Latino landowners who dominated Mexican California's cattle-ranching economy after 1821, Happersberger chose to honor Swiss immigrant John (Johann) Sutter, who—like a small but important number of Yankee businessmen—brought capitalism to Mexican California. Just as Johann Sutter anglicized his given name, Happersberger Anglo-cized this European immigrant, casting his private fiefdom, reliant on indigenous labor before gold was discovered at his mill site in 1848, as a great Anglo-American success story. Two mid-nineteenth-century Anglo-Americans round out Happersberger's pantheon of California founders: western explorer John C. Frémont and monument donor James Lick. In 1846, as war between the United States and Mexico loomed, Frémont encouraged a small group of Anglo-Americans to proclaim an independent Bear Flag Republic, and then declared himself the U.S. military governor of California. He later made a fortune in California real estate and was one of the state's first U.S. senators. Few of Happersberger's contemporaries believed the wealthy and eccentric Lick to be on par with the likes of Serra, Frémont, and Sutter.

Beneath these labeled portraits are a lesser pantheon of names associated with California history. Tellingly, the sculptor favored the English Drake over the Spanish soldier Juan Rodríguez Cabrillo, who was actually the first European to reach California. Spanish military leader Gaspar de Portolà paved a path for Junípero Serra and his fellow Franciscans. Californio José Castro was governor of California during the Mexican period and its military commander during the Mexican-American War. Californio General Mariano Guadalupe Vallejo became one of the leading dons in Mexican California's supposedly romantic, nearly timeless past, before acquiescing to the Americans—first militarily, then politically, and finally economically. The other half of the eight men in Happersberger's minor pantheon were somewhat less famous Anglo-Americans who directly contributed to American economic and military conquest of California: Yankee trader Thomas O. Larkin, Mexican-American War naval commodores John D. Sloat and Robert F. Stockton, and James Marshall, who discovered gold at Sutter's Mill. Like their Hispanic counterparts, these Anglo names reinforced the lessons of the more highly touted Serra, Frémont, and Sutter.

The Lick monument's tale of white dominance proved influential as other communities considered erecting their own pioneer statues. Communities across the United States celebrated the monument's design and erection. The *New York Times* published an article about its dedication, as did newspapers in smaller communities across the country, including the *Bloomington (Ill.) Pantagraph* and *Harrisburg (Pa.) Daily Independent.* Coverage also appeared soon after in weeklies such as the *Weekly Wisconsin* (Milwaukee), *Southport (N.C.) Leader,* and *Oakland (Calif.) Tribune.* While some printed only brief announcements that the dedication had occurred, others devoted significant column space to the monument's design and dedication, including illustrations. Wherever press coverage of the monument appeared, it was consistently laudatory of the work, including Happersberger's portrayal of white progress. The imagined march from Indian savagery to Anglo-American civilization would be celebrated in equally explicit ways in other monuments at the turn of the twentieth century; in fact, deviations from Happersberger's depiction of progress superseding savagery would spark vocal public protest.

PROPER DEPICTIONS OF PROGRESS

Interest in erecting monuments to early western settlers grew after 1900. Like fin de siècle monuments to ordinary soldiers, these western statues were designed by prominent sculptors in the Beaux-Arts style. Increasingly, though, the artists' visions conflicted with those of donors leading efforts to erect pioneer monuments. While artists were drawn to powerful images of Plains horse nomads and suffering Anglo overland migrants, donors insisted on explicit celebrations of white cultural dominance. For example, controversy would erupt in Denver over Frederick MacMonnies's plan to place an Indian warrior atop a pioneer monument in the city's commercial center. In 1904, as Portland cast its *Sacajawea* statue, the Denver business community hired MacMonnies, a distinguished and Beaux-Arts-trained artist, to design a pioneer monument to beautify the growing city. The sculptor persuaded the prominent donors to adopt a fountain, featuring elaborate bronze sculptures and architectural features that echoed the massive pillars and piers of the 1890s Lick monument.[16]

Despite MacMonnies's embrace of grand Beaux-Arts artistic tradition, when his design appeared in local newspapers, it sparked public outrage. Although it embraced many aspects of French heroic statuary, his depiction appeared to invert what whites assumed to be a God-given racial hierarchy. In keeping with contemporary conceptions of the noble savage and cultural evolution, the sculptor explained that his "idea in the design has been to make a gradual transition from civilization to savage life. . . . First, the Pioneer Settlers, Miners, Cowboys; then the Wild Animals; finally the Savage and the Buffalo (which are even now almost myths!), sacrificed to civilization and about to disappear forever into the Happy Hunting Grounds."[17] Critics read the monument in the traditional manner, expecting the pinnacle of American progress to appear atop the colossal central column, but MacMonnies seemed to glorify the "savages" displaced by Anglo settlers by placing a nude Plains Indian seated on a rearing horse at the pinnacle of the thirty-foot monument. An editorial in Denver's *Rocky Mountain News* insisted, "We have no prejudice against the noble red man. But history hath it that he faded away before the advance of the pioneers. . . . [W]e don't want the Indian dominating a structure erected to the men whose business was getting rid of Indians."[18] Viewers found it unacceptable for an indigenous warrior to be glorified over the sacrifices of white hunters, prospectors, and pioneer mothers. And the warrior's martial pose contradicted popular notions of Indians necessarily yielding to dominant white culture.[19]

Public criticism received extensive coverage in the local press. When the secretary of the Western Federation of Miners stood trial for his life, he used his notoriety to champion replacing MacMonnies's Indian with a Pony Express rider. The *Rocky Mountain News* complied with his request

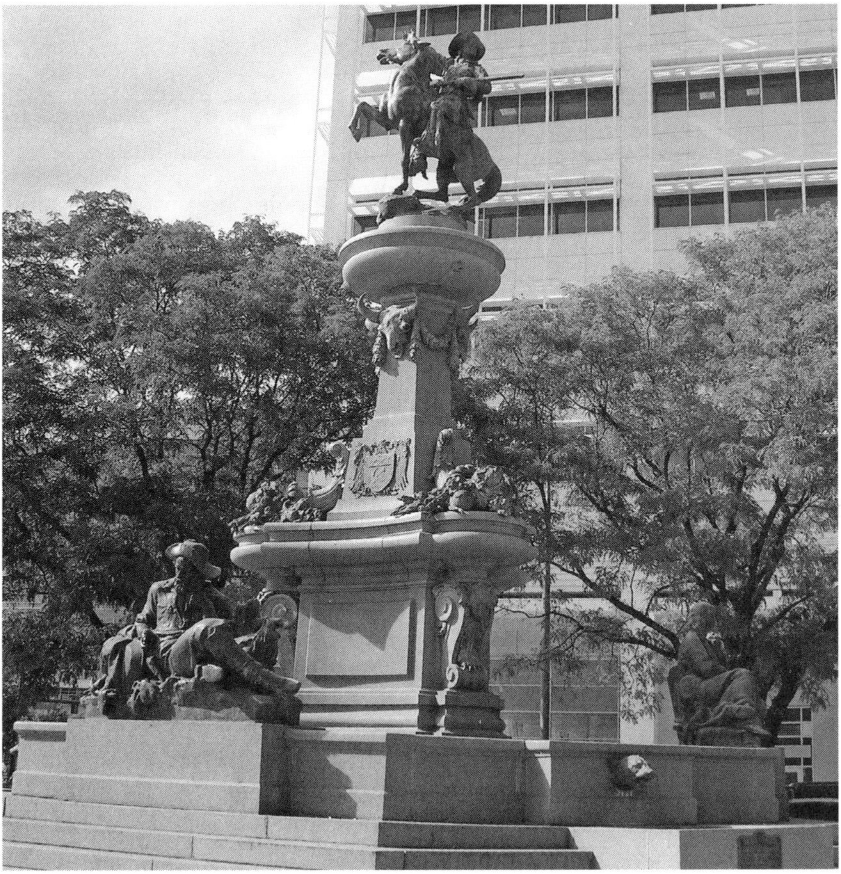

FIGURE 1.2. Frederick MacMonnies, *Pioneer Monument,* Denver, Colorado, 1911. Photograph by author.

that its staff sketch such a monument and compose a poem supporting his proposal.[20] Under pressure from the Colorado Society of Pioneers, MacMonnies ultimately replaced the heroic Indian figure with a sculpture of renowned frontiersman Kit Carson, grandson of Daniel Boone and guide to John C. Frémont's California expedition. The finished monument featured an equestrian figure of Carson towering above three other bronze figures representing frontier life: a Prospector, a Hunter, and a Pioneer Mother with child (figure 1.2). Lest there be any question about indigenous power to stop the march of white civilization, MacMonnies abandoned plans to sculpt a pioneer corpse lying at the Pioneer Mother's feet. MacMonnies thus acquiesced to the public's expectation that white progress would stand proudly and unchallenged atop the massive pillar, sacrificing his vision of civilization's gradual evolution for a newer emphasis on the conquest of western lands and peoples.[21]

MacMonnies's finished monument met with widespread approval. The American Federation of Arts' *Art and Progress* (which would soon change its name to the less value-laden *American Magazine of Art*) declared that the revised monument had "not only dignity but decorative quality."[22] The monument's 1911 dedication was celebrated by "hundreds of aged men who carried civilization into the Rockies . . . and aided in wresting what is now the great state of Colorado from the domain of 'savage beasts and still more savage men,'" along with Colorado's governor and members of the Pioneer Society, the Sons of Colorado, and the Grand Army of the Republic. So important was it for aging settlers, including those "unable to acquire a competency under the conditions of civilization which they helped to bring about," to attend the dedication of the monument in their honor that local newspapers and other "public spirited institutions" paid to bring them to Denver and give them "the time of their lives."[23] The racial ideology inscribed on MacMonnies's finished work for Denver and on the San Francisco Lick monument would become a central message of both Portland's 1905 Lewis and Clark Centennial Exposition and the Bay City's Panama-Pacific International Exposition a decade later.

INDIAN MOTHER TO A WHITE RACE

Following shifting tastes in sculpture more generally, pioneer monuments erected after 1900 abandoned nineteenth-century French grandiosity and allegory in favor of heroic-sized bronze Anglo-American figures standing on a simple stone base, which erased the ethnic diversity hinted at in Happersberger's Lick monument. Within a generation, western pioneer monuments consistently depicted generic frontier characters who embodied settler colonialism, exuded whiteness, and displayed desirable gender identities. Alice Cooper's 1905 *Sacajawea* (see plate H) represented a transitional model, featuring a realistic portrayal of an actual historic figure who embodied westward expansion and the white civilizing project. Created for the Lewis and Clark Centennial Exposition in Portland, Cooper's *Sacajawea* depicted the young Shoshone woman guiding the Lewis and Clark expedition westward, her young son, Jean-Baptiste, on her back. Cast with bronze donated by prominent early Oregon settler Henry Waldo Coe, the sculpture was paid for through a nationwide subscription campaign led by a group of Portland clubwomen.[24] Although *Sacajawea* was warmly received in 1905 Portland, westerners would soon reject its merging of racial identities and of conservative and feminist values.

Most early pioneer monuments were erected by white men to celebrate white male dominance. In contrast, western women's clubs became increasingly active not only in fundraising for monuments to white founding fathers, but also in erecting their own monuments to pioneer mothers. In Oregon and across the country, middle-class women were active in various organizations during the Progressive era. Prominent southern white women labored to erect many statues to the Confederate men in the late nineteenth century. Yet when veterans' groups sought to commemorate Confederate women, southern women resisted having a similar bronze and stone monument erected in their honor. The veterans' primary publication considered the women's resistance a sign of modesty, but some of the women to be honored proposed more constructive forms of commemoration instead, such as scholarships for young women. The veterans spurned the women's suggestions in favor of a series of public sculptures in southern states designed by male sculptors.[25] Yet of the hundreds of Confederate monuments erected, only a handful—such as Baltimore's *Confederate Women of Maryland Monument*—depicted Confederate wives and mothers. Though most early pioneer monuments likewise commemorated white men, progressive women actively promoted Pioneer Mother monuments beginning with Portland's 1905 *Sacajawea.*

Portland's *Sacajawea* statue was in many ways a feminist project. The white Pacific Northwest suffragists who sponsored the project deliberately chose to erect the first bronze public statue of a specific western woman. Rather than hiring a nationally renowned sculptor like Frederick MacMonnies, they sponsored a regional women-only sculpture competition to select the statue's design. Their chosen artist, Alice Cooper, like the female artists of the 1893 Chicago World's Fair, portrayed strong women dreaming of a better future.[26] Instead of an allegorical female figure like those used in Confederate monuments and in the Lick pioneer monument, the Portland suffragists presented a heroic depiction of a specific female historic figure, whose fame they aimed to enhance. Scholar Maureen Reed argues that the suffragist donors chose to honor Sacagawea because the increasingly famous "American Indian woman could demonstrate boldness, motherhood, and submission to civilization all at once."[27] The donors scheduled its dedication to align with a National American Woman Suffrage Association national convention in Portland, and national and regional suffrage proponents, including Susan B. Anthony and Abigail Scott Duniway, attended the sculpture's 1905 dedication.[28]

The white feminist leaders who helped to erect Cooper's *Sacajawea* considered it a fitting memorial to the thousands of white women who had migrated to Oregon about a half century earlier. Indeed, fundraising materials produced by the Sacajawea Statue Association declared that Sacajawea was "the first pioneer mother to cross the Rocky mountains and carry her baby into Oregon country."[29] Local writer and historian Eva Emery Dye, whose fictionalized biography of Sacagawea captured popular attention in the first years of the twentieth century, and Portland suffragist Sarah Evans, who led fundraising efforts for the statue, depicted Sacagawea as not only a nurturer to westering men and children but a civilizer. Local suffragist Anna Shaw went a step further, suggesting that it was white men, rather than Indian women, who were uncivilized.[30] In the Portland *Sacajawea*'s public sponsorship and reliance on fundraising by local elite women, it was like many other monuments erected in the American West in the years that followed. Later commemorations, however, would refuse to accept both its feminist agenda and its use of a woman of color to symbolize frontier motherhood.

While newspapermen dismissed the work as a "charming" illustration of a "little squaw," *Sacajawea*'s erectors apparently considered the statue to be a racially progressive project.[31] Cooper's heroic statue celebrated Sacagawea as a literal and figurative leader to white men. Her mixed-race son represented racial amalgamation, serving as an allegory of the diverse populations of the West becoming one American people. Yet by choosing Lewis and Clark's indigenous guide to commemorate white settler women, the monument also contributed to a national narrative about progress and the expansion of white civilization to the West. Indeed, the statue was erected at the center of the Lewis and Clark Exposition, which explicitly celebrated white westward expansion. Another statue created for that exhibition, Hermon MacNeil's *Coming of the White Man*, depicts the chief of the local Multnomah tribe standing with his arms crossed, staring haughtily as a young scout points toward whites arriving to displace them. After the fair, both statues were permanently installed in Washington Park, honoring the "noble savages" who yielded to white settler colonialism. No indigenous woman could serve as an allegory of virtues like liberty.[32] But as the mother of a young mixed-race child who paved the way to white settlement of Indian lands, Sacagawea *could*—at least in 1905 Portland—symbolically birth a more civilized nation. Within a decade, however, such a merging of Native and white memorializations would become unthinkable to western audiences.

CELEBRATING PROGRESS AT THE PANAMA-PACIFIC INTERNATIONAL EXPOSITION

Social Darwinism and the triumph of white civilization became organizing themes of the 1915 Panama-Pacific International Exposition (PPIE) in San Francisco, which celebrated the completion of the Panama Canal and the city's phoenixlike rise from the aftermath of the 1906 earthquake and fires. The PPIE art and architecture and the public speeches made at the exposition emphasized the same narrative of California history commemorated in the nearby 1894 Lick monument. In response to the concerns Turner raised at the 1893 World's Columbian Exposition about the closing of the frontier, the PPIE celebrated imperialism as the new American frontier. According to Sarah J. Moore, the PPIE fair repeatedly evoked the nineteenth-century white pioneer "as the national patriarch who articulated the model of progress for the nation that began with Europeans' first encounters with the New World and ended with America's ascendancy as imperial nation, made manifest by the Panama Canal and celebrated at the 1915 fair."[33] That narrative was repeated throughout the fair's visual arts display.

As a central ideological framework for the PPIE, social Darwinism's evolutionary ideology was carefully displayed through the fair's extensive use of sculpture. In Frank Morton Todd's five-volume report on the exposition, he explained that much of its sculpture represented man's evolution.[34] Two key works by prominent artists A. Stirling Calder, Frederick Roth, and Leo Lentelli, placed in the central Court of the Universe, emphasized the superiority of *The Nations of the West*—led by the spirit of Enterprise and a covered wagon—over *The Nations of the East*. While the western piece featured both white and black Heroes of Tomorrow, the group was led by a very white Mother of Tomorrow.[35]

The art of the PPIE also explicitly celebrated white conquest of the American West. Two of the most popular works at the fair were a pair of heroic equestrian statues by leading American artists teaching fairgoers that Indian savagery had given way to white civilization: Solon Borglum's *The American Pioneer* and James Earle Fraser's *The End of the Trail.* A rancher turned sculptor whose older brother would later carve Mount Rushmore, Solon Borglum favored symbols of white supremacy over historical accuracy in his portrayal of an American pioneer. The subject's dignified pose atop a prancing horse evoked nineteenth-century equestrian monuments to military leaders. Clad in rough Anglo-American clothing, the pioneer was armed with a rifle and an ax, which spoke to his work ethic, his economic aspirations, and his contributions to manifest destiny. With the rifle, he would hunt to support his family, and protect his family from both wild animals and wild Indians. With the ax, he would transform untamed forests into civilized farmland and build a log cabin, that lasting symbol of white civilization. The sculpture's contrast between martial pageantry and rough frontier realities honored white settlers for their willingness to face frontier privations and celebrated the mastery of civilized white society over the untamed wilderness and native peoples. The pioneer's advanced age evoked a national patriarch and indicated that the frontier period had passed, giving way to a more settled and civilized society.[36]

Borglum's *The American Pioneer* received a good bit of attention from fair visitors, including U.S. secretary of the Interior and California native Franklin K. Lane. In his remarks at the fair's opening ceremony, Lane argued that the spirit of the American pioneer lived on in twentieth-century imperialism. Lane pointed to Borglum's *Pioneer* statue as embodying those characteristics of civilized white manhood: "The greatest adventure is before us, the gigantic adventure of an advancing democracy, strong, virile, and kindly, and in that advance we shall be true to the indestructible spirit of the American Pioneer."[37] Borglum's *Pioneer* and its counterpart, Fraser's *The End of the Trail,* both portrayed the end of an era. San Francisco and the state of California declared at the exposition that the frontier spirit lived but that it was reborn and recast to lead the twentieth-century project of American imperialism.

James Earle Fraser's *The End of the Trail* received even more popular attention than Borglum's *The American Pioneer.* At a time when handheld cameras were becoming widely available among middle-class audiences, Fraser's statue "was abundantly photographed and was one of the official photographer's best sellers."[38] Moreover, models of Fraser's sculpture, depicting a tired American Indian man slumped over his weary pony, sold widely, helping spread the impact of the work far beyond the fair gates. Twenty-first-century scholars argue that Fraser intended *The End of the Trail* as pointed criticism of federal Indian policy, which devastated indigenous peoples by forcing them onto reservations, marking their survival in the face of suffering. Growing up on a ranch in Mitchell, South Dakota, Fraser witnessed federal soldiers forcing indigenous peoples from their native lands onto reservations. According to western art expert Patricia Broder, Fraser "developed a deep sympathy for" indigenous peoples.[39] In his memoirs, he explained, "As a boy, I remembered an old Dakota trapper saying, 'The Indians will someday be pushed into the Pacific Ocean.'" And Fraser later explained that he envisioned "making an Indian which represented his race reaching the end of the trail, at the edge of the Pacific."[40] Inspired by the 1893 Chicago Columbian Exposition's depictions of savagery and civilization, Fraser first modeled *The End of the Trail* in the 1890s, then enlarged it to monumental size for the PPIE.[41]

Fraser may in fact have intended to protest Indian removal policies. But given the fair's emphasis on social Darwinism and *The End of the Trail*'s pairing with Borglum's *The American Pioneer*, it is hardly surprising that fairgoers perceived the statue as declaring the disappearance of the vanishing Indian, in keeping with early twentieth-century ideas of social Darwinism. Any concern that viewers might have felt about the fate of these indigenous peoples likely aligned with what cultural anthropologist Renato Rosaldo refers to as "imperialist nostalgia."[42] Indeed, a published guide to sculpture at the fair depicted the piece as a "conception of the end of the Indian race."[43] While Fraser may have intended to challenge the mistreatment of Native peoples, the public clearly read his statue as celebrating the natural demise of those peoples in the face of a superior white culture.[44]

WHITE PIONEER MOTHERS

By the second decade of the twentieth century, most white Americans agreed that Anglo-American society represented the pinnacle of human evolution; failure to celebrate white supremacy continued to spark controversy, like that surrounding a PPIE statue, the first of many monuments portraying white Pioneer Mothers. Despite the growing influence of women's associations in the West and across the country, when feminine notions of decency and white racial ideology collided with artistic vision, the male-dominated art establishment upheld the artist's vision. But, as in Denver, proposed artistic elements in the San Francisco Pioneer Mother monument that failed to reinforce accepted notions of white dominance sparked vocal protest, which persuaded the artist to alter his design.

The sight of San Francisco's Lick monument towering over that city's smoldering ruins in the aftermath of the 1906 earthquake inspired San Francisco society matron Ella Sterling Mighels to conceive, and tirelessly promote the erection of, a monument to Pioneer Mothers in that city. As historian Brenda Frink has shown, Mighels embraced a racialized notion of Anglo-American women as civilizers of both Indian savages and white men. Mighels envisioned a monument to pioneer mothers not as gentle leaders who made great sacrifices but as a civilizing influence over the rough-and-tumble world of gold-rush California. Far from promoting women's suffrage—as did the Portland women who erected the Cooper *Sacajawea*—Mighels believed that women's influence should be channeled through motherhood within the domestic sphere. While many white Californians shared Mighels's belief in white supremacy, they were slow to embrace her vision of a monument depicting a seated pioneer mother providing presumably Protestant religious instruction to her children.[45]

Mighels's efforts to erect a statue of a gold-rush mother holding "church around her knees" birthed the Pioneer Mother Monument Association, one of many middle-class women's voluntary organizations established during the Progressive era.[46] That association raised funds to erect a monument "symbolizing Motherhood, to be dedicated to the Pioneer Mothers of the West—the self-sacrificing women who, with their little ones at their side, braved the dangers and underwent the hardships and privations that are always incident to pioneer life."[47] But not until that group's efforts were subsumed by the PPIE's Woman's Board did the project gain traction. Most PPIE sculpture, including Borglum's *The American Pioneer* and Fraser's *The End of the Trail*, was made from plaster and intended to survive only the duration of the fair. In contrast, the Pioneer Mother was to be cast in bronze and would remain as a permanent gift to the city of San Francisco. The Pioneer Mother Monument Association and various

California pioneer associations pledged to fundraise for the project. But tension soon developed between John Trask, chief of the PPIE's Fine Arts Department, and the clubwomen sponsoring the statue. Trask, a leading figure in the fine arts establishment, was convinced that no California artist was qualified for a project of this significance. Instead, he sought to give the commission to his friend, Beaux-Arts-trained sculptor Charles Grafly.[48]

Trask told Grafly that he and the Pioneer Mother Monument Association envisioned a sculpture of "a mother, two or three children, [and] a father with a pick and gold-miner's pan introduced as a back ground or bas relief on the pedestal." But despite Trask's suggestion that Grafly study U.S. history from "1848 to 1865 paying special attention to the sterling qualities of the [white] women who . . . showed themselves the worthy predecessors of the present suffragettes by enduring great hardships in order to come out here and boss the aforesaid husbands," Grafly's artistic vision was informed by French allegorical monuments and eastern romanticizations of the West.[49] Grafly abandoned both Mighels's conception of a hoop-skirted Anglo-American woman *and* the committee's familial vision in favor of a woman clad in the fringed buckskin and moccasins that many easterners associated with the Wild West, along with nude children symbolizing the future.

San Franciscans balked at Grafly's depiction of a white woman playing Indian. Eastern urbanites might put on Indian costumes and engage in wilderness activities as an antidote to modernity's inauthenticity, and Pacific Northwest feminists may have held up Sacagawea as an icon of maternalist leadership, but two generations removed from the unruly and ethnically diverse gold rush, Anglo-Californian women still felt a need to defend their civility.[50] Mighels's corsets and hoop skirts were optional, but modest Anglo costume was non-negotiable. Pressure from the Native Daughters of the Golden West and other women's pioneer associations persuaded the eastern artist to replace the "costume of a primitive Sioux Indian squaw" with a homespun gown, simple leather shoes, and sunbonnet.[51] While this change ensured that the white pioneer woman could not be mistaken for an Indian woman, it achieved little more historical accuracy. Most mid-nineteenth-century Anglo-American emigrants wore clothing sewn from manufactured cloth, contrary to the widespread homespun myth.[52] Under pressure from the female donors, Grafly also agreed to adjust the head covering, but even the final version (figure 1.3) lacked the wide brim

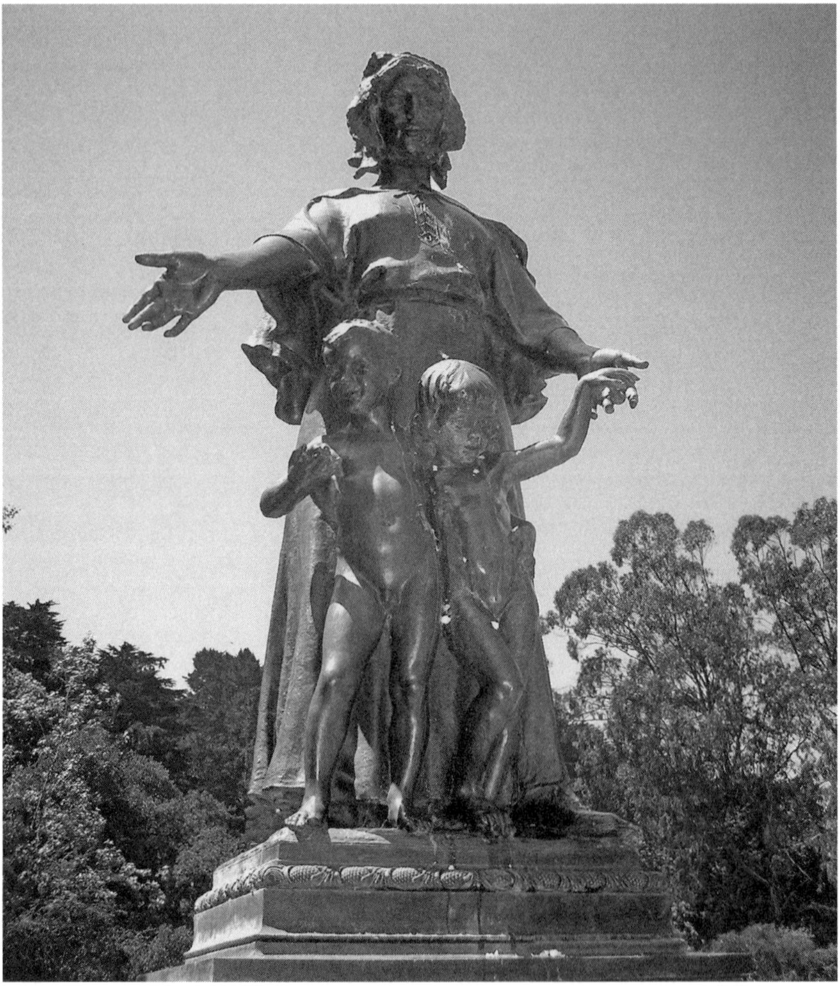

FIGURE 1.3. Charles Grafly, *Pioneer Mother*, San Francisco, California, 1915. Photograph by author.

characteristic of a mid-nineteenth-century sunbonnet. This is surprising because those wide-brimmed sunbonnets were designed to protect white women's fair complexions from the sun and thus prevent any resemblance to darker-complexioned indigenous women—a detail apparently lost on San Francisco's fashionable clubwomen, who (despite their determination that the monument be cast in bronze rather than the much whiter plaster used for the PPIE's temporary exhibits) remained more concerned about the monument's racial ideology than its historicity.

Some of the clubwomen sponsoring the monument—including Mighels—were outraged that Grafly insisted on including nude children in a monument intended to instruct California's children. Yet they understood Grafly's use of nudity to emphasize the children's innocence and vulnerability. While nudity in adults was closely associated with primitiveness at the time, it appears that the monument's white donors never questioned the children's whiteness. In keeping with the racialized maternal rhetoric in this period, Indian women like Sacagawea could bear mixed-race children, who might eventually assimilate into the dominant white society. But white viewers simply could not conceive of a white mother bearing nonwhite children. Happersberger's female allegories had been replaced by actual western women, and Sacagawea in turn yielded to a white Pioneer Mother. But that white Pioneer Mother's children could, for the time being, remain allegorical.

Both Trask and monument association president Helen Sanborn claimed to support the artist's vision, so long as the pioneer mother could not be mistaken for an American Indian. But Sanborn insisted that the children's nudity made it impossible for the organization to raise public subscriptions to support the monument. Trask confided in Grafly that he had given up trying to negotiate with Mighels. Philanthropist and honorary president of the PPIE Woman's Board Phoebe Hearst and U.S. Senator (and former San Francisco mayor) James Phelan finally brokered a compromise, persuading Grafly to make the boy's genitalia somewhat less conspicuous, and thus less offensive to the elite Anglo women donors' genteel sensibilities.[53]

Public opinion of the revised statue was generally positive. Remarkably, more than one thousand people visited the artist's eastern studio to view the completed statue, which they agreed was a "symbolical masterpiece."[54] Although at least some vocal California clubwomen feared exposing their offspring to nudity in public sculpture, actual children appear not to have been overly bothered by Grafly's creation.[55] In the context of other PPIE art, fairgoers appear to have overlooked the children's nudity and accepted Grafly's statue as simply one more celebration of the arrival of white civilization in the formerly savage West.

The bronze *Pioneer Mother* was overshadowed at the PPIE by Borglum's and Fraser's much larger and more temporary plaster works. Both *The American Pioneer* and *The End of the Trail* were prominently featured in the 1915 souvenir book of the fair's sculpture collection, while Grafly's bronze

Pioneer Mother barely received mention.[56] A quarter-century later it stood, weather worn and vandalized, in the near ruin of the Palace of Fine Arts. Within three months of its rediscovery, civic and historic groups helped to restore the monument, and it was displayed at the Golden Gate International Exposition before being installed at its final site among statues of famous white men in a meadow in Golden Gate Park on December 8, 1940, where it is largely ignored by the public. Meanwhile, although bronze models of Fraser's statue were sold as souvenirs—and countless copies have since been sold, including a heroic-sized reproduction erected in Waupun, Wisconsin, in 1929—the original plaster statues received less respect. Fraser's *The End of the Trail* and Borglum's *The American Pioneer* were saved from destruction along with most of the PPIE art and architecture when the city of Visalia accepted the exposition company's offer of free statuary for the cost of removing the pieces from the fair site. Few people knew about their location, though, and even Fraser assumed his statue had been destroyed.[57] In 1968, Oklahoma City's National Cowboy Hall of Fame and Western Heritage Center acquired and restored Fraser's *The End of the Trail* in exchange for providing Visalia with a bronze copy of the popular statue. Borglum's *The American Pioneer* survived until 1980, when it sustained substantial earthquake damage. The broken pieces eventually ended up in the town dump. Although some pieces are rumored to have been rescued by private collectors, there are no known surviving models of the complete statue, which had been the first representational monument to a generic white pioneer man.[58]

RUGGED MALE PIONEERS

In the 1890s, westerners sought to absolve white guilt over Indian conquest through depictions of the inevitable progression from savagery to civilization, but a generation later, indigenous dispossession appeared more or less complete, and federal policy shifted toward accepting assimilated Indians as citizens. Having achieved white dominance, Anglo settlers began to grapple with their own culpability in that dominance. While famous individuals like Brigham Young or John Sutter could conquer indigenes through their leadership, casting generic pioneer types as conquerors—as Solon Borglum did for the PPIE—meant that they had conquered someone. Artists, donors, and the public resolved this tension

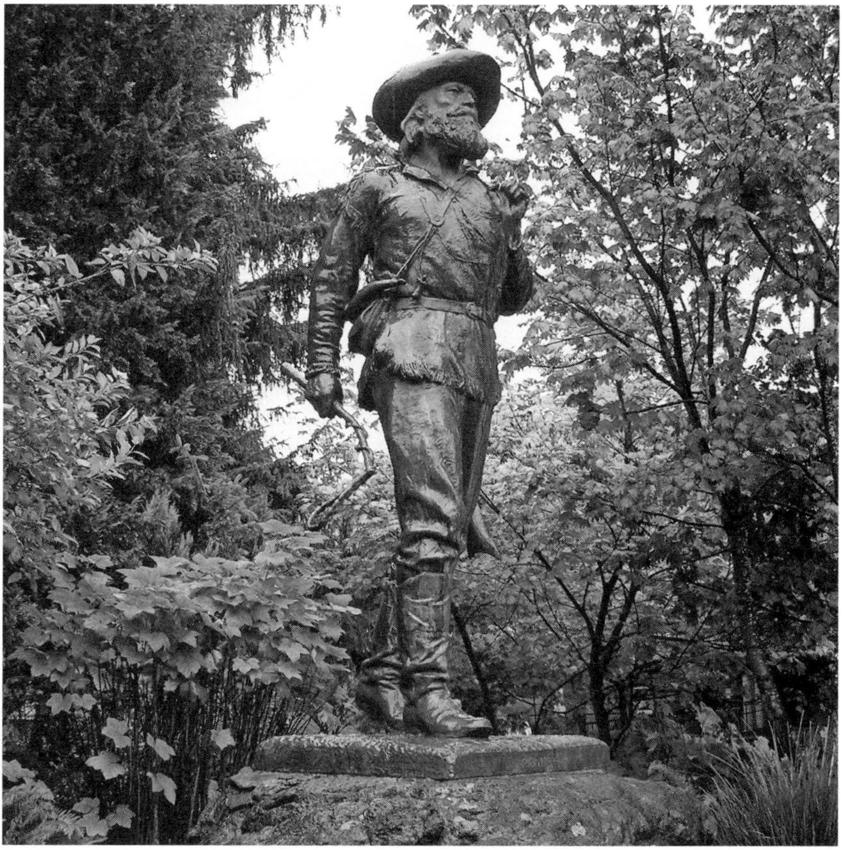

FIGURE 1.4. A. Phimister Proctor, *The Pioneer*, Eugene, Oregon, 1918. Photograph by author.

by emphasizing pioneers' success in dominating wild lands rather than wild peoples. Emphasizing settlers' struggles to conquer the landscape—whether in pioneer memoirs, fiction, or monumental sculpture—was a defense mechanism that allowed white Americans to deny their responsibility in the devastation of the Indians.[59]

Most monuments erected after World War I abandoned French Beaux-Arts statuomania, instead depicting a single generic pioneer figure—often playing Indian by wearing fringed buckskin—that more closely resembled Great War doughboy statues. Shortly after Solon Borglum's conquering *The American Pioneer* appeared at the PPIE, prominent western sculptor Alexander Phimister Proctor created such a bronze Pioneer for the campus of the University of Oregon, *The Pioneer* (figure 1.4). Born in Ontario, Canada, in 1860, Proctor migrated by covered wagon with his family, gradually traveling south and west until they arrived in Denver in 1871. Phimister Proctor, as he was known, considered himself a true frontiersman because of his passion for hunting and fishing—activities that, as a young man growing up in the shadow of the Rocky Mountains, Proctor prized ahead of his art. The Paris-trained artist devoted significant time and energy to studying living wild animals and dissecting dead ones—many of which he had shot himself—to precisely reproduce their musculature. Likewise, Proctor spent several summers living among and modeling Native Americans to produce realistic sculptures and paintings. Unlike former rancher Solon Borglum and eastern artist Charles Grafly, and as I explore in greater detail in the next chapter, Proctor was also committed to historical accuracy when depicting white pioneers.[60]

Yet Proctor's devotion to authenticity did not lead him to challenge much of the iconography typical of early twentieth-century western art. Instead, he embraced heroic representations of rough, strong cowboys and pioneers that mirrored early settlers' romanticized images of themselves. In fact, Proctor himself played Indian, even compiling his reminiscences under the title *Sculptor in Buckskin*. So when the artist was commissioned to sculpt a pioneer monument for the University of Oregon campus, in Eugene, instead of modeling it on Augustus Saint-Gaudens's famous 1899 bronze tribute to *The Puritans*, as donor and Portland timber baron Joseph N. Teal had requested, Proctor instead turned to imagery more typical of Frederic Remington's western soldiers and cowboys. The sculptor hired an old trapper to model for the work so that he could incorporate both his own memories and "first hand descriptions and impressions of those hardy men and women who crossed the plains."[61] Proctor's resulting 1918 monument to Oregon pioneers featured a buckskin-clad frontiersman with a rifle thrown over his shoulder, striding purposely into the West and the future, proclaiming his rugged frontier masculinity. Frederick V. Holman—president of the Oregon Historical Society and former president of two pioneer associations—approved, declaring at its dedication that the "statue symbolizes and immortalizes in a remarkable way the Oregon pioneer['s] . . . courage, his determination, his instincts and his high ideals."[62] Although old and grizzled like Borglum's pioneer for the PPIE, Proctor's pioneer appeared ready to conquer nature, American Indians, or anything else that might stand in his way. Yet by traveling on foot in his sturdy boots, he remained a hardworking yeoman, rather than riding in like a conquering hero. Teal, like other male donors of his generation, embraced swashbuckling solo white male pioneers as the embodiment of white civilization.

As the debate surrounding the PPIE's *Pioneer Mother* reveals, a white woman wearing clothing made from animal hides endangered both her racial and her gender identities, calling into question her domesticity and raising fears of racial amalgamation. This was particularly true in California, which despite the persistence of its towering *Lick Pioneer Monument*, still struggled to overcome its Indian, mestizo, and gold-rush past. But the Oregon public happily embraced Proctor's choice to dress his pioneer man in a suit of fringed buckskin, because—like Theodore Roosevelt's carefully orchestrated transformation from a northeastern dandy into a fearless rancher—a white man's choice to rough it in the wilderness or to play Indian enhanced rather than challenged his masculine image.[63] Indeed, in Proctor's sculpture, the Eugene pioneer's European-style coat of fringed buckskin and his long tousled beard marked him as a masculine backwoodsman, while his rifle and confident stride demonstrated his white racial superiority.

MARTYRS ON THE SNOW WHITE ALTAR

The Donner Parlor of the Native Sons of the Golden West was determined to erect a similarly celebratory monument in California's Truckee Pass to honor their namesake wagon train, but the ugly story that made the Donner party famous complicated its commemoration. In 1846–47 the ill-fated Donner party had faced a winter of exposure and starvation, and a few had famously survived by consuming the flesh of fallen fellow travelers. Plans to erect a simple commemorative shaft that would have conveniently skirted the issue of cannibalism soon gave way to calls for a heroic statue in keeping with recent monumentalization efforts in San Francisco and elsewhere. But artists and the monument's sponsors disagreed about how to celebrate white supremacy while commemorating the infamous Donner party's suffering. Native Son Chester Warren Chapman had asked San Francisco sculptor Douglas Tilden to design the Donner party monument, yet the Native Sons could not accept Tilden's conception of a "lone pioneer figure" on top of a pedestal, surrounded by "a dozen or so figures sitting, lying, creeping in different attitudes from cowering anxiety to resignation of death."[64] Instead, most Anglo-Californians imagined the California pioneer as "the seeker for gold, the argonaut, [who] was all conquering, all triumphant, sure, able, resourceful, unbaffled by storm or stress." Why, then, would they construct a monument to the misery—let alone the cannibalism—of the Donner party? The *San Francisco Call* insisted that the Donner party members were "martyrs," and asked its readers, "Had those victims not been sacrificed on the snow white altar of the Sierras, as the first born emigrants into the fair land of California, how many thousands might have perished in other winters?"[65] In honor of these martyrs, the Native Sons held a massive barbecue—offering an abundance of food in sharp contrast to the Donner party's starvation, yet oddly evocative of a few members' cannibalism—and sought to raise a memorial.[66]

Just as Denver business interests had sponsored impoverished early white Colorado settlers' attendance at the dedication of their pioneer monument, the Native Sons sought to honor the starving Donner party's role in paving a path to California. But Tilden's proposed sculpture placed too much emphasis on the Donner party's suffering (and raised the specter of cannibalism). Instead, as Doris Foley's history of the monument details, the Native Sons insisted on a generic pioneer figure whose victory over adversity was never in question—something similar to the heroic pioneer men sculpted by Solon Borglum and Phimister Proctor.

Breaking ties with Tilden, in 1913 the monument committee selected another Californian's depiction of a pioneer family: a bold pioneer man gazing westward, supporting his wife and baby with his strong right arm as their young child clings to his boots (figure 1.5). Unlike Borglum's and Proctor's rough-and-tumble frontiersmen, in John McQuarrie's *Pioneer Family (Donner) Monument*, a hardworking farmer dressed in homespun clothing guides his family to their new home in the land of gold. The president of the University of California composed the monument's inscription: "Virile to risk and find; kindly withal and a ready help. Facing the brunt of fate; indomitable—unafraid."[67] Only the 22.5-foot base (marking the depth of the snow pack during the Donner party's entrapment) hints at the tragedy. Newspapers from San Francisco to Eugene, Oregon (which was eagerly awaiting completion of Proctor's *The Pioneer*) to Deadwood, South Dakota, excitedly followed the monument's

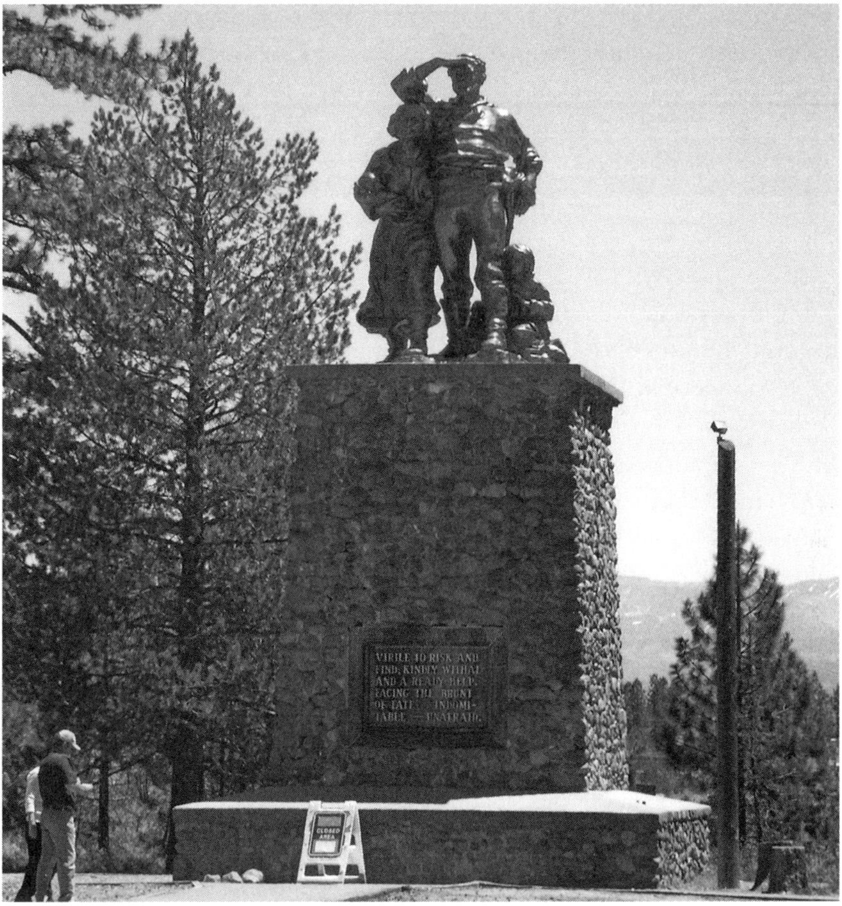

FIGURE 1.5. John McQuarrie, *Pioneer Family (Donner) Monument,* Truckee, California, 1918. Photograph by author.

progress, seemingly unaware of the controversy surrounding its design. The statue's 1918 dedication received extensive regional attention and was covered by press throughout the West, all of which cheered the heroic depiction of California pioneers. However, some Californians felt that the completed monument failed to sufficiently honor the suffering of the Donner party.[68] While its creators might have debated whether to portray the Donner party's suffering or a more positive generic pioneer family, only the land itself—and not its indigenous inhabitants—remained able to challenge Anglo-American dominance by the monument's dedication in 1918. The McQuarrie design, which, the *Santa Cruz (Calif.) Evening*

News insisted, "honor[ed] the pioneer women of California no less than the pioneer men," also helped to cement white westerners' depictions of pioneer men and, increasingly, pioneer women for future monuments.[69]

BIRTH OF THE PIONEER MOTHER MOVEMENT

The first pioneer monuments declared the arrival of Euro-American civilization to the Wild West and its vanquishing of Indian savagery. Pioneer monuments would continue to celebrate white dominance for decades to come. But whites' interest in noble savage mythology dwindled as they grew confident in their conquest of indigenous populations and western lands. Nearly four decades of assimilationist policies under the 1887 Dawes Severalty Act culminated in the Indian Citizenship Act of 1924. While meaningful citizenship was still decades away for most indigenous individuals, western settlers' anxieties about Indian savagery appear to have faded rapidly after World War I. Social Darwinist pillars yielded to swashbuckling white pioneers marching westward. Confident in their racial dominance, white westerners turned their attention to a new source of anxiety: white women's sexuality. Western men and women responded as they had to earlier racial anxieties: by erecting pioneer monuments that enshrined their gender ideals.

As we will see in the next chapter, private donors in communities from Kansas City, Missouri, to Ponca City, Oklahoma, embraced monuments that commemorated the triumph of white civilization over savagery embodied in statues of Anglo-American women. So popular did monuments to that white-woman-in-a-sunbonnet trope become that it deserves to be called the Pioneer Mother movement. With proper depictions of race clearly delineated, westerners embraced Pioneer Mother monuments in large numbers, but found themselves quibbling over the best way to represent white womanhood.

BIBLES, RIFLES, AND SUNBONNETS

Venerating Pioneer Motherhood, 1920–1940

As a Pennsylvania lawyer turned Oklahoma oilman, E. W. Marland hired artists Jo Davidson, Jo Mora, and Bryant Baker to sculpt iconic Oklahomans—cowboys, pioneers, and Ponca and Cherokee Indians—to line the driveway leading to his mansion in the mid-1920s, a friend supposedly asked, "Why don't you . . . make a statue to the vanishing American, a Ponca, Otoe, or an Osage—a monument of great size?" Marland, surrounded by women with bobbed hair, wearing "inadequate skirts," and smoking cigarettes, replied, "The Indian is not the vanishing American—it's the pioneer woman."[1] To combat the rise of those short-haired, short-skirted, smoking New Women, Marland borrowed from the plans Davidson had confided in him to create a heroic Sunbonnet Woman, sponsoring a competition to select the best portrayal of pioneer womanhood for his adopted hometown of Ponca City. The competition attracted nationwide attention. Reportedly, 750,000 Americans viewed the twelve entries that toured the nation in 1926, and many of those cast votes for their favorites.[2]

The twelve submissions to Marland's competition all depicted variations on a common theme of a sunbonnet-clad white mother. Moreover, the winning Ponca City *Pioneer Woman* statue (plate B) was just one of the two dozen monuments erected between 1927 and 1939 specifically honoring pioneer mothers for carrying civilization to the savage frontier. Eighty-four percent of the pioneer monuments dedicated during that period included pioneer mothers; more than half focused on pioneer mothers unaccompanied by men. In fact, more pioneer mother monuments were erected in those thirteen years than the total number of pioneer monuments erected prior to 1920, with far more similarity in iconography and artistic style among statues than in that earlier period. Those monuments erected in the late 1920s usually featured a realistically depicted pioneer

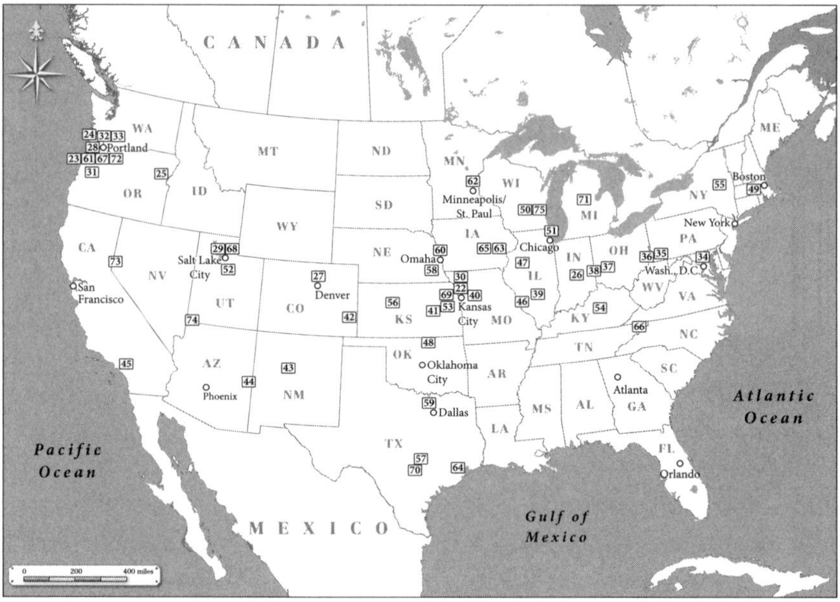

MAP 2. Pioneer Monuments Erected 1920–1939. Map by Gerry Krieg. Numbers on the map correspond with a chronological listing of monuments in the appendix.

mother and her children. In the 1930s, even those children were stripped away from many, leaving solo pioneer women.

So firmly did the canon of Pioneer Mother iconography become established in the late 1920s that any proposed variation sparked protest. As part of the 1936 lavish celebration of the one hundredth anniversary of its brief independence, the Texas Centennial Commission decided to erect a monument to pioneer women on the campus of the Texas State College for Women (currently, Texas Woman's University) in Denton. When the learned panel of judges announced its selection of a design, however, the people of Texas objected loudly. The stylized, modernist—and, even more shockingly, nude—model of a "pioneer family" was deemed an inappropriate representation of frontier womanhood (plate E). In the late 1920s and early 1930s, Americans had achieved widespread agreement that pioneer monuments should commemorate white settler women as the embodiment of white civilization. These Pioneer Mothers were consistently depicted as women clad in sunbonnets, armed with rifles with which to defend their innocent children, or Bibles symbolizing their role in carrying Anglo civilization to the western frontier. At the height of what I call the Pioneer Mother movement (1927–1939), western viewers did not tolerate sculptures that deviated from that dominant iconography. Around 1900, towers of social Darwinism predominated; twenty-five years later, adherence to accepted pioneer motherhood imagery became a popular and powerful way to inscribe racial hierarchy onto western lands.

The pure number of public monuments erected in this period (most of them sculpted by prominent American artists for growing U.S. cities) using consistent iconography of sunbonneted Pioneer Mothers speaks to the power and consistency of that imagery. The slight differences that appeared in depictions of white frontier women produced during the Pioneer Mother movement might therefore appear to be inconsequential variations on a theme. But those seemingly minor variations warrant our close attention, for they represent far more than mere artistic license. This chapter focuses on well-known pioneer woman statues by renowned artists Phimister Proctor, Avard Fairbanks, August Leimbach, Bryant Baker, and Leo Friedlander. Comparing these famous statues to each other and to lesser-known monuments, famous paintings, and contemporaneous visual culture reveals how artists, donors, and public audiences negotiated specific and at times subtle messages about expected gender and sexual roles, white racial supremacy, and the nature of American national identity. Some historical context is required before analyzing these distinctions among Pioneer Mother monuments.

Celebrations of early white settlement collided with rapid social change in the early twentieth century, inspiring white westerners to embrace a growing national trend of rural nostalgia. Declining availability of homesteading lands coincided with rising anxiety about dramatic shifts in American society. Urbanization, increasing immigration from Asia and southern Europe, falling birth rates among native-born Americans, new public roles for women, looser attitudes toward sexuality, and the highest divorce rate in the world all convinced many that the American family was in crisis. These fears inspired efforts to shore up white civilization by promoting more conservative domestic roles for white native-born women even as they tended toward nostalgia for an idyllic rural frontier past. Female progressive reformers seeking to improve living conditions for poor and rural mothers viewed their own standards of modern "scientific motherhood" to be a route to Americanization. But those standards were increasingly challenged by more conservative women, who hearkened back to the antebellum "moral motherhood" ideology that had characterized mothers as the "angel of the house." These 1920s conservatives adapted nineteenth-century moral motherhood to encompass a patriotic, exclusionary form of native-born white motherhood.[3] Meanwhile, prominent men such as Theodore Roosevelt and sociologist Edward Ross celebrated the traditional (rural, white) American family, embracing a racialized form of Jeffersonian agrarianism.[4] Rurality—particularly that embodied by white farmers' wives in the midwestern heartland and recently settled portions of the Far West—seemed to offer a crucial alternative to the dangers of modernity.[5]

Prominent Americans warned that white Americans' falling fertility rates amid massive immigration would produce "race suicide," and they celebrated rural families' fertility and traditional cultural values. Meanwhile, conservative elements throughout the United States embraced public sculpture as a way to remember what had been lost and to instruct future generations. As we saw in chapter 1, public opinion played a key role in shaping—or at least constraining—the design of pioneer monuments. In the early twentieth century, the dominant culture expected western monuments to celebrate the arrival of white civilization and perhaps mourn the demise of savage indigenous cultures. The obsession with the supposedly vanishing Indian, which had motivated many pioneer monuments erected from the 1890s through World War I, faded in the face of rapid social change. By the 1920s, white Americans were more concerned about race suicide and flappers than they were about Anglo dominance over indigenous peoples. Anxiety over the decline of (white) western families and communities drowned out narratives recounting the triumph of white civilization.[6] That anxiety played itself out in the creation of a veritable Pioneer Mother movement—the focus of this chapter—that emerged during the Jazz Age and lasted until the start of World War II.

As American women gained new political, economic, and social opportunities and increasingly embraced their sexuality—and as concern with new immigration from southern and eastern Europe and from Asia grew widespread—monuments erected by conservative groups such as the Daughters of the American Revolution (DAR) and western pioneer organizations celebrated an earlier golden age of clearly defined gender roles and Anglo-American dominance. In fact, the nativist DAR embraced pioneer monuments as a means to resist rapidly changing gender norms and to celebrate white civilization simultaneously. Like earlier towers of western progress, the Pioneer Mother symbolized the arrival of white settlement, advanced civilization, and Anglo-American gender norms to the savage frontier. But in contrast to white southerners' contemporaneous calls for monuments depicting popular "Mammy" imagery, western Pioneer Mother monuments carefully avoided any hint of Indianness of the sort embraced by Portland's 1905 *Sacajawea* or that elicited outrage in Charles Grafly's design for San Francisco's 1915 *Pioneer Mother* (both discussed in chapter 1).[7] For southerners in the 1920s, celebrating a fictional grandmotherly black slave woman devoted to her white "family" at once justified segregation and constructed domesticity in a way that freed white women from household labor to participate in the public sphere.[8] But in western states, which had been among the first to grant women suffrage, and where white civilization was predicated on the recent removal of the racialized Other, white women's engagement with the public sphere and embrace of their own sexuality proved more problematic for those determined to maintain the recently established racial order. Western monuments therefore depicted chaste, nurturing white Pioneer Mothers. Lest those Pioneer Mothers be suspected of doing hard physical labor on the frontier (as many female settlers did out of necessity), or of challenging male leadership in the public sphere (while western states led the nation in enfranchising women), most western monuments depicted white women walking westward. Always en route to the West and never arriving, Pioneer Mothers carried white civilization westward without being tainted by the frontier's racial mixing and flexible gender roles. Inspired by a combination of fine art traditions and popular fiction portraying the Wild West, the monuments of the Pioneer Mother movement in turn shaped not only later pioneer monuments, but also American popular imagination about rural women more broadly for generations to come.

In art historian Annette Stott's 1996 essay, "Prairie Madonnas and Pioneer Women: Images of Emigrant Women in the Art of the Old West," she demonstrated that late nineteenth- and early twentieth-century artists consistently portrayed western women as young white mothers clad in long dresses and sunbonnets. Stott argued persuasively that between 1890 and 1930, the closing of the frontier, the growing prominence of artists living in the West, and changing gender norms led to stronger, more active roles for women in western painting and sculpture than had been typical during the nineteenth century. Nineteenth-century images of Prairie Madonnas—westering women whose "piety, purity, submissiveness, and domesticity," as well as their role in fulfilling manifest destiny, were merged in Marian imagery—now were replaced by new, more robust images of active Pioneer Women after 1890.[9] Yet, Stott's formal analysis of painting, sculpture, and public statuary disguises important distinctions between art produced for personal consumption and that concretized through public commemoration. Public monuments—which are intended to serve multiple audiences and to permanently enshrine certain cultural values—are inherently more conservative than art produced for more private, individual purposes. A close examination of the four dozen western monuments erected to frontier women during the Pioneer Mother movement shows that these changes appeared more gradually and infrequently in public monuments than they did in western paintings intended for private consumption. At the height of the Pioneer Mother movement, private donors and the American public alike demanded pioneer monuments that reinforced long-held beliefs in women's moral superiority in the face of rapid social and demographic change.

Elite white women were among the first to embrace this Pioneer Mother imagery. While towers of white male progress sculpted and erected by men had included pioneer women in very minor supporting roles prior to 1920, suffragists sought out a female artist to sculpt *Sacajawea* as a tribute to Oregon's pioneer mothers, and San Francisco's clubwomen erected a bronze *Pioneer Mother* among the plaster creations of the PPIE in 1915 (see chapter 1). That monument in turn inspired Indiana clubwomen to commission a Pioneer Mother statue of their own in the early 1920s (see chapter 5), and other women's clubs followed. But just as elite women's monument building peaked in the mid-1920s, American gender dynamics shifted dramatically. Early excitement over women's nationwide enfranchisement fractured amid debates over the Equal Rights Amendment (ERA), and as it became apparent that women did not consistently vote for maternalist reform (as many progressive reformers had hoped), nor did they simply follow their husbands' political preferences (as many men had assumed they would). At the height of the Jazz Age, western men embraced Pioneer Mother iconography to combat pervasive flapper imagery. Seizing the reins from western clubwomen, beginning in the mid-1920s, elite white men commissioned renowned white male artists to produce prominent tributes to pioneer motherhood.

In this chapter, I argue that the famous male artists producing pioneer monuments in the late 1920s adapted earlier ideas about westering True Women (characterized by their morality and domesticity). Beginning in the 1890s, New Women began enjoying greater freedom to embrace public roles ranging from paid clerical work to eventually voting. By the 1920s, New Women became associated with even greater social and sexual freedom. Artists responded by returning to the mid-nineteenth-century Prairie Madonnas described by Stott to combat these images of New Women, while also evoking the romance of western adventures typical of fin de siècle dime novels and early Hollywood westerns. By coopting Catholic Madonna imagery, these prominent male artists simultaneously proclaimed the moral superiority of Protestant Anglo-American women over Catholic women (many of whom were Latina or European immigrants) in the West.[10] Although most stood heroically tall on their own two feet, the Anglo-American Protestant women portrayed in Pioneer Mother monuments did not completely abandon the protection of their covered wagons. Instead, sculptors surrounded these young pioneer women with young children, armed them with guns or Bibles, and placed these sainted Pioneer Mothers on pedestals bearing bas reliefs of their covered wagons. Examining small but significant differences among these remarkably similar Pioneer Mother monuments reveals the power of that iconography as well as its limits. This chapter begins by comparing how prominent (and some less prominent) artists balanced Prairie Madonna and Pioneer Woman imagery in their monuments to pioneer mothers. I then focus on artists' depictions of weaponry in 1920s and 1930s pioneer monuments, before turning to competing visions of pioneer motherhood for Denton, Texas, in the mid-1930s.

While Pioneer Mother monuments continued to appear throughout the West during the 1930s, my comprehensive study reveals that representations of western settlers became somewhat more diverse once more. Some artists depicted pioneer women unaccompanied by their children, casting them as virginal women rather than mothers, while others chose to design monuments illustrating groups of western characters. And Mormon sculptures emphasized patriarchal father figures rather than lone women. But as the Denton nude pioneer family controversy made clear, monuments to Pioneer Mothers remained important, and public audiences expected those pioneer mothers to wear prairie dresses and sunbonnets.

PRAIRIE MADONNAS AND PIONEER WOMEN

Early pioneer monuments were modeled to varying degrees after cosmopolitan European monumental sculpture of the late nineteenth century. Western towns and cities continued to stake claims to their urbanity by erecting pioneer-themed statuary by prominent American artists throughout the 1920s and 1930s, but the design of those monuments changed significantly. Rather than pairing portraits of famous men with allegorical female figures, by the mid-1920s, pioneer monuments consistently included relatively realistic depictions of generic western women. Prominent pioneer monument sculptors were increasingly inspired by contemporary American visual culture. In the mid-nineteenth century, eastern artists trained in European romantic traditions, such as Albert Bierstadt, produced popular paintings of sublime western landscapes. One's ability to appreciate their sublimity became a marker of class status at a time when "taste had become a tool of cultural hegemony."[11] But around the turn of the century, American painting and illustration abandoned romantic portrayals of the Rocky Mountains as the American Alps in favor of more documentary representations of western lands and peoples—albeit images still more informed by imagination than reality.[12] Painting images of bold men surviving and dominating western landscapes enabled American artists to differentiate themselves from their effete European counterparts. Those stronger western images appealed powerfully to Americans grappling with a crisis of masculinity.

Immediately after World War I, those masculine anxieties encouraged westerners to erect monuments to hardy male pioneers. But by the late 1920s, western monuments focused almost exclusively on Pioneer Mothers. The monuments of the Pioneer Mother movement borrowed and adapted imagery from both nineteenth- and twentieth-century western-themed American paintings. In Stott's study of western women in American art, she identified stronger Pioneer Women in western paintings beginning in the 1890s. For example, Harvey Dunn, who studied at the Chicago Art Institute and Howard Pyle's Brandywine School of illustrators, drew on his childhood on a South Dakota homestead in his paintings and illustrations of frontier life. Dunn's frontier New Women were resilient and spirited women of their times, who worked hard outdoors alongside their husbands. Eschewing constraining corsets and sunbonnets, they wear dark skirts and shirtwaists (blouses), with their hair in a loose wind-blown bun. Lest viewers think their looser hairstyle reflects loose morals, these frontier women's pure white shirtwaists and determined expressions reassure the audience of their virtue. But sculptors producing inherently conservative public monuments to pioneer women in the 1920s combined the grit of Dunn's hardy women with more demure mid-nineteenth-century Prairie Madonna imagery.[13]

Reconstructing the precise intentions and influences that shaped sculptors' designs for pioneer monuments is often difficult, but leading American sculptor Alexander Phimister Proctor—who was recognized as the nation's leading sculptor of western monuments, and who produced two of the nation's best-known Pioneer Mother monuments in the late 1920s—recorded his artistic and personal influences in a book-length autobiography published after his death.[14] The availability of Proctor's autobiography and other archival sources related to his art, combined with the nationwide attention paid to his pioneer monuments, make those works—and those that influenced or borrowed from them—worthy of especially close attention.

PRAIRIE MADONNAS

Phimister Proctor, as he was known, produced a pair of Pioneer Mother monuments in the late 1920s, one of which would remain one of "the best-known monuments in the nation" throughout the twentieth century.[15] Both monuments display more traits of the older Prairie Madonnas described by Stott than of her New (Pioneer) Women. Rather than embracing Dunn's hardworking New Women, Proctor drew his inspiration for his 1927 and 1928 *Pioneer Mother* statues from another Howard Pyle student, William H. D. Koerner, whose enormously popular illustrations of westering women hearkened back to 1850s Prairie Madonnas.

Koerner's *Madonna of the Prairie* illustration quickly attracted public attention when it appeared on the cover of the *Saturday Evening Post* in 1922 for the first of eight serial installments of Emerson Hough's novel *The Covered Wagon*. The instantly popular image then appeared widely on the cover and advertising for the book version. Koerner's illustration portrays the beautiful young heroine seated on a wagon box, with the opening of the wagon cover forming a halo around her face. Koerner's illustrations inspired the costuming for a silent film adaptation of Hough's novel, which became the first western "epic" film. According to Koerner biographer W. H. Hutchinson, "The impact of the film version of *The Covered Wagon* on the popular conceptions of the people, events, and settings of the West-That-Was cannot be overemphasized."[16] In the year before *The Covered Wagon* was released, only 50 identifiable western films had been made; in the year following its release, 150 westerns were made—and the industry maintained that level of production until it was eclipsed by television in the 1950s.[17] Adaptations of Koerner's covered wagon imagery pervaded the massive advertising for the movie, giving *Madonna of the Prairie* a significant role in shaping public perceptions of settler women. The beautiful and pure Prairie Madonna of the novel at times stepped into the more active role of a robust Pioneer Woman in the 1923 silent film. But while movie posters showcased both sides of Hough's heroine, popular attention remained focused on the covered wagon Madonna. Phimister Proctor's bronze public monument inspired by Koerner's illustration also clung to more traditional imagery.

Proctor wrote in his autobiography that for many years he had wanted to create a monument to female pioneers, but that desire had remained unformed until 1922, when Koerner's *Madonna of the Prairie* grabbed the nation's—and Proctor's—attention. Rather than "show her . . . plodding westward in a calico dress," Proctor insisted that he depict "another, no less heroic side."[18] Proctor's 1927 *Pioneer Mother* grouping for booming Kansas City (plate C) became one of the earliest and most prominent works of the Pioneer Mother movement. Most monuments of the movement featured a sunbonnet-clad Pioneer Mother walking westward on the overland trail, carrying a baby or accompanied by her young children. In contrast, Proctor placed his Prairie Madonna on horseback, demurely riding sidesaddle with her baby in her lap and her sunbonnet hanging down her back, accompanied by her husband and a grizzled mountain man guide and his pack mule. While Proctor was inspired by Koerner's Prairie Madonna, in his monumental work he also looked back to mid-nineteenth-century painting, adapting maternal imagery from George Caleb Bingham's famous 1851 painting *Daniel Boone Escorting Settlers through the Cumberland Gap*. Bingham's famous painting used the Renaissance image of Mary and Joseph's flight to Egypt, placing the Madonna at the apex of the grouping's triangular shape. Proctor adapted this pyramidal structure in his sculpture, likening Pioneer Mothers to the Virgin Mary and emphasizing his Pioneer Mother's role in bringing white civilization to savage Indian lands. To further emphasize his Prairie Madonna's self-sacrifice in migrating westward, Proctor encircled his larger-than-life bronze grouping with a text from the book of Ruth: "Whither thou goest I will go. Thy people shall be my people and thy God my God." Proctor was convinced that his monument, which employed ancient scripture and Renaissance imagery (interpreted through mid-nineteenth-century American painting), authentically depicted the spirit of frontier women who followed their pioneer husbands westward.

AUTHENTIC COWBOY ART

Phimister Proctor prided himself on the authenticity of his western-themed sculptures. Like other leading western artists of his era and future generations of cowboy artists, he clung to a fantasy of authenticity, while incorporating—and at times relying on—mythology and artifice in his work. For example, to work on the Kansas City *Pioneer Mother,* Proctor moved his family from Palo Alto to Southern California, because he was "certain that western characters would be easier to find in Hollywood than anywhere else"—including recently settled regions of the northern plains, where frontier conditions persisted in the early 1920s.[19] In Hollywood, Proctor sought someone to pose for the westering family's trapper guide and soon selected "an old bewhiskered gentleman" who had recently completed work as a body double for Ernest Torrence in the film adaptation of *The Covered Wagon.*[20] Similarly, the young woman Proctor chose to represent the pioneer mother in the Kansas City monument wore a costume of questionable historical accuracy sewn by the artist's wife. The model sat on a sidesaddle given to the artist by a woman who claimed—rather unconvincingly—to have ridden across the plains on it as a bride in 1852.[21]

Proctor's concern for authenticity in many ways paralleled that of the most famous "cowboy art" sculptors of his generation, Frederic Remington and Charles M. Russell. Like many painters and illustrators of their generation, Remington (who rejected the eastern political realm in favor of sculpting in the West) and Russell (who grew up on the frontier) depicted a Wild West in which savage Indians fought brave cowboys and the U.S. Cavalry. Like the generations of cowboy artists their work inspired, while Remington and Russell sought to faithfully document western life, the scenes that they chose to reproduce were inspired more by romantic tales than by the realities of diverse peoples' lives in the early twentieth-century West. Rather than producing portraits of famous individuals, Remington's twenty-five bronze statues portrayed generic heroic figures of the mythic West: soldiers, broncobusters, and Indian savages. Russell's sculptures—again like Proctor's—focused more on the daily life of cowboys, Indians, and western wildlife. But where Remington and Russell produced art for museums and private collections, Proctor became best known for his commissioned public monuments, and increasingly for depictions of pioneer mothers.[22]

PROCTOR'S PIONEER MOTHERS

Both Proctor's equestrian group and his second monument for the University of Oregon campus depicted passive, pious Pioneer Mothers. Proctor's 1927 *Pioneer Mother* (plate C), which presented a pioneer family as the holy family, and the central pioneer mother as being as faithful as the biblical Esther, was enthusiastically received by most viewers from its inception to its erection in Kansas City. Howard Vanderslice was so taken with Proctor's vision that he was determined to give the larger-than-life bronze grouping to his hometown of Kansas City, despite its enormous price tag of $250,000 ($3.4 million in 2015 dollars—a cost so exorbitant that Vanderslice kept it out of the newspapers).[23] Newspaper coverage of the monument was extremely enthusiastic. Several local residents agreed, "This is the only kind of statuary worth a damn."[24] Thousands attended its 1927 dedication.[25]

Proctor then sculpted a solo *Pioneer Mother* statue for Eugene, Oregon (figure 2.1). Intended to complement his earlier *The Pioneer* (see figure 1.4) standing on that university campus—and to fit within the burgeoning Pioneer Mother movement—it depicted an elderly woman who sat gazing contemplatively at the partially open book resting in her lap. In contrast to Proctor's Kansas City grouping and Ponca City's famous *Pioneer Woman* discussed below, donor Burt Brown Barker requested a statue that did not perpetuate the hardships that pioneer mothers faced. Instead, the University of Oregon vice president wanted to remember all pioneer mothers as he personally recalled his mother and grandmothers, as "pioneers of the true type, in the sunset of their lives, after the hardships and

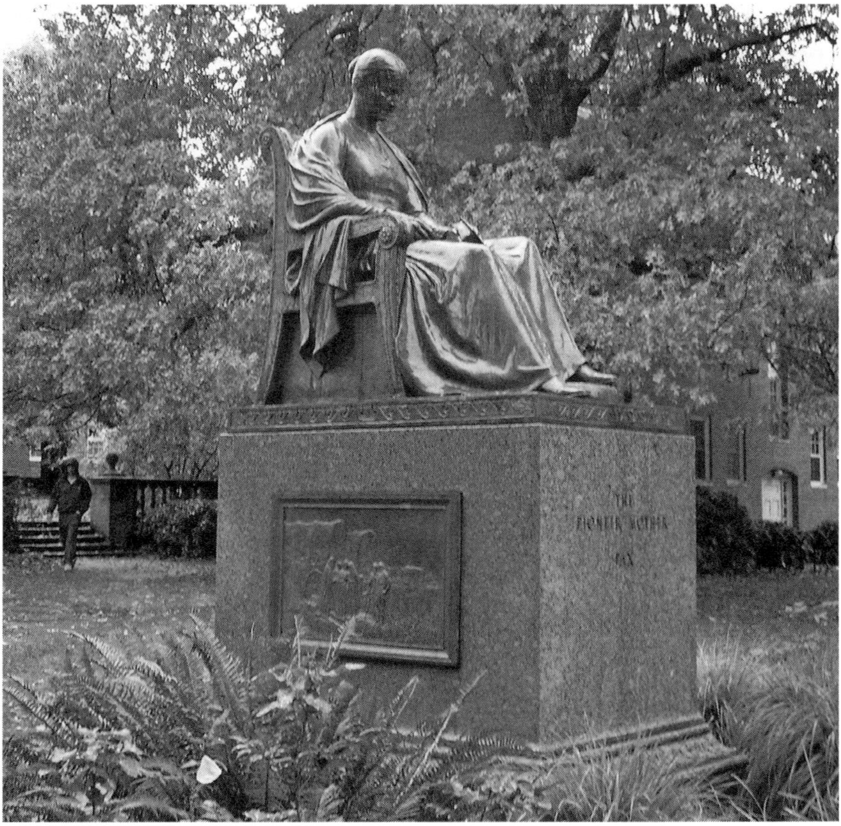

FIGURE 2.1. A. Phimister Proctor, *Pioneer Mother*, Eugene, Oregon, 1928. Photograph by author.

battles and sorrows of pioneering were past."[26] This memorial emphasized elderly pioneer women's continued domesticity, in marked contrast to her brave male companion across the quad, who stood poised to conquer the frontier.

Phimister Proctor's two well-known *Pioneer Mother* monuments depict the beginning and the end of a single story: the persistent domesticity and maternity of white women engaged in the mid-nineteenth-century overland migration. In an ironic choice typical of the Pioneer Mother movement, to celebrate pioneer women's heroism, Proctor employed more passive imagery than was typical of contemporary artists, such as Dunn. Proctor's devotion to artistic authenticity did not extend to historical accuracy regarding his settler subjects' daily lives. Yet his embrace of mid-nineteenth-century domestic ideology, with its celebration of stalwart men and nurturing mothers, aligned neatly with the idealized portraits of pioneer life in numerous pioneer memoirs and western print and visual culture as early western settlers reached their golden years. And it was echoed by several other pioneer monuments erected in the 1920s, including the work of Avard Fairbanks.

MATERNAL MEMORY

Avard T. Fairbanks, who had taught at the University of Oregon and was an active member of the Old Oregon Trails Association, sculpted a bronze group for Vancouver, Washington, that played to white Pacific Northwest residents' determination to believe—however inaccurately—that their ancestors had maintained distinct gender spheres while traveling West on the Oregon Trail.[27] In fact, he depicted a domestic ideal that had been closely held by westering men and women in the 1840s and 1850s (and the many eastern artists who embraced Prairie Madonna imagery in that era), but that their children in late nineteenth-century Oregon and Washington abandoned.[28] That memory, combined with Fairbanks's Mormon identity (which I explore in greater depth in chapter 4), inspired a highly domestic Pioneer Mother more similar to Proctor's work than Dunn's active Pioneer Women or even Ponca City's more famous *Pioneer Woman.*

Fairbanks balanced nostalgia for separate gender spheres with more modern, active forms of motherhood. Rather than striding purposely into the unknown and uncivilized West, Fairbanks's Vancouver *Pioneer Mother* (figure 2.2) rests demurely against a shoulder-high concrete backdrop whose shape evokes domestic features. The ruffled neckline of her flowing gown emphasizes her femininity and suggests 1920s clothing styles' abandonment of Victorian structure without the asexuality of flappers' shapeless shift dresses. Meanwhile, the shawl on her shoulders gently echoes the Madonna-like headscarves typical of western art from when the cult of domesticity reached its height nearly a century earlier, rather than the sturdy sunbonnet, designed to protect and contain white womanhood in the western wilderness, so popular among other male sculptors in the 1920s. She stands with a flintlock rifle in her right hand but appears unprepared to use it; her left rests tenderly in what Erving Goffman terms a "feminine touch" on the head of her eldest child, a daughter.[29] This daughter, in turn, reassures the youngest child, while a son grasps their mother's skirts timidly.

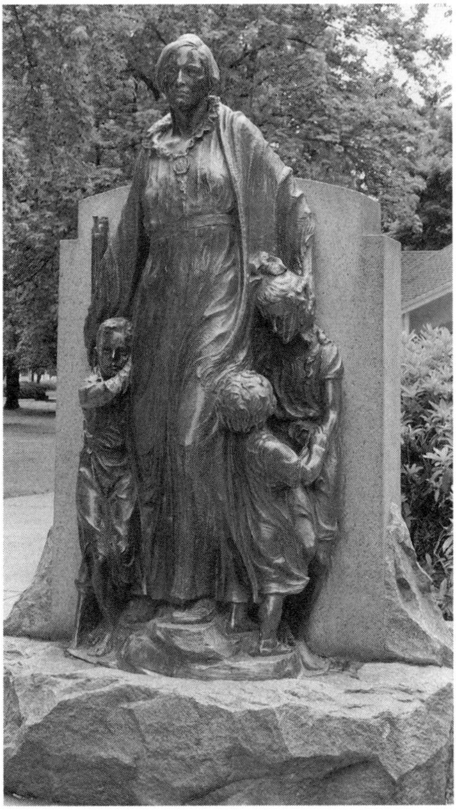

FIGURE 2.2. Avard T. Fairbanks, *Pioneer Mother*, Vancouver, Washington, 1928. Photograph by author.

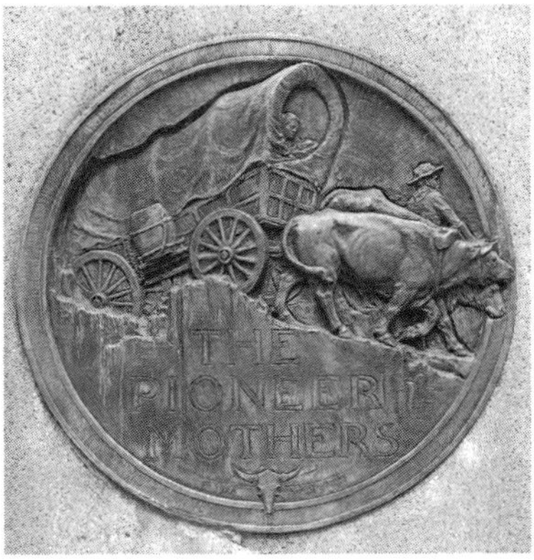

FIGURE 2.3. Avard T. Fairbanks, *The Pioneer Mothers*, Vancouver, Washington, 1928. Photograph by author.

The sculpture's gentle domesticity was further reinforced by the waterfall and flowering shrubs surrounding it and a medallion affixed to its back (figure 2.3): a recasting of Fairbanks's earlier *Old Oregon Trail* bas-relief, retitled *The Pioneer Mothers*.[30] Those bas-reliefs depict a hardy pioneer guiding his covered wagon and ox team over rough western terrain, while his bare-headed wife holds their baby in a Madonna-like pose, the arc of the wagon cover forming a halo encircling her head, echoing W. H. D. Koerner's *Madonna of the Prairie* painting and antebellum maternalism. Historians have generally assumed that the antebellum ideal of moral motherhood—which emphasized maternal sacrifice and viewed motherhood as the basis of female citizenship—was replaced by the rise of scientific motherhood during the 1920s, but Rebecca Jo Plant argues convincingly that traditionalists continued to view "American motherhood" as a national social and political institution throughout the interwar period.[31]

Fairbanks's balancing of women's domesticity and heroism mirrors the tension between the realities of settlers' lives and the celebratory notes struck in pioneer tributes and early settlers' published reminiscences. At least one daughter of Oregon settlers disagreed with the balance Fairbanks struck. Izella Surfus Osterud viewed the Fairbanks monument in the late 1960s. "T'wasn't like that at all. Not at all," she informed her granddaughter, Grey Osterud. "'First thing is, the baby would be dead. . . . The danger wasn't wildcats or Indians, but cholera,' she replied, speaking as much to the statue as to [her granddaughter]. 'Guns weren't any use for that. And a mother couldn't protect her children, either.' She concluded, 'Should have waited a couple of years and taken the train.'"[32] Historical research confirms Osterud's claim that communicable diseases carried West by white settlers were more dangerous to them (not to mention Native peoples) than were predatory animals or humans. But most white westerners preferred myth to reality, and celebration to commiseration.

Far from evoking strong women, the Pioneer Mothers sculpted by Proctor and Fairbanks hearkened back to mid-nineteenth-century domestic ideology. By evoking nineteenth-century Prairie Madonnas they combated modern, stronger images of New Women. Yet at the same time, these new Madonnas evoke the romance of western adventures typical of fin de siècle dime novels. Meanwhile, elite white clubwomen erected monuments that featured bolder Prairie Madonnas braving the Old West depicted in those dime novels.

CLUBWOMEN AND CIVIC MATERNALISM

Of course, prominent white men designed and erected most pioneer monuments, particularly prior to 1900. But elite white women—often operating through the civic-minded women's clubs that were a hallmark of middle- and upper-class women's lives and their primary means of influencing public affairs at the turn of the century—helped to shift western commemoration toward celebrating pioneer mothers through highly maternalist imagery.[33] World War I and the 1920s brought new occupational, political, social, and sexual opportunities to American women. As growing numbers of American women rejected Victorian mores, elite and middle-class white women applied their growing public roles to commemorating what they characterized as traditional maternal sacrifice. Women's clubs throughout the West exerted growing political and social influence, but clubwomen seeking to erect pioneer monuments had to negotiate their visions for Pioneer Women commemoration with powerful men who controlled public spaces and both civic and household purse strings. Linking Ella Sterling Mighels's vision of a Pioneer Mother statue in San Francisco to plans for the 1915 Panama-Pacific International Exposition brought greater fundraising power but required the PPIE Woman's Board and its Pioneer Mother Monument Association to accept a compromise between the female donors' desires for an explicitly white maternal figure and the prominent male sculptor's and PPIE fine arts director's artistic vision. In the 1920s, empowered by the growing Pioneer Mother movement, other women's clubs succeeded in erecting slightly bolder Prairie Madonnas.

In 1912 the businessmen of the Westport (Missouri) Improvement Association sponsored a carnival and published a seventy-six-page booklet recounting local white-male-dominated history to raise funds to erect "a full-sized prairie schooner with wagon master and bullwhackers and the faithful dog in the rear" in Westport's business district to mark the centennial of commercial traffic on the Santa Fe Trail.[34] But local clubwomen's greater commitment to erecting a monument to family migration enabled them to shape its message. After the businessmen's centennial events, women belonging to the Kansas City Historical Society, the DAR, the Daughters of the Confederacy, and the National Old Trails Road Association formed the Daughters of Old Westport, which succeeded in erecting a permanent monument by well-known male artist Robert Merrell Gage in 1920. Their efforts to erect a boulder affixed with bronze commemorative plaques aligned with equally modest trail-marking efforts mounted by the DAR in neighboring Iowa around the same time, but maternalism took precedence over more masculine imagery on the Westport monument. While the reverse plaque features a white trader and an Indian trapper, as well as noting that the monument was "erected by the Daughters of Old Westport in honor of the pioneers of Westport," the obverse plaque depicts *The Pioneer Mother*: a white woman holding both a rifle and an innocent infant, with a young child at her side.[35] As the erectors of San Francisco's *Pioneer Mother* encountered, the Daughters of Old Westport had to balance their favored maternalist imagery with male business and political leaders' expectations for more masculine scenes. Yet the balance of power—and the resulting vision for pioneer commemoration—was shifting by the

1920s. Clubwomen increasingly erected highly maternal Pioneer Mother monuments, and male artists and donors began to embrace to varying degrees the clubwomen's visions of sunbonneted Pioneer Mothers.

MADONNA OF THE TRAIL

One of the most powerful early twentieth-century women's clubs, the Daughters of the American Revolution (DAR), commissioned twelve identical Pioneer Mother monuments in the late 1920s for a dozen states, stretching from Maryland to California. August Leimbach's design for those dozen statues combined the Madonna label popularized by Koerner's painting with the stronger images of the New Women depicted by Dunn and others in the early twentieth century. In part because so many of Leimbach's statues were spread across the nation, they would become arguably the best-known American Pioneer Mother monuments ever erected, influencing the design of many later statues and helping shape popular memory of the frontier. But the DAR did not set out to erect pioneer monuments at all.

In the first years of the twentieth century, California's Auto Club and the Native Daughters of the Golden West erected cast-metal bells to mark El Camino Real, the supposed route traveled by the Spanish missionaries who were the stars of the state's mythic Spanish past.[36] Meanwhile, a group of Missouri women belonging to the DAR formed a committee in 1909 to locate and mark the old Santa Fe Trail within their state, using boulder plaques or monuments. From that project grew plans for a national highway that would mark the historic migration route. By 1911 the committee had dedicated twenty-nine markers in Missouri to indicate parts of the Santa Fe Trail, and DAR chapters in other states along the proposed highway campaigned actively for the project. Within a year of its 1912 founding, some seven thousand men had joined the National Old Trails Road Association, which, in keeping with gender norms of the period, "handle[d] the basic and practical side of the question," while the DAR's national committee "handle[d] the historic and sentimental side."[37] Members of both organizations worked to paint telegraph poles along the route in the red, white, and blue colors of the DAR, and advocated the project with their state legislatures. In 1927, association president (and future U.S. president) Harry S. Truman and President Calvin Coolidge received congressional approval for creating a national memorial highway stretching from the Atlantic to the Pacific. Like local commemoration efforts in Westport, Missouri, to which the National Old Trails Road Association and the DAR had contributed, economically and politically powerful men were an important early driving force for the national road project, but clubwomen did much of the practical work and selected maternalist imagery for the completed monuments.[38]

Conservative white clubwomen ensured that gendered imagery dominated the National Old Trails Road campaign. The DAR's early efforts emphasized the evolution of that route from bison path to Indian footpath to wagon road, a history that emphasized the roles of male hunters and settlers in building and migrating along the route. But, again as in Westport, such masculine images of tough pioneers soon gave way to an emphasis on the supposedly female space within those covered wagons. In 1913, the DAR's National Old Trails Road Committee adopted as its symbol an image of a woman seated within the interior of a covered wagon, holding a young child on her lap. Originally dubbed "The Pioneers," the DAR renamed it "The Madonna of the Trail," and adopted it as a symbol of their committee.[39]

Inspired by Alice Cooper's 1905 *Sacajawea* statue (plate H) and the sentiments expressed at that statue's dedication, the DAR soon abandoned its initial efforts to erect roadside markers in favor of life-sized monuments to an allegorical Pioneer Mother. DAR member Arlene B. Nichols Moss and her artist son worked with architectural sculptor August Leimbach for six months to develop a design for the twelve identical statues. Although inspired by *Sacajawea*, the DAR—an organization that limits its membership to women who can trace their lineage to a (presumably white) veteran of the American Revolution—embraced an image of an Anglo-American woman for its celebration of frontier motherhood. Leimbach's Pioneer Mother strides purposely westward, dressed in a simple homespun prairie-style gown and wide-brimmed sunbonnet (plate D). Clad in heavy boots, with a determined set to her jaw and a rifle clutched in her hand, she appears less feminine than either of Proctor's youthful or elderly Prairie Madonnas. But Leimbach's title—*Madonna of the Trail*—evokes the earlier Prairie Madonna image for this monument, created for a conservative women's organization.[40]

In Moss's dedicatory address, she declared that the Old National Trails honored both "the fortitude of the Pioneer Fathers who opened the way and the enduring faith and ever-abiding hope of the Mothers." But Moss declared the Leimbach statues to be a national shrine, paying tribute to those "Madonnas of the Trail" who "erected an altar" in their new western homes "to country and to God," whose "sacred history" paralleled that of Mary, the mother of Jesus.[41] The ladies of the DAR thus invoked Catholic Marian imagery similar to that used by Proctor in his 1927 family grouping for Kansas City. But while the DAR dedicatory language and the statues' title directly evoked antebellum Prairie Madonnas, August Leimbach's sculpture more closely aligned with the stronger Pioneer Woman imagery that was emerging in other forms of western art. As the DAR women labored to erect their twelve Madonnas, those rival notions of pioneer motherhood came into direct competition under the sponsorship of oil magnate E. W. Marland.

COMPETING NOTIONS OF PIONEER MOTHERHOOD

Like monument erectors elsewhere in the West, oil magnate E. W. Marland believed that erecting a prominent work of fine art would also raise the status of his adopted state. The monument design competition that Marland sponsored attracted unprecedented public attention to pioneer woman imagery and to his adopted hometown of Ponca City, Oklahoma. While other scholars have written about this competition, the opportunity it provides to compare different artists' conceptions of pioneer womanhood, and the availability of sources documenting public reception of those competing depictions, make it worthy of extended attention here to uncover competing gendered cultural memories of the frontier.[42]

Public monument erectors of this era typically either commissioned a prominent regional artist or perhaps selected a design from among small clay sketches. But Marland asked Reinhardt Galleries in New York City to commission the nation's leading sculptors to each produce a three-foot-tall bronze model. Marland paid each of the twelve male artists who responded—Bryant Baker, A. Stirling Calder, Jo Davidson, James Fraser, John Gregory, F. Lynn Jenkins, Mario Korbel, Arthur Lee, H. A. MacNeil, Maurice Sterne, Wheeler Williams, and Mahonri Young—$10,000 commissions ($136,000 in 2015 dollars).[43] (Female sculptors Gertrude Whitney and Anna Vaughn Hyatt were invited but declined to participate.) Due to popular demand, an exhibition displaying the twelve entries appeared not only in Reinhardt's New York galleries, but also in Boston and major cities across the Ohio Valley, Great Plains, and Far West before reaching Ponca City. The 750,000 people who reportedly viewed the exhibition were encouraged to cast votes for their three favorites to help guide Marland's choice. It soon became clear that Marland and the wider public (but not art critics) agreed about the appropriate design of Pioneer Mother monuments.[44]

Most prominent pioneer monuments erected at the turn of the century, as we have seen, were designed by Paris-trained sculptors in the Beaux-Arts style adapted from French statuomania. But the citizens who voted in Marland's 1927 competition clearly favored designs drawn out of portraiture and pop culture rather than Parisian fine art traditions. While some other entrants drew on personal experience in the West, winning sculptor Bryant Baker drew on childhood reading about pioneers' "fights against Indians behind barricaded wagons, and the struggle for a living in a new country."[45] Presumably he was also influenced by dime novel illustrations, like Koerner's illustrations for *The Covered Wagon*, and other Wild West visual media, which circulated widely in his native England and in the United States in the early twentieth century. That Baker and F. Lynn Jenkins (another crowd favorite) focused on sculpting portraits accurately—albeit shaped by popular culture—rather than holding to the strict rules of classicism or the Beaux-Arts tradition, or seeking the historical accuracy pursued by Proctor, apparently made their work particularly appealing to popular audiences and to Marland.

Despite growing up a Pennsylvania urbanite and not "know[ing] much about art," Marland actively sought to shape the participating sculptors' works.[46] Like donors in several other western cities in the second half of the 1920s, Marland explicitly envisioned a realistic statue of a pioneer *mother* in a sunbonnet, "the maker of civilization, [and] the mothers of the men of the west."[47] Marland instructed the competitors to depict that pioneer mother without men, and sent supposedly authentic sunbonnets to each sculptor to inspire them.

According to the *New York Times*, "The exhibition included at least one figure to please almost every taste. And every great school as represented by the technique of the sculptors, from a figure suggesting the Greek [Arthur Lee's *Faithful*] to another embodying the last phase of modernism [Maurice Sterne's *Determined*]."[48] Despite these stylistic differences, the twelve entries bear striking similarities that responded to Marland's preferences and speak to the power of the Pioneer Mother movement: all twelve pioneer women are young white women wearing long dresses. Nine wear sunbonnets, in keeping with Marland's expectations. Only one is solitary. Ten of the twelve entries hold babies. Significantly, the winning entry was the only one that featured a young son but no baby (plate B). Janet Galligani Casey suggests that this young son offset the pioneer woman's femininity and reminded viewers that pioneer women's primary role was to raise sturdy sons.[49] I would add that Baker's highly respectable woman and cheerful son minimize concerns other renditions raise about hardships on the frontier. Baker's youthful conception was the overwhelming public favorite, receiving the most votes in eleven out of fourteen cities. Nationwide, his design received 42,478 votes for first choice, and a clear plurality overall with 123,000 total votes.[50]

Those artists who deviated from popular Pioneer Mother imagery or from the Beaux-Arts style typical of monumental sculpture at the time were soundly defeated. In a comment that echoed the controversy surrounding Grafly's buckskin-clad Pioneer Mother for the PPIE, one journalist observed, "The great American public may not know much about art, but it certainly knows what the well-dressed pioneer should wear."[51] Public audiences voiced little support for Maurice Sterne's modernist woman draped in a classical gown, despite his inclusion of a child on her arm and a bonnet on her head. The public cared even less for Lee's nearly nude female figure, wrapped in a sheer garment that seemed at odds with the sunbonnet, the infant on her right arm, and young boy at her left hip. As the *Denison (Tex.) Herald* reported, "Arthur Lee got his wires crossed and dressed grandma in tulle—and nothing else. That will never, never do!"[52] Adding children, sunbonnets, and a rifle could not overcome the sculptures' stylistic departure from the cheerful realism—and supposedly historically accurate costumes—that Americans had come to associate with Pioneer Mother monuments.

Votes cast by the public indicate that the presumably middle-class audiences in the chosen urban centers were more interested in embracing stereotypical images than in the artistic creativity or fame of its creator. Even in supposedly sophisticated New York City, Baker's design was the clear favorite, receiving six thousand votes. MacNeil's *Challenging*—whose windswept hair, active pose, and merging of motherhood with outdoor work evoked Harvey Dunn's paintings—was second in the New York vote count. Third place went to A. Stirling Calder's *Self-Reliant,* whose subject, like August Leimbach's in *Madonna of the Trail,* grasps a baby and a rifle with which to defend it.[53] Intriguingly, New Yorkers' second and third choices both accentuated the pioneer woman's bust. But even New Yorkers rejected James Earle Fraser's *Affectionate,* which showed the pioneer mother in the act nursing her infant and included an exposed nipple. White audiences continued to love Fraser's depiction of an Indian man and his pony at *The End of the Trail,* but by emphasizing pioneer mothers' biological role, the sculptor's *Affectionate* called into question white women's moral superiority over indigenous women.

As Janet Galligani Casey detailed, the professional art community strongly opposed holding a popular vote, and especially disliked Bryant Baker's entry, which they thought was "too sweet."[54] But western audiences and American youth loved Baker's emotive young woman armed with religion, which was the clear nationwide favorite. They were also captivated by John Gregory's emotional portrayal of a pioneer woman taking her husband's rifle after he was killed in an Indian attack, which New York high school students preferred because it "tells a story."[55] Gregory won the most votes in three western cities, including Fort Worth, Texas, where Gregory's design dominated Baker's (3,599 votes to 2,529), and Jo Davidson's came in a distant third (858).[56]

In the context of the Pioneer Mother movement, Baker's *Pioneer Woman* was likely favored by the public and selected by the competition's sponsor because it skillfully balanced Marland's desire for a sunbonneted mother with the bolder Pioneer Woman imagery that had emerged in western painting and illustration more than twenty-five years earlier. Other entries depicting the strong Pioneer Woman types, such as John Gregory's *Protective* and H. A. MacNeil's *Challenging,* were also popular, but they were soundly defeated by Baker's design in the overall vote. More independent than a Prairie Madonna, but more feminine than Harvey Dunn's portrayals of active prairie women, Baker's winning entry struck a balance among the varied images of western women that appeared in many public monuments during the Pioneer Mother movement.

Baker's winning statue was unveiled in 1930, before a crowd of around forty thousand. Although the plaque on *Pioneer Woman*'s base dedicates the monument to "the woman who braved the dangers and endured the hardships" of the frontier, the woman's well-tailored gown looks more suited to a schoolteacher than a farmer's wife, and her presumably pale complexion is protected by her sunbonnet halo. The son at the side of the winning woman, and the Bible that she carries in her right arm, reassure viewers that this genteel young woman has braved dangers and endured hardships to spread white Christian civilization in keeping with 1920s familial and civic maternalism. The scale and popularity of Marland's competition ensured that Ponca City's winning design would linger in the American imagination and, as I explore in future chapters, heavily influence the design of later monuments. But during the Great Depression, the Pioneer Woman's reliance on God's word to spread white civilization soon gave way to more pioneer mothers armed—however grudgingly—with rifles.

ARMING PIONEER MOTHERS

The American public responded enthusiastically to the combination of youthful beauty and refined civilization embodied in Baker's winning design for the Ponca City monument. The Bible tucked under the woman's arm in his *Pioneer Woman* more subtly evokes the "church around her knees" that Mighels envisioned for San Francisco's Pioneer Mother monument. Books became even more powerful images in the aftermath of the infamous 1925 Scopes Monkey Trial, which pitted conservative Victorian values against Jazz Age modern ideas over the question of teaching evolution in public schools. Seven pioneer mothers erected during the Pioneer Mother movement, including Proctor's elderly subject in *Pioneer Mother*, hold Bibles or other books. Some pioneer mothers relied on rifles to protect their children—and by extension the nation's future—from wild animals and Indian savagery.

Artists routinely depicted pioneer men carrying axes or guns to indicate their technological, sexual, and racial dominance. For a pioneer man to wield a steel ax—as Borglum's heroic subject does in *The American Pioneer*—symbolized his ability to transform a forested wilderness into a settled home and farm, as well as his technological dominance over Indians' stone tools. Similarly, in Karl Gerhardt's 1892 *Pioneer Statuary Group* for Iowa's capitol (figure 2.4), a white father and son stand poised to conquer the land, as in Borglum's *The American Pioneer*, using a manufactured ax, rifle, and bowie knife. Behind and below them to their left, their indigenous guide, armed only with a primitive stone tomahawk and

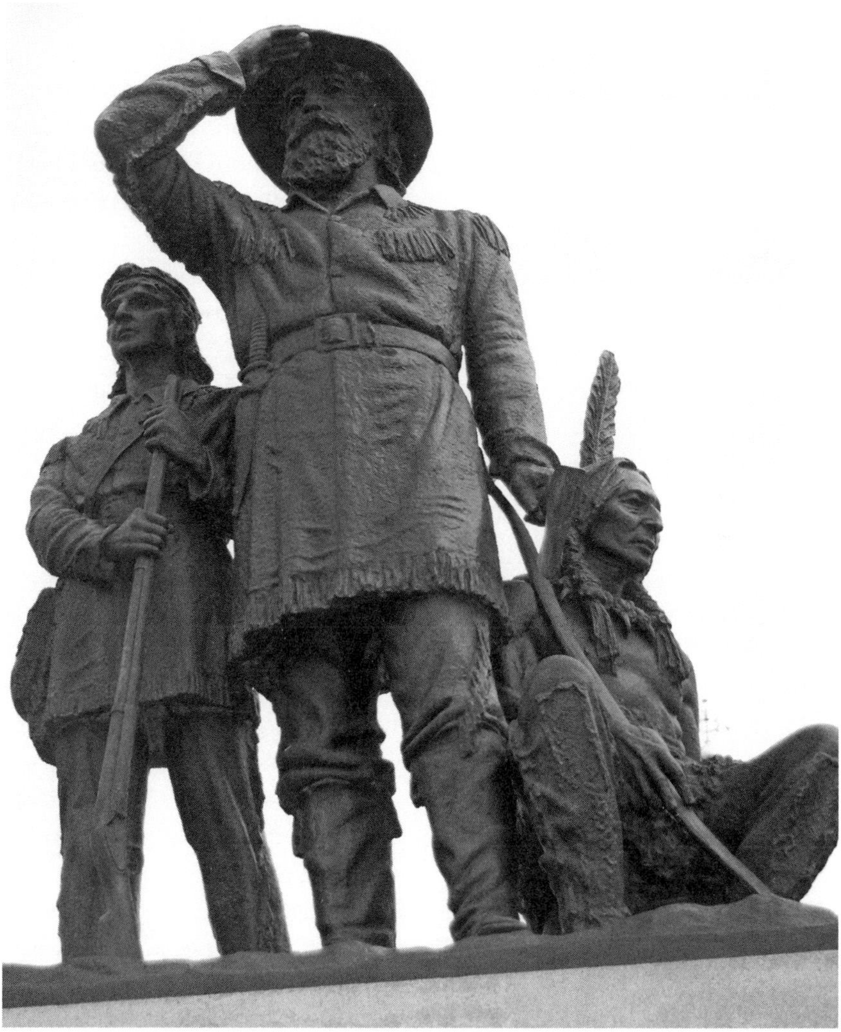

FIGURE 2.4. Karl Gerhardt, *Pioneer Statuary Group*, Des Moines, Iowa, 1892. Photograph by David Culver.

unstrung bow, sits on a rock, gazing back toward the life he has lost to white progress.

But a woman with an ax carried very different meanings. Holding an ax suggested that she did hard outdoor labor—a deviation from the separate spheres gender ideology that early settlers and their descendants chose to forget. Wielding an ax in self-defense would involve close contact with her attacker and require physical strength that Americans in the

1920s would have assumed she lacked. Even worse, a woman's ax could resemble a tomahawk, evoking centuries of captivity narratives in which savage Indians scalp white men and ravage white women. Thus, for a woman to wield an ax challenged not only her femininity but her whiteness, and it might even evoke troubling questions about her sexual purity. The only entry in the Ponca City competition depicting a pioneer woman with an ax was much less popular than those armed with Bibles or rifles, particularly among western audiences.

Male artists gave guns to pioneer women to reinforce their vulnerability amid wild animals and wild men. For example, August Leimbach's sturdy pioneer woman "grasped [her] gun" and children and "ran out in the field to look for the father" because she believed him to be in danger (plate D).[57] Yet in the years following famed sharpshooter Annie Oakley's death in 1926, Americans remained wary of arming pioneer mothers. Fifteen of twenty-five statues erected in the 1920s and 1930s depicting pioneer women unaccompanied by men include rifles, but none appear prepared to fire their weapons, even in self-defense. Avard Fairbanks's *Pioneer Mother* (figure 2.2) holds a flintlock rifle but looks completely unprepared to use it. August Leimbach's twelve Madonnas and two of the twelve Ponca City competition entries seem to use their rifles as walking sticks. Three other Ponca City competition entries hold rifles in defensive postures. Although Mario Korbel's Pioneer Mother balances a rifle across her knees while holding an infant in her arms, the viewer is left to wonder whether the statue's title, *Heroic*, describes her or the loyal guard dog seated attentively at her feet. Only Robert Garrison depicted women shooting at marauding Indians as well as doing domestic work, in his art-deco-inspired *Covered Wagon Frieze*, created for a Denver bank (figure 2.5). Settler men wielded guns to hunt wild game (both as sport and to provide for their families), to drive "wild" Indians off their supposedly available lands, and to defend their families. But at the height of the Pioneer Mother movement, pioneer women wielded firearms reluctantly to protect their children and their own purity.

The appeal of guns as defensive weapons for pioneer women can be seen particularly clearly in the Pioneer Mother monument erected by the people of Kansas on the Topeka statehouse lawn in 1937. Kansas Pioneer Women's Memorial Association first vice chair Lilla Day Monroe was initially inspired to pursue a pioneer woman monument out of a belief in

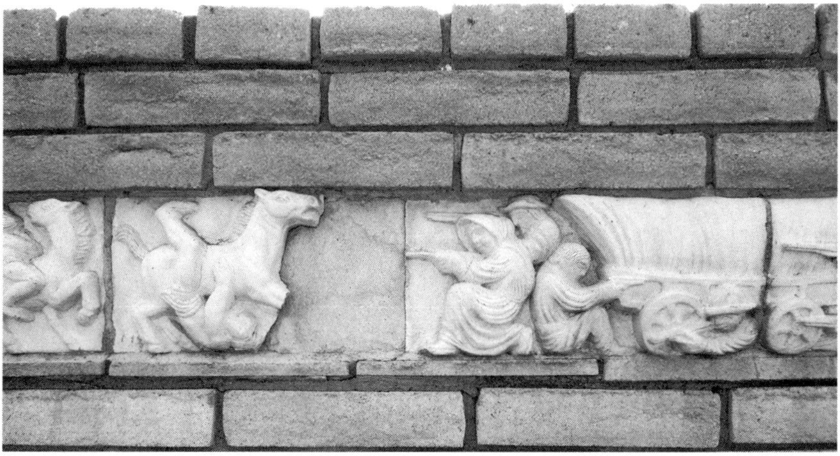

FIGURE 2.5. Robert Garrison, detail of *Covered Wagon Frieze*, Denver, Colorado, 1925. Photograph by author.

women's equality.[58] But the memorial association, which grew out of the Woman's Kansas Day Club, gained the support of the male-dominated Kansas state government to erect the monument on the statehouse grounds and succeeded in public fundraising (including donations from Kansas schoolchildren) by appealing to maternalist ideology. The memorial association selected Bryant Baker's design featuring a sunbonneted pioneer woman holding a scythe, which in many ways resembles that artist's winning Ponca City design. Apparently learning from criticism of his Ponca City model, Baker this time depicted the boy barefoot and clad in rough clothing, and sculpted more reticent gazes for both mother and son. But a request for Baker to replace the scythe with the more common iconography of a gun gained enough traction that by 1935, Baker's model was on display in the capitol rotunda, and the association gave a $10,000 contract for a bronze monument to former Kansan (and sculptor of the Westport *Pioneer Mother*) Merrell Gage instead.[59]

Gage's final design, *Pioneer Women of Kansas*, not only replaced the pioneer woman's scythe with a gun, but it moved her from an active outdoor pose to a domestic scene that emphasized her defensive role (figure 2.6). His depiction of a seated mother with a resting rifle across her lap, a son reading beside her, and a dog at her feet echoed his earlier celebrated bas-relief *Madonna of the Plains*, which appeared in the Palace of Fine Arts at the Pacific Southwest Exposition in 1928. It also bore a striking

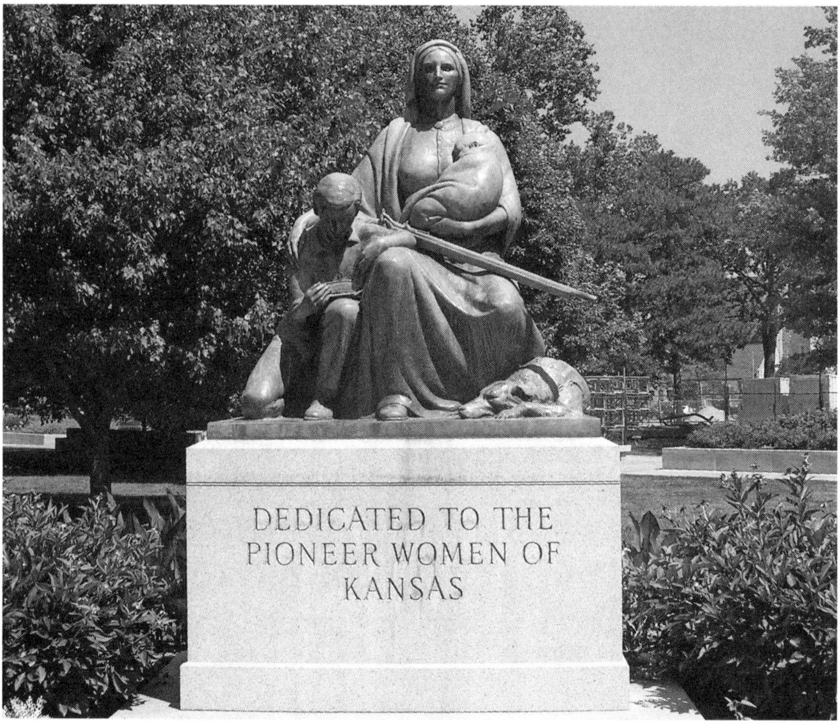

FIGURE 2.6. Robert Merrell Gage, *Pioneer Women of Kansas*, Topeka, Kansas, 1937. Photograph by author.

resemblance to a rival entry in the Ponca City competition, Mario Korbel's *Heroic*. But where Korbel's *Heroic* pioneer mother appears ill at ease with both the child in her arms and the rifle in her lap, Gage's cradles an infant at her breast, and her other arm reaches around her strapping son. Even the guard dog in *Pioneer Women of Kansas* is more at ease, resting contentedly at her feet. In all these ways, Gage portrayed a gentle Pioneer Mother at rest within her domestic space. Indeed, when a few protested Gage's depiction of a "pioneer lady holding a gun," claiming that *their* mothers never hunted for game or fought Indians, the *Topeka (Kans.) Capital Journal*'s editors defended the sculptor, insisting that pioneer women had to be ready to defend their homes if necessary in the absence of their husbands. Of course, nineteenth-century women were supposed to be the *moral* defenders of the home. While pioneer men struck boldly into the savage wilderness to build new homes and communities, pioneer women were supposed to sit within those rough cabins protecting their civility.[60]

Male artists' tendency to arm Pioneer Mothers also suggests men's concerns about containing female sexuality during the Jazz Age. In the 1920s, many American men shared E. W. Marland's anxiety about women bobbing their hair and wearing knee-length sheath dresses. Victorian mores had emphasized white women's maternal role. Nineteenth-century women were expected to be emotionally expressive but sexually reserved, even passionless. But by the 1920s, women were throwing away their corsets and tailored dresses in favor of shorter, looser-fitting gowns. Young people increasingly moved their courtship out from under the watchful eyes of their elders. Birth control became more widely available, and married women began expecting sexual pleasure.[61] In the face of such rampant sexuality, westerners lost interest in lurid captivity narratives, instead embracing images of chaste Pioneer Mothers. These virtuous pioneer women could rely on firearms if necessary to contain explosive western sexuality. Whether armed with Bibles or guns, as the Great Depression seized control of the nation, Americans commemorated pioneer women for taming the wild frontier with their sexual purity.

PROPER PIONEER WOMEN

At the height of the Great Depression, the Texas state legislature appropriated a remarkable $3 million for an enormous statewide celebration of the centennial of Texas's brief independence and appointed the Texas Centennial Commission of Control (led by the lieutenant governor and the Speaker of the Texas House of Representatives) to plan it. The commission planned statewide events to celebrate the 1936 centennial, including the erection of several major public monuments. Texas State College for Women president L. H. Hubbard proposed that a statue honoring Texas pioneer women be placed on the women's college campus. The centennial commission then sponsored an open competition to select the statue's design.

The people of Texas objected loudly to the design selection of the learned panel of judges. American studies scholar A. Joan Saab argues that American art was democratized in the 1930s by New Deal policies. But public monuments—unlike Federal Art Project murals that embraced a trend toward folk art—tended to remain within the purview of the intellectual elite. As both the Ponca City competition and the uproar in Denton demonstrate, the American public felt qualified to assess the authenticity and appropriateness of pioneer monuments. While the "general public repeatedly and passionately embraced the possibility that art was important and that it could transform American society in positive ways," as Saab argues, they expected public monuments to reinforce what they considered traditional values.[62]

Professional artists, such as those appointed to the Commission of Control's jury, appreciated Zorach's depiction of close family relationships in a harsh environment, but the public zealously objected to the stylized nude figures.[63] A Zorach biographer recounted Texans' "anguished protests" that *Pioneer Family Group* (later renamed *The Family* at its installation in 1964; plate E) featured a family rather than a pioneer mother, and that the Daughters of the Republic of Texas declared it "the greatest insult that could be offered to these women who believed and practiced the virtue of modesty."[64] Texas artist Waldine Tauch insisted that nudity was appropriate for classical figures but not for American pioneer women.[65] Others complained that the figures "'looked like apes' and that a 'nude statue was not appropriate to a woman's college.'"[66]

Although the director of the Dallas Museum of Fine Arts publicly defended the sculptor and the aesthetic value of his work, the people of Texas were not easily mollified. Zorach attempted to salvage his design by creating a new model in which the figures were lightly draped in a manner reminiscent of ancient Roman togas. But the draped figures—like Maurice Sterne's modernist submission to the Ponca City competition—remained far from the public's mental image of respectable Pioneer Mothers. That this move did not satisfy the public suggests that people were more concerned with Zorach's modernist style (which evoked the socialist realism produced in the Soviet Union during this decade) and his rejection of standard Pioneer Mother iconography than they were with the figures' nudity. Amid the scarcity of the Great Depression, the centennial commission broke its contract with Zorach and hired another prominent sculptor, Leo Friedlander, to produce an appropriately demure Beaux-Arts Pioneer Mother (plate I).

Friedlander, who had not submitted a sketch to the original competition but had created massive marble pioneer-themed sculptures for the new Oregon statehouse, provided a much safer interpretation of pioneer life than the modernist family modeled by Zorach. Dressed in a high-necked jacket and ankle-length skirt, Friedlander's Pioneer Woman carries neither a rifle nor a Bible but demurely holds her left hand over her heart in a feminine touch. Both her childlessness and the white marble from which she was sculpted suggest purity, even virginity. Friedlander's *Pioneer Woman* thus safely suited the public's expectations for a proper statue on a woman's college campus, aligned with popular memory of frontier womanhood.

The prominent men on the selection committee apparently failed to anticipate the public outcry that Zorach's design would elicit. William Zorach was a prominent early twentieth-century American artist, but the sculptor found himself embroiled in several controversies surrounding major commissions in the mid-1930s. While his sculptures were less avant-garde than his earlier fauvist and cubist paintings, they were inspired more by primitive African sculpture than by the Beaux-Arts school that informed most pioneer monuments in this era. Unfortunately, the official minutes of the centennial commission do not record the selection committee's rationale and utterly ignore what was apparently a very public controversy. Only the execution of a contract with Leo Friedlander for the replacement statue and a single telegram from the president of the San Antonio Woman's Club, protesting a New Yorker "demoralizing the Texas pioneer woman with a nude statue," hint at the debate.[67]

Though the controversy apparently raged through much of 1938, newspaper coverage appears inaccurate and incomplete. Papers in Denton and nearby Dallas appear to have largely avoided commenting on the design and placement of the statue. *Lass-O*, the student newspaper, did cover funding and site selection for the coming pioneer monument, but writers discussed the controversy only inaccurately and after the fact. "One can only guess that this was a matter of such delicacy that stories could not be printed in too much detail," reporter Tom Kirkland speculated in the *Denton (Tex.) Record-Chronicle* in far racier 1958. "One gets the impression, though, that all of Denton sighed 'of all things' in unison." According to Kirkland, the Texas Centennial Commission of Control insisted that the pioneer woman be fully clothed before they would pay the sculptor's fee.[68] It is unclear how much the public knew at the time—or later—about the state's involvement in selecting the controversial design. Regardless, public outcry—however ill-informed—clearly pressured the state Commission of Control into rejecting the design selected by their own committee of experts and replacing it with another artist's design that was more similar to other Pioneer Mother monuments erected during the 1920s and 1930s. (Twenty-five years later, Zorach brought his pioneer family grouping back to life, as I explore in detail in chapter 3.) Leo Friedlander's more demure image became well known in Denton and across the state of Texas "as an embodiment of the strong and independent spirit of the legacy of [Texans'] forebears."[69] Similar values would be embodied by other Pioneer Mother monuments at the height of the Great Depression, including two quite similar solo pioneer women that were erected by other Great Plains communities during the Dust Bowl years: a white marble pioneer woman carrying two books in the Mount Hope Cemetery in tiny Ellis, Kansas, and Ellis Luis Burman's white *The Pioneer Woman* erected by the Lincoln (Nebraska) Woman's Club. The sculptors stripped these three frontier women of the accompanying children that were so typical of maternalist 1920s Pioneer Mother monuments. Abandoning the darker hue of bronze, the sculptors work in white materials to further emphasize their subjects' purity and whiteness.

PRAIRIE MADONNAS AND PIONEER WOMEN

Annette Stott argued persuasively that nineteenth-century Prairie Madonnas gave way to stronger images of Pioneer Women in western paintings and sculpture produced after 1890, but this shift from Prairie Madonna to Pioneer Woman appeared more gradually in public monuments than they did in other works of western art. Even August Leimbach's sturdy pioneer woman was called a *Madonna of the Trail* and was promoted by the DAR using Marian references. A burst of Pioneer Mother monument building in the late 1920s, including DAR statues stretching from coast to coast and a nationwide competition to select a monument for Ponca City, Oklahoma, enshrined a particular image of pioneer womanhood: a young mother, clad in a prairie gown and sunbonnet, carrying or leading her children westward, armed only with a rifle or Bible. So accepted did that iconography become that attempts to stray from it sparked controversy in the 1930s. As concerns about flappers and independent women gave way to anxiety about lost breadwinners during the Great Depression, maternalist imagery began to yield to virginal white women stripped of their children and their rifles. At the same time, Pioneer Mothers, plural, became more common in monuments ostensibly dedicated to prominent pioneer men. The trend toward depicting pioneer families would grow far more pronounced after World War II.

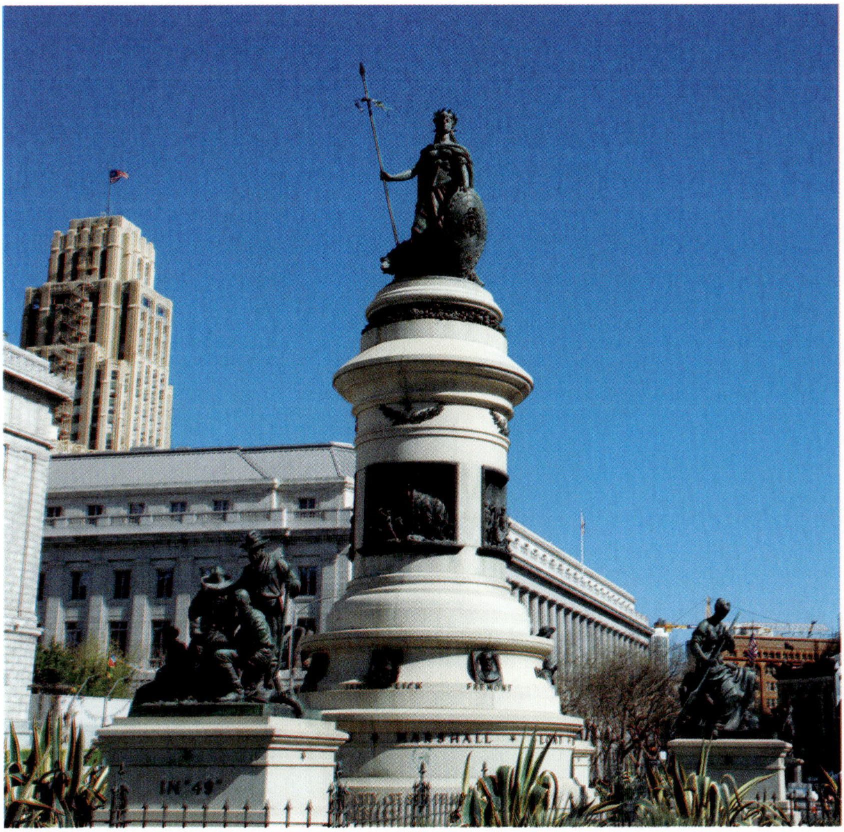

PLATE A. Frank Happersberger, *James Lick Pioneer Monument,* San Francisco, California, 1894. Photograph by Lisa Allen. This social Darwinist depiction of the Americanization of California was lauded across the nation in the 1890s but has sparked controversy in recent decades.

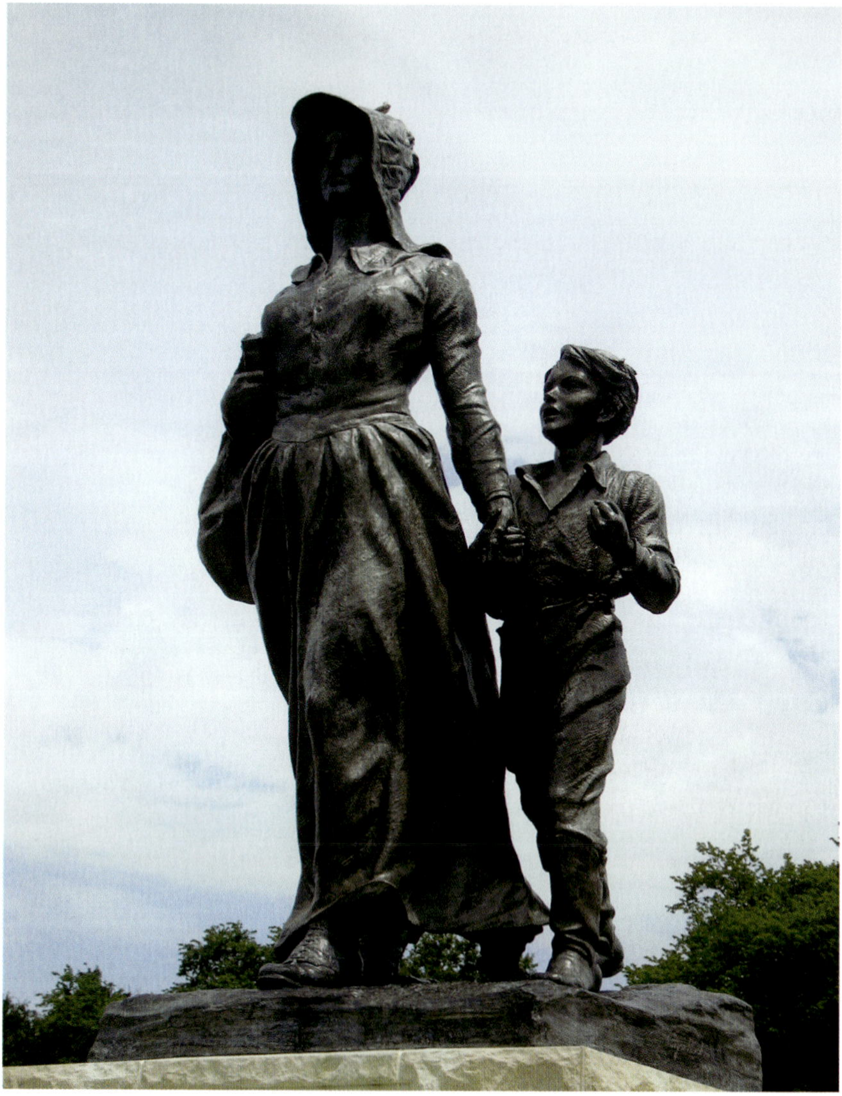

PLATE B. Bryant Baker, *Pioneer Woman*, Ponca City, Oklahoma, 1929. Photograph by author. This was the winning design in oilman E. W. Marland's sculptural competition. The twelve bronze models entered in Marland's competition toured the nation. Baker's design was the overwhelming public favorite.

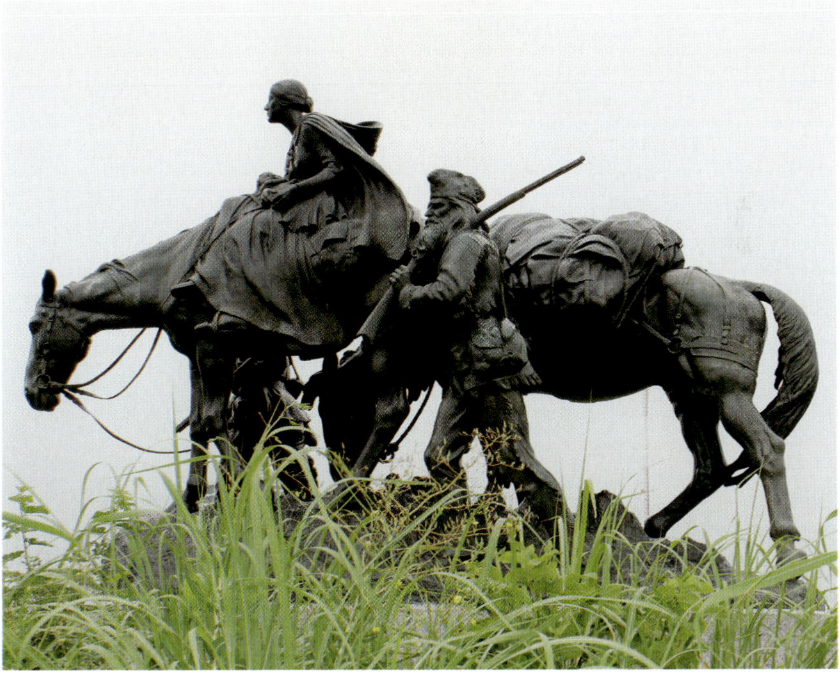

PLATE C. A. Phimister Proctor, *Pioneer Mother*, Kansas City, Missouri, 1927. Photograph by author. After a warm public reception in the 1920s, this monument was soon forgotten by the people of Kansas City. But residents of nearby Westport tried repeatedly to have the massive statue moved to their small downtown area.

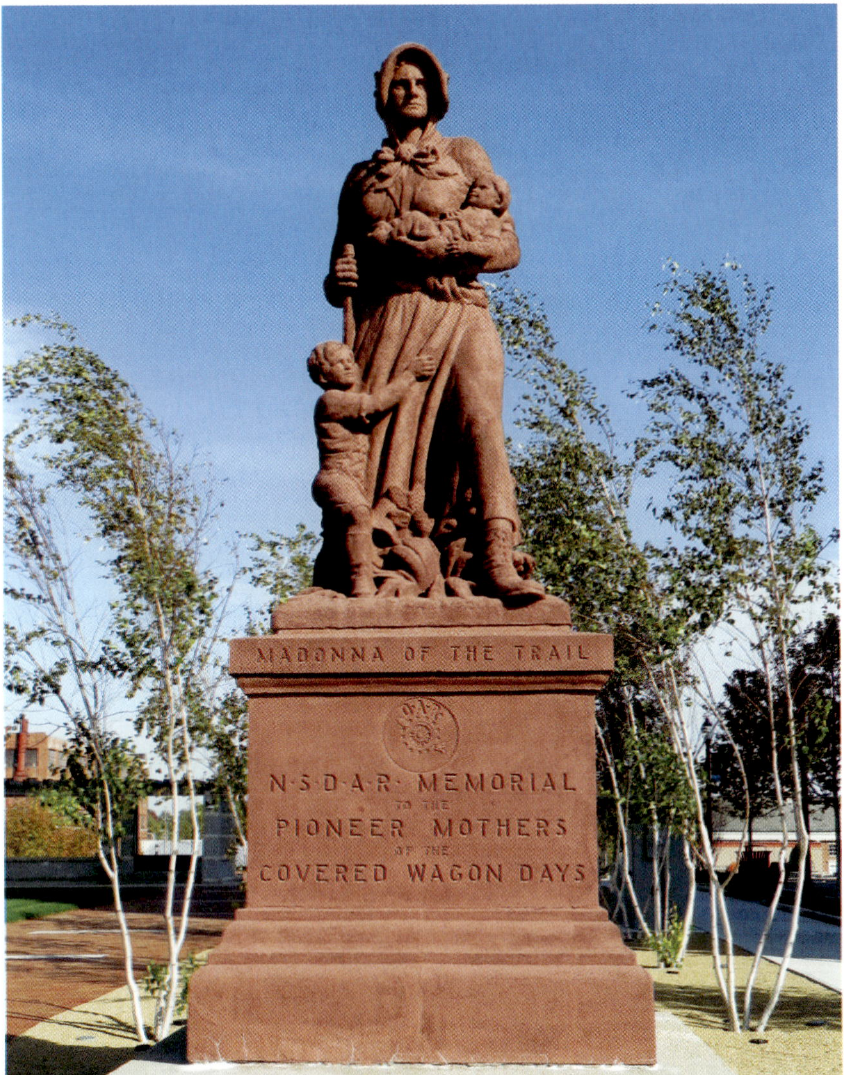

PLATE D. August Leimbach, *Madonna of the Trail*, Springfield, Ohio, 1928. Photograph by author. One of twelve identical statues erected in different states to mark western trails. This statue was moved twice—in the 1950s to accommodate highway construction, and again in 2011 to the newly created National Road Commons (pictured here) in downtown Springfield.

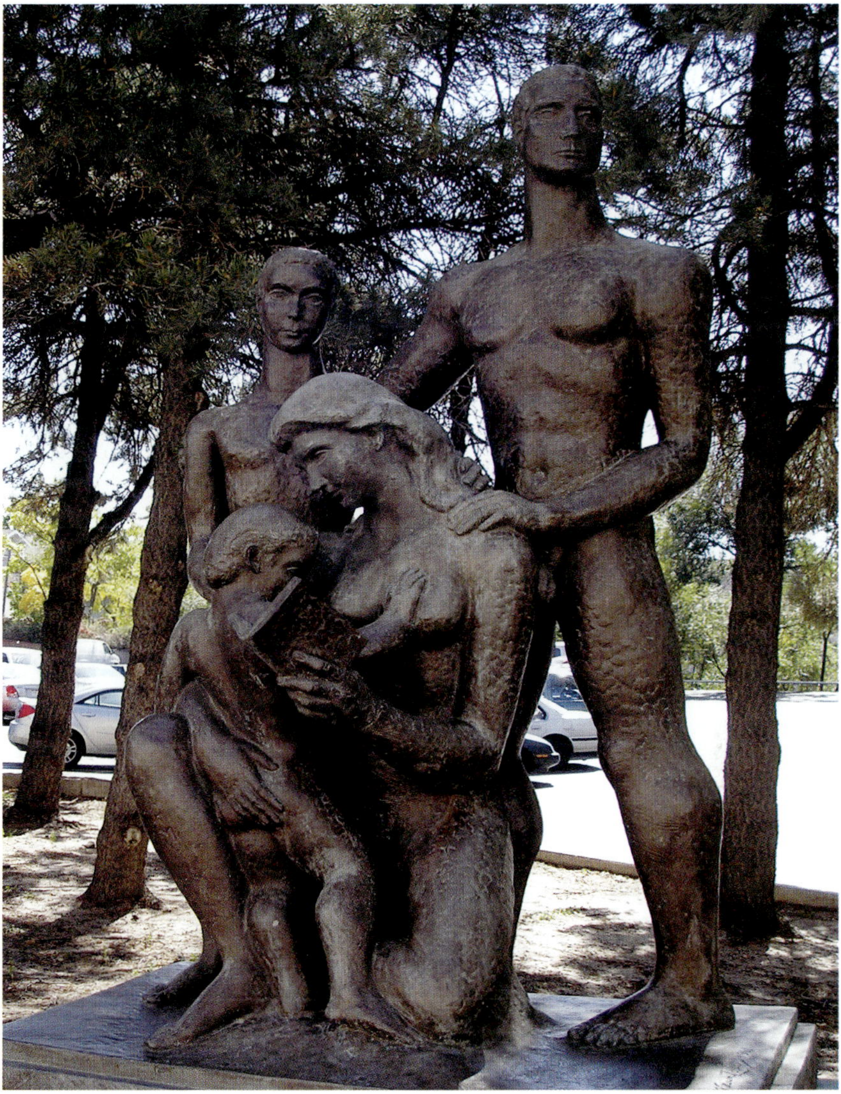

PLATE E. William Zorach, *The Family*, Colorado Springs, Colorado, 1964. Photograph by author. This work was selected as a tribute to pioneer women as part of 1936 Texas centennial celebrations under the title *Pioneer Family Group*. Public controversy convinced the selection committee to reject Zorach's work and substitute Leo Friedlander's far more demure *Pioneer Woman* (plate I). Zorach's design was finally cast in heroic bronze under the more general title *The Family* in the 1960s.

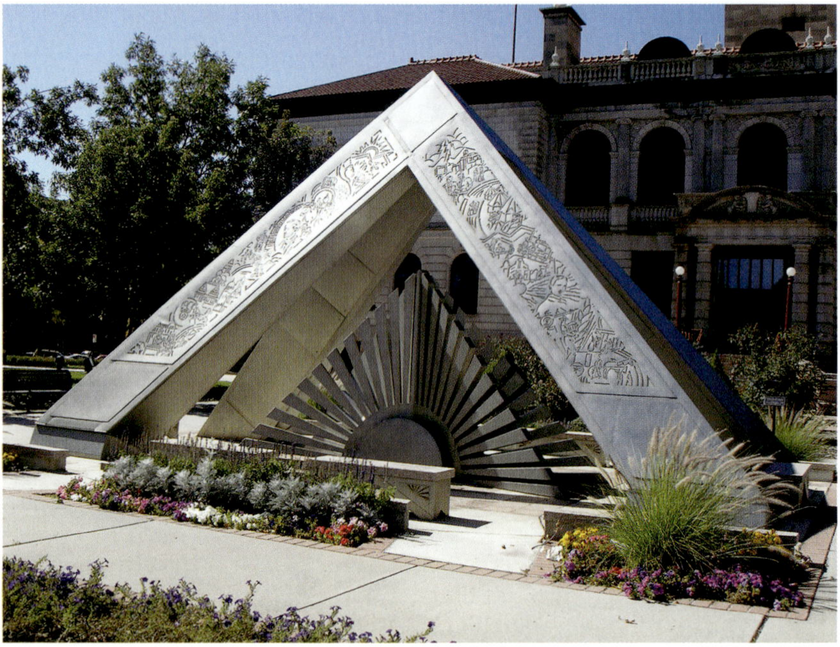

PLATE F. Harriet Lee, *Follow the Setting Sun*, Colorado Springs, Colorado, 2005. Photograph by author. The El Paso County Pioneers' Association wanted to erect a concrete covered wagon monument in front of Colorado Springs's Pioneer Museum. Instead, community debate persuaded them to erect Harriet Lee's stainless steel pyramid, imprinted with images telling a more inclusive history of the region.

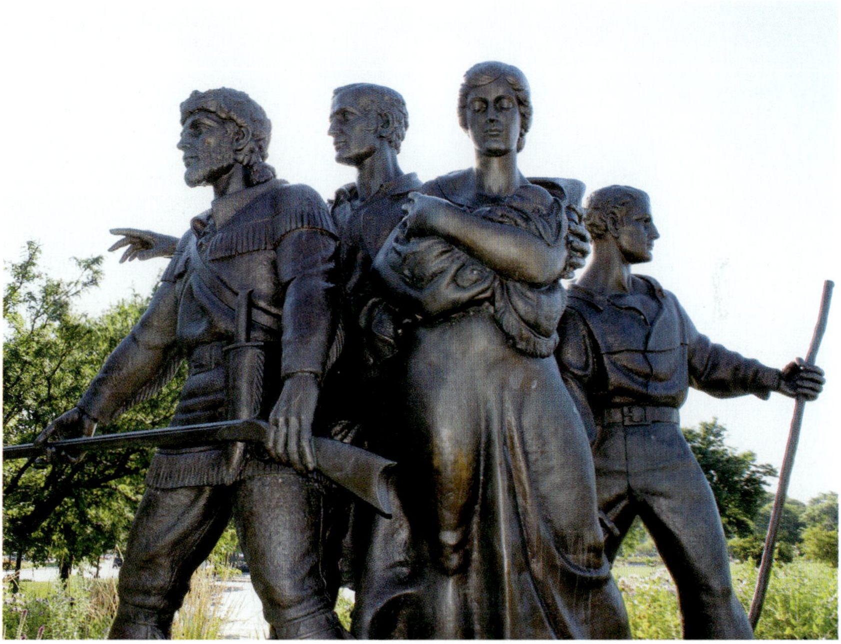

PLATE G. Trygve Rovelstad, *Pioneer Family Memorial*, Elgin, Illinois, 2001. Photograph by author. This work was conceived during the 1930s but not erected until 2001, when income from entertainment tourism enabled long-struggling Elgin to redevelop its riverfront.

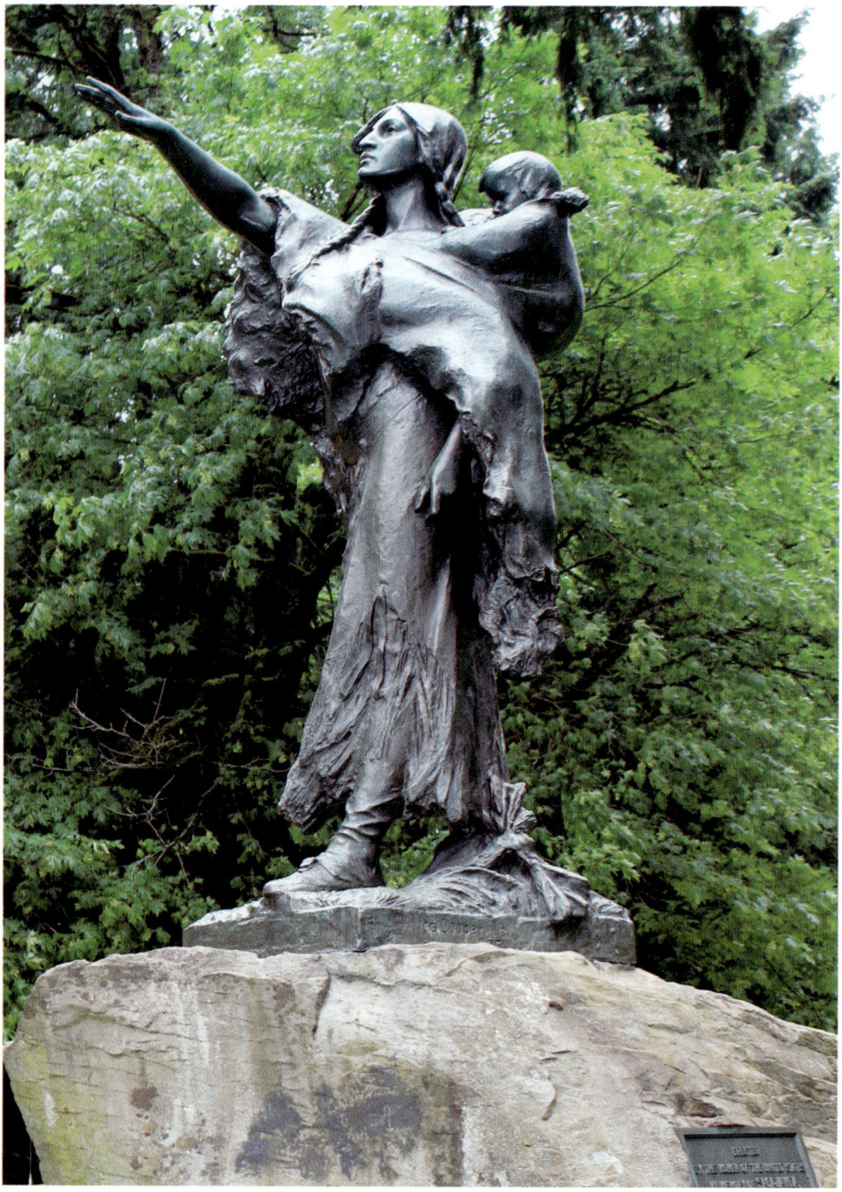

PLATE H. Alice Cooper, *Sacajawea,* Portland, Oregon, 1905. Photograph by author. This statue of the famed guide for the Lewis and Clark expedition was sculpted by a female artist and erected by suffragists. It was dedicated to Sacagawea and to "the pioneer mother of Oregon."

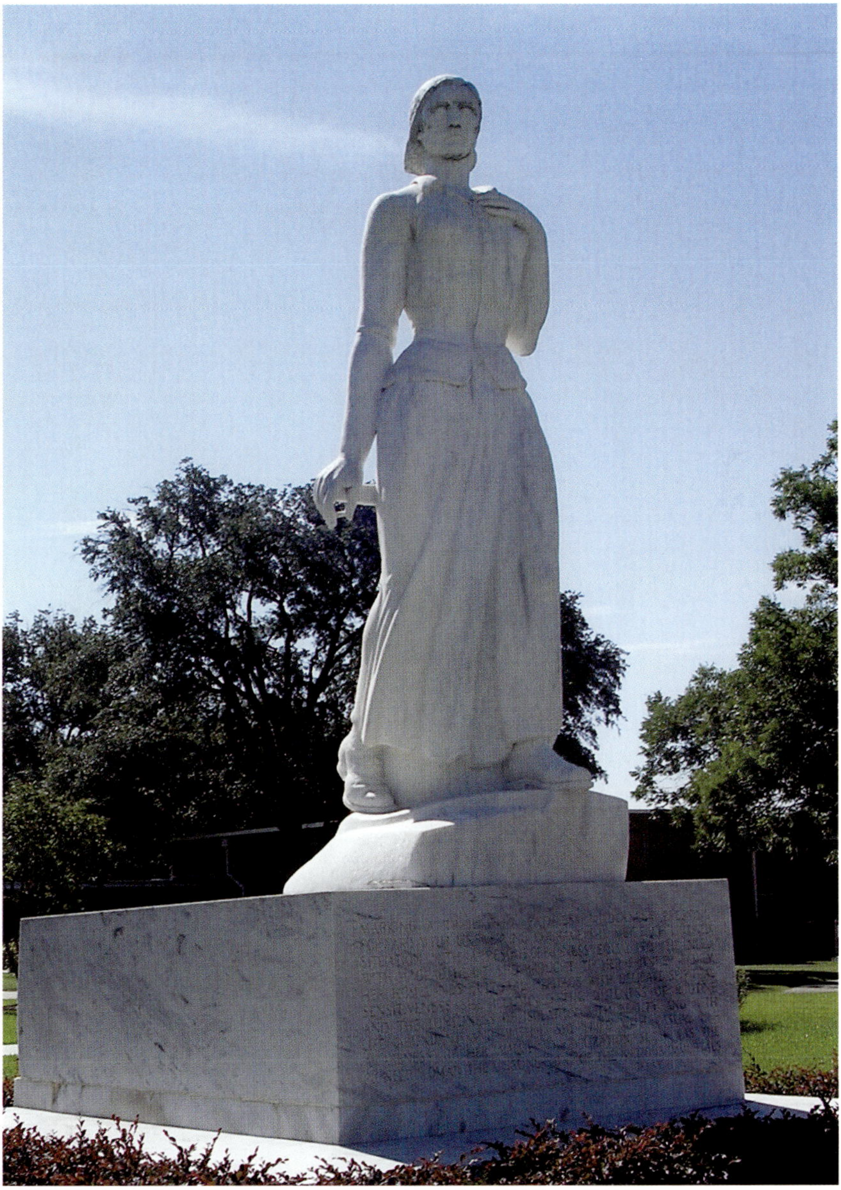

PLATE I. Leo Friedlander, *Pioneer Woman*, Denton, Texas, 1936. Photograph by author. This statue was chosen to replace William Zorach's controversial nude pioneer family grouping (plate E) for the Texas centennial celebration in 1936.

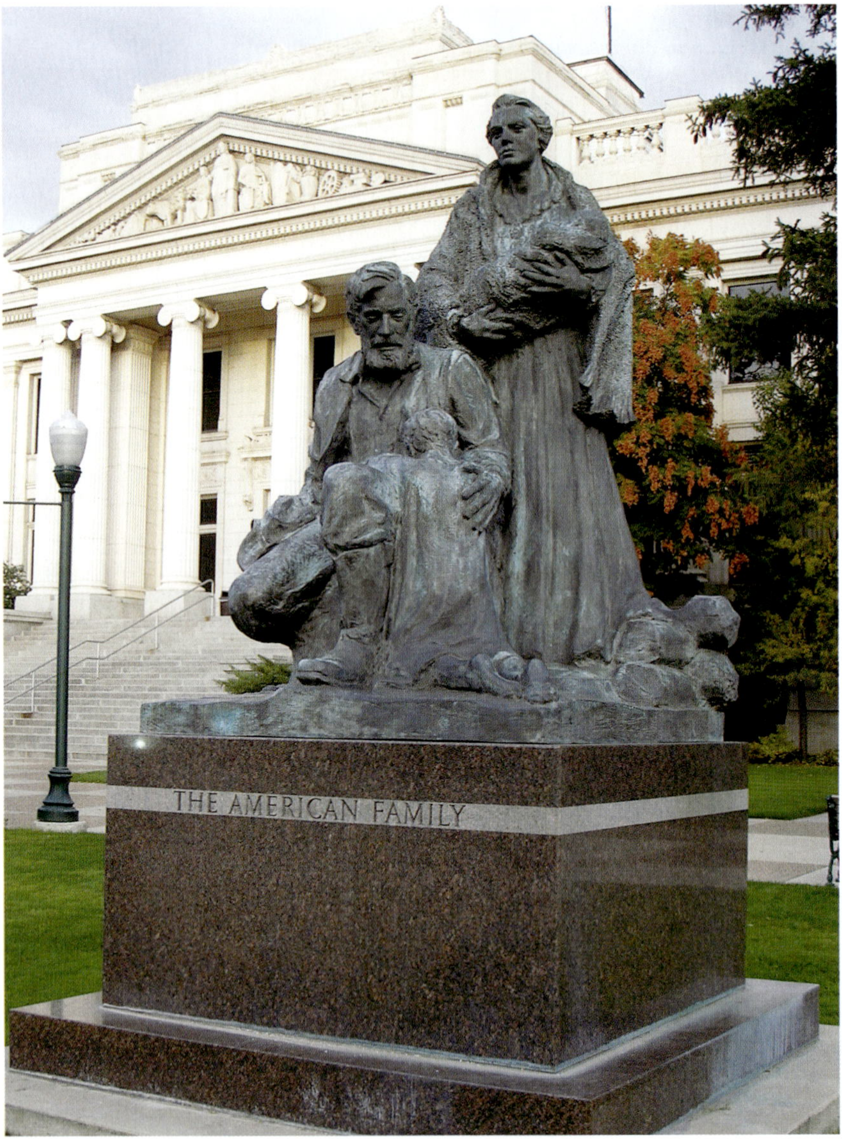

PLATE J. Avard T. Fairbanks, *The American Family*, Provo, Utah, 1978. Photograph by author. First conceived by the Mormon artist in the 1940s, this work was known as *God Bless Our Home* or *The Eternal Family* until shortly before it was erected on the county courthouse grounds in Provo, Utah, at the heart of the Mormon cultural area.

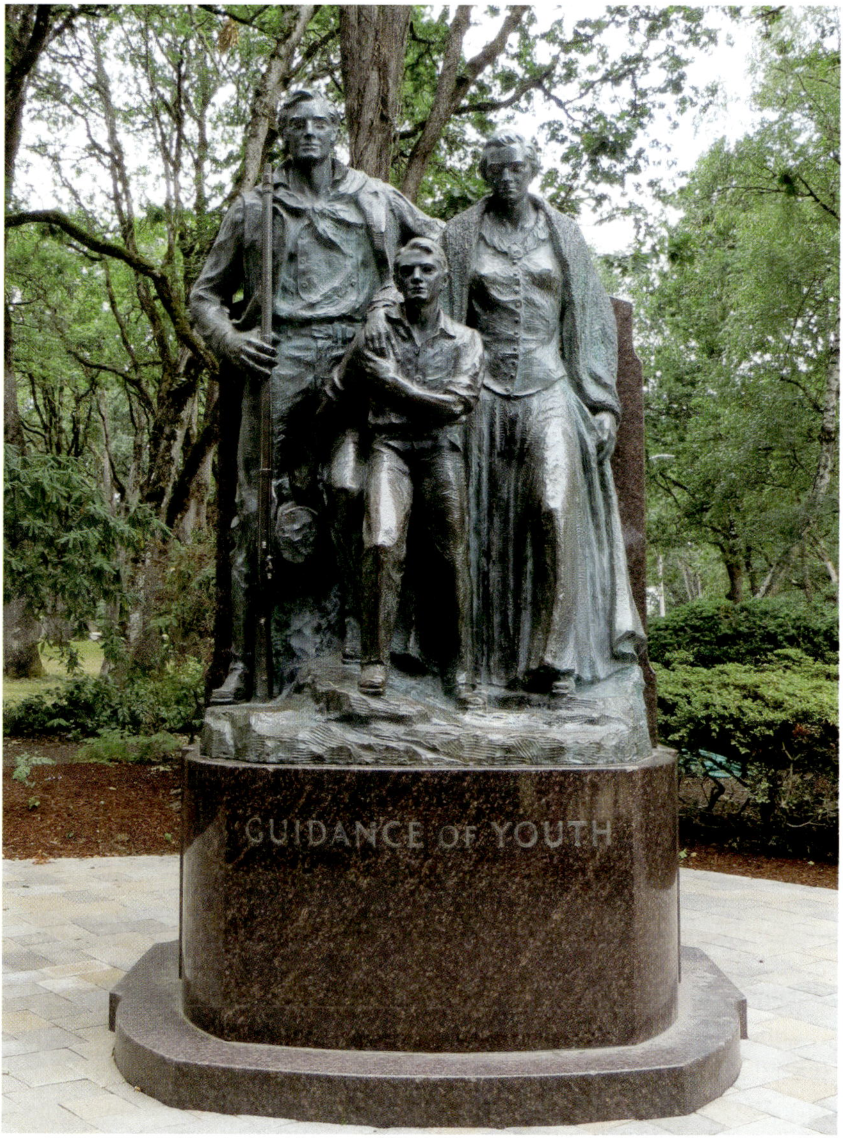

PLATE K. Avard T. Fairbanks, *Guidance of Youth*, Salem, Oregon, 1958. Photograph by author. In contrast to earlier pioneer monuments, this work emphasizes the pioneer couple's son as the hope for the future.

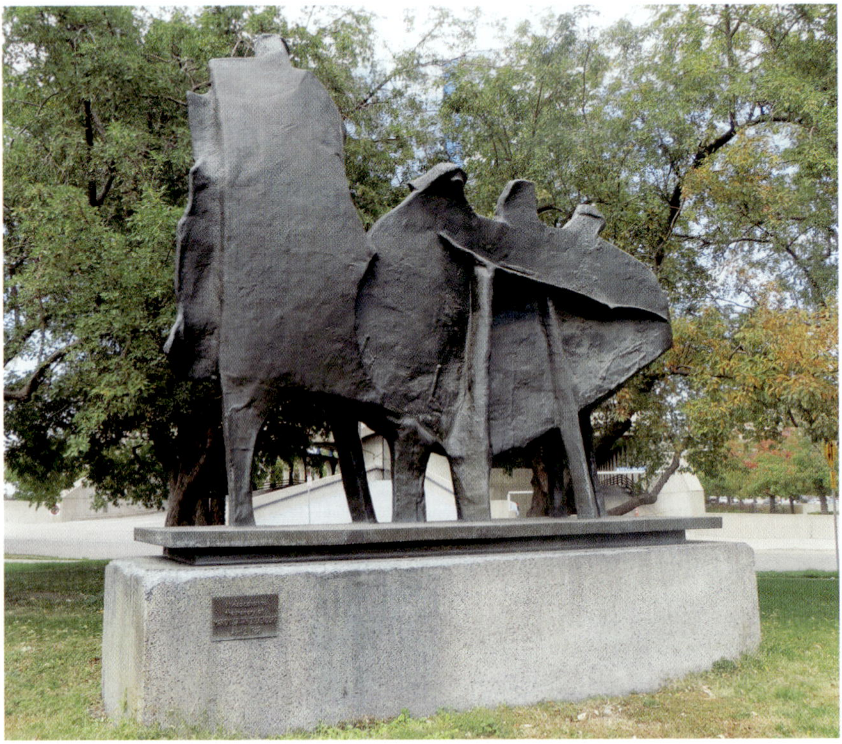

PLATE L. Susan M. Pogzeba, *Homage to the Pioneer,* Denver, Colorado, 1968. Photograph by author. Pogzeba refused to assign a meaning to her abstract work, but others saw it as evoking family relationships or an outline of the Rocky Mountains.

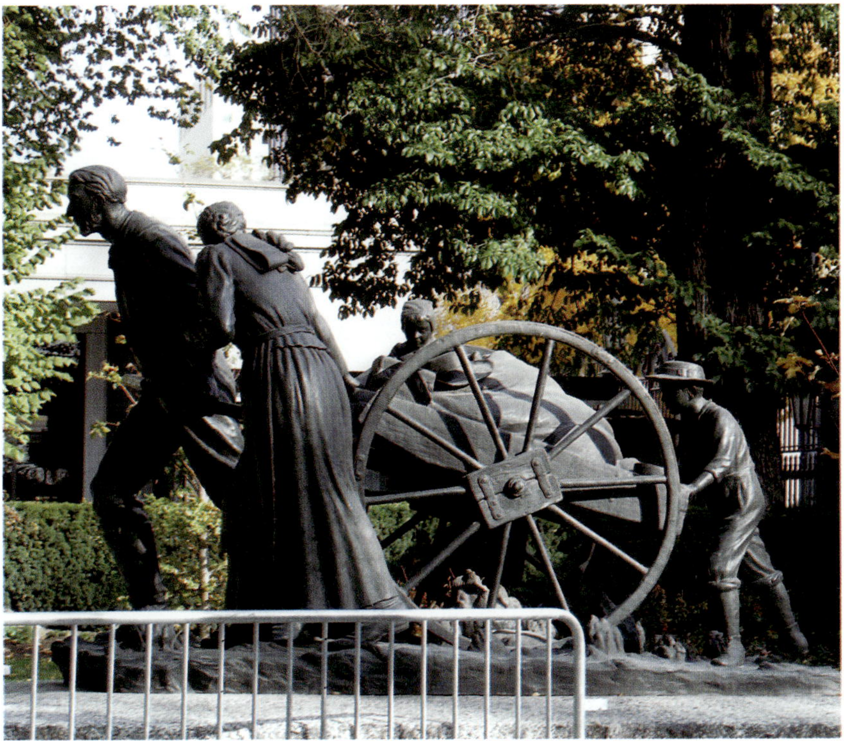

PLATE M. Torleif S. Knaphus, *Handcart Pioneer Monument*, Salt Lake City, Utah, 1947. Photograph by author. First sculpted in 1926, the artist expanded it to heroic size for the LDS church's Temple Square in 1947. The monument soon became a popular gathering spot for Mormons, shaping generations of Mormons' ideas about the handcart brigades. Knaphus's design also inspired several more recent handcart monuments.

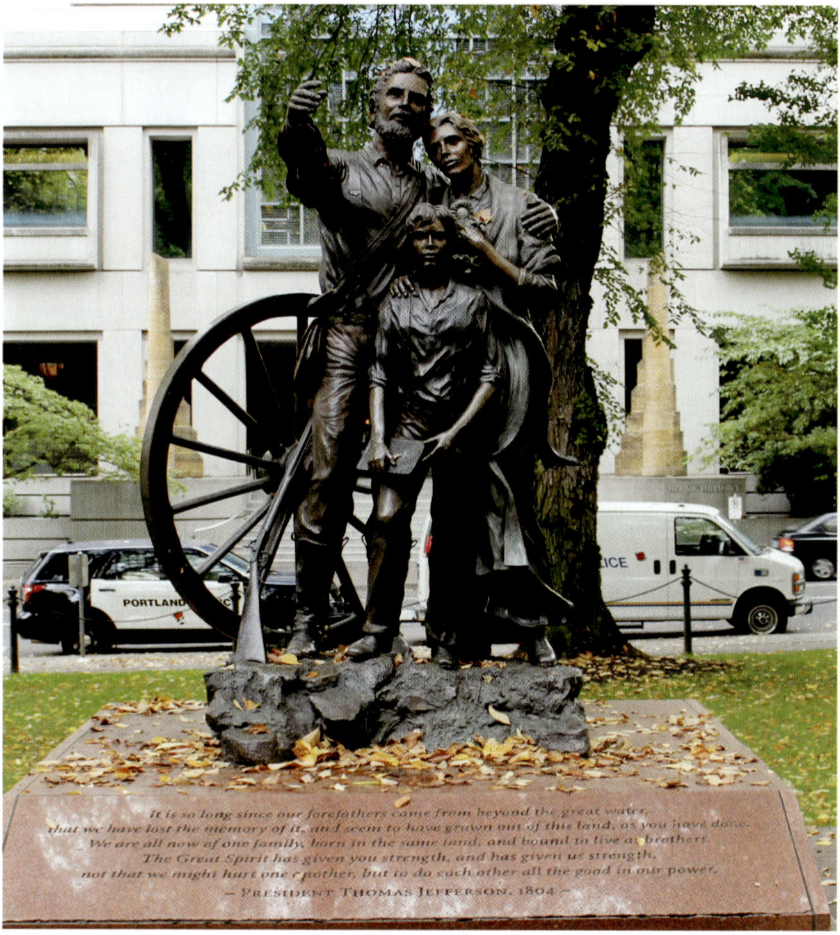

PLATE N. David Manuel, *The Promised Land*, Portland, Oregon, 1993. Photograph by author. Manuel's design borrowed heavily from earlier pioneer monuments, and many Americans found it appealing. But it sparked controversy in progressive Portland, Oregon, for celebrating white conquest of Native lands and peoples.

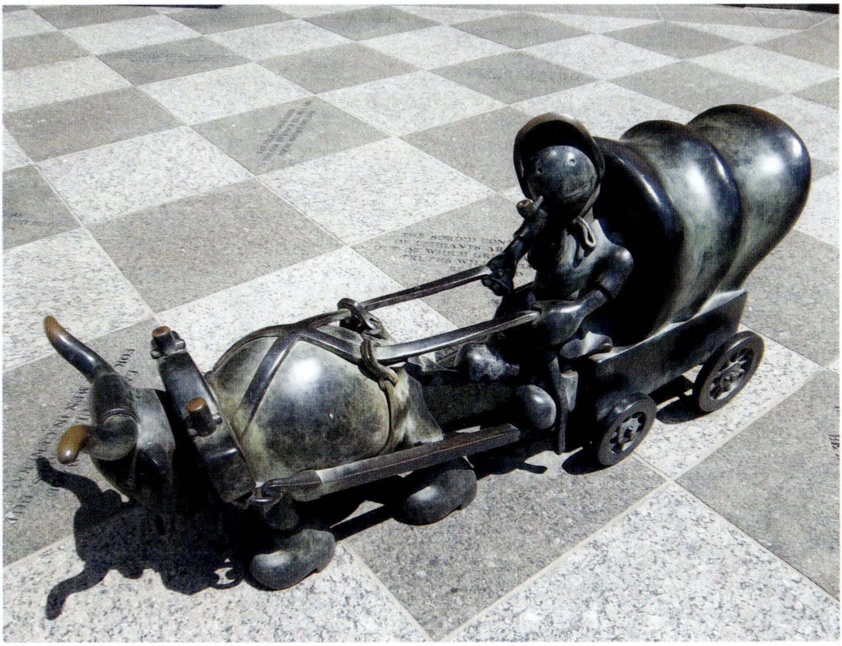

PLATE O. Tom Otterness, *The Covered Wagon*. Detail of *Gold Rush* installation, Sacramento, California, 1999. Photograph by Aimee Duchsherer. The artist humorously challenged traditional gender roles and conflated mid-nineteenth-century overland migrations with mid-twentieth-century family vacations.

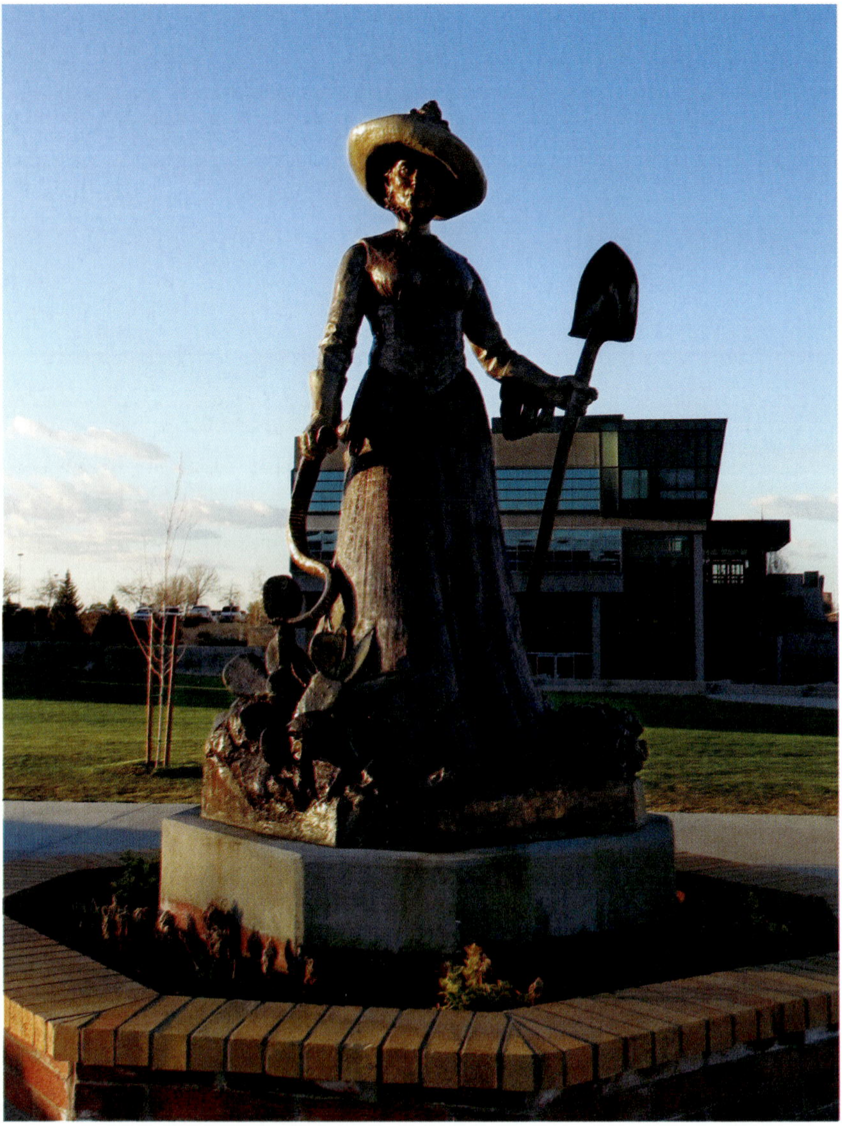

PLATE P. Debbie Gessner after Bob Boze Bell, *Not-So-Gentle Tamer,* Prescott Valley, Arizona, 2013. Photograph by author. This sculpture was adapted from a painting by Bob Boze Bell. Although it celebrates more active roles for women, it softens that stronger depiction with humor and ultimately portrays western women as responsible for taming western lands and western men.

CHAPTER 3

MEMORY AND MODERNITY IN POSTWAR FAMILY MONUMENTS, 1940–1975

A former janitor bequeathed the bulk of his modest estate to fund a pioneer memorial for Salem, Oregon, in 1940. Carroll Moores presumably envisioned a heroic Pioneer Mother statue to complement the pioneer-themed architectural sculpture that decorated the new state capitol in his hometown—perhaps something similar to the bronze Avard Fairbanks *Pioneer Mother* statue erected in nearby Vancouver, Washington, a decade earlier (see figure 2.2). But as World War II raged in Europe and the Pacific, Americans lost interest in erecting bronze and marble monuments to Pioneer Mothers. Instead, in keeping with a growing emphasis on utilitarian solutions to society's needs, Salem residents suggested practical uses for Moores's bequest: everything from establishing a pioneer museum to purchasing a new ambulance or building a municipal golf course. Understandably, the officials of the aptly named Pioneer Trust Company, which managed the funds, remained committed to erecting a statue as Carroll Moores's monument to Oregon pioneers. But the people of Salem were shocked to learn that, rather than erecting another Beaux-Arts Pioneer Mother statue, the trustees intended to purchase a 1914 Pierre-Auguste Renoir bronze statue of the Roman goddess Venus with Moores's bequest. While the trustees leaped at the chance to purchase such a prominent artwork for the city of Salem, the public was appalled by the notion that a nude goddess could commemorate Oregon's pioneer women. Ironically, significant public support developed for a local artist's model *Spirit of the Oregon Pioneer*, which included a male nude figure symbolizing that frontier spirit. But city officials rejected Frances Kells MacCollin's modernist allegory in favor of a far more traditional pioneer family.

Popular support for innovative portrayals of pioneering, like MacCollin's *Spirit of the Oregon Pioneer*, had grown in the generation since the nationwide Ponca City competition Bryant Baker won with *Pioneer Woman* (plate B), at the height of the Pioneer Mother movement. But while avant-garde artists stretched creative boundaries after World War II, many westerners remained committed to traditional representations of pioneer women in long dresses and wide-brimmed sunbonnets as an antidote to what they perceived to be the ills of modernity. In Salem, the local park commission rejected the male nude *Spirit of the Oregon Pioneer* in favor of a much safer choice: a family group in frontier garb, *The American Family*, by longtime pioneer monument sculptor Avard T. Fairbanks (plate J). Like several other postwar pioneer monuments, Fairbanks's work for Salem embraced 1950s America's obsession with the new nuclear family while clinging to traditional Beaux-Arts style. Yet modernism continued to make inroads into pioneer monuments. Interest in more innovative depictions of early white settlers increased in the 1960s, and by the mid-1970s, residents of another fairly conservative midsize western city eagerly embraced a nude pioneer woman even more pioneering than the Renoir *Venus Victorieuse* Oregonians had rejected two decades earlier.

From the 1880s to the 1920s, westerners sought to concretize white supremacy and celebrate the passing of the frontier era by erecting monuments to white pioneers. During the 1920s and 1930s, communities across the American West focused on commemorating the sacrifices of white female settlers. Then the craze faded—especially in the Far West's growing metropolises, which no longer felt a need to declare their cultural sophistication by erecting grand public monuments. Pioneer narratives about self-made men increasingly became part of the nation's foundational postwar myths.[1] A growing number of high schools, colleges, and universities in the Midwest and West adopted pioneers as their sports team mascots. Bronze tributes to pioneer women's sacrifices gave way to television and film westerns, celebrating masculine adventure. Commemorations of pioneers planting white civilization in fertile western soil yielded to fictional tales of cowboys fighting and outsmarting Indians. White Americans felt confident enough in their dominance of the West by the 1950s that stories of cowboys and Indians became a popular way to process new anxieties about unwinnable wars in Korea and Vietnam and about losing personal identity as organization men living amid suburban sameness.

As western cities ballooned, and suburban subdivisions became the West's new wide open spaces in the 1950s, westerners joined eastern residents in embracing efficiency and rationality, and they began to erase or reimagine frontier memory. Technology promised solutions to the world's problems, from feeding the growing global population to maintaining a cleaner suburban home.[2] This preference for practicality and simplicity also influenced postwar art and architectural styles: Beaux-Arts and neoclassical sculpture yielded to nonrepresentative abstract expressionism and minimalism's simplified geometric forms, and midcentury modern architecture stripped away art deco's lavish decoration, leaving only clean, simple lines. But Jackson Pollock's drip paintings also captured public attention, contrasting sharply against Norman Rockwell's nostalgic vignettes of American life.[3] Meanwhile, pioneer monuments fell out of favor in rapidly growing cities, as urban westerners abandoned the Pioneer Mother movement's backward gaze in favor of pursuing modern structures closely resembling those in eastern cities, ranging from downtown office buildings housing growing bureaucracies to suburban fast food restaurants and enclosed shopping malls. Plans to erect pioneer monuments stalled amid contestation over how to represent early settlers. Some newly sprawling urban areas, such as Denver, Colorado, and Minnesota's Twin Cities, experimented with different ways to commemorate their earliest settlers. Some placed pioneer mothers within modern nuclear family units, while others applied new materials or unconventional designs to frontier commemoration. Yet conservative commemoration remained dominant in most places: fiberglass pioneer mothers and new nuclear family monuments still held up mid-nineteenth-century households as models for modern youth. This chapter's close examination of pioneer-themed monuments from the 1950s and 1960s reveals Americans gradually accepting avant-garde artistic sensibilities through contestation and commemoration. Yet while the avant-garde came to dominate the fine arts world in the postwar era, experimentation in pioneer commemoration remained a fringe movement. Traditional representations still predominated, particularly in more conservative rural areas.

Interest in Beaux-Arts pioneer monuments declined in booming western cities but grew in some smaller communities and in areas rediscovering their frontier heritage, as both urban and rural Americans embraced colorful characters such as Davy Crockett. While film and television

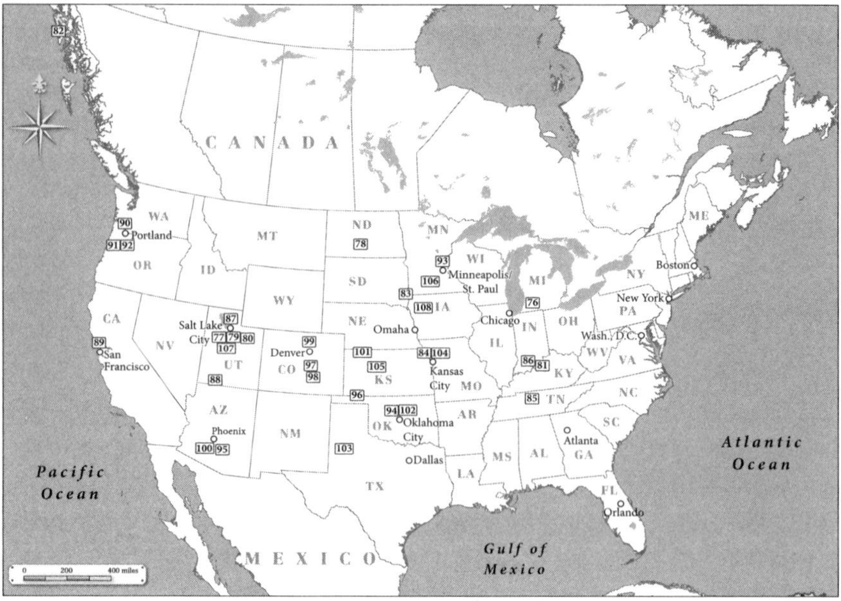

MAP 3. Pioneer Monuments Erected 1940–1974. Map by Gerry Krieg. Numbers on the map correspond with a chronological listing of monuments in the appendix.

westerns focused on cowboys, Indians, and outlaws, western pioneer monuments increasingly depicted premodern nuclear families. Pioneer Mother movement statues erected in the 1920s and 1930s typically portrayed a pioneer woman, perhaps with a babe-in-arms or accompanied by young children. In contrast, more than half of all Cold War–era pioneer monuments depicted white nuclear families. Those nuclear families—characterized by a father, a mother, and a strapping young son—were a mid-twentieth-century innovation developed in response to urbanization and postwar suburbanization. Rather than emphasizing women's distinct maternal roles, these nuclear family monuments embraced new family norms, while pointing to antebellum white frontier households as the ideal American family. In so doing, they ignored significant shifts that had occurred in American family structure between the 1840s and the 1950s. That transformation was particularly striking in the West, as large frontier families gave way seemingly overnight to atomized suburban households. These postwar pioneer family monuments designed by different artists and erected thousands of miles apart resembled one another to a remarkable degree, even though the smaller communities' statue projects lacked the media saturation typical of the Pioneer Mother movement. This remarkable similarity suggests the power of this postwar family ideal throughout rural America. By tracing changing depictions of men, women, and children in pioneer monuments erected in the 1940s and 1950s, this chapter reveals shifting American gender and family norms during those decades. While the characters portrayed in these sculptures still spoke to local communities, the familial roles represented in pioneer monuments shifted along with the nation's evolving social and aesthetic conventions.

In this chapter I demonstrate that pioneer monuments reflected and reinforced the dominant culture's changing conceptions of the ideal American family between 1940 and 1975. As Natasha Zaretsky argues, shared ideas about the family are "intrinsic to a sense of [American] national identity," but "during periods of large-scale social transformation," those "familial values [have] undergone revision."[4] Amid Cold War fears of atomic attack, an early twentieth-century emphasis on maternal roles gradually gave way to celebrations of the child-centered nuclear family as a bulwark against the spread of communism. That decidedly modern nuclear family form became enshrined in pioneer monuments portraying supposedly premodern family norms. As I show in this chapter—which is organized topically rather than chronologically—the white women, children, and men in western pioneer statues transcended mere frontier commemoration and came to represent the ideal contemporary American family.[5]

Even as pioneer monuments exchanged 1920s maternalism for 1950s nuclear family relations, the Pioneer Mother movement's preference for Beaux-Arts realism continued to influence most of the sculptures. But postwar pioneer monument erectors also grappled with modernism in various ways. Some artists experimented with new materials, ranging from copper to state-of-the-art fiberglass, for sculpting otherwise traditional Pioneer Mothers. Others embraced more avant-garde artistic styles or depicted bronze pioneer women in contemporary clothing or even no clothing at all. And by the 1960s, some erectors had abandoned plans for a monument altogether in favor of nonrepresentational sculpture or a practical commemoration that nonetheless played on traditional gendered tropes. In this chapter I first explore the ways in which Americans experimented with new expressions of pioneer motherhood. Next I examine the tension between changing family norms and traditional family values in pioneer family monuments, before turning attention to more daring experimentation during the 1960s and early 1970s. Throughout this chapter, I demonstrate that, whether westerners enshrined new nuclear family norms in traditional artistic style, embraced a nude pioneer mother, or rejected representative sculpture altogether, after World War II, they responded to modern life by adapting accepted pioneer tropes and artistic conventions to meet contemporary needs.

MODERN PIONEER MOTHERS

Whereas cultural shifts during the Jazz Age had inspired a Pioneer Mother movement, far fewer monuments to pioneer mothers were erected in the forties, fifties, and sixties, and those that were created sought to engage with modernity in various ways. Urban westerners turned their attention from frontier commemoration to more cosmopolitan concerns, forgetting the prominent Pioneer Mother statues in their midst. A growing number of those monuments were moved to accommodate wider roads and bigger buildings. Yet while urban populations pushed aside reminders of their frontier past, rural folk held on to their nostalgia for pioneering, and early white settlers featured prominently in postwar centennial celebrations. John Bodnar argues that postwar centennial (Wisconsin, Minnesota) and sesquicentennial (Ohio, Illinois) commemorations celebrated ethnic communities' and women's contributions to society to emphasize broader cultural conformity in the face of a perceived communist threat.[6] State and local centennials inspired some new efforts to memorialize pioneer women, and a handful of sculptors looked back to the Pioneer Mother movement for inspiration for new monuments. Decades after sculpting the gentle *Pioneer Mother* for Vancouver, Washington, discussed in chapter 2, Avard Fairbanks continued to visit smaller communities throughout the interior West, producing tributes large and small to white pioneer mothers.[7] But even as pioneer commemoration offered an alternative to modernity, artists increasingly incorporated strikingly avant-garde elements into their pioneer monuments, creating tensions between modernity and popular frontier memory. Modernism and traditionalism collided in pioneer monumentalization, producing some surprising results.

Some artists experimented with sculpting traditional Pioneer Mothers from novel materials. Large urban areas typically welcomed these artistic

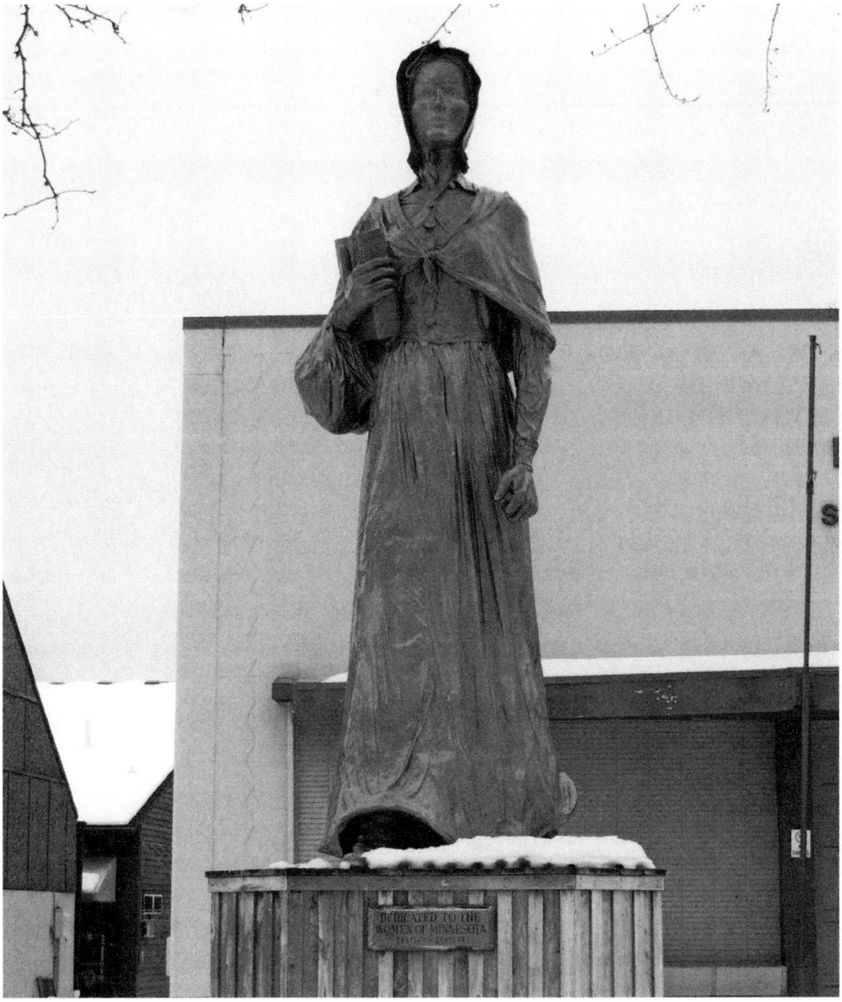

FIGURE 3.1. Gordon Shumaker, *Pioneer Woman*, St. Paul, Minnesota, 1958. Photograph by author.

experiments, but over time they faded from the public eye, just as older monuments were forgotten in postwar cities. The Minnesota Centennial Women's Committee hired local artist Gordon Shumaker to sculpt the twenty-foot-tall *Pioneer Woman* for the state fairgrounds.[8] Shumaker dressed his highly traditional pioneer woman in both a sunbonnet and a Marian shawl across her shoulders (figure 3.1). The book in her right hand and the satchel hanging from her right elbow replicate Bryant Baker's famous *Pioneer Woman* in Ponca City, Oklahoma (plate B). But unlike

Baker's statue, which included a young boy to balance those burdens artistically and symbolically and to represent hope for the future, Shumaker depicted a woman striding placidly westward, solo like the woman in Leo Friedlander's *Pioneer Woman* (plate I), erected in Denton, Texas, in the 1930s. Yet in an apparent nod to the more avant-garde art movements of the 1950s, such as pop art's focus on consumerism, Shumaker produced his *Pioneer Woman* from oddly modern and ephemeral fiberglass, which he then painted to resemble the enduring bronze that had been favored at the height of the Pioneer Mother movement.[9] Existing records do not reveal whether Shumaker and the donors sought to play with modernity and tradition in this monument, or whether postwar civic frugality inspired him to paint state-of-the-art fiberglass to resemble traditional bronze. But newspaper coverage suggests that support for Shumaker's efforts to adapt the iconography of that movement to the postwar era was similarly ephemeral. Prior to 1940, monument dedications were major events typically receiving extensive newspaper coverage, particularly when mounted to mark a local anniversary. By contrast, although Shumaker's *Pioneer Woman* was featured prominently in advertisements for the fair, the statue itself appears to have elicited little excitement. Its dedication became just one of many events that occurred amid the circus-like atmosphere of centennial celebrations centered at the Minnesota State Fair—all of which lost much of their luster amid heavy rainstorms.[10] As the fiberglass statue aged over the next several decades, however, it became widely accepted—and widely photographed—as a supposedly traditional feature of the fair.

Meanwhile, aging reduced both the novelty of an Arizona pioneer monument and its ability to attract public attention. As its shiny copper tarnished, Charles B. Martin's 1968 *Arizona's Pioneer Women* blended in among a growing array of memorials placed in a plaza next to the state capitol in Phoenix. The innovative materials that once made these monuments cutting edge gradually faded, causing them to more closely resemble their traditional predecessors. Over time, the shiny surfaces of these once-avant-garde statues faded, and the sculptures were both accepted and forgotten just like more traditional pioneer monuments.

Some efforts to modernize pioneer monuments "worked" better than others.[11] In the late 1950s, Trygve Rovelstad sought to resurrect a pioneer monument design, for his hometown of Elgin, Illinois, that had fallen victim to the Great Depression and changing cultural expectations for public monuments. As other cities had erected Pioneer Mother monuments in the 1920s, Elgin leaders had approached Rovelstad to create their own pioneer monument. But at the height of the Great Depression, city leaders abandoned his statue in favor of building a log cabin replica, and Rovelstad's independent fundraising efforts floundered. Two decades later, as suburban sprawl transformed Elgin into a bedroom community of nearby Chicago, Rovelstad reimagined his heroic work for the state capitol in Springfield. He even sponsored a 1958 essay contest for Illinois high school students to help him select twenty famous Illinoisans for commemoration on the new granite backdrop of his proposed statue, but the sculptor's promotional efforts failed to inspire interest in his outdated design. Rovelstad did find greater success with a new design, though: his 1968 Illinois sesquicentennial coin featured new skyscrapers towering over nineteenth-century frontier scenes, successfully marrying frontier narratives with modern urban life.[12]

While Pioneer Mother imagery gained little traction in 1950s urban Illinois, a design that had seemed too avant-garde in the 1920s found new life in rural southwestern Kansas. Grain dealer and grower D. K. Baty's pioneer commemoration efforts had stalled in his rather conservative small town of Liberal, Kansas, as similar efforts had in Salem, Oregon, and across much of the country. Finally in 1959, perhaps motivated by the approaching state centennial, Baty and his wife commissioned a local art student to create a monument to the pioneer mothers of Kansas for the local library. According to area newspaper coverage, Baty offered to pay Carlos Frey enough to enable him to complete his master's of fine art at the University of Kansas. Learning about Baty's project, nationally renowned sculptor Wheeler Williams "offered his aid and advice to the Liberal artist in this undertaking."[13] Williams would supply far more than advice. The Batys abandoned Frey in favor of resurrecting Wheeler Williams's *Fearless* pioneer mother, which he had entered in E. W. Marland's 1927 monument competition for Ponca City, Oklahoma.

Newspaper coverage does not explain why the donors abandoned the young art student in favor of a thirty-year-old Pioneer Mother design. Perhaps they leaped at a chance to acquire a work by a much more famous artist, much as the Pioneer Trust Company had seized an opportunity to purchase Renoir's nude *Venus Victorieuse* as Carroll Moores's gift to Salem.

At a time when avant-garde movements increasingly dominated university fine arts departments across the country—even making inroads at University of Utah against lingering conservativism led by none other than fine arts dean Avard Fairbanks—it seems even more likely that the young student's proposed design was too experimental for the Batys' goal of "glorify[ing] the qualities of these [Kansas pioneer] heroines which enable[d] them to triumph over the rigors of frontier life."[14] But if the Batys sought a return to the pioneer monuments of the 1920s, so willingly embracing Wheeler Williams's *Fearless* is surprising. Although Williams's design featured a woman in a long gown and bonnet cradling a swaddled infant in her arms, *Fearless* strayed significantly from the standard 1920s Pioneer Mother trope invoked by the Batys. The wide-rimmed bonnet on her head evokes a stereotypical Indian brave's warbonnet as much as it does a white woman's calico sunbonnet. And even though the skirt of the woman's long gown is heavily pleated, it clings to her legs in a manner that viewers in both the 1920s and the 1950s would have considered indecent. Williams's 1920s artistic wedding of classical and cutting-edge depictions of frontier womanhood tested the limits of 1950s decorum, but it was apparently preferable to the far more avant-garde styles being taught in art academies and universities across the nation. A copy of another, particularly conservative entry to the Ponca City competition, Jo Davidson's *Trusting*, was placed on a marble pedestal at the Pioneer Pipe Line Company's terminal at Woods Cross, outside Salt Lake City, in 1953.[15] But Davidson's *Trusting* had been too reserved to gain popular or critical attention in 1927, and thus the statue represented an extremely safe choice for adoption in risk-averse 1950s Utah.

Just as August Leimbach paired a relatively strong depiction of a pioneer woman with a gentler Madonna title, Liberal, Kansas, balanced a somewhat risqué pioneer mother with Marian interpretive text straight out of the 1920s: "With faith in God, she built a home for her family in the wilderness."[16] According to newspaper coverage in Amarillo, Texas (an urban center 150 miles from Liberal), the Williams sculpture "succeeded in portraying womanly tenderness, sweetness, patience and courage as well as purposefulness and capability," and "Baty is well pleased with the result."[17] Whether erecting contemporary-looking pioneer women, pioneer mothers of golden fiberglass, or monuments rejected in the 1920s as too cutting edge, westerners in the 1950s responded to Cold War anxiety by embracing a new kind of pioneer mother. Pioneer mother commemoration took an even more surprising turn in Indiana, where the urban Pioneer Mother movement faded and was replaced by a pragmatic solution to diverse rural concerns.

MULTIETHNIC MOTHERS AND VIRGIN FOREST

Pragmatism profoundly shaped the outcome of Indiana's pioneer mother tribute efforts from the 1910s to the 1950s. The roots of Indiana's rural 1950s homage to pioneer motherhood reached back to the first decades of pioneer commemoration. As people traveled from across the nation to San Francisco's Panama-Pacific International Exposition (PPIE) in 1915, Indiana prepared to celebrate its statehood centennial in 1916. Reading about Charles Grafly's *Pioneer Mother* and other social Darwinist art at the PPIE, Indiana residents decided to commemorate their own pioneer mothers. Intriguingly, while world's fairgoers marveled at sculpted tributes to white supremacy, at least some Indianans envisioned a more ethnically inclusive frontier narrative. But nativism soon increased across the nation, and early enthusiasm for erecting a Pioneer Mother monument in Indiana faded. When Indiana finally dedicated a tribute to pioneer motherhood in the 1950s, that commemoration substituted a postwar emphasis on utilitarian solutions in place of the elaborate but ephemeral plaster sculptures of the PPIE or the more lasting bronze pioneer monuments. Yet their practical tribute to pioneer women called on gender ideology more typical of 1915 than of 1950.

Early efforts to commemorate Indiana's pioneer mothers had closely resembled those in western states. The male-dominated Indiana Historical Commission supported the establishment of the female-led Pioneer Mothers Memorial Association of Indiana. As part of state centennial celebrations in 1916, Perry Township High School dedicated a Pioneer Mother memorial boulder, which mirrored those placed across the country in that decade and the next. But the newly formed memorial association argued that, in addition to dedicating civic buildings and creating parks, the state should erect a statue to commemorate its centennial, and that one honoring "the Pioneer Mother of Indiana" would have the "widest appeal."[18] To raise funds for such a statue, the association sold a thirty-page memorial booklet edited by Charity Dye of the

Indiana Historical Commission, reproducing "sentiments expressed by various Indiana authors" related to Indiana pioneer mothers, for twenty-five cents a copy.[19] Its epigraph placed the proposed statue on par with Grafly's *Pioneer Mother* and the Statue of Liberty, and its editor claimed that donors large and small "consider[ed] themselves the true daughters of the Pioneer Mother."[20] Yet, if that memorial booklet is to be believed, those Indiana donors interpreted pioneer motherhood to be far more diverse than most Americans assumed during the interwar period.

According to the booklet, Indianans of varying cultural backgrounds found something to value in the proposed statue of an idealized Anglo-American woman. Working-class women embraced the Pioneer Mother as a symbol of the hard work of their frontier predecessors. African Americans who had been born into slavery and Anglo-Americans raised by a "colored 'Mammy'" supposedly considered the proposed "memorial of the Pioneer White Mother" to be a fitting tribute to "The Pioneer Black Mother."[21] This is surprising because, though "Mammy" monuments were proposed by several southern communities in the 1920s, their focus on black women's nurturance of white children was ultimately intended to reinforce white supremacy rather than to suggest any degree of equality between black and white women.[22] Other individuals viewed the statue as a way to honor any respected women of the past or present. One Indianan reportedly contributed to the statue to honor (presumably Anglo-American) frontier women who moved to "Bleeding Kansas" to promote the antislavery cause. Another sought to commemorate their (western European) ancestors who came to America as indentured laborers in the seventeenth century in pursuit of religious freedom. Yet another donated money "in honor of the mothers and daughters of my country, Armenia," arguing that "All the mothers of the world should be included in the thought of this memorial to the Pioneer Mother of Indiana."[23] Unfortunately, it is impossible to verify the veracity of these remarkably inclusive statements attributed to a diverse range of Indiana residents. Moreover, even if they are legitimate, it is unclear how widespread such views might have been.

Despite the apparent ethnic inclusivity of the association's significant fundraising efforts, they were unable to accomplish their mission as part of the state's 1916 centennial celebration. Thereafter the Pioneer Mothers Memorial Association began to look more and more like the many other women's clubs operating in Indianapolis at the time. Society pages announced their monthly meetings and recorded their various social activities, including a joint social event to welcome soldiers from World War I and a children's Christmas party. Association president Charity Dye continued to devote "all of her strength" to the cause, though, promoting the organization's historical perspective through speeches to other women's clubs and serving on prize committees for historical essay contests.[24]

Dye was so devoted to this project that the proposed monument to Indiana pioneer mothers gradually morphed into a tribute to her upon her death in 1921. The association commissioned Indianapolis artist Myra Reynolds Richards to produce both a death mask of Dye and a bronze group depicting a pioneer woman resembling Dye for a memorial fountain. But just as suffrage organizations fractured after achieving the Nineteenth Amendment, the Indiana group lost its way after losing its fearless leader. The association managed to raise about 40 percent of the $10,000 ($132,000 in 2015 dollars) required to erect their memorial before again losing momentum.[25]

Meanwhile, another wealthy Indianapolis socialite commissioned the same local female artist to design a new decorative fountain in memory of her late husband. The resulting Fountain Square grouping featured a father armed with a musket, a son carrying a heavy ax, and a shy young daughter struggling to carry her mother's distaff and flax—a reference to nineteenth-century mythology that inaccurately remembered frontier women as having been active in making homespun cloth.[26] She and her mother wear narrow-rimmed bonnets, which continue this reference to colonial womanhood and resemble Charles Grafly's compromise design for San Francisco's 1915 *Pioneer Mother*. In contrast to later pioneer family groupings, Richards's Pioneer Mother, clutching a Bible to her chest, rather than the well-armed father and son, leads white civilization westward in this female artist's sculpture.

Meanwhile, the memorial association continued to struggle as Indiana descended into the Great Depression. Yet at least a few Indianans remained committed to their cause—albeit in revised form. As the Pioneer Mother movement faded, the memorial association's remaining membership voted in 1940 to commemorate pioneer mothers by donating the group's $5,900 (nearly $100,000 in 2015 currency) to help purchase a ninety-acre tract of "virgin" timber, near the recently established Hoosier

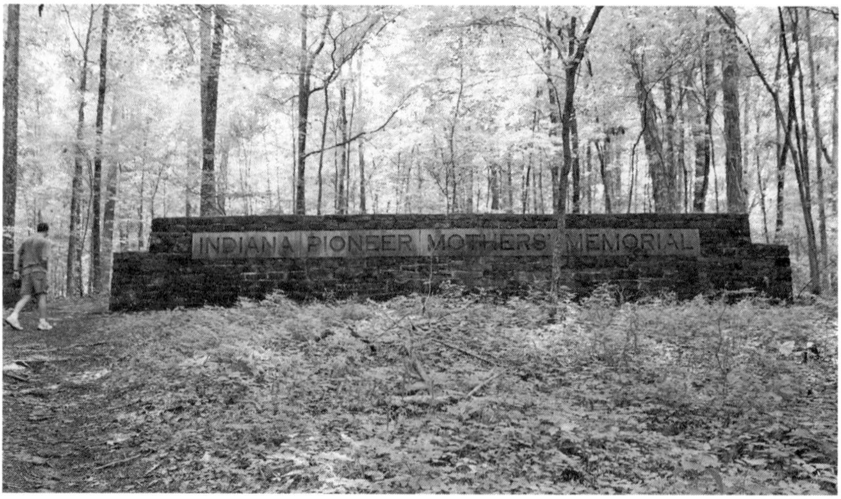

FIGURE 3.2. Indiana Pioneer Mothers Memorial Forest wall, Paoli, Indiana, 1951. Photograph by author.

National Forest, that had been threatened by logging.[27] As Americans forgot existing Pioneer Mother monuments, like the one in Indianapolis's Fountain Square, memorial association members abandoned their longed-for statue, choosing instead to participate in growing nationwide efforts to conserve the environment, which anticipated 1970s ecopolitics. This practical postwar solution simultaneously saved the forest tract, fulfilled (in a sense) the mission of the memorial association, and absolved its remaining members of further responsibility to manage their treasury. The plan also conveniently avoided competing with the Fountain Square pioneer monument and followed a nationwide shift from urban to rural frontier commemoration.

On the surface, the Indiana group's practicality paralleled that of Salem residents' suggestions for using Carroll Moores's funds to construct a public building or acquire a new ambulance. Yet on a symbolic level, the association's actions stayed truer to Charity Dye's original vision. In place of a sculpture depicting a Pioneer Mother's purity, they substituted the supposed virginity of woodland that had been farmed by Native peoples since about 1380 C.E. Instead of erecting a female artist's statue of clubwoman Charity Dye as a pioneer woman, the memorial association substituted a memorial wall built from reclaimed foundation stones cut by actual frontier men (figure 3.2).[28] That these foundation stones had been laid by settlers in the region some five generations earlier clearly belied the memorial forest's virginity and that of the white women who settled in those frontier homes. It is unclear how effectively the new memorial forest truly "help[ed Indianans] remember the courage, personal integrity, and faith of the pioneer women."[29] Some Indianans still clung to early twentieth-century glorifications of pioneer motherhood. But by the 1950s, others were seeking ways to modernize those depictions of sunbonneted pioneer women or to embrace more practical means of commemoration. Increasingly, communities believed that their nation's greatest values were embodied not in maternalism but in the togetherness of the American nuclear family.

PIONEER FAMILIES

During the 1950s—an era that many consider to be the golden age of the American family—pioneer monuments shifted from celebrating solo pioneer women to portraying nuclear families. By the time the Pioneer Mothers Memorial Association finally erected its memorial wall to Indiana's pioneer mothers, in the 1950s, most other donors and sculptors had embraced pioneer families that resembled the Myra Reynolds Richards grouping erected in Indianapolis's Fountain Square in 1924. But in 1950s pioneer monuments, as in popular culture, mothers and even fathers faded to the background as children stepped forward, ready to lead their parents and their society toward "new frontiers." Raised on a steady diet of television westerns, and grappling with the realities of commuting male breadwinners, housebound young mothers, and Cold War anxieties in the age of Sputnik, baby boomers, and their parents, unsurprisingly came to view the Old West as a golden age for the American family. Rather than the Wild West imagery typical of film and television westerns in this era, monument builders instead embraced Laura Ingalls Wilder's depiction of a solitary nuclear family surviving and thriving on the frontier. Ignoring the physical hardships, isolation, flexible gender roles, and reliance on child labor typical of nineteenth-century frontier life, postwar Americans embraced the mythic West as a place of manly men, nurturing mothers, and, increasingly, children embodying hope for the future.[30]

Baby boomers not only dominated popular culture, but they even took over family dynamics in many western pioneer monuments. Just as urbanization and growing roles for women and immigrants following World War I inspired xenophobia and nostalgia for an imagined agrarian past, suburbanization and economic and baby booms following World War II inspired an idealization of the white native-born nuclear family. Prior to 1900, Americans had generally viewed children as miniature adults who should contribute to the household economy. In the early twentieth century, progressive reformers instead argued that children were precious creatures who deserved protection from labor and physical danger. By the 1950s, many Americans came to view children as the center of the American family. Advice books and popular magazines taught that family life should revolve around the needs of young children.[31] Women were expected to find fulfillment in their roles as wives and mothers, and—in the words of family historian Stephanie Coontz—a woman was "pitied if she did not *want* what was expected of her."[32] Scholars Joanne Meyerowitz, Jessica Weiss, and others have demonstrated that many families, both white and nonwhite, failed to fit this prescribed pattern of a male breadwinner, female homemaker, and three or more young children, all united in family "togetherness."[33] Nonetheless, many Americans—and particularly those in the growing middle class—accepted the new glorification of the white nuclear family so prevalent in the mass media and aspired to live it out.

This emphasis on the nuclear family unit can be seen in pioneer monuments erected throughout the postwar period. Immediately following World War II, as most other sculptors and monument donors abandoned Pioneer Mothers, Avard Fairbanks explicitly embraced the Madonna-like imagery typical of mid-nineteenth-century western paintings, which he had previously used only in bas-relief panels, adapting it to new social conditions. The North Dakota Federation of Club Women (NDFCW) began fundraising for a memorial to pioneer women in 1927, as newspapers across the country followed the casting and erection of A. Phimister Proctor's Kansas City *Pioneer Mother* (plate C). In keeping with Pioneer Mother movement ideology, NDFCW president Nina Farley Wishek declared that pioneer life was full of isolation and hardship. Yet rather than evoking the Prairie Madonna that Proctor, Fairbanks and others sculpted in that era, Wishek insisted that the realities of frontier life on the northern plains called for a statue of a strong, mature woman. But the NDFCW's fundraising efforts lagged as hard times hit farmers in the American heartland;

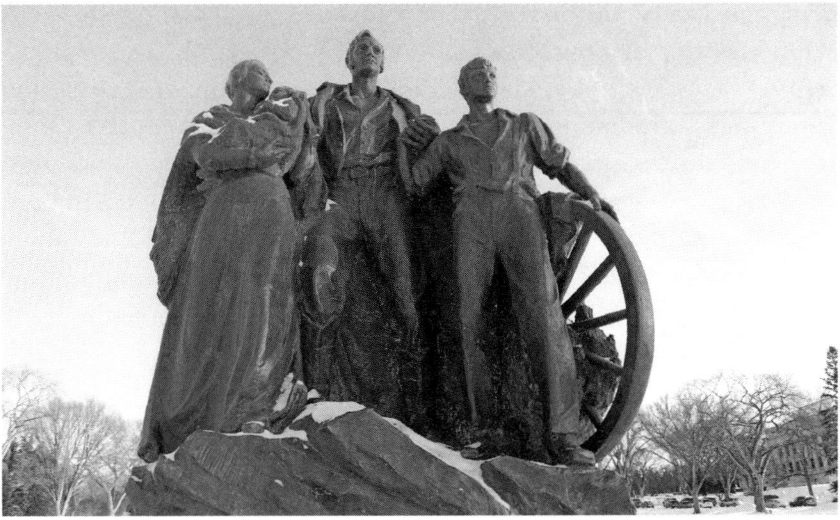

FIGURE 3.3. Avard T. Fairbanks, *Pioneer Family Group*, Bismarck, North Dakota, 1946. Photograph by author.

Wishek's insistence on stronger Pioneer Woman imagery also may have discouraged potential donors. Predictably, the NDFCW's funds dwindled further during the dust bowl years. For reasons that remain unclear, the project was then taken up during World War II by a Canadian businessman, who hired Avard Fairbanks, the sculptor of particularly maternal pioneer mothers, to produce a pioneer *family* monument.[34]

Erected on the lawn of North Dakota's new art deco capitol, Fairbanks's *Pioneer Family Group* (figure 3.3) united postwar ideas about the importance of the nuclear family and suburban domestic life with nineteenth-century domestic ideology. "My desire in this monument," Fairbanks explained to the governor of Idaho, "was to express the family as a unit with the individual characteristics of each. The feminine qualities in the figure of the mother of tenderness and love, strength and dependability in the father and the suggestion of adventure in the adolescent youth who holds to his father for guidance are universal ideals and the latter expresses the father and son relationship particularly."[35] In this postwar family group, Fairbanks replaced the pyramidal structure of his earlier pioneer monuments with a seemingly more egalitarian father, mother, and teenage son standing in a semicircle. But the baby that Fairbanks placed in its nurturing mother's arms drew her attention aside to domestic matters, while her husband stepped into a clear leadership role. While the strapping son looks to his father for guidance, his other arm rests on a wagon wheel, symbolizing the progress of white civilization and indicating his readiness to depart from the family unit and embrace the future.[36] Fairbanks thus depicted an idealized white family life as it was (re)defined in the immediate postwar era: family togetherness, mothers' domesticity and nurturance of young children, fathers' central role as breadwinner, and young men embodying hope for the future.[37]

Several smaller towns also erected pioneer family monuments during the Cold War, typically turning to local artists to celebrate local history. Rural populations continued to erect such pioneer family statues long after the cultural revolutions of the 1960s and the culture wars of the late 1970s through the early 1990s inspired more progressive communities to challenge such pioneer commemoration. Rather than rugged frontiersmen, these monuments celebrated Jeffersonian yeoman families as antidotes to modernity and models for Cold War family life. While many adapted the traditional Beaux-Art imagery, a few used more avant-garde styles, formats, and materials, just as those erecting postwar pioneer mothers had done.

Given Hollywood's emphasis on westerns at the height of the Cold War, and particularly the popularity of shows like *Davy Crockett*, residents of Kentucky and Tennessee unsurprisingly experienced renewed interest in their frontier heritage in this period. But well-known local artists produced pioneer-themed art with a decidedly contemporary geometrical flair for Louisville and Nashville. In *Early Kentucky Settlers*, Marshall M. Fredericks depicted the "spirit of Kentucky" for the *Louisville Courier-Journal*'s new building (figure 3.4), with a modernist "pioneer family" surrounded by signs of white industry: thoroughbred horses, sheep, tobacco, riverboats, and a giant catfish. Instead of a strapping young son, in this scene deer, bear, and raccoon families frolicking at the frontier man and sunbonneted woman's feet symbolize the land's promise for the future.[38] Similarly, when Nashville, Tennessee, built the new Cordell Hull State Office Building a few years later, the city surrounded the massive midcentury modern structure with four bronze sculptural groupings, depicting different aspects of Tennessee history, by local artist Thomas Puryear Mims. Using stylized human figures, Mims forsook realism in favor of modernist "oversimplification, exag[g]eration and intensification

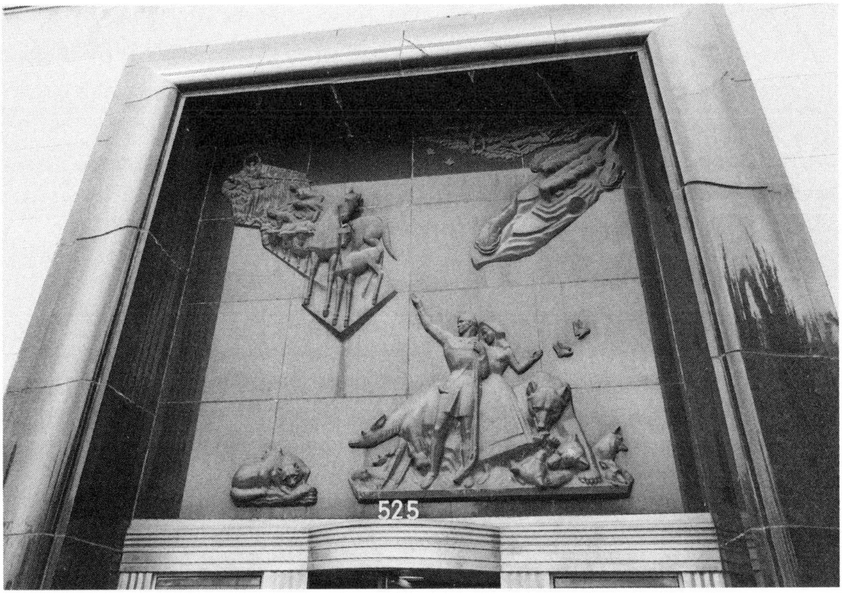

FIGURE 3.4. Marshall M. Fredericks, *Early Kentucky Settlers*, 1948. Photograph by author.

of vertical lines" to elicit emotion in the viewer.[39] Mims's stylized *Mountain Group* (also known as *Pioneer Family*) features a pioneer couple and their adolescent son. But while the father and son wear frontier buckskin, Mims gave his pioneer mother a contemporary twist: barefoot and bare headed, she wears a 1950s-style knee-length dress. Even more unconventional pioneer sculpture gained public support as Carroll Moores's monument for Oregon's capital city.

SOPHISTICATED MISREPRESENTATION

Not all American communities in the 1950s were prepared to accept avant-garde depictions of pioneer women or families, which many felt misrepresented American cultural heritage. Salem residents' debate regarding Carroll Moores's pioneer monument pitted the fine arts establishment's embrace of the avant-garde against postwar pragmatism and a rich local tradition of Beaux-Arts pioneer memorials. Unable to satisfy everyone, civic leaders ultimately chose safety over modernity.

Salem residents grew up imbued with frontier memory and surrounded by Beaux-Arts pioneer monuments. The Oregon capital sits in the heart of the fertile Willamette Valley, which was the primary destination for Anglo-American farming families migrating over the Oregon Trail in the 1840s and 1850s. Alice Cooper's 1905 *Sacajawea* and Avard Fairbanks's 1928 *Pioneer Mother* stand near Portland about fifty miles north, and A. Phimister Proctor's 1918 *The Pioneer* and 1928 *Pioneer Mother* sit on the University of Oregon campus some sixty-five miles south. Allen G. Newman's zinc *Pioneer* stood near the capitol from 1903 until it was toppled by a windstorm in 1917, and Proctor's monument to frontier circuit-riding missionaries had been mounted in Salem since 1924. Pioneer monumentalization was also central to Oregon's new state capitol design. After Oregon's statehouse was destroyed by fire in 1935, a jury rejected the gilded domes typical of other state capitols, selecting from among 123 design submissions what the winning architects described as a "forceful and vital modern structure with broad and masculine feeling."[40] Placing Leo Friedlander's Beaux-Arts white marble Lewis and Clark relief to the left of the entrance and covered wagon family to the right, with Ulric Ellerhusen's gold-plated *Pioneer* atop a spire, on the otherwise simple PWA moderne building encouraged visitors to read Oregon history—as westerners had done since the 1890s—as one of progress from savagery to civilization, accomplished through the efforts of white men. While each individual work mounted on the new capitol fit easily within the Pioneer Mother movement during which it was erected, and both Friedlander and Ellerhusen had recently completed other prominent pioneer monuments, the building as a whole read like a pillar of civilization circa 1890. Proctor's *Circuit Rider*, painted murals, and marble reliefs inside the capitol and in the adjacent new state library reinforced this gendered and racialized message.[41]

As the presence of these major pioneer monuments in the area suggest, the people of Oregon were heavily invested in their state's pioneer heritage. Despite Leo Friedlander's and Ulric Ellerhusen's faithfulness to Beaux-Arts traditions in their sculptures for the new capitol and their experience sculpting other pioneer monuments, Oregon residents—particularly competing artist J. Leo Fairbanks, who had replaced his brother Avard on the faculty of the University of Oregon—penned numerous complaints about the artists' work during the 1930s. They questioned the works' historical accuracy, as had been typical in the two previous decades, and complained of the sculptures' perceived modernism. One woman declared that she had "received great inspiration" from Phimister Proctor's *Pioneer* on the University of Oregon campus (see figure 1.4) and *Circuit Rider* near the capitol, Alice Cooper's *Sacajawea* in Portland (plate H), "and above all," Bryant Baker's *Pioneer Woman* at Ponca City (plate B), and in comparison, she found Friedlander's reliefs lacking.[42] Another complained that an "eastern sculptor [Ellerhusen] has pictured our Oregon pioneer as a smooth shaved gent, probably wearing rayon underwear."[43] Friedlander and Ellerhusen defended their designs on artistic grounds, and Capitol Reconstruction Commission member Robert W. Sawyer insisted that the work was not "modernistic stuff. It is good, clean pictures."[44] But those depictions of good, clean frontier men and women were in fact a central part of the new capitol's PWA moderne design.

Janitor Carroll Moores made his decision to fund a pioneer monument as that new capitol was being completed. His bequest of $25,000 was specifically for "a monument or memorial to be erected in memory of the early Oregon pioneers" and empowered the city council to determine its location.[45] But by the time of his death in 1937, public will to erect Pioneer Mother statues was waning across the country, particularly in cities along the Pacific slope. In the absence of a shared public vision, the city of Salem put off making a decision for more than a decade.

By the early 1950s, the fund had grown to about $30,000 (about $275,000 in 2015 dollars), and Salem residents had begun to debate how best to spend Moores's bequest, after the outgoing mayor invited suggestions from the public. In keeping with postwar practicality, he suggested some kind of "living memorial."[46] Most ideas from the public, however, seemed to promote the proposers' pet projects rather than innovative forms of pioneer commemoration, including a playground, an ambulance for the fire department, a branch city library, and a municipal golf course.[47] A special commission named by the city favored traditional statuary in keeping with the donor's intent, but popular opinion appeared to strongly favor erecting a memorial in the Odd Fellows cemetery, where a number of prominent pioneers were buried.[48] Rather than investing in a prominent statue, though, residents wanted most of the funds to endow cemetery maintenance—apparently motivated more by frugality than ancestor veneration.

When the Pioneer Trust Company announced its intention to purchase Renoir's nude *Venus Victorieuse* with Moores's funds, the opinion page of the *Salem Daily Capital Journal* filled with outraged letters from church boards, garden clubs, and individuals who believed that the impressionist nude sculpture of the Roman goddess of love did not represent Oregon pioneers, and was not appropriate to erect in front of the modern county courthouse under construction near the PWA moderne state capitol.[49] Although San Franciscans had embraced a (clothed) Roman goddess of war, embodying the spirit of California, in the 1890s and nude children in 1915, a nude goddess of love sculpted in 1914 was simply too much for 1950s Salem. The national media soon picked up the story, and a local Lions Club member told *Time* magazine, "What we want . . . is a statue of a pioneer woman in a gingham dress and a sunbonnet . . . not this trash."[50] It mattered little that the piece in question was a major work by a world-famous sculptor, and that its style was by no means cutting-edge four decades after its creation. Although the popularity of Beaux-Arts monuments had declined after World War II, many of Salem's forty-three thousand residents seemed to want and expect yet another 1920s-style white Pioneer Mother. Presumably, the blue-collar donor had also envisioned a prairie gown and sunbonnet.

Members of the memorial selection committee stood by their decision, believing that they were acting in the public's best interest by purchasing such a prominent work of art. Prominent architect Pietro Belluschi was not surprised that their choice produced complaints, but he remained convinced that "with a proper inscription and in the proper setting," the Renoir *Venus* "will be a more suitable memorial to the pione[e]rs than a little man with a rac[c]oon hat," as in the monuments created for Louisville, Kentucky, and Nashville, Tennessee.[51] Former governor Charles Sprague declared that Salem already had plenty of pioneer statues and insisted that "future generations [would] be grateful" if the city spent Moores's money on a beautiful work of art rather than one more traditional pioneer statue.[52] But the loud public protest soon persuaded the selection committee to reconsider.

Community leaders remained committed to Beaux-Arts traditionalism. A special mayoral committee developed new "guiding principles to govern the search for an appropriate memorial," focused on "pioneers and pioneer activities," to commemorate "the spirit of all those whose dreams, toil and sacrifices laid the foundations for the community."[53] The *Daily Capital Journal* printed a photograph of *Pioneer Family Group*, the

North Dakota monument sculpted by Avard Fairbanks, who had taught at the University of Oregon for seven years, sculpted *Pioneer Mother* for nearby Vancouver, Washington, in the 1920s, and by this time become well known for his pioneer-themed monuments. That Fairbanks had not been approached to produce the Moores monument was, according to the *Capital Journal*, a "somnolent mystery."[54] The committee ultimately recommended the erection of a log cabin "of pioneer type . . . plus a piece of statuary depicting a pioneer family group," thus merging common frontier imagery of the 1920s and the 1950s.[55]

The public was invited to vote on twenty-four entries, including a reproduction of a log cabin, a relief map of the Oregon Trail, illustrations of a Pioneer Mother and of the Oregon Trail, and other pioneer family groups by local artists and Bryant Baker, the Ponca City *Pioneer Woman* sculptor. Given the public resistance to the Renoir *Venus*, it is surprising that viewers strongly favored local artist Frances Kells MacCollin's allegorical *Spirit of the Oregon Pioneer* over both Fairbanks's and Baker's more conventional works. More than fifty of the nearly seventy people who entered opinions in the exhibit visitor's book commented favorably on MacCollin's work, which portrayed the Oregon Trail embodied in a nude male form that echoed the female forms often found on the prow of nineteenth-century sailing ships. Viewers greatly preferred this design over MacCollin's other, safer submission, *Tall Timber*. MacCollin, in pursuing compromise between her artistic style and the trustees' and public demands for a traditional monument, pleased no one—including herself. *Tall Timber*'s merging of traditional and modernist elements, a style that had been accepted cheerfully in Louisville and Nashville only a few years earlier, was soundly rejected by Salem residents. Despite all the demands for a gingham dress and sunbonnet, those who viewed the entries strongly preferred the more avant-garde *Spirit of the Oregon Pioneer*, and the Salem Art Association voted unanimously to recommend its selection. Tellingly, the public's second choice was not the vaguely modernist compromise *Tall Timber* but Avard Fairbanks's much more traditional rendition of a fully clothed pioneer family, in which his only innovation was to emphasize the couple's strapping young son as society's hope for the future.[56]

Perhaps those who viewed and commented on the twenty-four entries were less representative of public opinion than those who had attended exhibits and voted in the Ponca City competition three decades earlier.

One resident wrote an indignant letter to the editor insisting that Salem needed to leave to future generations "a magnificent monument" in the "exact likeness" of the "stalwart" and "honest, Christian people of the best lineage" who had migrated to Oregon.[57] The Salem Park Commission's decision to identify four proposals it deemed "most appropriate for the park site" suggests that public dissent persisted.[58] The commission's short list included MacCollin's compromise *Tall Timber*, Baker's pioneer family group, and Portland sculptor Frederic Littman's depiction of a pioneer family centered between two massive walls, all of which fit the committee's guidelines but excluded MacCollin's much more highly regarded and more daring *Spirit of the Oregon Pioneer*.

The Pioneer Trust Company ultimately chose the most popular of the four traditional options identified by the park commission. An *Oregon Statesman* columnist described Avard Fairbanks's design for *Guidance of Youth* (plate K) as "'safe,' well within the orbit of history and of art and of morals," and "indulg[ing] in no abstraction."[59] Fairbanks, who had been "very anxious to make a beautiful Pioneer woman statue" for Salem, was overjoyed that his traditional pioneer imagery prevailed.[60] "This is a very great triumph in America," he commented, "because at one time there were art interests and those directing the new movements and isms who made recommendations for the erection of a nude 'Venus' by the French modernist, Renoir. Had it been completed Oregon would have had a French female nude to represent the pioneer mothers of the great Oregon Trail. What a travesty. . . . Fortunately, we have real Westerners and true Americans who still believe that our cultural heritage is well worth memorializing with true and sincere presentations rather than by sophisticated misrepresentations."[61] It speaks volumes that Fairbanks declared the iconic white pioneer woman as representing not only "real Westerners," whose ancestors had carried Anglo civilization westward, but also all "true Americans," whose identity had become inextricably linked to western mythology by the 1950s. No longer simply sites of local or even regional memory, supposedly self-made pioneers had come to represent the heart of American national identity at the height of the Cold War.

Echoing monuments erected during the Pioneer Mother movement, Fairbanks again adapted his 1924 *Old Oregon Trail* medallion to become a 1958 Oregon centennial bas-relief, which he attached to the reverse of the pioneer monument's marble backdrop. Yet Fairbanks's model for the Salem sculpture focused not on a popular Pioneer Mother character, nor on a rugged male settler, but on a child the *Oregonian* described as "the personification of red-blooded, American boyhood."[62] Fairbanks explained that he chose to place a young man at the center of the 1950s Salem monument because (in keeping with mainstream family norms of that era) "all life and our ideals are centered in youth, for therein lies the great futures."[63] The boy's tender and loving "ideal mother" (with no babe-in-arms requiring her intensive nurturance) stands just behind him and to one side, her "guiding hand" on the youth's shoulder.[64] His clean-shaven "rugged, strong and firm" father stands in the background, providing a firm foundation while allowing the younger generation to lead.[65] This father's farmer role would enable him to train and mentor his young son, rather than abandoning him for long hours each day at the office, as many postwar middle-class fathers did.[66] At the same time, his guidance would protect his growing son from the danger of excessive emotional dependency on his nurturing mother.[67] Yet this postwar pioneer father also steps aside and encourages his son to lead. Amid Cold War uncertainty, mainstream America's energetic youth, rather than its mothers' civilizing influence or even its fathers' steadfastness, represented the nation's greatest hope for the future. But the nineteenth-century frontier myth—and Beaux-Arts traditionalism—still underpinned American national identity.

1960s EXPERIMENTATION

Cultural changes in the 1960s shattered many Americans' steadfast faith in pioneer mothers and families, encouraging more experimental representations of frontier life. Western frontier mythology and the promise of America's youth lost much of its cachet in the 1960s and early 1970s, when the 1950s' appearance of cultural conformity splintered amid student activism, calls for civil rights, and the sexual revolution. As baby boomers reached adolescence, they began to reject 1950s conformity, questioning their elders' authority and anything associated with tradition. Rather than holding young people up as the nation's hope for the future, older generations began to question what was wrong with America's youth. Amid this growing generational gap, previous decades' longing for the supposed golden age of the 1850s appeared outdated and even wrong-headed.

Significantly, no major Beaux-Arts-style pioneer monuments were erected during the 1960s. Even die-hard Pioneer Mother sculptor Avard Fairbanks failed to receive a commission to produce a major Pioneer Woman monument (though he would return to sculpting traditional pioneers in the 1970s). Instead, he produced several heroic-sized sculptures celebrating the centennial of the short-lived Pony Express, which fit more easily with persistent popular interest in film and television westerns. As sculptors strayed from accepted Beaux-Arts styles and the iconography of the Pioneer Mother movement, westerners began to question just what made something a pioneer monument.

AVANT-GARDE PIONEERS

By the 1960s, avant-garde design had become commonplace in urban communities, including in smaller cities on the Great Plains. But what artists widely accepted remained contested among plains residents, some of whom clung to more traditional pioneer imagery. Avard Fairbanks's 1946 Bismarck *Pioneer Family Group* (figure 3.3) so impressed the president of the University of North Dakota (UND), George Starcher, that he created a sculptor-in-residence position for Fairbanks in the mid-1960s. But conflict soon arose between the highly traditional Fairbanks and UND's avant-garde art department in that conservative state. UND faculty and students found trite Fairbanks's proposal to adapt his typical pioneer woman figure to embody learning in a heroic work for the campus, titled *Alma Mater*.[68] More conservative North Dakotans found the woman in Fairbanks's sculpture to be indecently clothed, and suggested that the work's title should be revised to "Invitation to earning and permissive lasciviousness."[69] In the face of such resistance, Fairbanks fled his UND studio under cover of darkness and returned to even more culturally conservative Utah and to sculpting Beaux-Arts pioneers for Utah's Mormon population.

Just as the perspectives of North Dakota residents and UND artists clashed over Fairbanks's work, conservative pioneer messages persisted amid widely publicized political protests. Pioneers figured in to many Illinois sesquicentennial events in 1968, even as demonstrations outside the Democratic National Convention in Chicago devolved into a police riot. As the civil rights movement morphed from fighting southern desegregation to battling poverty and inequality in Chicago and nationwide, midwestern communities showed little interest in erecting heroic bronze statues of pioneers and increasingly forgot those already standing in their city centers. For example, Minneapolis, Minnesota, constructed an apartment tower on the site of its downtown Pioneer Square park and moved its 1936 John K. Daniels *Pioneers Monument* from that park to a small, oddly shaped lot in a residential neighborhood. But in response to the lingering public appeal of frontier mythology and the longing for idealized mid-nineteenth-century families, a few Colorado cities experimented with more abstract designs amid the social experimentation of the 1960s. And as several western communities merged pioneer family imagery with avant-garde artistic and architectural forms, they blurred the boundaries of what qualifies as a pioneer monument.

The local arts community pushed Denver to experiment with a new form of pioneer commemoration. In the mid-1960s, the city named a small triangular park after real estate developer William Zeckendorf, and the honoree's foundation offered a $5,000 prize for a sculpture dedicated to Colorado pioneers and produced by a Colorado artist.[70] Zeckendorf presumably expected a monument that continued the Beaux-Arts tradition of the previous half century. Instead, the selection committee chose a design, *Homage to the Pioneer*, by a young local artist, Susan Pogzeba, who "refuse[d] to ascribe any particular meaning to" her abstract design (plate L), "although other people have tried to pin such meanings as 'family' on it." The artist explained that she "was just working with forms and this was the result."[71] Pogzeba's forms echo the standing figures in Avard Fairbanks's semicircular *Pioneer Family Group*, but her abstract flat shapes bore little resemblance to Fairbanks's realist pioneer characters. That Pogzeba's abstract figures also evoked the forms of the Rocky Mountains towering to the west of Denver may have increased the design's appeal for the selection committee.

The committee—consisting of the directors of the Denver and Colorado Springs art museums and a University of Colorado art history professor—acted within the standards of the fine art establishment of the time, which focused on nonrepresentational art, such as that of the abstract expressionists and minimalists. Abandoning a New Deal–era emphasis on art for the masses and social reform, beginning in the 1940s, abstract expressionists focused instead on personal expression through a free-form aesthetic. Then in the 1960s, minimalists traded abstract expressionism's emotion for cold, simple forms made from industrial materials such as steel and concrete.[72] The minimalism of Pogzeba's abstract metal forms appears to have made her entry stand out to the Zeckendorf monument's selection committee, which awarded second prize to a series of engraved tablets, and third prize to a "stylized metal sculpture of tree forms."[73]

Pogzeba's minimalism was far less warmly received by the general public. The *Kenosha (Wisc.) News* printed a United Press International photo of its 1968 unveiling, with three older women clad in wool coats and headscarves in the foreground, skeptical looks on their faces, under the title "We Don't Like It."[74] Like those three women, most westerners still expected American pioneer monuments to embody traditional values rather than new artistic styles. Colorado residents rejected the Denver fine arts establishment's claim that Pogzeba's abstract figures represented an homage to the pioneer. But the public appears to have rejected the work's pioneer label rather than the design itself. Indeed, it was appreciated widely enough to justify installing a fiberglass copy—painted to resemble bronze as Minneapolis's *Pioneer Woman* had been a decade earlier—in Dallas's Reverchon Park that same year, under the more generic title *Family Group*. There, the copy remained until 1991, when it was destroyed by vandals.[75] The original bronze work—displayed without its pioneer title—survived but was gradually forgotten as downtown Denver was redeveloped around it.

WHAT'S IN A NAME?

By the 1960s, a growing number of Coloradans and other westerners were willing to embrace abstract or stylized depictions of the American family, so long as those sculptures evoked—but did not explicitly claim to commemorate—western pioneers. The Columbia Savings and Loan Association erected heroic-sized bronze castings of William Zorach's *Pioneer Family Group*, the design originally favored to win the 1936 Denton, Texas, competition for a memorial to the Pioneer Woman (plate E). Zorach's stylized nude family grouping had sparked outrage during the Pioneer Mother movement when it was chosen to honor pioneer women on the state women's college campus. But by the 1960s, the public appeared to embrace the familial relationships that had initially won over the Denton monument selection committee—as long as the statue claimed to represent the "traditional" American family and not a pioneer woman.[76] Zorach's nude family grouping was "warmly received" in 1966, when Columbia Savings erected the castings under the more generic title *The Family*—one in a niche specially designed for it in the Mining Exchange Building in downtown Colorado Springs and another at the bank's Pueblo, Colorado, office.[77] The *Colorado Springs Gazette-Telegraph* described it as "a sensitive and impressive work."[78] Two years later, it was boldly featured in the bank's print advertising campaign: "William Zorach sculpted this bronze *Family* to symbolize strength and unity. . . . To us they [also] symbolize the idea on which we have built our business. The idea is this: You should get something more than efficiency from a savings and loan association or a bank. . . . And while you may not save with us simply because of our antiques and art, you might because we make saving an art."[79] Thirty years after Zorach's design had sparked public scandal, it no longer appeared avant-garde; in fact, it read as just the opposite. While Coloradans were not ready to consider the work a tribute to a Pioneer Mother, the piece gained widespread acceptance as a beautiful portrayal of familial values.

While Americans continued to associate nuclear families with "strength and unity," idealized American family units—and monuments celebrating them—became increasingly divorced from frontier imagery amid the growing social divides of the 1960s. Over time, Columbia Savings and Loan ceased celebrating its Zorach family monuments, and like many other people across the country, Coloradans gradually stopped noticing the bronze pioneer statues—at least until someone decided to move them. Three decades after they were installed in Colorado Springs and Pueblo, Zorach's statues were removed from the banks that had once so proudly displayed them. One now appears outside the Fine Arts Center in Colorado Springs, its original pioneer moniker replaced with the vaguer title *The Family*.[80] Zorach's design, which had been rejected so strenuously in the 1930s only to be embraced amid the experimentation of the 1960s, had by the 1980s and 1990s culture wars once more lost its cache in urban Colorado.

Meanwhile, pioneer commemoration, modern art, and monument naming collided in a nearly opposite manner in 1960s Reno, Nevada. In 1966, Reno demolished its old state building to accommodate a new performing arts center, which would offer high culture as an alternative to gambling in the city's many casinos. Builders salvaged a 1939 Byron S. Johnson bronze sculpture, *Humanity*, from a drinking fountain on the

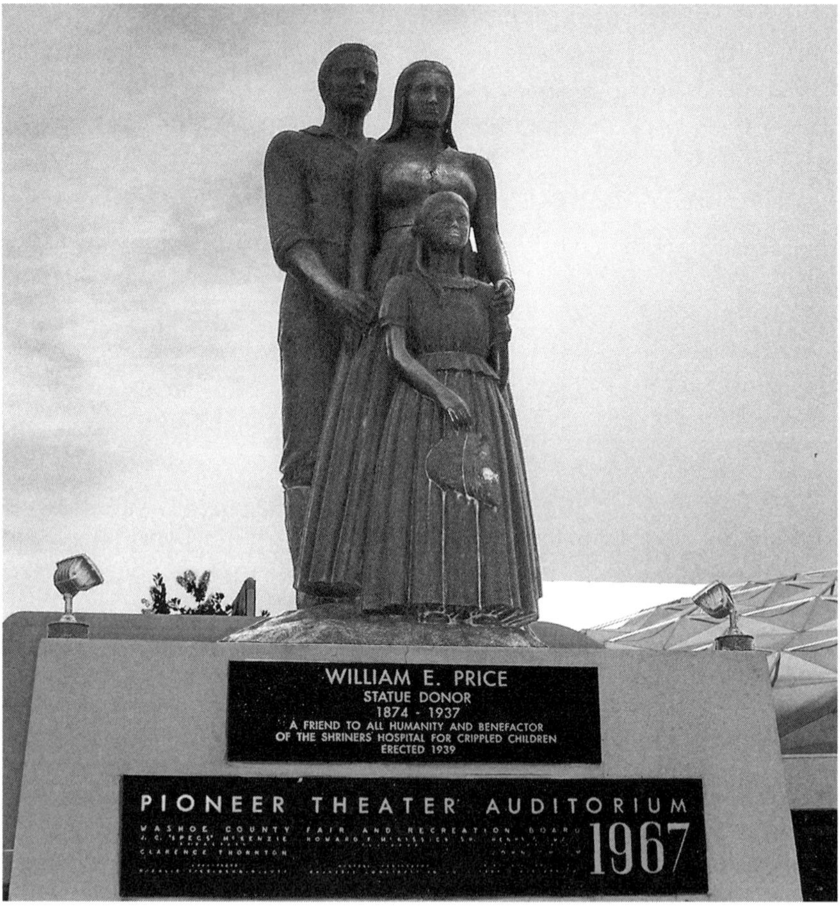

FIGURE 3.5. Byron S. Johnson, *Humanity*, Reno, Nevada, 1939. Photograph by author.

site (figure 3.5). When Johnson had sculpted the father, mother, and daughter dressed in frontier garb at the end of the Pioneer Mother movement, the artist and its philanthropist donor had intended it to depict timeless Humanity. But as pioneer family monuments grew popular in other smaller cities after World War II, local residents began to interpret Johnson's universal grouping as a pioneer family and referred to it as such. The new auditorium, with a gold-anodized geodesic domed roof, was officially named the Apollo Theater, but it soon became known as the Pioneer Theater-Auditorium (now the Pioneer Center for the Performing Arts) after the locals' interpretation of whom *Humanity* portrayed.

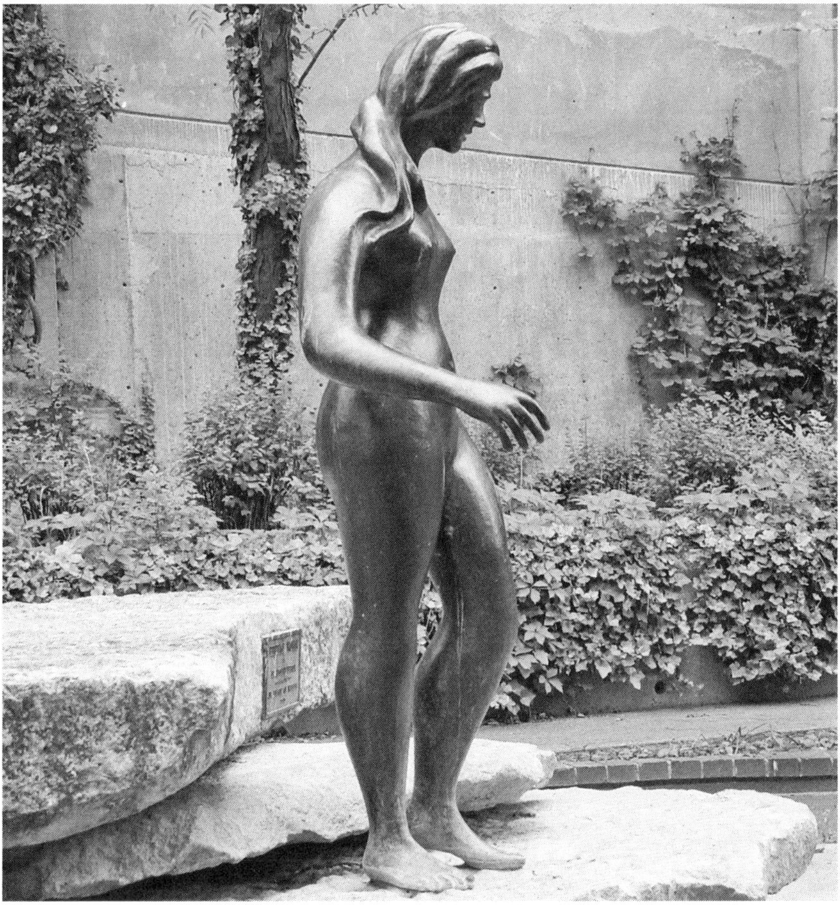

FIGURE 3.6. Richard Bergen, *Heritage Woman,* Wichita, Kansas, 1976. Photograph by Rich Bergen.

The innovative performing arts center sculpture in turn became known locally by the affectionate title *The Golden Turtle,* in reference to its innovative gold-domed roof, rather than the pioneer affiliation earlier locals had assigned to the supposedly universal *Humanity.*[81]

A decade after all these naming shenanigans in Colorado and in Nevada, a similarly vague title apparently persuaded Wichita, Kansas, residents to accept a nude pioneer woman statue commissioned by the city council for a new pocket park under construction behind the former city hall and Carnegie Library. Local artist Richard Bergen described his work as "an abstracted nude figure of a pioneer woman preparing herself for a cool dip in a Kansas stream." Demonstrating more empathy for western settlers than historical knowledge, Bergen explained, "When you've been walking across the plains on a hot, windy, dusty day and you come to a river . . . [y]ou'd probably strip off your clothes and jump in. That's what I think the pioneers probably did, too." Although *Heritage Woman* (figure 3.6) was highly stylized, the artist claimed, "It has a classical feeling to it."[82] Indeed, the nude woman's pose echoed Renoir's *Venus Victorieuse,* which had been cutting-edge art when sculpted in 1914 but was far less so when it was rejected as a Pioneer Mother monument for 1950s Salem, Oregon—and even less so by the mid-1970s, when Bergen was sculpting *Heritage Woman.* The Wichita Heritage Square Advisory Committee unanimously approved the Bergen sculpture, which the chair called "very effective and just right for the setting"; the director of Wichita's Community Arts raved that he "love[d] it. No question, she is a stunning person."[83] They appeared to embrace the juxtaposition of a nude figure representing a pioneer woman—a hot, dusty settler—with a Victorian-style urban park. Perhaps because the artist chose to name the sculpture after its site in Heritage Square Park rather than explicitly identifying the nude figure as a pioneer woman, the broader public seemed to share the arts community's appreciation. The citizens of Wichita apparently viewed Bergen's *Heritage Woman* within a long-established fine arts tradition of nude female forms. In contrast to the outrage expressed in Texas in the 1930s and in Oregon in the 1950s, newspaper coverage of Wichita's *Heritage Woman* did not reveal any protests to her nudity. Instead, local residents appeared to welcome the work's merging of classical and contemporary aesthetic for their new Victorian-inspired urban park, overlooking the artist's conception of a nude pioneer woman revealing herself in downtown Wichita.

MOTHERS, FAMILIES, AND AMERICAN MEMORY

During the golden age of monumental sculpture in the late nineteenth and early twentieth centuries, monuments to early western settlers gradually coalesced around a common image of a sunbonneted Pioneer Mother. That imagery fell out of favor in the postwar period. Artists experimented in various ways with modernizing Beaux-Arts pioneer imagery, while communities explored more pragmatic tributes to their frontier forebearers. Those western cities that erected pioneer monuments in the 1940s and 1950s favored depictions of frontier yeoman families that mirrored the kind of family togetherness conveyed in TV sitcoms and celebrated youth as their hope for the future. Modern art movements gained inroads among some audiences, while others clung fervently to sunbonnets and prairie-style gowns. Interest in pioneer monuments increased again amid the culture wars of the late 1970s through the early 1990s, offering a way for smaller western communities to claim significance within a larger national story. This was particularly true in Utah, where Mormon visions of an independent theocratic state gradually gave way to claims of being the most American of Americans. In the next chapter, I focus in depth on how Mormon Utah grappled with its place in the American nation through pioneer statuary.

MORMON EXCEPTIONALISM, ASSIMILATION, AND AMERICANNESS, 1890–1980

Shortly before the start of World War II, inspiration struck prominent Mormon artist Avard T. Fairbanks as his young son prayed at his knee. Fairbanks sketched the scene as a sculpture beseeching fellow Latter-day Saints (LDS) to trust and obey both their earthly and their heavenly fathers. The Church of Jesus Christ of Latter-day Saints had been a strong supporter of LDS visual arts for fifty years, had paid for Avard Fairbanks's father to study art in Paris, and had commissioned Avard Fairbanks himself to produce a number of important sculptures. But the LDS First Presidency showed little interest in Fairbanks's spiritual family scene. The sketch for *The American Family* only gained traction decades later, when Fairbanks populated that religious scene with his stock frontier characters, a strong patriarch and a self-sacrificing mother, which were popular across the United States but bore special meaning to Mormons, and as the LDS church increasingly sold itself as representing traditional values amid rapid social change. The sculpture would ultimately be erected as a seemingly secular monument to the American Family in the artist's hometown, Provo, Utah (plate J).

The family's nineteenth-century garb and the log cabin fragment behind them mark them as western settlers who embody the values of hard work and self-sacrifice—as well as traditional gender roles—that late twentieth-century Americans associated with pioneer families. Placed on the front lawn of the county courthouse, this bronze father, mother, young son, and babe-in-arms declared their frontier family to be the foundation of American democracy. At a time when many Americans feared the breakdown of what they imagined to be traditional family values, Fairbanks's statue declared this frontier household to be the ideal American family. Yet the monument spoke differently to local audiences at the heart of the Mormon cultural area. By depicting distinctive LDS doctrine about the persistence of earthly families in the afterlife, Fairbanks's sculpture also promoted a new form of Mormon exceptionalism. Rejecting both the taint of nineteenth-century polygamy and the early twentieth-century assimilation efforts, the devout Mormon sculptor declared this patriarchal LDS household to be the true American Family. Examining the Mormon subculture's use of pioneer monuments to define itself highlights LDS efforts to balance their cultural distinctiveness against assimilation into mainstream society. Isolating the substantial mass of monuments erected by Mormons in Utah and along Mormon migration routes highlights the centrality of pioneer memory within the LDS subculture and suggests the importance of frontier memory to American national identity.

Soon after Brigham Young led the Mormon migration out of religious persecution in the Midwest (which had climaxed in the killing of LDS founder and prophet Joseph Smith) to the Salt Lake Valley in 1847, the LDS church embraced music and the performing arts as a means of instilling both sacred teachings and communal identity among the LDS faithful. The Mormon Tabernacle Choir became an instrument that mediated the tension between Mormon exceptionalism and assimilation into mainstream American society.[1] A few decades later, as Mormons built the Salt Lake Temple, church leaders turned their attention to the visual arts, going so far as to sponsor several "art missionaries" to obtain art education in Paris.[2] There, John Hafen, Lorus Pratt, Edwin Evans, Herman Hugo Haag, and John B. Fairbanks studied at the famed Académie Julian, honing their skills before returning to Utah to paint murals within the LDS temple under construction in Salt Lake City. LDS artists also produced artworks commissioned by the church, which were intimately related to LDS doctrine or church history and were carefully scrutinized by church leadership.

Like secular art buyers and monument erectors, the church repeatedly had to choose between hiring the most famous artists or supporting local talent, and between political expediency and support for local tastes. As a church commissioning religious art, though, the LDS leadership also sought to balance those common artistic and political issues against the spirituality of both the subject and the artist. The art missionaries that the church sent to Paris in the 1890s were devout Mormons who expressed their religious devotion through temple murals and sculptures. But in commissioning sculpture for temple exteriors and historical works for other LDS sites, the church appears to have been more concerned with the artists' artistic reputation than with their religiosity, and the selected sculptors typically avoided even the faux religiosity of secular references to the Virgin Mary. While the church's artist and design choices avoided Catholic iconography that had limited relevance to LDS theology, they also suggest that Mormons often prioritized gaining acceptance from mainstream society over maintaining religious purity in public-facing statuary.

The church's role in erecting Mormon-themed monuments also changed over time, as the LDS church's and Mormon believers' growing efforts to assimilate into mainstream American society were punctuated with moments of retrenchment. Indeed, the LDS church commissioned religious artwork most actively when constructing new temples in Utah and beyond, while conversely, it commissioned public sculpture most actively in periods of Mormon assimilation into mainstream American culture. Rejecting even the limited experimentation of artists such as William Zorach and Thomas Puryear Mims, LDS leaders gravitated toward respected American artists with Mormon ties who used widely accepted secular iconography. The works the church commissioned tended to be even more conservative—artistically and in their depiction of gender norms—than contemporaneous mainstream monuments.

The impulse to enshrine westward migration was particularly strong for the LDS church. In the late nineteenth and early twentieth centuries, it sought simultaneously to integrate large numbers of immigrant converts (many from the British Isles and Scandinavia—groups considered relatively assimilable by mainstream American society) and to preserve Mormon doctrine as Utah embraced assimilation into the American nation. Mormons believed that they played a crucial, distinct—and even holy—role in American westward expansion. Even after Utah transformed itself from an LDS theocratic state to a member of the United States, its politics and public life were heavily influenced by Mormon culture and the LDS church. That influence can be clearly seen in how LDS leaders shaped nominally public commemorations. Pioneer Day, which celebrated Brigham Young's 1847 arrival in the Salt Lake Valley, has been celebrated statewide as a religious holiday since 1857; it became an official state holiday in 1882.[3] Beginning in the 1880s and continuing throughout the twentieth century, LDS, community, and nominally secular government leaders worked together to erect monuments to those early settlers. In contrast to mainstream Christian denominations, Latter-day Saints believe in ongoing revelation from the time of Joseph Smith. The mid-nineteenth-century Mormon overland migration therefore represented a kind of sacred history of the LDS church. For Latter-day Saints, that story became not only a central part of the national frontier narrative, but also a reminder that the LDS faithful had been led by Brigham Young out of mainstream American society to their promised land. As the LDS church moved away from independence toward annexation by the United States, Mormon interpretations of Utah's frontier past shifted, and so did depictions of pioneer men, women, and children in LDS-sponsored public monuments.

In the late nineteenth century, Mormon leaders abandoned their dream of building an LDS theocracy and communal economy in Utah—and the increasingly embarrassing practice of polygamy—in favor of the practical advantages of American statehood. Most scholars agree with sociologist Armand L. Mauss's argument that at the same time, Latter-day Saints moved from emphasizing Mormon cultural distinctiveness to pursuing assimilation into mainstream American culture. Indeed, most scholars frame Mormon history from the late nineteenth century to the present in terms of this tension between Mormon exceptionalism and assimilation.[4] Stephen Prothero suggests that Mormons increasingly "found their identity as a 'peculiar people' in more socially acceptable markers, including prohibitions against tobacco, alcohol, tea, and coffee they refer to as the Word of Wisdom. These compromises bought Mormons some measure of respectability."[5] Just as Mormon families managed to escape the shadow of polygamy and gain acceptance in American society after World War II, however, mainstream American culture began to fragment along racial, gender, and generational lines in the 1960s and 1970s. Meanwhile, the internationalization of the LDS church exaggerated cultural divides between those living in the Mormon cultural area and those outside it. Outwardly, the LDS church coupled its increased evangelism efforts with a public relations campaign promoting Mormonism as a mainstream religion built on "clean living and the importance of family."[6] Within heavily Mormon Utah, however, as Mauss and others argue, the church responded to these shifts with retrenchment in the decades following World War II. The LDS headquarters assumed control of auxiliary organizations, and "correlation" efforts standardized doctrinal teachings. Yet the LDS church also reached out to like-minded people outside their faith and beyond the Mormon cultural area. By the late 1970s many—though certainly not all—LDS leaders and lay Mormons joined Protestant fundamentalists in fighting the Equal Rights Amendment (ERA) and embracing the religious right.[7]

I argue in this chapter and those that follow that commemorating the Mormon migration has been one way for Latter-day Saints to negotiate the competing demands for exceptionalism and assimilation that have helped shape Mormon culture for the last 150 years. Early Mormon monuments emphasized an LDS canon of famous white men, such as Brigham Young, who were founders of both LDS faith and Mormon society in Utah. Over time—but more slowly than in mainstream monuments—that emphasis on famous white men faded in favor of generic pioneer families. In Utah, persistent emphasis on the patriarchal family as the basic unit for LDS society, both on earth and in the hereafter, muted the Pioneer Mother movement's influence. Focusing on white westering families—who represented Mormon religious calling and moral uprightness as well as the mainstream narrative of manifest destiny—rather than sainted Pioneer Mothers enabled Mormon sculptors like Avard Fairbanks to create public monuments that operated on several levels simultaneously. Through frontier-themed sculptures, the LDS church encouraged Mormon audiences to hold fast to LDS religious and cultural traditions, while encouraging non-Mormons to accept Mormons as part of an American nation built on the hard work and sacrifice—and racial purity—that Americans associated with white pioneers. Meanwhile, by appropriating the LDS religious symbol of the frontier family, modern conservatives promoted their own vision of the traditional family, a family that they saw as under attack by social forces.

Mormons' frontier history and cultural memory, like their cultural values, have served as both centripetal and centrifugal forces in that negotiation. The mid-nineteenth-century overland migration carried Mormons out of persecution in the United States and into their promised land. But that overland migration can also be seen as participating in the American national project of manifest destiny. Distinctive Mormon gender and family norms—particularly polygamy—were a primary justification for their persecution in the nineteenth century, although many

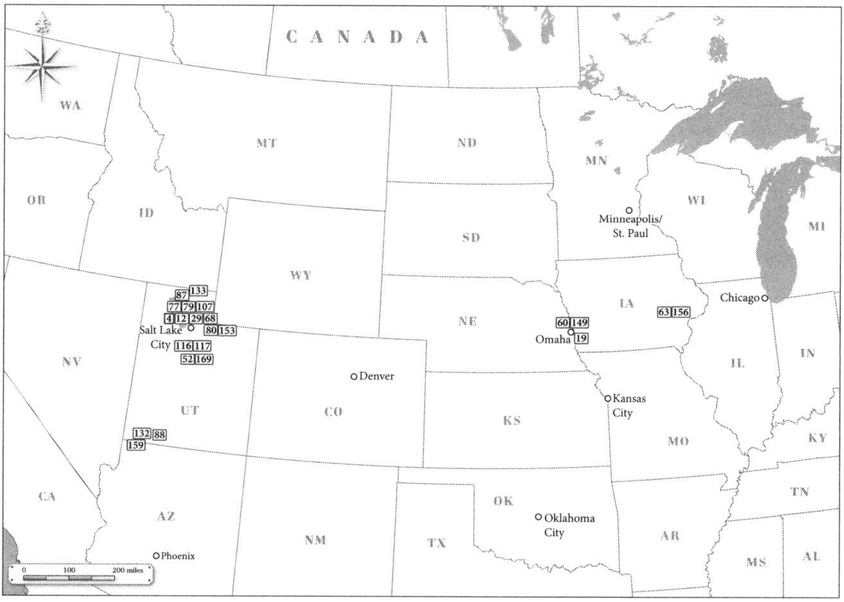

MAP 4. Mormon Pioneer Monuments. Map by Gerry Krieg. Numbers on the map correspond with a chronological listing of monuments in the appendix.

Mormons never practiced plural marriage, and the church officially abandoned polygamy in the 1890s. Mormons also moved away from theocracy and communal economic structures at the turn of the century. In this chronologically organized chapter, I argue that Mormon Utah embraced pioneer commemoration along with the rest of the nation at the turn of the twentieth century, albeit with a greater emphasis on LDS patriarchal leadership and prophecy. By the 1920s, and continuing through the 1970s, Mormons held up the LDS emphasis on so-called traditional families as a bulwark against rapidly changing mainstream gender and family roles. Even as other Americans increasingly forgot the frontier-themed monuments in their midst after World War II, Mormons continued to erect new statues and to feature existing monuments in statewide Pioneer Day commemoration events. Through their selection of sculptors and monument designs from the 1890s through the 1970s, the church and LDS-dominated public bodies shaped pioneer-themed public monuments that depicted the Mormon migration as a crucial part of the national project of western conquest and settlement, while holding up Mormon frontier families as models for the American nation.

CHURCH LEADERS AND PIONEERS IN EARLY MORMON MONUMENTS

Late nineteenth-century calls for pioneer commemoration were particularly powerful in Utah. Pioneer monuments offered Mormons an opportunity to celebrate their forefathers' arrival in Zion. Perhaps more important for Mormons in the 1890s, however, was that pioneer monuments also provided a means to publicly declare their whiteness, at a time when, as W. Paul Reeve argues, the polygamy debates called their racial identity into question.[8] Calls to celebrate generic Mormon pioneers and to declare their racial superiority over American Indians—and thus their equality with other Anglo-Americans—converged with efforts to commemorate early LDS leaders and the sacred history of their church's founding. By the 1880s, public sentiment in Salt Lake City favored erecting a monument to city founder, LDS prophet, church leader, and frontier politician Brigham Young. Examining the process by which the Brigham Young monument was erected illuminates how the LDS church and public institutions were intertwined in nineteenth-century Utah. It also reveals ways in which the LDS church and local Mormons adapted common monumental forms to celebrate the singular LDS gathering to Zion while declaring Mormons' whiteness and their place within the broader project of white settlement of the West.

In the decades following the 1847 establishment of the LDS church in Utah, as church leaders commissioned LDS artists to produce imagery from the Book of Mormon for Temple Square, they also actively supported art for public spaces outside the temple commemorating the achievements and recalling the suffering of early Mormon migrants to Utah. Early sculptural works supported by a combination of church and public funding celebrated the founding of the Mormon state of Deseret, emphasizing the distinctiveness of theocratic Mormon Utah even as they depicted white settler experiences that strongly paralleled those of non-Mormon westward migrants.

Utah's first major public monument to the pioneer era was dedicated to Brigham Young. Like many Confederate monuments also erected in the 1890s, Salt Lake City's Young monument celebrated a prominent leader. Young was revered among Utahans not only as a prophet and church leader, but as a dedicated and savvy civic leader and founder of the growing Salt Lake City. But the Young statue would also serve as a monument to early Mormon settlers of Utah—and thus to white colonization. The quasi-church organization Brigham Young Memorial Association unanimously approved Utah native Cyrus E. Dallin to design and sculpt a monument to Young; around the same time, the LDS church also invited Dallin to sculpt the angel Moroni to top the spire of the Salt Lake Temple.[9]

Cyrus Dallin was in some respects the natural choice to sculpt this monument to Young and the early LDS settlers. Dallin's grandparents were English converts to Mormonism who joined the mid-nineteenth-century migration to Utah. The sculptor's father, Thomas, chose to be baptized into the LDS faith in 1848. He met his future wife, Jane Hamer, at Winter Quarters (present-day Omaha, Nebraska) as their respective families prepared to cross the plains to Utah in 1851; they later married and settled in the frontier town of Springville, some fifty miles south of Salt Lake City. Their son Cyrus had displayed early artistic talent as he grew up in the Mormon town, eventually leading Thomas Dallin to mortgage their family's home to support his son's travel to Boston to study sculpture. Cyrus would later became one of the first Utah artists to study in Paris. Although Cyrus spent much of his adult life in the Boston area, he remained committed to visiting and providing art to his beloved Utah. Dallin crafted portrait busts of the church presidency and a statuette of Brigham Young, which he exhibited at Savage's Store in Salt Lake in an effort to raise interest in commissioning a monument-sized version of the work.[10] As such, he was a logical choice to sculpt an angel for the temple and a heroic statue of the church and civic leader.

On another level, though, it is surprising that Dallin received these major commissions from the LDS church and the Brigham Young Memorial Association. The Utah-born artist had traveled east at a young age to pursue his art training, and he rarely returned west. Following several failed business schemes during Cyrus's youth, his father sought to support his growing family through mining—a pursuit that LDS church leaders discouraged. Since Thomas's arrival in Utah, he had become a "free thinker," questioning the existence of God, and was "labeled a 'renegade' by the orthodox members of the Mormon Church."[11] Thomas's challenges to church authority eventually led to his excommunication and his family's ostracism from the close-knit Mormon community of

Springville. Cyrus would also come to question the teachings of the LDS church, making his commissions for sculptures of religious significance even more surprising. LDS president William Woodruff first approached Dallin to design a statue of the angel Moroni for the east central-tower of the LDS temple—a highly visible location of great religious significance. Although Dallin was desperate for work, he initially declined the Moroni commission, declaring that he did not believe in angels. But Woodruff eventually persuaded Utah's best-known sculptor to sculpt Moroni, and Dallin undertook intensive study of Mormon theology to inform his work. In this, he appears to have lived out his later declaration: "My work is my religion." Rejecting Mormonism and organized Christian churches as having "too many intermediaries between me and God," Cyrus Dallin eventually "adapted" what he described as "a somewhat personal version of the [American] Indian form of worship."[12] Thus, Woodruff appears to have sought the most talented local artist to sculpt the highly visible Moroni, despite the sculptor's disbelief in angels and rejection of the LDS priesthood.

Although Dallin remained hesitant to sculpt LDS angels, he appears to have been much more comfortable creating the relatively secular Brigham Young monument. Indeed, he had publicly advocated for such a commission. In that work, religiosity took a back seat to messages of manifest destiny and a tribute to the mythic noble savage, which appeared in much of Dallin's later work. Local newspapers did not record any concerns from local Mormons about the artist's religious faithfulness. Dallin even persuaded the memorial association to broaden the scope of their intended monument to honor those who had traveled overland with Brigham Young in 1847 and to all pioneers who—like the sculptor's parents and grandparents—had migrated to Utah in the mid-nineteenth century.[13]

Whereas San Francisco's 1894 James Lick statuary originated as a pioneer monument and secondarily became a tribute to its donor (plate A), Salt Lake City's contemporaneous monument began as a tribute to a famous man and then, under Dallin's influence, came to stand for a much broader class of early white settlers and the white colonization project. Dallin based his design for the Brigham Young monument on the massive sculptural tribute to French politician Léon Gambetta erected in Paris in 1888.[14] That monument, designed by sculptor Jean-Paul Aubé and

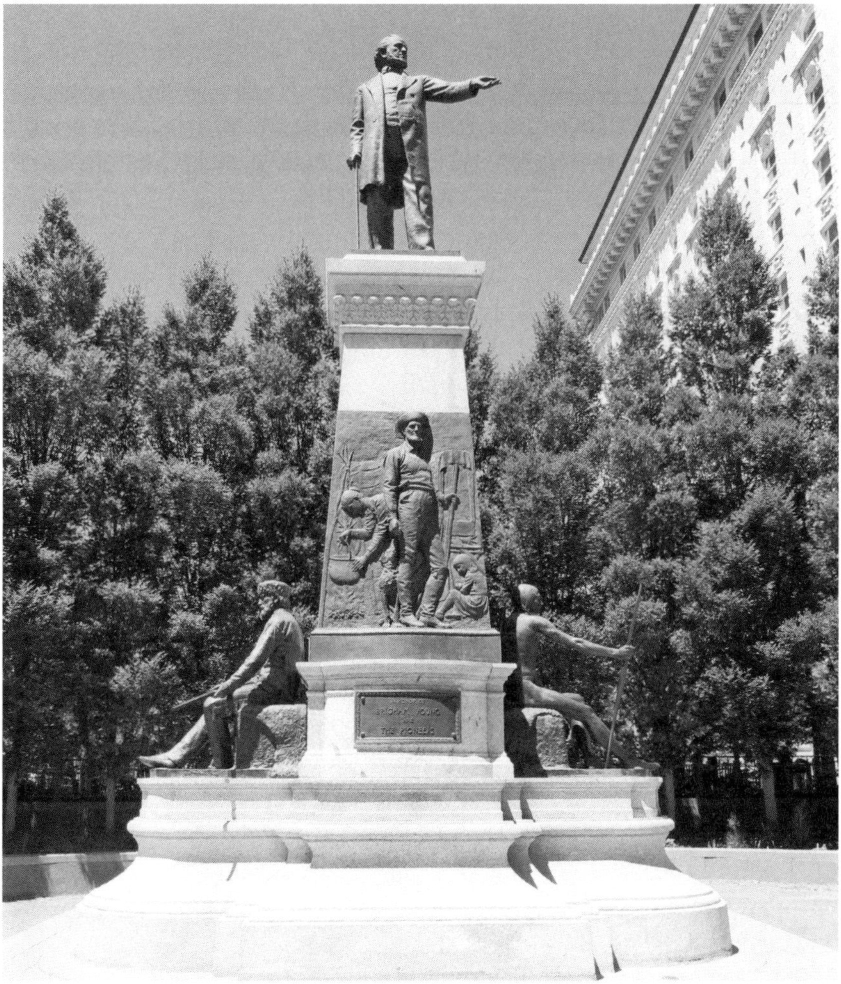

FIGURE 4.1. Cyrus Edwin Dallin, *Brigham Young Pioneer Monument*, Salt Lake City, Utah, 1897. Photograph by author.

architect Louis-Charles Boileau, featured bronze allegorical figures atop a massive stone pillar as well as on its base. The honoree was sculpted out of stone and placed in front of the massive pillar, beneath the allegories of Glory and Democracy. The Gambetta monument was erected in the courtyard of the Louvre Palace (today the site of Ieoh Ming Pei's controversial pyramid) as part of late nineteenth-century French statuomania.

Dallin's design for the *Brigham Young Pioneer Monument* echoed the Gambetta monument's massive pillar topped by bronze figurative statues, with a stone carving at mid-height and additional bronze figures around its base (figure 4.1). Instead of Jean-Paul Aubé's allegorical figures, however, Dallin chose to depict representative frontier characters. He symbolically elevated the Mormon religious leader and politician, placing him at the pinnacle of his column. At its base Dallin placed a pioneer family relief as well as bronze sculptures of the white fur trapper and indigenous scout who had paved the way for Mormon settlement of Utah. Dallin's portrait of a famous leader thus became a pioneer monument. Paralleling San Francisco's social Darwinist James Lick monument, it declared Utah's white men—particularly the LDS faithful following Prophet Brigham—to be the pinnacle of civilization.

Dallin's representational bronze statue of Brigham Young was the first part completed of the massive monument he designed. The statue depicted Young standing in Emigration Canyon, pointing to the Salt Lake Valley and declaring it to be where the LDS faithful would settle. The bronze Young stands tall despite supporting himself with a staff in his right hand. While the staff hints at Young's illness on his arrival in Emigration Canyon, Dallin's portrayal of Young standing upright makes the item in his hand more suggestive of military swagger than of illness. In Dallin's initial sketch, Young's left arm had been outstretched, pointing his people toward the Salt Lake Valley, in a commanding gesture reminiscent of Aubé's Gambetta sculpture. Dallin later adjusted the figure's hand position to one that welcomed all new Mormon Utah residents and even non-Mormon travelers and settlers. Dallin's welcoming bronze portrait of Young was well received when displayed on a temporary pedestal in front of the Utah Building at the 1893 Columbian Exposition in Chicago (home to the famous White City, celebrating white racial dominance over supposedly inferior peoples).[15]

A combination of church and private contributions funded the monument. The LDS church contributed $8,000 (more than $200,000 in 2015 dollars) to help fund production of the granite pedestal. The Salt Lake City Council gave the association deed to the monument's final location at the intersection of Main and South Temple Streets, just beyond the wall enclosing Temple Square. Prominent local citizens supported the project when it was first launched, but fundraising efforts soon lost momentum during the hard times that struck Utah in the early 1890s, as the federal government cracked down on LDS church power in the name of battling polygamy amid a massive nationwide recession. Empowered by the 1887

Edmunds-Tucker Act and the 1890 *Mormon Church v. United States* Supreme Court decision, the federal government dissolved the corporation of the LDS church and confiscated most church property.[16] Although the LDS First Presidency issued a circular urging that the monument "be given first place[,] and other considerations of a public nature be regarded as secondary until the work in hand shall be completed," and extending an invitation through the church "to every man, woman and child throughout our mountain home to contribute something in commemoration of the pioneers and their great leader, President Brigham Young, whose genius has left its impress on every part of this favored land," fundraising efforts stalled.[17] To increase interest in the project, the association wanted to dedicate the unfinished monument on the fiftieth anniversary of the arrival of pioneers to Salt Lake Valley on July 24, 1897.

Moving forward with the unveiling in 1897 required a substantial change to Dallin's plan for the monument, forcing him to deemphasize its commemoration of generic pioneers. To save time and money, the memorial association insisted that Dallin produce the relief of the covered wagon family as a bronze bas-relief panel, rather than carving it into the central column as in the Aubé Gambetta monument that had inspired Dallin's design. Dallin wrote to Governor Heber Wells in May 1897 vehemently opposing this change, which he felt would weaken the monument's artistic merits. The completed monument more closely resembled Frank Happersberger's 1894 Lick monument, which emphasized a progression from Spanish padres to Anglo California. Substituting a bronze plaque also deemphasized the monument's celebration of the broader class of pioneers, which Dallin had campaigned to include (not to mention decreased income for the impoverished sculptor, who had to pay for the bronze casting out of his commission).[18] The design change instead focused attention on the social Darwinist progression from Indian and trapper to Brigham Young, which likely pleased LDS leaders focused on commemorating the prophet and church leader at a time when Mormons struggled to be accepted as white by mainstream American culture—largely because of their beliefs in the principles of plural marriage and communal economy, both of which non-Mormons associated with uncivilized primitive cultures.[19]

The completed monument features a bronze bas-relief plaque depicting an overland trail scene, which emphasizes the centrality of the patriarchal family to turn-of-the-century Mormon culture. Dallin's sculpture of the man and his dog standing guard over his family and covered wagon in many ways resembles mainstream portrayals of overland trail life. Behind the Mormon patriarch, his wife and daughter prepare the family meal, but the daughter's posture underscores her obedience to her father more than her labor contribution. While later non-LDS monuments often featured women striding westward accompanied by a young son, this scene emphasized the Mormon patriarch's leadership and westward migration itself. A smaller plaque dedicates the monument "In Honor of Brigham Young *and* the Pioneers" (emphasis added). On the reverse of the pedestal is an honor roll of the male-dominated "PIONEERS who arrived in this valley July 24, 1847," with a list of the names of all 143 men, 3 women, and 2 children in the company; a horizontal line emphasizes the whiteness of the 148 Mormon names distinguished from 3 others labeled as being "colored servants"—a designation that would later spark protest amid the black power movement of the 1970s.

Cyrus Dallin flanked Brigham Young's pedestal and the pioneer family scene with two large seated figures "illustrative of the primitive conditions which existed in this region before the advent of the pioneers": an Indian scout dressed only in a loincloth and moccasins, and a grizzled white trapper wearing fringed buckskin and a coonskin hat.[20] Dallin—like many American artists of his time—was fascinated by the indigenous peoples of the American West. He later created a powerful series of sculptures of Indian men that were immensely popular among whites and generally respected by indigenous peoples. Indeed, Dallin had rejected Christian denominations in favor of his personal interpretation of Native religious belief, yet he was a product of his time, who embraced and enshrined the popular narrative of the vanishing Indian. Although he might have been more willing than most white men of his era to acknowledge indigenous peoples' humanity, his monument to Brigham Young nonetheless argues that, just as fur trappers had given way to Mormon farmers, indigenous culture would ultimately yield to that of whites settling the West.

When the Brigham Young Memorial Association unanimously selected Cyrus Dallin to sculpt the Brigham Young monument, they sought to mark the founding of Salt Lake City and honor its founder. Yet at a time when the LDS church was choosing to abandon the principle of plural marriage in favor of assimilation into the American nation, they also sought to commemorate the short-lived LDS theocracy, and to remind and instruct local Mormons to follow the prophet's teachings. Dallin produced a memorable Brigham Young monument that unarguably celebrated that local hero. Yet by including pioneer-themed plaques and heroic-sized sculptures of an Indian man and a white trapper, this son and grandson of early Utah settlers and lapsed Mormon also broadened the scope of the monument, tying the fledgling Mormon settlement to the artistic achievements of western Europe and mainstream American ideas about social Darwinism. Moreover, although the finished monument did not emphasize generic settlers as much as he had planned, Dallin successfully linked Young's expedition not only to later waves of the Mormon migration, but to the broader national project of westward expansion and manifest destiny and to a national conversation about white dominance. As the polygamy debate called Mormons' racial identity into question, Dallin declared Mormons and the LDS church to be the natural bearers of white civilization and white male patriarchal authority in the Great Basin and beyond.

MARKING THE MORMON MIGRATION IN THE EARLY TWENTIETH CENTURY

Between the world wars, the LDS church and secular organizations were active in marking important sites in LDS history and along the Mormon migration routes. Marking the Mormon Trail emphasized the national character of the overland migration. But for the LDS leadership, commemorating the Mormon frontier experience also became an effective way to deflect attention from the polygamy debate, hearings on whether to seat (non-polygamous) Reed Smoot in the U.S. Senate, and contentions that the church held an economic and political monopoly within the new state of Utah. It was also an effective means to promote assimilation into mainstream culture, while still celebrating Mormon religious and cultural achievements. Rather than remembering their migration to Utah as a distinctive experience in which the faithful escaped from persecution and left the United States to establish a distinctive religious settlement, the Saints increasingly framed Mormon history as part of a larger story of American western settlement.[21]

The first monument to mark the route of the Mormon Trail from the

Midwest to Utah, completed in 1918, was not an LDS project. The Council Bluffs chapter of the Daughters of the American Revolution (DAR) erected *Mormon Trail Memorial*, by Norwegian American artist Paul Fjelde, to mark the end of the Mormon Trail through Iowa. Like other non-LDS bas-reliefs erected during the interwar period, Fjelde's memorial portrays a man and his son driving an ox team hitched to a covered wagon, on which rides a pioneer woman holding an infant. The mounted, armed man who dominates Fjelde's relief emphasizes the arrival of white American power to an untamed wilderness, a common theme in several prominent male pioneer sculptures erected around the time of World War I. Mounted on a boulder by an exclusive colonial heritage organization, this bronze relief was part of the DAR's efforts to link all western trails to white settlement of the West and the building of the American nation, indicating that the DAR was willing to include migration along the Mormon Trail—if not exactly the LDS faithful—within their broad conception of the westward march of white civilization.[22]

In the 1920s, the DAR erected August Leimbach's dozen *Madonna of the Trail* statues, which dodged Mormon Utah by following the Santa Fe Trail. Meanwhile, the Daughters of Utah Pioneers commissioned Norwegian immigrant Torleif S. Knaphus to sculpt a three-foot-tall monument speaking more directly to the Mormon migration experience. Knaphus was a Mormon convert determined to use his artistic abilities to promote his new faith and to serve the LDS church. After training at the Académie Julian and the Art Students' League in New York City, he sculpted baptismal fonts and reliefs for LDS temple interiors in Laie, Hawaii; Cardston, Alberta; Mesa, Arizona; Idaho Falls, Idaho; and Salt Lake City, Utah. But he is best known for his more secular 1926 *Handcart Pioneer Monument*, which became one of the most recognized symbols of Mormonism, influencing popular understanding of the Mormon migration for nearly a century.[23]

The use of handcarts was unique to the Mormon migration. Whereas non-Mormons traveled overland as families and companies at their own expense throughout the nineteenth century, at midcentury the LDS church sponsored the mass migration of Saints from the eastern United States and Europe to Utah through its Perpetual Emigration Fund. Unable to both pay passage across the Atlantic and provide wagons and ox teams for the many poor European immigrant converts because of financial setbacks, beginning in 1855, the church instead organized companies that would use human power to push or pull wooden carts from Iowa City to Salt Lake City. Five handcart companies set out during the 1856 travel season. Three companies arrived safely, but the last two companies suffered through harsh winter conditions because of their late start, and more than two hundred people (nearly a quarter of the emigrants) perished. Despite those difficulties, additional handcart companies successfully crossed the plains in 1857, 1859, and 1860, before the church abandoned that model.[24]

Many late nineteenth-century Mormons, beset by racial and religious discrimination as well as economic hardship triggered by the polygamy debate and nationwide economic downturn, appeared eager to forget the handcart brigades. Handcart stories, like those of the Donner party in the mainstream migration to the West Coast, evoked poverty, tragedy, and perhaps an element of embarrassment. In this context, Cyrus Dallin understandably chose to depict a covered wagon family, rather than handcart emigrants, in the overland trail relief for his 1897 *Brigham Young Pioneer Monument.* But that careful disregard of the handcart brigades began to change in the early twentieth century, as Mormons increasingly assimilated into mainstream American culture. The Native Sons of the Golden West erected a monument in California that transformed the Donner party story from one of failure, in which wagon train members literally consumed others in their party, to one celebrating the arrival of white families—and thus white civilization—in the West (see figure 1.5). Likewise, avoiding Mormons' infamous suffering, Torleif Knaphus hailed Mormon hard work and the unity of LDS families in his *Handcart Pioneer Monument,* completed in the mid-1920s and unveiled by LDS president Heber J. Grant. Surviving handcart pioneers "declared the monument to be a most accurate portrayal of the conditions under which they and the other handcart pioneers labored across the plains."[25] The bronze sculpture was proudly displayed for many years in the Temple Square Bureau of Information, where it attracted lots of attention. Plans to enlarge it were derailed amid metal shortages during World War II, but an enlargement of Knaphus's work was finally unveiled on Temple Square as part of the 1947 centennial of Mormon settlement in Utah (plate M). That hero ic-sized monument soon became a center of Mormon memory, instructing Temple Square visitors in the devotion of nineteenth-century LDS converts and serving as a popular meeting place for the LDS faithful.[26] By the late twentieth century, many Mormons came to embrace handcart images—heavily influenced by Knaphus's sculpture—as symbols of Latter-day Saints's heritage of hard work and unwavering faith in God and the LDS church.

Knaphus's handcart family monument (and those that followed it) celebrated distinct gender roles that were more myth than reality. Of course, even families traveling west by covered wagon frequently found it necessary to cross accepted gender boundaries. But flexible work roles were the norm among the handcart brigades. Men and women of all ages worked hard side by side to push and pull handcarts over the Mormon Trail in the 1850s. Frequently, a man would pull the cart while his wife pushed from behind. But Knaphus's Mormon patriarch strides purposefully forward, pulling the family's handcart over the rock-strewn trail, while his young son pushes from behind. Despite being unencumbered by pregnancy or carrying an infant, as would have been typical for women on the Mormon Trail, his wife walks beside but slightly behind him, showing deference to the patriarch. Their young daughter rides perched atop the family's few belongings in the center of the handcart. The woman's nurturing posture contrasts sharply against her husband's and son's forward movement and obvious labor. Instead, she more closely resembles women in the works of the Pioneer Mother movement of the 1920s and 1930s, which were erected mostly in the years immediately following the dedication of Knaphus's original handcart monument model, to commemorate self-sacrificing Madonnas of the trail, except that in Knaphus's portrayal, the pioneer mother's domesticating sunbonnet hangs down her back.

THE PIONEER MOTHER MOVEMENT IN UTAH

Latter-day Saints embraced many aspects of mainstream American culture in the early twentieth century. Mormon women's economic power declined as Utah's home industry faded, leading women to shift from sanctioned activism within their domestic sphere to participation in secular women's clubs, which by the 1920s—like other clubs for middle-class American women—centered on maternalism.[27] But distinct Mormon cultural elements limited the social changes that fueled the Pioneer Mother movement elsewhere in the United States during the 1920s and 1930s.

While others across the nation feared the arrival of hordes of supposedly unassimilable immigrants from southern and eastern Europe, Asia, and Latin America, few such immigrants sought to settle in Utah. And Utah eagerly welcomed poor Mormon converts arriving from the British Isles and Scandinavia, like sculptor Torleif Knaphus.[28] Conservative Americans elsewhere may have feared the repercussions of the Nineteenth Amendment, but women had been able to vote in Utah territory since 1870. While most non-Mormons and even many Mormons cheered the decline of plural marriage, assimilation into mainstream culture in some ways represented a loss of Mormon women's cultural authority, as social gender roles hardened, and an early emphasis on familial exaltation and a mother in heaven faded. And lingering conservative Mormon gender roles mediated against the modern sexual mores sweeping the rest of the nation.[29] Pioneer Mother monuments were therefore less common in Utah than in other western states during the 1920s and 1930s.

But Cyrus Dallin's hometown, Springville, was eager to erect a Pioneer Mother monument. Seven years after the DAR erected Paul Fjelde's *Mormon Trail Memorial,* as the group prepared to erect a dozen identical *Madonna of the Trail* statues marking western trails from Maryland to California but bypassing Utah, members of the Springville Daughters of Utah Pioneers (DUP) chapter initiated a movement to commemorate their town's founding fathers and mothers by erecting a monument in Springville's city park. They sought to "leave something" to future generations that would "put respect and reverence in all hearts for these pioneers and the work they accomplished."[30] They reached out to Dallin, who—since completing the *Brigham Young Pioneer Monument* for Salt Lake City twenty-five years earlier—had found national fame through his series of four equestrian statues, *The Epic of the Indian.* Dallin by this time had rejected the LDS church but embraced the ideals and imagery of the nationwide Pioneer Mother movement, and he claimed to be eager "to do something in recognition of the pioneer mothers, as I had one."[31] But the sculptor, who struggled financially for most of his life, repeatedly put off submitting a proposal to the monument committee, apparently favoring paid commissions over this work, which he had promised to do for free.

The committee suggested that Dallin use his mother's likeness as a model for a central figure representing the universal Pioneer Mother type. Dallin claimed to have had the same idea himself. Energized by

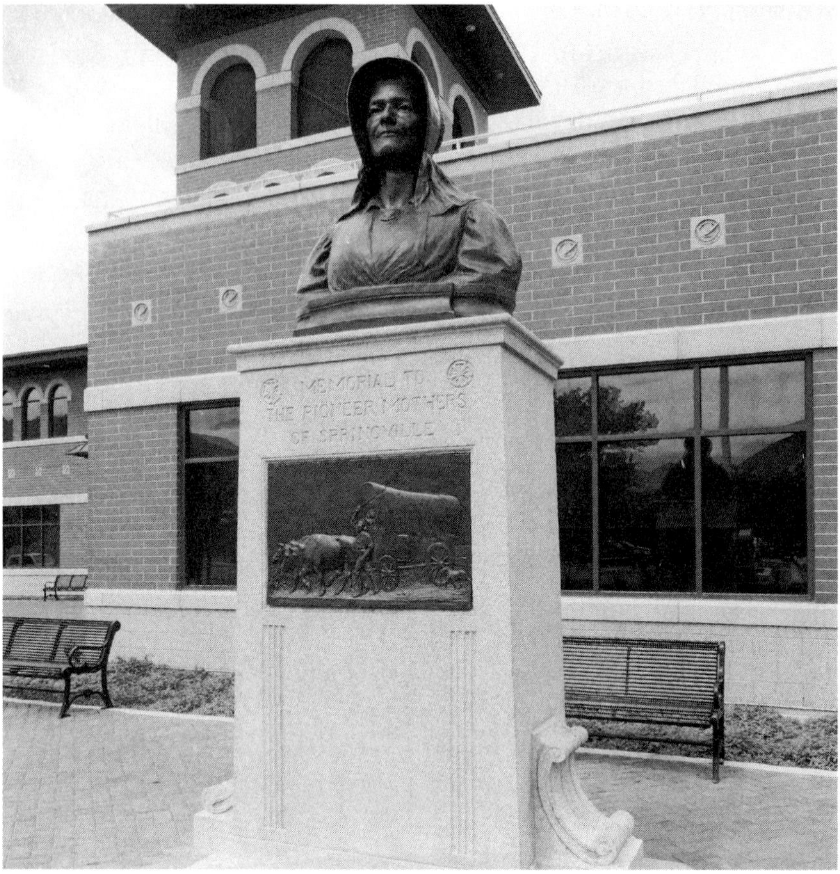

FIGURE 4.2. Cyrus Edwin Dallin, *Pioneer Mother (End of the Trail)*, Springville, Utah, 1931. Photograph by author.

this concept (and likely pleased to discover a shortcut to fulfilling his promise to the DUP), Dallin went to work revising a half-figure bust of his mother and a bas-relief of a covered wagon that he had modeled years earlier, adding a sunbonnet and replacing her Edwardian costume with one more appropriate to the 1850s. Cyrus's mother believed that he had encapsulated the spirit of a pioneer woman, yet whether her feelings matched those of the typical Pioneer Mother remained open for debate in Springville.

Dallin's portrait turned Pioneer Mother was in many ways an oddly fitting Mormon contribution to the Pioneer Mother movement. Whereas many other Mormon pioneer monuments incorporated religious overtones, the Marian-like imagery typical in Pioneer Mother monuments erected outside the Mormon cultural area in this period had little place in Mormon theology, and the secular Dallin also avoided them in his *Pioneer Mother* (figure 4.2). At the height of the Pioneer Mother movement, redressing his mother's bust in a prairie gown and sunbonnet was enough to mark her as a Pioneer Mother for many viewers. Utah Mormons had little use for the new, stronger roles for women represented in August Leimbach's *Madonna of the Trail* (plate D) and Bryant Baker's *Pioneer Woman* (plate B). Rather than depicting a woman boldly striding westward, Dallin's use of a disembodied bust ensured that Springville's Pioneer Mother symbolized the heart of white Mormon civilization; in keeping with 1930s Mormon gender norms, she most decidedly was not a trailblazer.

The only motion conveyed in the work was enclosed in the covered wagon relief that Dallin placed on the concrete pedestal. That plaque's male pioneer, swinging a whip to urge his ox team westward, closely resembled Avard Fairbanks's 1920s depictions of the Oregon Trail. But Dallin's wagon cover is not angled to echo the pioneer mother's sunbonnet and suggest a halo, as in Fairbanks's *Old Oregon Trail* plaque and William H. D. Koerner's famous painting *Madonna of the Prairie.* Instead, Dallin's relief emphasizes the Pioneer Mother's—and his own mother's—unchanging nurturance regardless of location or circumstance. Like the bust that it supports, Dallin's plaque assures viewers that Utah's pioneer women did not challenge their proper place as mothers within the domestic sphere.

Despite Dallin's success in capturing his (pioneer) mother's spirit in ways fitting for LDS Utah and the monument committee's embrace of his design, fundraising for the monument proved challenging. Dallin's donation of his time and labor reduced the cost from above $15,000 to somewhat under $2,000 to cast the monument. But the committee struggled to raise even that relatively modest sum at the onset of the Great Depression, much as fundraising efforts for Dallin's Brigham Young project had lagged amid economic hard times three decades earlier. With their work and Dallin's finally complete, the sculptor persuaded the committee to dedicate the finished monument "to perpetuate . . . the lives of sturdy pioneer women" on Pioneer Day, July 25, 1932—a move that further aligned Dallin's portrait with Mormon pioneer memory.[32]

The completed monument was unveiled with much pomp and—as seems to have been typical of any major monument sculpted by Cyrus

Dallin—an overlay of controversy. While Dallin's status as an outsider to the fine art establishment sparked conflicts surrounding several of his secular works, controversies surrounding Dallin's Utah monuments centered on a different type of outsider status. Although he was born in Springville to Mormon migrants who met at Winter Quarters, and he had contributed major sculptural works to the LDS church (including the *Angel Moroni* and *Brigham Young Pioneer Monument*), Cyrus and his father's rejection of certain LDS teachings left them outside the church and on the outskirts of polite society. Although the monument committee had encouraged Cyrus to look to his own sainted mother for inspiration, and she clearly met the DUP's membership qualifications, other Springville residents questioned whether Jane Hamer Dallin, who had immigrated to Utah in 1851 but had not settled in the Springville area until nearly a decade after the town's founding, and—perhaps more important—whose husband had been excommunicated by the LDS church, truly qualified as a Springville pioneer.[33] Springville residents were likely more concerned, however, about the artist's lack of faith, his father's excommunication, and their family's resulting social ostracism than they were about his mother's arrival in the town a decade after its founding.

Tensions surrounding religious faithfulness, family heritage, and social class boiled to the surface at the monument's dedication. The LDS church played a prominent role in the ceremony, as it had in the dedication of other nominally secular monuments. President Anthony W. Ivins of the LDS First Presidency was the day's orator, and George Albert Smith of the Quorum of the Twelve Apostles offered the dedicatory prayer. The local Pioneer Day queen unveiled the monument. Young Springville resident Virginia Dallin missed out on the opportunity to unveil her uncle's statue—much to Cyrus Dallin's disappointment and disgust—when she lost her campaign to be crowned Pioneer Day queen. Virginia had been selected as the First Ward candidate, but the queen was elected by votes costing one penny each. She and her family were of modest means as well as outsiders within Springville because of family members' religious views. Not surprisingly, Virginia lost to the popular daughter of a wealthy merchant and LDS bishop, a granddaughter of one of Springville's original settlers. Cyrus, angry over what he saw as an unjust system, prefaced his prepared dedicatory remarks before a crowd of ten thousand with a harangue about the election process. And rather than emphasizing the donors' intent that the monument represent a universal pioneer type, Dallin referred several times to the statue being based on his mother. This seemingly minor slip sparked controversy because some in Springville did not believe that Jane Hamer Dallin qualified as a Springville pioneer—and thus was not a fit model for a Pioneer Mother monument. Some local Saints also apparently disliked erecting a Mormon pioneer monument sculpted by a famous local son who, since sculpting a monument to Prophet Brigham three decades earlier, had quite publicly rejected their faith. Whether or not Dallin was intentionally provoking the crowd, his impolitic remarks revealed his motivation in creating the statue. In the aftermath of the Pioneer Day dedication, Dallin remained convinced that his mother had displayed the courage and righteousness that marked a Pioneer Mother. A few Springville residents held a grudge against the sculptor, insisting that only devout Latter-day Saints represented true Mormon pioneer heritage. But over time, as Mormons continued to embrace assimilation into mainstream American society, most in the town came to appreciate the reinvention of his unpopular mother as a universal Pioneer Mother.[34]

A GENEALOGY OF MORMONNESS

Like Knaphus's popular handcart family monument, the *This Is the Place Monument*—the largest and arguably most well-known monument to Mormon settlement in Utah—began modestly in the 1920s and then was greatly expanded for the 1947 centennial. Although the sculpture was conceived and erected amid the Pioneer Mother movement, *This Is the Place* pointedly rejected both the Madonna-like iconography of that era and the generic pioneers of earlier Utah monuments. It also explicitly avoided references to the Mormon handcart companies Knaphus had immortalized in his popular monument. Instead, the massive centennial monument looked back a half century for inspiration and iconography to Cyrus Dallin's 1897 *Brigham Young Pioneer Monument*, with its merging of social Darwinism and statuomania (see figure 4.1). Like that work, San Francisco's contemporaneous *James Lick Pioneer Monument* (plate A), and many 1890s Confederate monuments, *This Is the Place* explicitly celebrated famous white men. And as with the Brigham Young monument, LDS church leaders pushed for *This Is the Place* to be designed by a prominent

Utah-born sculptor who had strayed from the LDS faith. But this time, they ensured that their chosen artist had the correct pioneer and LDS pedigree. At a time when other Americans were commemorating pioneer mothers and beginning to honor pioneer families, while urban Americans were losing interest in pioneer monuments altogether, Utah once again erected an enormous monument to LDS patriarchs and to Mormons' whiteness that celebrated the Saints as the fulfillment of American manifest destiny.

In 1920, the church decided to erect a monument called *Coming of the Pioneers* in Emigration Canyon, the location from which Brigham Young had famously declared that emigrating Mormons would settle in Salt Lake Valley. The *Coming of the Pioneers* pillar, produced by a cemetery monument association, served as a landmark for local residents, but the monument itself received little attention. J. Leo Fairbanks, son of Mormon art missionary John B. Fairbanks and an accomplished artist in his own right, soon advocated for a more substantial monument to the prophet's "momentous pronouncement."[35] J. Leo envisioned "elevated sculptured figures supported by four Grecian pillars," but his idea gained little traction in the 1920s. He then persuaded his brother Avard—who was active in the Sons of Utah Pioneers and the American Trails and Landmarks Association, while building a reputation as a sculptor of pioneer monuments—to join him in calling for a monument in Emigration Canyon. J. Leo's design received little support (even from Avard), but the Fairbanks brothers' broader goal of building a large monument did gain traction. The Utah Pioneer Trails and Landmarks Association (which by 1934 had erected forty-three monuments), Daughters of Utah Pioneers, Sons of Utah Pioneers, and Utah State Historical Society petitioned the state government to erect a fitting monument in time for the 1947 centennial of Mormon emigrants' arrival in the Salt Lake Valley.[36] Nephi Morris, president of the Sons of the Utah Pioneers, declared that the proposed location, in the mouth of Emigration Canyon, "mark[ed] the spot where 'western civilization and culture' began."[37] The state and LDS church leadership soon joined forces to erect a more elaborate monument.

Although the monument was ostensibly public art, erected with a combination of state, church, and private funds, LDS church leaders tightly controlled its conception, design, and promotion. Utah governor Henry H. Blood formed the monument committee in the mid-1930s, with, among others, Brigham Young University professor Alice L. Reynolds and LDS president Heber J. Grant, who led the group. That committee, which met in the church office building, invited two prominent Utah-born sculptors, Mahonri Mackintosh Young and Avard T. Fairbanks, to submit proposals. Although Avard's brother J. Leo had pursued the monument for many years, had won prizes in painting and sculpture at Académie Julian in Paris, and by this time was chair of the Art Department at Oregon State University, he was not invited to participate.[38]

Avard Fairbanks's advocacy for the project and his artistic and LDS pedigrees apparently earned him an invitation to compete for the lucrative and highly visible commission. Avard was the best-known son of art missionary John B. Fairbanks. He had studied sculpture in Paris as well as under James Earle Fraser (sculptor of *The End of the Trail*), earned a bachelor of fine arts degree from Yale, and held a prestigious Guggenheim Fellowship in Europe. By 1938 he had produced several prominent and popular pioneer monuments that contributed to the secular Pioneer Mother movement, including *Pioneer Mother* in Vancouver, Washington, and various renditions of a covered wagon family. Moreover, he had worked with his father and brother to design the well-received LDS church exhibit for the Chicago World's Fair and had recently delivered a bronze casting of *Tragedy at Winter Quarters* to the Nebraska Mormon cemetery. A highly traditional realist, Avard Fairbanks sought to portray history accurately in his memorials.[39] As Cyrus Dallin had done with the Salt Lake City Brigham Young monument fifty years earlier, Fairbanks envisioned a monument not just to LDS or Utah leaders, but to the vast westward migration of the nineteenth century. He proposed a large shaft supporting a "representative pioneer family . . . with their covered wagon. In the foreground would be Brigham Young . . . rising up from his carriage [despite his illness], saying 'This Is The Place.'"[40] Fairbanks showed his model to the monument committee "and labored with them. Some had promised even to vote for his model without seeing" his competitor's.[41]

But the committee instead chose to commission Mahonri Young to design their "shrine honoring Brigham Young and other Utah pioneers."[42] Nephi Morris confided in Young, "There is a project on foot to put up a real Pioneer monument and we want you to do it Another party is after it and we don[']t want him to do it We want [you] to."[43] Indeed, President Grant had apparently wanted Young to produce the monument since the project was conceived, some sixteen years earlier, and Grant told Young, "Everybody wants you to get it."[44] According to Young, there were thirty-two members on the selection committee, and the only one who voted for Avard Fairbanks was related to him.[45]

Mahonri Young was arguably the best-known Utah-born artist of his generation, but like Cyrus Dallin, and unlike his competitor Avard Fairbanks, he was not an observant Mormon. Whereas Avard Fairbanks had served as LDS branch president in Ann Arbor, Michigan, Mahonri Young, as an adult, did not attend church, contribute to the church financially, or observe the LDS Word of Wisdom. He appears to have been chosen for the *This Is the Place* commission primarily because of his strong familial ties to a church that cares deeply about genealogy and to the Mormon leader to be commemorated in the monument. According to historian Wayne K. Hinton, "President Grant's support for Young's model was critical, since he was so influential in determining who would be awarded the commission."[46] Grant apparently believed that Mahonri Young's genealogy—if not his lapsed LDS faith—made him a natural choice to enshrine sacred LDS history on the Utah landscape. The *Salt Lake Tribune* found it "singularly fitting that a grandson of Brigham Young has given to the world the pioneer churchman's most striking monument."[47] But the committee might have also believed that Young's fame as a secular artist would make the work more acceptable to non-Mormons at a time when the LDS church was determined to claim its place within the American nation.

Although Young was not an observant Mormon, he maintained a kind of Mormon folk religiosity and actively pursued art commissions from the LDS church, including the popular 1913 *Seagull* monument in Temple Square, which included pioneer scenes on its base. But Young's best-known depiction of pioneer life was his submission to the Ponca City Pioneer Woman competition, which apparently was too sturdy and stolid to appeal to critics or the American public. A social realist, Young sculpted, painted, and etched a wide range of subjects, but he was perhaps best known for his sculptures of athletes and manual laborers.[48]

Mahonri Young rejected the classical architecture envisioned by his friend J. Leo Fairbanks. He also avoided the pioneer woman imagery typical of the Pioneer Mother movement and the more familial designs pioneered by his competitor, Avard Fairbanks. His proposal even strayed from his own expertise in the musculature of prize fighters and wage

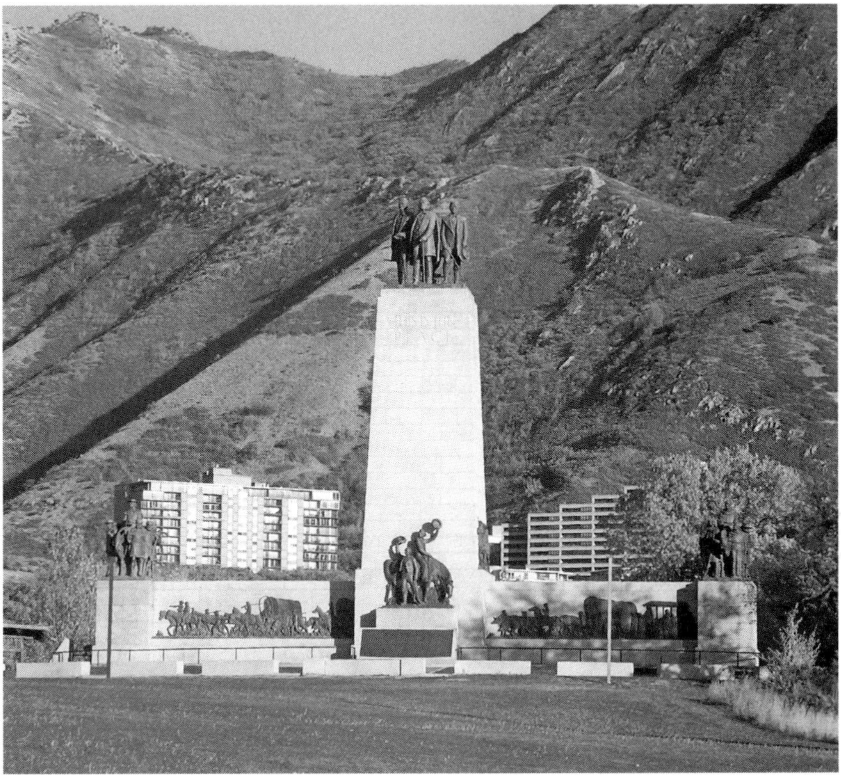

FIGURE 4.3. Mahonri M. Young, *This Is the Place Monument,* Salt Lake City, Utah, 1947. Photograph by author.

laborers. Instead, Young's design represented a return to the statuomania, social Darwinism, and cult of famous white men that had been common during the late nineteenth century. His design for *This Is the Place Monument* (figure 4.3) was even more grandiose than Cyrus Dallin's earlier monument to the LDS prophet (see figure 4.1). Mahonri placed bronze figures of Brigham Young; Heber C. Kimball, Brigham Young's first counselor; and fourth LDS president Wilford Woodruff atop a massive granite base. The sculptor assured the selection committee that, while his depiction of the triumvirate of Young, Kimball, and Woodruff did not accurately portray the moment that an ill Brigham Young had viewed Salt Lake Valley from Woodruff's wagon, the proposed design featuring three of the best-known patriarchs of the LDS church captured the spirit of that event. President Grant concurred, reminding the committee that "they weren't erecting a monument to a covered wagon."[49] Instead, they erected a monument that portrayed specific LDS figures—and by extension, Mormon society in Utah—as the fulfillment of American manifest destiny.

Like Dallin's 1897 *Brigham Young Pioneer Monument*, Mahonri Young's *This Is the Place Monument* represents Indian and white non-Mormons paving the way for Mormon settlement in Utah. But whereas Dallin's monument copied French statuomania's verticality, Young used a broad granite base to convey a more extensive history of Utah exploration and settlement, laying a sound foundation for the central pillar's genealogy of Mormonness. The massive base beneath Brigham Young, Kimball, and Woodruff depicts an orderly progression within the Great Basin from American Indians to Spanish padres, mountain men to white settlers, and finally Mormon leaders. Echoing Frank Happersberger's monument to James Lick, erected in San Francisco a half century earlier, Mahonri Young's massive commemoration includes bas-reliefs of twenty named western figures. Most are prominent non-Mormons who paved the way for the Mormon migration, including early Catholic missionaries Fathers Silvestre Vélez de Escalante and Francisco Domínguez (the Spanish men who "discovered" the Great Salt Lake), Father Pierre-Jean De Smet (a Jesuit missionary whom many credit with persuading Sitting Bull to participate in the Treaty of Fort Laramie, creating the Great Sioux Reservation), and nearly a dozen fur traders and explorers. Among the latter are John C. Frémont, who appears among the California pantheon on Happersberger's 1894 Lick monument (plate A); Kit Carson, who replaced a defeated Indian warrior atop Denver's 1911 *Pioneer Monument* spire (see figure 1.2); and Jim Bridger, who also appears on a 1986 pioneer monument in Westport, Missouri (see figure 6.2). Above these famous non-Mormons, on the pillar supporting the three LDS patriarchs, stand Orson Pratt, Erastus Snow, and the other nine horsemen who were the first LDS to enter the valley. Mahonri Young chose to commemorate only one nonwhite man within his march to Mormondom: Chief Washakie, a respected warrior and Shoshone leader, who reportedly welcomed Mormons onto Shoshone lands, and later in life was baptized in the LDS church.[50]

Taken together, Mahonri Young's genealogy of Mormonism traces an evolution from Indian savagery to Christian faith, and from untamed mountain men and doomed Anglo migrants to devoted Mormon leaders, that parallels 1890s monuments in Salt Lake City and San Francisco. And like those monuments, *This Is the Place* emphasizes famous individuals rather than a generic class of pioneers. Although its reliefs are not organized as hierarchically as those in San Francisco's Lick monument, erected a half century earlier, they nonetheless represent a return to turn-of-the-century monuments' social Darwinist focus on an orderly progression from Indian savagery to white civilization. By standing on an unusually broad granite base beneath a hierarchical tower of Mormon leaders, the reliefs declare particularly clearly that non-Mormons prepared the way for Mormon settlement while holding up LDS church leaders as the pinnacle of Mormon and—more broadly—American society.

Like Cyrus Dallin's monument to Brigham Young, *This Is the Place Monument* locates Indians and mountain men squarely within that orderly progression. But Mahonri Young also prominently features the infamous Donner party, blazing a trail through the Wasatch Mountains to the Great Salt Lake in 1846. The artist, echoing LDS histories, emphasizes that their decision to pull their wagons up "Donner Hill," rather than continuing through what would become known as Emigration Canyon, exhausted their teams, and that their resulting exhaustion greatly contributed to their later entrapment in the Sierra Nevadas. The Donner party thus served as literal trailblazers for Brigham Young's vanguard of Mormon settlers the following year, who were able to cut a road through the canyon in less than four hours. Mahonri thus accepts the Donner party as martyrs to the cause of white civilization—as many had characterized them at the time the Donner monument was erected in Truckee, California, thirty years earlier (see figure 1.5)—and uses them and the other non-LDS figures on his monument to highlight the superiority of Mormon civilization. Besides the back-breaking labor in the Wasatch Range and an unusually early snowfall in the Sierra Nevada range, two factors delayed the Donner party and contributed to their suffering: the group's discord and some members' insistence on traveling in relative comfort—characteristics that contrasted sharply with the LDS church's reliance on military-style order and frugality in its overland companies and Utah settlements.

By including the Donners, Brigham Young's 1847 pioneer company, and later church leaders in the monument but excluding later waves of Mormon migrants, Mahonri Young pointedly avoids commemorating the suffering of the ill-fated handcart companies celebrated by Torleif

Knaphus (plate M), and places in greater relief the distinctiveness and success of Mormon settlers in Utah. Nineteenth-century Mormon settlements had succeeded in arid Utah in part thanks to the communal nature of their society, building cooperative ventures ranging from irrigation systems to manufacturing centers. But beginning in the 1890s, Mormons abandoned both theocratic governance and cooperative enterprises, instead embracing the American capitalist economic system and attributing their success to a combination of hard work and divine provision.[51] As Utahns celebrated the centennial of Mormons' arrival in the region, many likely joined Mahonri Young in commemorating aspects of their distinctive political, economic, and religious heritage. At the same time, by placing LDS leaders on the central pillar, towering over its broad base of western exploration and settlement, Young's design also declares to non-Mormons that LDS church history played a crucial role in the westward march of white civilization and should be central to American national identity. LDS church president and president of the Utah Pioneer Trails and Landmarks Association George Albert Smith agreed, declaring that the monument "ought truly to be a national instead of even a state project."[52]

The *This Is the Place Monument* commemorates both the golden anniversary of Utah statehood in 1946 and—perhaps more importantly—the centennial in 1947 of Brigham Young's pioneer party arriving at the Salt Lake. Church leaders exerted significant influence over the monument's design and played key roles in its public dedication on Pioneer Day in 1946. The governor, county commissioner, and mayor of Salt Lake City also delivered speeches, but the *Salt Lake Tribune* credited the church with laying the monument.[53] Soon after its dedication, the State of Utah asked Mahonri Young to produce what would become his final major work: a sculpture of Brigham Young as the state's representation in Statuary Hall in the U.S. Capitol. In contrast to the powerful colonizer and prophet featured atop the *This Is the Place Monument,* Mahonri Young's grandfather appears as a wise and even gentle leader in the seated portrait his grandson created for Statuary Hall, uniting the statuomania of *This Is the Place* with the domestic imagery that was more typical of Mahonri's chief competitor for LDS monument commissions and an increasingly prominent sculptor of pioneer monuments outside the Mormon cultural area, Avard Fairbanks.

MORMON PIONEER FAMILIES

Throughout his long career, Avard Fairbanks created sacred art for the LDS church in Salt Lake City, Utah, and for LDS temples and religious sites throughout the United States. He also created many iconic images for mainstream American society, ranging from popular portrayals of Abraham Lincoln to Dodge Ram hood ornaments. American frontier mythology permeated many of Fairbanks's works, but particularly his monuments to pioneer families, created for both Mormon and non-Mormon audiences. For more than fifty years, Fairbanks created memorials to western pioneers in communities stretching from the Great Plains to the Great Basin, and from the Midwest to the Pacific Northwest. Like Dallin's pioneer plaque emphasizing a strong patriarch in his 1897 *Brigham Young Pioneer Monument,* Fairbanks's monuments for Mormon Utah highlighted fathers' roles earlier and more explicitly than monuments outside Utah—including those sculpted by Fairbanks for secular audiences. His Utah sculptures, through their portrayals of Mormon family life, mirrored Latter-day Saints' efforts to assimilate into twentieth-century American society, while remaining true to distinct LDS doctrine and cultural values.

The committed Mormon created many sacred works depicting LDS history and religious teachings, including sculptures of Mormon pioneer families that emphasized family unity and patriarchy. But whereas Cyrus Dallin and Mahonri Young honored prominent Mormon men, Fairbanks consistently included generic pioneer types typical of the Pioneer Mother movement. One of his best-known sculptures memorializes a particularly tragic episode during the 1840s Mormon migration to Utah: the encampment at Winter Quarters, near present-day Omaha, Nebraska, where the artist's ancestors John Boylston and Sarah Fairbanks buried three of their parents and an infant son. *Tragedy at Winter Quarters* (figure 4.4) was commissioned by the LDS church for the Hall of Religion at the second Chicago World's Fair. The 1933 fair's Hall of Religion emphasized religious differences through individual exhibits paid for by various religious groups; Mormons and others viewed the fair as an opportunity to proselytize.[54] According to Fairbanks's son and hagiographer, Eugene F. Fairbanks, Avard initiated the inclusion of an LDS exhibit in the hall and helped to conceive a display of LDS history and ideals—plans approved by the First Presidency. The resulting LDS exhibit was a family affair.

Avard, his father, and his older brother J. Leo (who had advocated for a pioneer monument in Emigration Canyon) produced artworks for the fair that represented Mormon history as part of a broader national history of westward expansion, while emphasizing distinct LDS cultural values. The Hall of Religion and larger Chicago fair were so successful—despite widespread suffering at the height of the Great Depression—that the fair reopened the following year.[55]

When the LDS church expanded its exhibit in 1934, Avard Fairbanks offered to create two additional pioneer-themed statues to augment the display—one symbolizing sorrow, and the other representing hope. *Tragedy at Winter Quarters* commemorates the hardships of the Mormon migration. Not even the scant protection of a covered wagon domesticates this scene, in which the artist's ancestors bury their baby. The sturdy pioneer husband encircles the grieving Mormon pioneer woman with his strong arm and heavy overcoat. The sculpture's emphasis on the male patriarchal role set this work and Fairbanks's other sacred works apart from those of his non-LDS contemporaries, who continued to sculpt monuments to solo pioneer women.

Avard Fairbanks also depicted a strong patriarch in a more uplifting companion piece. The artist described the mother in *Youth and New Frontiers* as "the central figure," whom Fairbanks placed "upon a pedestal, [as] an evidence of the high esteem in which Latter-day Saints hold womankind and especially mothers." Yet even if the woman "is honored" in this statue, "and it is her husband's desire to keep her thus," her "courageous" husband's active pose and proximity to the viewer eclipse both the honored mother and their young son, for whom the statue was named. While the mother is responsible to "guide and direct" her infant child, the father literally "supports the child" with his left hand, even as he provides for the family's physical needs through his field labor.[56] While an esteemed mother apparently can represent all LDS women, the LDS man's dual roles of provider and patriarch—and his son's preparation to assume those dual roles—dominate the viewer's impression of this work. The son stands with his hand in his pocket, distancing himself from his mother both physically and psychologically. But the father, standing at the forefront of his family with veins bulging in his massive forearms, appears unready to yield his authority to youth amid the promised new frontiers, as would fathers in non-Mormon pioneer monuments, including

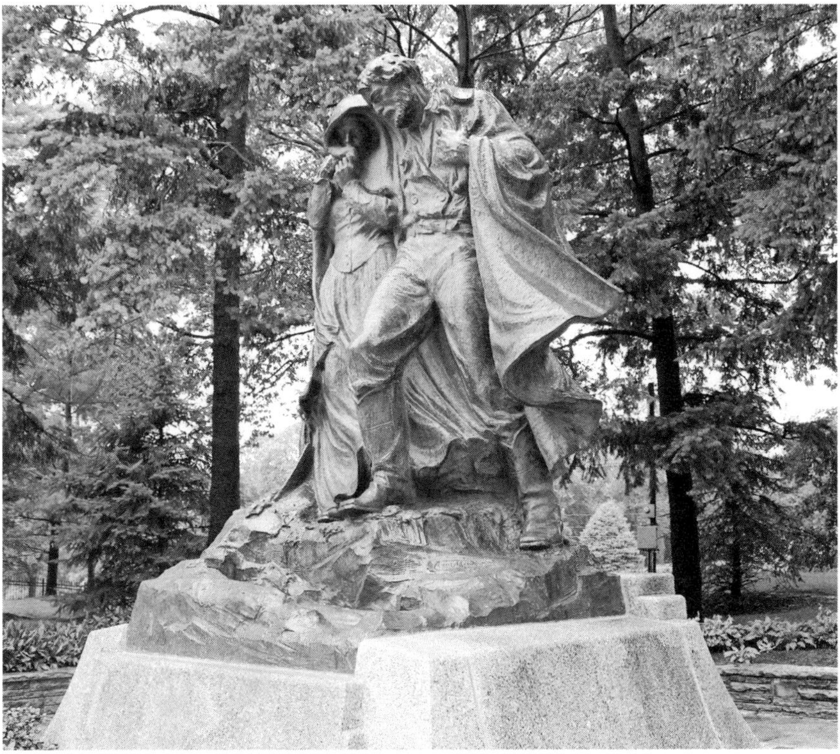

FIGURE 4.4. Avard T. Fairbanks, *Tragedy at Winter Quarters,* Florence, Nebraska, 1936. Photograph by author.

Fairbanks's secular pioneer family in *Guidance of Youth,* erected in Salem, Oregon (see plate K).

The artist's written commentaries describing the work—and its later bronze casting under the title *New Frontiers* (figure 4.5) for the LDS church conference center in Salt Lake City —inadvertently highlight the tension between Mormon and mainstream values that Avard Fairbanks and his LDS audiences sought to negotiate amid cultural assimilation. A 1937 article about the coming monument, in the "Church Section" of the LDS-owned *Deseret News,* reproduced the artist's explanation of the statue, which described the mother as "the center about which the family life is grouped." Four years later, in a cover story for *Relief Society Magazine* (the official publication for the primary LDS women's organization), the artist repeated this description of the woman in the bronze *New Frontiers,* but he inserted the phrase "symbolic of our *American* concept of the

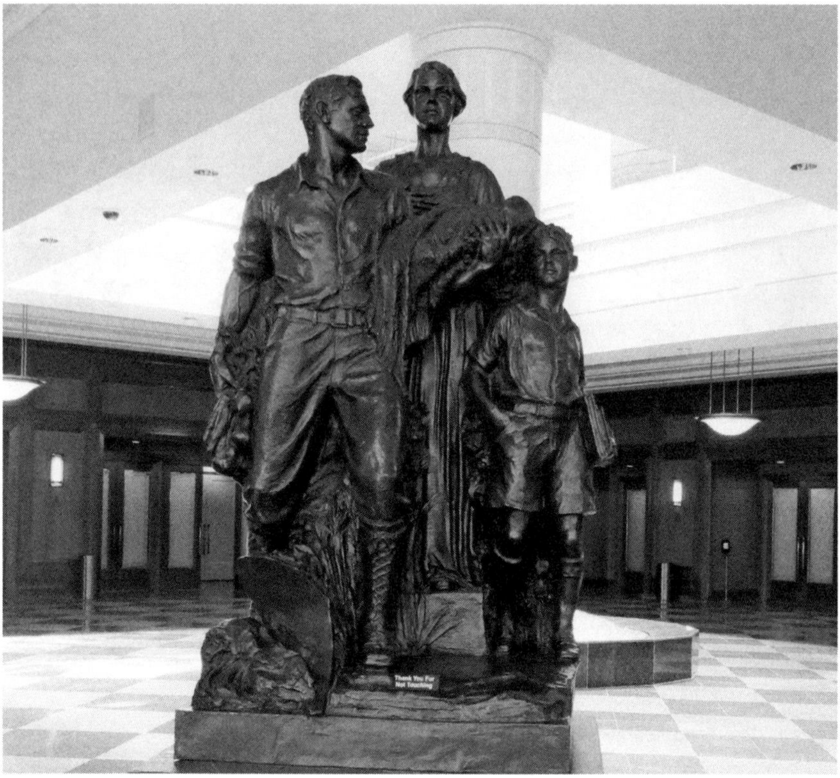

FIGURE 4.5. Avard T. Fairbanks, *New Frontiers*, Salt Lake City, Utah, 1937. Photograph by author.

mother."[57] Yet *Relief Society Magazine* also included language adapted from Fairbanks's original draft statement, emphasizing that "our religion's teachings point out that progress is eternal and that 'the glory of God is intelligence.'" Indeed, according to Fairbanks, "The youth of today seeks to further advance the culture established by the great [Mormon] pioneers."[58] Fairbanks imagined the sacrifices of LDS Pioneer Mothers to typify the ideal *American* mother. But the sculptor associated progress and hope for the future not with mainstream American values, but with LDS religious teachings about the eternality of cultural progress and of Mormon family relationships. While American mothers and maternalism still belonged on a pedestal, Fairbanks's American mother yielded her Mormon audience's attention to LDS doctrine and patriarchy.

With an eye toward proselytizing, Avard Fairbanks had emphasized a universal theme of parental love and national expansion in his works for the world's fair, while subtly instructing viewers in specific LDS theology. But in a 1942 bas-relief created for Temple Square in Salt Lake City, the headquarters of the LDS church, Fairbanks focused even more attention on the LDS patriarch's dominant role. The artist explained *Pioneering* in the pages of *Relief Society Magazine*: "A stalwart father, a tender mother, an infant child, a sturdy boy—typifies the Mormon family as it ventured forth into the unknown West."[59] Surprisingly, this pioneer father clearly held the young baby, taking an active role in nurturing the infant as well as providing for and guiding the young family. Rather than being honored on a pedestal, this *Pioneering* mother seems almost an afterthought, sandwiched between her husband and infant on one side and their young son on the other. While both father and son gaze forward toward their wagon and the future, like Knaphus's handcart Pioneer Mother, Fairbanks's mother looks backward toward the infant in her husband's arm. The spinning wheel hanging from the back of the family's wagon—a reference to both "age of homespun" pioneer mythology and Deseret's efforts at self-sufficiency—makes clear that the Mormon mother's role will remain unchanged upon their settlement in Utah. Although Fairbanks placed this man behind his wife and children, the father's animated pose and greater dimensionality again focuses the viewer's attention on his centrality in the ideal LDS family.

Several monuments erected in the United States in the years immediately following World War I celebrated pioneer couples or families. But in the late 1920s and 1930s, few pioneer statues depicted couples or family units. Thus, Mormons' efforts to assimilate into American society by erecting extremely traditional American-style public art actually placed them outside the American mainstream at the height of the Pioneer Mother movement. In the decades that followed, however, mainstream audiences would also embrace monuments to western farming families. After World War II, Avard Fairbanks's traditional Mormon pioneer monuments would become models of family unity amid evolving American gender and family ideals.

MORMON FAMILIES AS EXAMPLES TO THE NATION

Nuclear families appeared more consistently in Mormon and secular pioneer monuments after World War II. Throughout Avard Fairbanks's fifty-year sculpting career, he adjusted his portrayals of white pioneer families in keeping with changing American cultural ideals—albeit without changing his conservative realist style. When creating pioneer monuments for Mormon audiences, however, he also responded to changes in LDS religious teachings and cultural values. LDS church leaders and most Mormon believers actively pursued assimilation into mainstream American society, especially from the 1890s—when church president Wilford Woodruff proclaimed an end to plural marriage—through the 1950s. Amid rapid social change in the 1960s and 1970s, however, new tensions developed between Mormon assimilation and LDS exceptionalism. The art and belief movement promoted innovative Mormon art that strayed from the long tradition of pioneer-themed works like those of Avard Fairbanks. Aligning with one side or the other of the culture wars sparked in the late 1970s became a way for individual Saints to integrate into an increasingly divided nation. While some Mormons embraced the social changes brought by the civil rights and women's rights movements, many others joined church leaders and evangelical Protestants in embracing social conservatism and calling for a return to what they considered traditional family values. Indeed, some evangelicals even began to hold Mormons up as examples of true American values.[60]

As the culture wars heated up in mainstream society and within the LDS church in the late 1970s, Avard Fairbanks joined many Americans—Mormon and non-Mormon—in embracing renewed calls for so-called traditional family values. His 1978 *American Family* monument (plate J) spoke powerfully on several different levels simultaneously. A statue some four decades in the making, *American Family* was inspired by a moment in Fairbanks's personal life that highlighted for him the spiritual importance of the Mormon family. He first proposed a monument depicting "one of my boys in prayer at my knee" in a 1941 letter to the First Presidency of the LDS church.[61] No response from the First Presidency survives among the artist's extensive personal papers, and the idea remained in sketch form for decades, long after Fairbanks settled in Salt Lake City as the dean of the University of Utah's new College of Fine Arts. Fairbanks ultimately realized his vision in bronze as one of the aging sculptor's final monuments. Instead of becoming a sacred work sponsored by the LDS church, however, it was erected on the lawn of the county courthouse in Provo, Utah, through public fundraising efforts of the Utah County Family Living Council—a countywide organization of representatives from various communities and organizations, including the city council of neighboring Spanish Fork.[62]

What began as a moment of "profound spiritual significance" eventually became a public monument "commemorat[ing] the significance of the family in American history" on a county courthouse lawn.[63] The bronze statue became a monument to "the pioneer American family and the strength and determination shown by these settlers."[64] Although the title does not explicitly indicate a tribute to western settlers, Avard Fairbanks clearly drew the family members depicted in the statue from his stock pioneer characters: a hardworking yeoman father, a shawl-wrapped mother cradling an infant, and a young child, each garbed in Fairbanks's conception of mid-nineteenth-century western attire. The base of a log cabin at their feet marks them as pioneers and domesticates the intimate scene. For a generation of people who grew up watching 1950s television westerns, such as *The Lone Ranger*, and later watched *Little House on the Prairie* with their children, the portrayal of a western frontier family as the American Family perhaps seemed natural. Indeed, Fairbanks's 1937 LDS *New Frontiers* and his 1958 secular *Guidance of Youth* both present the sons of pioneer men and women as the hope for American society's future. Yet offering a Mormon spiritual scene figuratively cloaked in buckskin as the American family ideal represented something both new and complex. Not only did *The American Family* commemorate the strength and determination of early frontier settlers in traditional Beaux-Arts style, but it also embraced the competing trends of LDS exceptionalism and Mormon assimilation into American culture. It responded to conservative critiques of changing gender norms by representing this traditional portrayal of a pious, patriarchal LDS family as the embodiment of the national family ideal. Conservative Mormons—Avard Fairbanks declared in this statue—had become the most American of Americans.

As in Fairbanks's earlier sacred sculptures, the father plays the central role in *The American Family*. The Mormon patriarch gazes tenderly at his young son praying at his knee. Kneeling before the seated patriarch, the barefoot boy yields to his father's leadership role in ways that sons in Fairbanks's postwar mainstream monuments would not have dreamed. While the loving Pioneer Mother remains in her rightful place behind her husband and young son, and once again holds her infant child tenderly, she is eclipsed by her husband's familial and religious roles.

The devout Mormons in *The American Family* clearly resonated for Utah County residents on a spiritual and historical level at a time of LDS doctrinal retrenchment and increasing local interest in social conservatism. "Avard Fairbanks's statue does more than just remind us of our pioneer heritage. It represents the family as a spiritual unit," Governor Scott M. Matheson declared at its unveiling. "Just as the young boy prays at his father's knee, learning the same spiritual values which guided the pioneers, those same values have brought us here today and guide us in the future."[65] The son—clad in a dressing gown that emphasizes both his youth and his submission to his father's masculine authority—kneels before his earthly father while praying to his heavenly Father. That earthly father, in turn, fulfills his proper role as the patriarch of his family, modeling for his wife and children their proper roles within the LDS church and God's kingdom. Amid rapidly changing racial and gender norms sweeping the nation and the LDS church, Fairbanks's portrayal of his prewar religious experience promised that the traditional Mormon family had survived and would continue to provide an earthly model of the heavenly realm.

The emergence of this work's multiple meanings were perhaps most clearly indicated by the endurance of multiple titles for the statue. Fairbanks's son Eugene included a clay model of this work under the title *God Bless Our Home* in his 1972 book about Avard's sacred sculpture, explaining that the "statuette honors the love, hope, faith, and unity of the Latter-day Saint family."[66] The sculpture's other working title, *The Eternal Family*, highlights its creator's careful merging of American family and frontier histories with Mormon theology of family life. LDS doctrine increasingly emphasized the eternality of family relationships and their centrality in the afterlife to emphasize the distinctiveness of Mormon family roles after the church officially abandoned polygamy in 1890. The twentieth-century LDS church taught that earthly marriages and parent-child relationships would persist—and largely shape—one's experiences in the afterlife. This LDS doctrine departs significantly from mainstream Christian teaching that earthly relationships will have no meaning in heaven. The Mormon belief in the eternality of family relationships (and church-sanctioned marriages) apparently enjoyed great appeal beginning in the 1970s as offering a bulwark against the breakdown of the traditional family.[67] The *Provo Herald* described the "Eternal Family Monument" as a "sacred monument symbolizing family unity."[68] Both the *Provo Herald* and the LDS-owned *Deseret News* (whose "Church News" editorials represented the First Presidency's viewpoint) persisted in referring to the sculpture as *The Eternal Family* even as its unveiling as *The American Family* neared. This indicates the perseverance of LDS religious teachings and widely held conservative cultural values in what appeared to be a secular setting, the county courthouse lawn, at the heart of Mormon Utah.[69] While mainstream society could embrace *The American Family* as a symbol of American democratic virtue and "traditional" family values, to the LDS faithful in Provo, it also represented a call for doctrinal purity and offered a way to balance competing demands to assimilate and remain distinctive. In Avard Fairbanks's capable hands, the eternal LDS patriarchal family offered a way to reimagine and remember conservative Mormons as ideal Americans. The white paternal and maternal images that Fairbanks pioneered in his 1920s and 1930s pioneer monuments had, by the late 1970s, come to represent not only Mormon or western families, but *the* American family.

EXCEPTIONALISM AND ASSIMILATION

Soon after the LDS church settled in Utah, it became an active sponsor of sacred music and art. Religious devotion was important for art missionaries and later artists called to decorate the inner sanctum of LDS temples. But for public monumental works intended to teach LDS traditions to non-Mormons, the church was less concerned with the sculptor's religious devotion than it was with their artistic ability and their willingness to portray the church's conception of its place within the world. The church's struggle between its call to remain separate and various pressures to assimilate into mainstream American culture played out in many venues, including the selection of artists and designs for public monuments. In the late nineteenth century, the church relied on lapsed Mormon Cyrus Dallin to present its history to its members and to the American people.

The Pioneer Mother movement shaped monuments across the nation, but the influence of the LDS church muted its influence in Utah. The Daughters of Utah Pioneers brought a Cyrus Dallin Prairie Madonna to Springville, *Pioneer Mother* (see figure 4.2), but religious and class tensions lingered around its dedication by Springville's native son. The

LDS church celebrated Torleif Knaphus's depiction of the explicitly Mormon trail experience and rejected Avard Fairbanks's efforts to place the Mormon migration within the national monument movement. Instead, the church clung to nineteenth-century statuomania, social Darwinism, and honor rolls of famous white men in the publicly sponsored *This Is the Place Monument,* declaring the church's early leaders to be the pinnacle of American civilization.

Yet the church embraced Avard Fairbanks's depictions of Mormon pioneer families in other contexts. More so than secular sculptors, Fairbanks incorporated strong patriarchal characters into the pioneer monuments he sculpted for the church and the Mormon cultural area. The artist incorporated generic patriarchal father figures in Mormon pioneer monuments even as his peers were shifting their attention toward solo pioneer women or abandoning the Pioneer Mother movement altogether. At the height of the Great Depression, Fairbanks paired memories of past grief with future hope, all the while celebrating the centrality of the Mormon family unit. Although mothers faded to the background in all his postwar sculptures, the sculptor never permitted Mormon children to eclipse their fathers' leadership as they did in his secular works. Instead, conservative anxieties about the breakdown of the so-called traditional family merged with a longstanding LDS commitment to patriarchal authority. Moreover, renewed calls for maintaining traditional LDS values and Mormon exceptionalism combined with a celebration of American democracy within the multiple meanings of *The American Family / The Eternal Family.* Through his sculptures, Avard T. Fairbanks skillfully navigated complex cultural tensions that simultaneously extolled LDS distinctiveness and Mormons as a shining example to the wider society. As the nation celebrated its bicentennial and struggled with rapidly changing cultural norms, Fairbanks led the people of Utah to remember Mormons as the most American of Americans.

From the late nineteenth century onward, Mormons grappled with opposing cultural trends toward distinctiveness and assimilation. Mormon pioneer monuments reflected that tension in embracing certain national trends—such as statuomania, Euro-American civilization, and an emphasis on white male founders—while rejecting others. The largest and perhaps best-known Mormon work, Mahonri Young's *This Is the Place Monument,* relied on outdated iconography and gigantism while ignoring the nationwide Pioneer Mother movement. By selecting Young's design, church leaders favored that artist's fame and LDS familial connections over Avard Fairbanks's religious devotion and tried-and-true Pioneer Mother imagery. But long after Mahonri Young's death in 1957, Fairbanks persisted in producing monuments that reinforced LDS religious teachings from a very conservative perspective. Shifts in the traditional realist's works for Mormon audiences actually anticipated shifts in pioneer monuments nationwide, offering Mormon families as models for the American nation. As Fairbanks's longer than fifty-year career ended with his death in 1987, popular and church interest in marking the sesquicentennial of the Mormon migration aligned with the rise of heritage tourism, inspiring communities throughout Utah to commission less prominent artists to produce pioneer monuments that carried on Fairbanks's artistic legacy.

CHAPTER 5

CONSERVATIVE COMMEMORATION AND PROGRESSIVE PROTEST IN THE CULTURE WARS, 1975–1995

In 1992, the Oregon Trail Coordinating Council (OTCC) commissioned well-known Oregon artist David Manuel to sculpt a bronze "memorial to the spirit of the pioneers" for downtown Portland to commemorate the trail's sesquicentennial.[1] Manuel's design employs imagery common to the dozens of pioneer monuments erected across the United States over the course of the twentieth century: a strong male pioneer guiding his family westward, a nurturing Pioneer Mother, their sturdy young son, a wagon wheel, a rifle, and a Bible (plate N). The composition's emphasis on the father's guidance and the son as the heart of the family are particularly reminiscent of western pioneer monuments erected since World War II. The mother's gentle gaze, meanwhile, hearkens back to better-known sculptures of the Pioneer Mother movement of the 1920s and 1930s, depicting a generic Pioneer Mother carrying white Christian civilization to the savage frontier.

Despite the long roots of Manuel's design in western popular commemorations, however, it quickly sparked controversy. Inspired by the New Western history (which argues that U.S. western history was dominated by conquest of western lands and peoples) and multiculturalism's efforts to include various cultures and viewpoints, outspoken Portlanders decried the sculpture's glorification of white settlers' seizure of Native lands. While Portland debated whether to accept the statue and where it should be installed, however, many smaller Pacific Northwest towns declared their desire to prominently display the controversial piece within their communities. This divide between Portlanders' hesitancy to accept and rural communities' eagerness to embrace this statue reflects the growing divide between progressives and conservatives and between urban and rural communities amid the culture wars of the late 1970s through the 1990s, while highlighting the varied forms "the work of memory" has taken in how we relate to America's frontier past at the turn of the twenty-first century.[2] This chapter and those that follow reveal the untold story of how western communities, both large and small, have used pioneer commemoration to redefine themselves in a rapidly changing world.

In Avard Fairbanks's pioneer family monuments for mid-sized cities like Bismarck, North Dakota; Salem, Oregon; and Provo, Utah, the long-time pioneer monument sculptor has adapted the iconography of the Pioneer Mother movement to fit postwar notions of modern family life. But Fairbanks was the last of his breed. The monuments of the Pioneer Mother movement were primarily created by internationally renowned artists for growing cities seeking to declare both their frontier roots and their newfound urban sophistication. In contrast, those of the postwar period were generally sculpted for smaller western towns by local "cowboy artists." Whether or not they belong to the elite invitation-only Cowboy Artists of America, these artists seek to preserve and perpetuate the culture of the Old West, typically modeling their work after turn-of-the-century western artists Frederic Remington and Charles Russell.[3] But when cowboy artists turned to sculpting pioneer families in the 1980s and 1990s, they borrowed and adapted the Pioneer Mother imagery of Avard Fairbanks, A. Phimister Proctor and Bryant Baker.

Those late twentieth-century cowboy artists, like the earlier artists of the Pioneer Mother movement, celebrated explicitly white western settlers. As Jason E. Pierce argues in his study of whiteness and the intellectual construction of the trans-Mississippi West, "the West had long been the crucible of American desires and dreams, and its swaggering heroes had always been white."[4] And, I would add, so had its sainted Pioneer Mothers. In response to growing concern about rural outmigration, I argue in this chapter that smaller, predominantly white communities embraced pioneer commemoration to create a "topography of remembering."[5] Centennial celebrations inspired many smaller towns to erect monuments to their frontier ancestors. Pioneer monuments offered a way for rural people to shore up local identity amid urbanization and rural outmigration and to write themselves back into national narratives of western expansion. After World War II, pioneer mothers and families came to represent ideal American family life, tying pioneer monuments into a rhetoric that was no longer specific to the West as a region. Beginning in the 1970s, those representations grew more politically charged as conservatives advocating so-called traditional family structures invested similar statues with new power.

Westerners who fled those conservative communities and flocked to the region's burgeoning cities were exposed to increasingly diverse peoples and ideas. The fine arts world rejected representational art and embraced the avant-garde beginning in the 1950s; in the 1960s, similarly dramatic changes started to spread through American society. Baby boomers raised to believe that they were both the center of the family and the hope for the nation's future began to demand a greater voice in American society. Nonviolent protests against segregation in the South inspired student activism nationwide on a wide range of issues, from protests against the Vietnam War to calls for women's liberation. By the early 1970s, identity politics rose in prominence, with calls for black power, American Indian sovereignty, Chicano identity, and gay rights; conservative backlash also escalated. Conservative religious groups, ranging from fundamentalist Protestants to Roman Catholics to Mormons, reached across doctrinal differences to defeat the ERA. This nascent religious right also found common cause around issues such as abortion rights and school prayer.[6]

During the 1970s and 1980s, in response to identity politics and changing household structures, many Americans became convinced that the traditional American family and the values that it represented were under attack. But the nuclear family was actually an invention of the 1950s. Although rates of divorce and female-headed households did increase beginning in the 1970s, the prevalence of blended families was more of a return to premodern patterns. And of course, women of color and working-class women had always worked outside the home. Nonetheless, many Americans perceived the supposedly timeless nuclear family to be in danger.[7] This fear helped to fuel the rise of the religious right, and, I argue, it also motivated some westerners to inscribe monuments to that nuclear family on their landscape.

Pioneer monuments have generally been welcomed with open arms into small, predominantly white towns from the Great Plains to the Great Basin. In the 1970s, pioneer monuments continued the postwar trend toward enshrining white nuclear families. But even as political rhetoric increasingly emphasized so-called family values, most pioneer monuments erected in the interior West in the 1980s and 1990s returned to an earlier emphasis on pioneer women and pioneer couples (except in Utah, where profamily

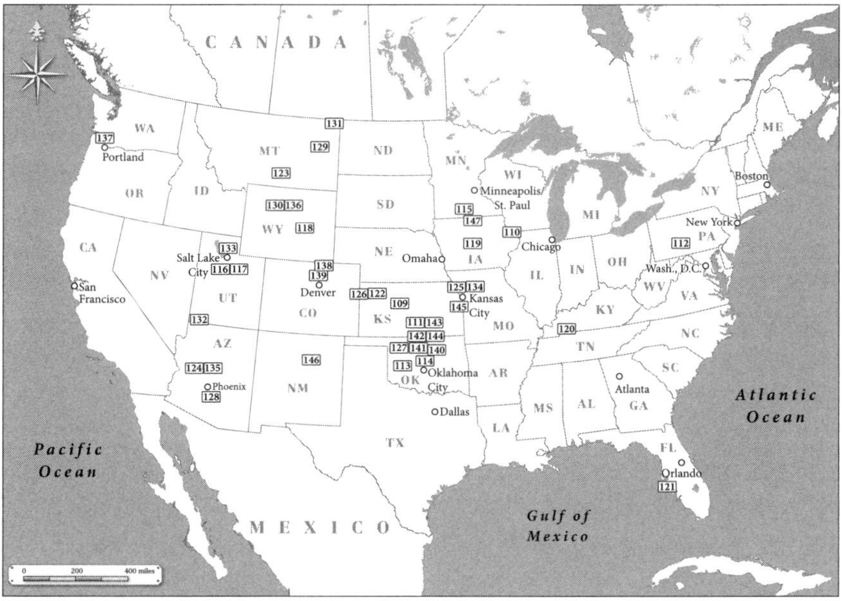

MAP 5. Pioneer Monuments Erected 1975–1995. Map by Gerry Krieg. Numbers on the map correspond with a chronological listing of monuments in the appendix.

ideology remained powerful). Feeling betrayed by the student activism of the 1960s, conservatives began abandoning the Cold War emphasis on youth as the nation's hope for the future. Rural pioneer monuments of the 1980s and early 1990s reassured viewers that their communities would persist in the face of a growing farm crisis and outmigration, just as their white settler ancestors had survived amid harsh frontier conditions. And in Oklahoma, pioneer commemoration became a powerful tool to erase the region's earlier identity as a federally designated Indian Territory—a move increasingly contested by the region's Native populations.

Even as Great Plains and southwestern towns sought to claim their place in a national story of westward expansion in the 1970s and 1980s, in the nation's growing cities and on college campuses, identity politics inspired growing numbers of people to challenge that accepted narrative of manifest destiny. As the United States prepared to celebrate the five hundredth anniversary of Christopher Columbus's supposed discovery of the New World in 1492, activists and academics recast traditional narratives of European discovery and colonization as conquest and genocide. Beginning in the late 1980s, proponents of the New Western history decried

Frederick Jackson Turner's nearly century-old "frontier thesis" as cultural imperialism. Instead of a repeated process of frontier development that enabled the growth of American democracy, they argued, U.S. western history should be understood as a story of white conquest of western land and peoples. They therefore rejected tributes to white pioneers—including pioneer monuments—as triumphalist and demeaning to peoples of color.

Fueled by this New Western history, disagreements over how history should be interpreted, remembered, and commemorated became important battlegrounds in the late twentieth-century culture wars. Progressive protestors in Portland and in other western cities decried what they perceived to be celebrations of white racism within pioneer statues. In response, cultural conservatives protested against being hamstrung by what they dismissed as political correctness. Caught in the crossfire, some monument sculptors struggled to tell more inclusive narratives or sought to stave off the mythical PC police. A few even countered Turnerian narratives with monuments to indigenous men and women. But other artists—like many westerners—remained true believers in frontier mythology. Because western attitudes toward inclusivity varied by locale, this chapter is organized geographically. I begin by examining early efforts at inclusivity in the Midwest during the 1970s and the conservative backlash that fueled increased interest in cowboy art in the Great Plains during the 1980s. I then take a closer look at the reactions of individual small towns and cities to pioneer monuments in their midst in the early 1990s, before turning attention to the racial dynamics of more recent frontier commemoration in Oklahoma, where brazen cowboy imagery encouraged many to forget the state's history as a federally designated Indian Territory. Throughout, this chapter demonstrates that western memory became an important battleground in the late twentieth-century culture wars. Over the last three decades of that century, pioneer monuments became both the vehicle and the occasion for expressing conservative and progressive ideologies.

ATTEMPTED INCLUSIVITY IN THE MIDWEST

Throughout much of the twentieth century, Americans thought of their nation as a cultural melting pot. But by the 1970s, progressive voices argued for greater multiculturalism, while conservatives denounced the fragmentation of society. Tensions between reformers and a supposed silent majority of conservatives undermined efforts to plan a unifying national celebration of the 1976 bicentennial of American Independence. Instead, bicentennial planners encouraged a decentralized approach that emphasized cultural diversity and local community identity.[8] Western communities welcomed representations of ethnic heritage that contributed to building a diverse America, but, as Laura Barraclough argues, "the overwhelming thrust of bicentennial activities in the region affirmed the legitimacy and importance of Anglo-American westward expansion for the development of the nation-state."[9] Although some projects expanded archives, created public artworks, and financed student scholarships serving communities of color and indigenous communities, Colorado bicentennial projects disproportionately supported projects that reenacted the Anglo-American settler experience.

Several smaller American communities, as part of their local bicentennial celebrations, chose to erect conventional pioneer monuments, such as W. Walter Campbell's *Pioneer Family* in Hollidaysburg, Pennsylvania. Others erected monuments that incorporated northern European immigrants within their pioneer memory, such as Ann Opgenorth and Donna Marihar's *Five Figures for Five Flags* in Dubuque, Iowa. The nation's bicentennial also inspired many smaller communities to erect monuments commemorating local centennials, through which western towns claimed a place within the national story of frontier settlement. As had become increasingly common since World War II, instead of commissioning famous artists or sponsoring competitions, these midwestern and western towns typically hired lesser-known artists from their community or region to depict local history. These local centennials in the 1970s tended to inspire a return to the white settler iconography of the 1920s Pioneer Mother movement. But the more culturally inclusive national bicentennial inspired a few communities to experiment with modern aesthetics—albeit in a limited way—and to erect more ethnically diverse monuments, such as a centennial relief mural in New Ulm, Minnesota.

New Ulm's sculptural brick mural established local German immigrants' whiteness by setting those immigrants against an indigenous Other. New Ulm's 1974 mural depicted relative interracial harmony that preceded a local armed racial conflict: the 1862 U.S.-Dakota War (more commonly known by the culturally biased title the Great Sioux

Uprising). Like many other Indian wars, the U.S.-Dakota War was caused by decades of broken promises and encroachment by white settlers resulting in destroyed traditional lifeways, physical removal of Native peoples, and cultural erasure. Fearing widespread starvation when the U.S. Civil War delayed a federal treaty payment, bands of Dakota (Sioux) warriors lashed out at local settlers, many of whom were recent immigrants from Germany and Scandinavia, killing more than six hundred whites (many of them unarmed civilians) and devastating the German town of New Ulm. Local militias and the Union Army soundly defeated the Dakota warriors, and thirty-eight were hanged in the largest mass execution in American history. The Dakota people—most of them noncombatants—were driven out of Minnesota and into internment camps and reservations in surrounding territories.[10]

Having forcibly removed the Dakotas from Minnesota, local whites joined far western cities in memorializing their racial superiority. As San Francisco and Salt Lake City erected towering social Darwinist pioneer monuments in the 1890s, New Ulm dedicated a state-sponsored monument honoring the whites—both immigrant and native born—who had "defended" their settlement "against the savage Indians." At the dedication of the obelisk, mounted with battle scenes, John F. Maegher declared that the "defenders . . . saved our state and its lovely women."[11] Well into the twentieth century, local whites commemorated white victims of what they called the Sioux uprising or massacre. They expressed little sympathy for the plight of the Dakota people, although they did erect a monument to Dakota men who saved whites during the war.[12]

That history of Indian removal came to the fore when, in preparation for the 1976 national bicentennial celebration, the New Ulm Business District and Southwest Minnesota State College commissioned a mural depicting frontier life in the town, which had been settled by the socialist German American Turner Society in the 1850s. In keeping with the town's German cultural identity and standard American representations of technology and progress, the Historic Trail Committee envisioned a mural portraying beer wagons, trains, and a steamboat. As artist Gordon Dingman, who was born in New Ulm, began sculpting the relief mural, however, he became captivated by the 1973 violent showdown between American Indian activists seeking to reclaim indigenous lands and federal law enforcement at Wounded Knee, South Dakota. By the early 1970s, indigenous rights

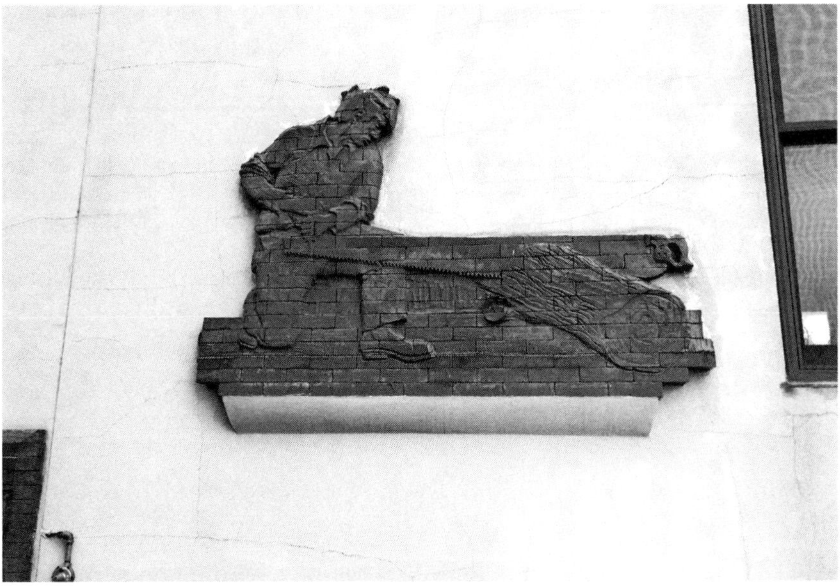

FIGURE 5.1. Gordon Dingman, detail of *Life Sketches*, New Ulm, Minnesota, 1974. Photograph by Michael Lansing.

activism such as that at Wounded Knee had persuaded some Minnesotans to reconsider the history of the Dakota War, recognizing that the conflict represented a desperate response to white conquest of Native lands and mistreatment at the hands of the U.S. government. Dingman sought to depict German settlers and Santee Sioux living in relative harmony on the Minnesota frontier prior to the 1862 war, but his interpretation stopped well short of challenging the long-accepted narrative of Indian savagery. Although Dingman completed archival research to inform his portrayal of both immigrants and indigenes, the artist's design flattened out the German immigrants' ethnic identity, and his depictions of Dakota people were modeled on Euro-American representations of American Indians by George Catlin, Seth Eastman, and Karl Bodmer that were themselves informed as much by myth as historic reality.[13]

Although the artist sought to celebrate peaceful coexistence, his New Ulm mural actually reinforced the logic of manifest destiny (figure 5.1). Dingman intended his design to critique uncompromising "national attitudes of the period leading to broken treaties, exploitation and ultimately war," but he portrayed westward expansion as the central narrative in local history.[14] The final scene presents a Dakota man dressed in Anglo-style clothing using the wrong end of a saw, waiting for "another man/cultural group to help him transition into a changed world."[15] While Dingman's mural certainly presented the Dakotas more humanely than the 1891 *Defenders* monument did, it fell well short of the artist's intent to depict "racial and cultural openness." Rather than celebrating traditional indigenous culture and gender norms, its primary message was one of white dominance. Meanwhile, communities farther west on the Great Plains lacked even Dingman's intent to portray the "oneness of man."[16] Rejecting even New Ulm's attempts at inclusivity, they instead applied pioneer commemoration to more conservative goals.

GREAT PLAINS SETTLEMENT AS A NATIONAL STORY

In the years following the national bicentennial, a strong conservative backlash developed to 1970s identity politics. As urbanites on both coasts rejected cultural conformity and popular melting pot metaphors in favor of celebrating diversity, many conservative white rural residents responded by clinging more tightly to traditional pioneer imagery. Whereas the Pioneer Mother movement that developed amid an earlier culture war, in the 1920s and 1930s, consisted primarily of monuments by famous artists for growing cities seeking to be cosmopolitan, three-quarters of those erected during the late 1970s and 1980s were sculpted by local artists for smaller towns. As new interstate highways increasingly bypassed small towns, and many rural areas were losing population to growing urban centers, erecting pioneer monuments became a way for smaller communities to claim their place within a national story of westward expansion. Marking a town's or county's one hundredth birthday also represented a way to naturalize white settlement by distancing current residents chronologically from the project of colonization. At the same time, a return to Beaux-Arts-inspired pioneer monuments offered conservative communities a way to reclaim old-fashioned values that they felt were under attack amid the late twentieth-century culture wars.

Monuments erected in the 1970s, as conservatives decried the breakdown of the traditional American family, tended to continue the postwar pattern of celebrating pioneer families. Like Avard Fairbanks's 1978 *American Family*, however, monuments to pioneer families in the 1970s focused on the family unit rather than following the 1950s trend of celebrating strapping young sons stepping forward into the future. Then, as rural America faced a growing farm crisis in the 1980s, defenses of family values took a back seat to promising (white) men's and women's persistence amid adversity. Although a few sculptors applied a veneer of cultural inclusion, most pioneer monuments erected during the 1970s and 1980s were sculpted by cowboy artists to celebrate white settlers' persistence. These monuments represented a form of conservative backlash against the spread of what many westerners dismissed as political correctness. In fact, Great Plains pioneer monuments increased in number and grew increasingly conservative as the culture wars heated up.

This pattern was particularly pronounced in centennial and sesquicentennial monuments erected in the interior states of Utah, Kansas, Montana, Wyoming, and Oklahoma. Altogether, fifty-four monuments—more than one-quarter of the 185 included in this study—were erected between 1970 and 1999. That rate was exceeded only by the Pioneer Mother movement of the 1920s and 1930s; this second age of memorialization would persist into the first two decades of the twenty-first century. Moreover, of those fifty-four monuments erected in the United States between 1970 and 1999, half were erected in just those five interior states, and several more were erected in adjoining areas. A substantial minority (11.1 percent) of those fifty-four monuments focused on Mormon history, and they did not flirt with modernism in the 1960s and 1970s, as did those in non-Mormon cities. Instead, the LDS faithful consistently embraced extremely traditional depictions of frontier families well into the twenty-first century.

Meanwhile on the Great Plains, centennial celebrations at the height of the late twentieth-century culture wars inspired smaller communities to erect monuments to pioneer women and pioneer couples. Altogether the southern plains received more than one-quarter of all pioneer monuments erected between 1970 and 1999. Ten pioneer monuments (18.5 percent) appeared in north-central Oklahoma alone. Five were erected in the heavily rural northwestern quadrant of Kansas during this period, two in Wichita near the Oklahoma border, and three more just across Kansas's eastern border, in Kansas City, Missouri. While the three pioneer monuments erected in Montana constituted only 5.6 percent of those erected during this period, that all three were erected on the western edge of the Great Plains within a four-year period (between 1985 and 1989), with two others appearing in neighboring northern Wyoming shortly thereafter, demonstrates the importance of centennial celebrations in shaping local pioneer commemoration, and makes that area also worthy of special attention.

Great Plains monuments grew more conservative as the culture wars grew more hotly contested in the 1980s and early 1990s. Early on, the artistic and cultural breaks of the 1960s combined with the bicentennial's emphasis on diversity to produce some modest artistic experimentation on the southern plains during the 1970s. Wichita's residents appear to have welcomed a new artistic vision of the frontier in Richard Bergen's nude *Heritage Woman* (see figure 3.6). In 1971, *Pioneer Family Statue,* created by Pete Felten Jr. for the small town of Oberlin (figure 5.2), was far less hierarchical than those typical of 1950s pioneer family monuments. And Oklahoma experimented with racial inclusivity. But as rural northwestern Kansas continued to erect pioneer monuments in the later 1970s and 1980s, those monuments increasingly relied on quite traditional depictions of pioneer men and women—a trend that continued in monuments erected in Montana and Wyoming in the late 1980s and early 1990s.

In the 1970s, Pete Felten Jr. produced several frontier-themed monuments for communities near his hometown in western Kansas, which grew more conservative as the culture wars intensified. For the earliest in 1971, Felten sculpted a frontier father, mother, daughter, and son, standing in a circle facing outward (figure 5.2). In contrast to 1950s monuments, which offered strapping sons as the nation's hope for the future, the Oberlin family stands in a circle with their backs toward one another and their arms linked, a defensive posture suggesting the pioneers' reliance on the family unit for survival. The Oberlin pioneer family circle suggests a greater degree of equality among the characters than the pyramidal shape typical in earlier decades. Indeed, the father in the Oberlin family bends his knees to embrace his children, decreasing the extent that he towers over the rest of the family. In keeping with earlier pioneer family monuments, the mother leans gently backward into the family circle, maintaining its core. But in a gesture toward feminism's growing influence, their teenage daughter leans slightly outward to embrace the future. As in the covered wagon family that Leo Friedlander sculpted for the Oregon statehouse some forty years earlier, the young son in Felten's

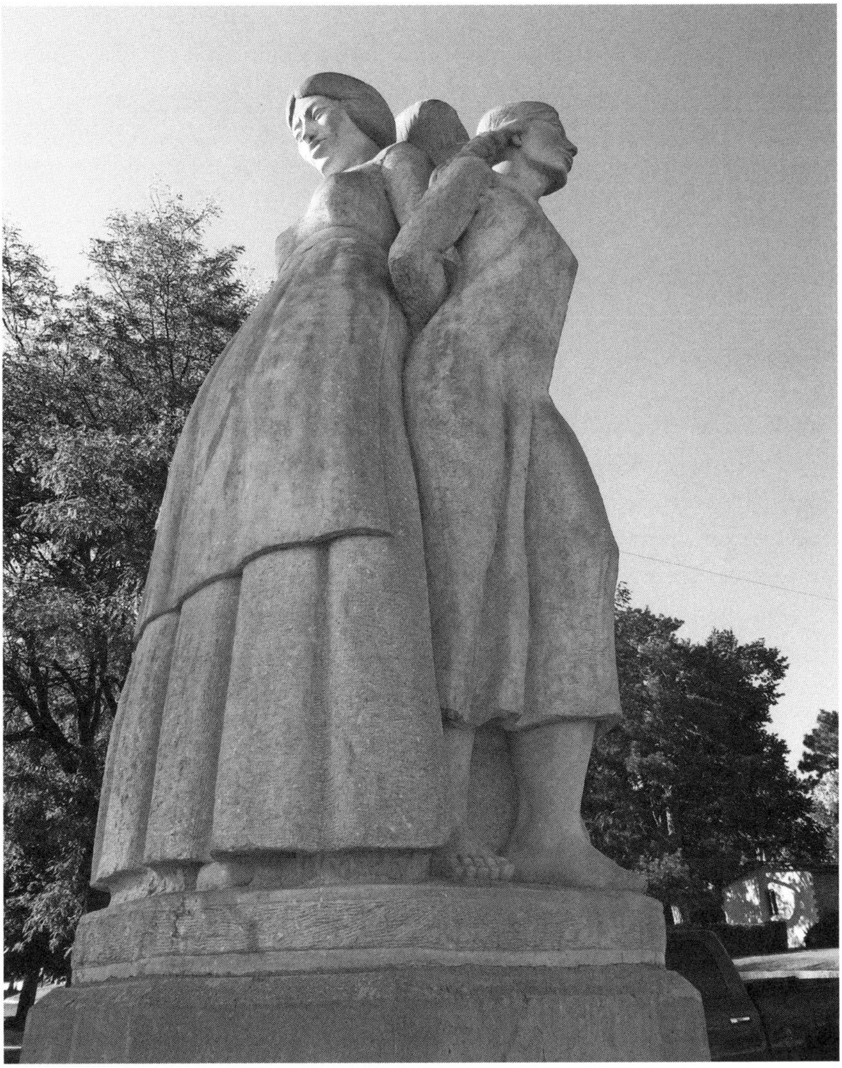

FIGURE 5.2. Pete Felten Jr., *Pioneer Family Statue*, Oberlin, Kansas, 1971. Photograph by author.

sculpture bends his knees, mimicking his father's posture, and appears ready to leap outward at the first opportunity. Public reactions to Felten's initial proposal had been mixed, but many skeptics apparently agreed with Ira Laidig: "When I first saw it I didn't like it, but the longer I sit here the better it looks."[17] What initially felt to many rural Kansans like too much of a departure from established pioneer family imagery soon grew more comfortable. But as conservative backlash against identity politics grew in America's heartland in the 1970s and 1980s, Great Plains pioneer monuments returned to their early twentieth-century roots.

As the global Cold War faded in the 1980s, the domestic culture wars heated up. Abandoning 1950s-style celebrations of the nuclear family, communities on the western plains returned to earlier depictions of pioneer men and women. Pioneer mothers and young pioneer couples by Pete Felten Jr. and other cowboy artists were erected more or less interchangeably in smaller communities in the interior West to commemorate local centennials in the 1980s and early 1990s. Rather than celebrating the guidance of youth, as did Avard Fairbanks's 1958 monument for Salem, Oregon (plate K), or women as symbols of white civilization, these rural monuments declared local communities' persistence during the 1980s farm crisis.

For example, amid Montana's brief pioneer monument boom, a Billings bank erected outside its new office building a local cowboy artist's take on a pioneer family. First Interstate Bank's chief financial officer told the *Billings Gazette* that the statue's purpose was "to honor the oldtime customers who really founded Billings."[18] Through its pioneer monument, the bank claimed frontier roots and a long-term commitment to the local community—paralleling earlier pioneer commemoration efforts at Columbia Savings in Colorado Springs and in Pueblo, Colorado, in the 1960s; at Midland Savings in Denver; and at United States Bank in Portland in the 1920s. To link local artist Mike Capser's settler family, *Pioneer's Vision* (figure 5.3), to Billings's ranching history, First Interstate added a plaque featuring a poem by rancher and cowboy poet Wally McRae.[19]

First Interstate, belying the company's name, sought to emphasize its distinctly Montanan identity by installing local Montana cowboy poetry and cowboy art. Architectural designer-turned-artist Mike Capser enjoyed a nationwide reputation, but the primary appeal of Capser's art remained his depictions of Montana people and places, which fit with popular notions of the West.[20] In fact, M. Solberg, who built a database of nearly 1,700 sculptures located in Washington, D.C., and across the country, declares that *Pioneer's Vision* "is among my very favorite pieces anywhere. The father paints the distant vision with outstretched hand. The son rapt, eyes glued to dad, worshipful. The sweet, carefree little girl & her dog. And momma: Grounded, practical, knowing. She recognizes

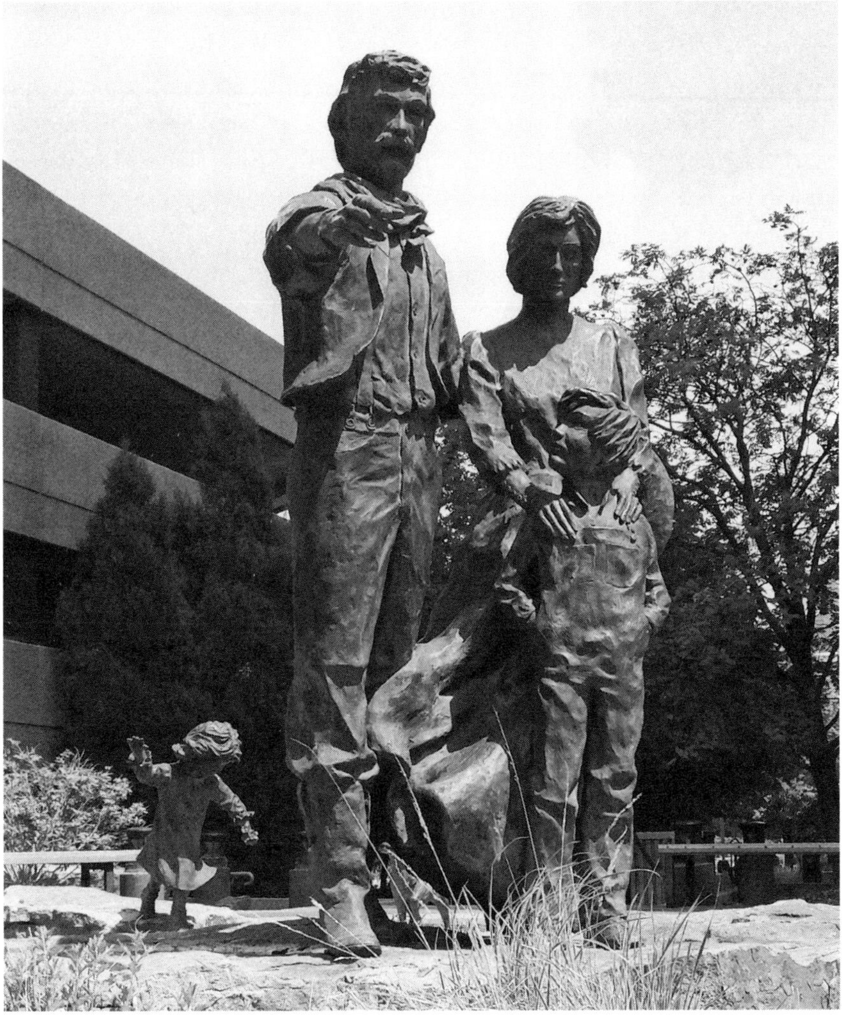

FIGURE 5.3. Mike Capser, *Pioneer's Vision*, Billings, Montana, 1985. Photograph by Pamela Pierce.

the vision, she's heard it many times before. But her concern is more immediate. 'What can I prepare for supper?' barely crowding out, 'How in God's name will I keep these children alive in this wasteland?'"[21] On one level, Solberg and other viewers connect to this statue for reasons similar to those of Americans who connected to pioneer family statues in the 1950s. The white father gazes into the distance with a vision of the West and the future, his arm encircling and gently guiding his equally white wife; the son looks at his father with rapt and worshipful eyes, and the mother's hands rest protectively on their young son's shoulders. But on another level, this piece, and particularly Solberg's analysis of it, also contains gendered perspectives that appear to have been influenced by the feminist movement. Rather than emphasizing women's passivity and maternalism by including a babe-in-arms, Capser's 1985 sculpture prominently features a young girl who strays from her family unit to romp with the family dog, which serves as playmate rather than bodyguard. Capser's girl resembles adventurous Laura Ingalls from the perennially popular *Little House* books, while the few other twentieth-century pioneer monuments featuring school-aged daughters more closely resemble Laura's dutiful older sister, Mary. Capser's pioneer mother appears more concerned about her practical responsibilities on the frontier than with her husband's and son's visions for the future. But in the end, both the girl's adventures and her mother's anxieties separate them from the real business of the family, which remains the passing of vision—and newly claimed western land—from father to son. Despite its seeming feminism, then, the work reinforces traditional Euro-American gender and family relationships as well as—like most pioneer monuments—white settler colonialism. That imagery had predominated throughout the twentieth century and appeared in dozens of pioneer monuments on the Great Plains, but beginning around 1990, it met with opposition in some more ethnically diverse or politically progressive communities in the Southwest and Pacific Northwest.

LOCATION, LOCATION, LOCATION

Monuments enshrining traditional frontier memory were welcomed in conservative small-town America, but they sparked protest in some more diverse and progressive communities. The pioneer monuments erected in western Kansas and eastern Montana in the 1980s marked local centennials and declared those rural places as significant in a larger national story of westward expansion. Yet they also shored up local conservative cultural values in the face of a perceived onslaught of political correctness.

A decade after the United States' supposedly inclusive bicentennial commemorations, the question of how to mark a national anniversary once more sparked nationwide debate. As the five hundredth anniversary of Spanish exploration in the Americas approached, Native activists denounced the traditional narrative of Christopher Columbus discovering the New World. Meanwhile, New Western historians embraced Patricia Limerick's reframing of western history around Euro-American conquest of western lands and peoples.[22] These cultural critiques quickly caught on in progressive circles, making interpretation and commemoration of western history an important battlefield in the larger culture wars. As progressive voices protested some pioneer monuments for celebrating white supremacy, more conservative communities embraced traditional pioneer monuments or built on 1970s efforts at ethnic inclusivity.

Anthropologist Michael Rowlands argues that some monuments "work," while others spark condemnation.[23] Rowlands suggests that for war memorials to work, they must serve certain functions for the living. But regional variations in frontier commemoration, particularly different communities' responses to the same pioneer monuments in the early 1990s, reveal how a statue's physical and cultural context shape how well a given monument works. In studying public monument reception, as in real estate, location is crucial. As activists and academics challenged the traditional narratives embraced by many rural whites, western communities disagreed about how—and even whether—early white settlers should be commemorated.

ATTEMPTED INCLUSIVITY IN THE SOUTHWEST

Pioneer memorialization during the 1970s and 1980s, as we have seen, was particularly active—and particularly conservative—in Kansas and Montana. Similarly, conservative pioneer monuments appeared in neighboring Wyoming and Oklahoma. But pioneer commemoration took a somewhat more inclusive form in the desert Southwest, where Native and Hispanic cultural influences were clearly felt.

The city of Prescott, Arizona, located about one hundred miles north of Phoenix, was overwhelmingly white in 1990 (92.9 percent non-Hispanic white).[24] Then, as now, Prescott actively marketed the legendary Old West, with three museums highlighting western heritage and the World's Oldest Rodeo, which celebrates a Spanish fantasy past and co-opts the centuries-old Mexican *charrería* tradition on which modern American rodeo is based.[25] As New Western history critiqued traditional frontier narratives and imagery, Prescott attempted to be more gender

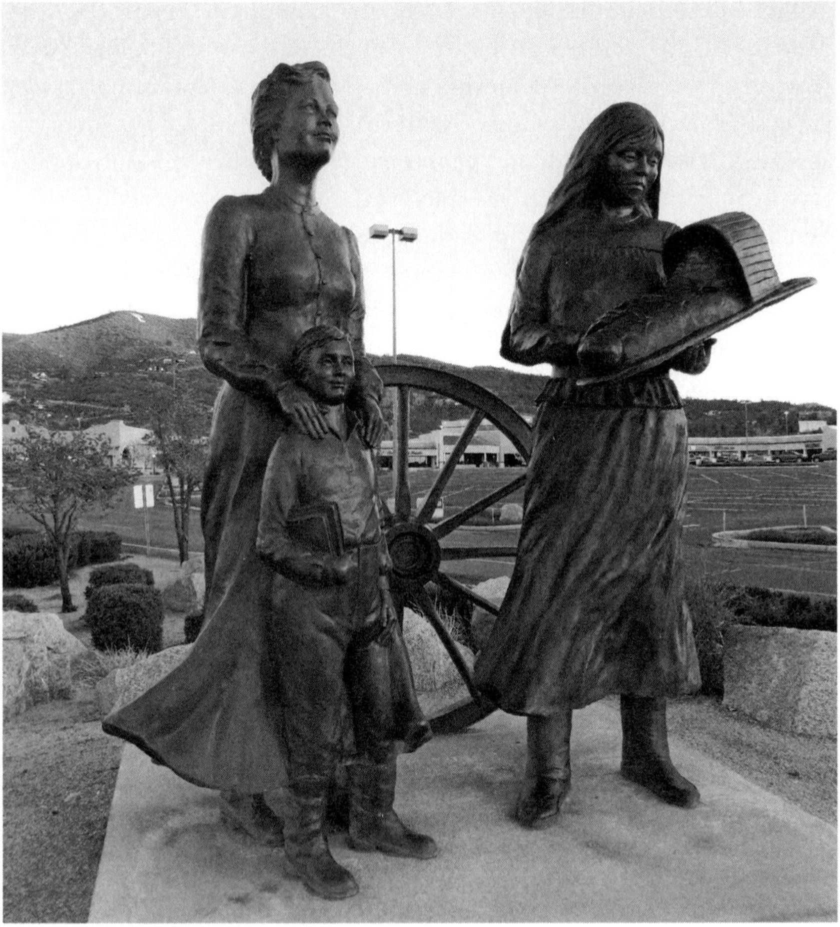

FIGURE 5.4. Pat Mathiesen, *Spirit of the Frontier*, Prescott, Arizona, 1990. Photograph by author.

and ethnically inclusive. While Prescott cowboy artist Bill Nebeker's 1985 *Early Settlers*, featuring a white mule skinner, a miner, a cowboy, and a pioneer mother, was placed in a prominent location in the heart of tourist-oriented Prescott, Pat Mathiesen's 1990 *Spirit of the Frontier*, an ethnically balanced portrayal of a pair of mothers—one indigenous, the other Anglo-American—was relegated five years later to the parking lot of a local strip mall, on the outskirts of town, fittingly known as Frontier Shopping Village (figure 5.4). Mathiesen depicts both women as relatively strong maternal figures but promises very different futures for them. The white pioneer gazes confidently into the future, her hands resting proudly on the shoulders of her school-aged son. Like boys in 1950s pioneer family monuments, the books clasped in his arm and the proud expression on his face assure the viewer that he is preparing to lead the nation. But the indigenous mother—wearing an Anglo-style cloth blouse and long skirt, her long hair hanging loose—gazes down at her infant, tied tightly to a cradle board, suggesting that both woman and infant were constrained by the backwardness of cultural persistence. The Yavapai infant will not grow into an equally strapping scholar prepared to lead its people, let alone the white-dominated nation. The wagon wheel that unites the Anglo and Indian figures visually promises progress toward a more white and civilized future—a message that likely appealed to Prescott's predominantly Anglo-American population.

Comparing different communities' reactions to identical statues highlights how racial dynamics shaped progressive and conservative perspectives on frontier memory at the height of the culture wars. Two castings of Burke Rutherford's 1992 *Pioneer Woman* were erected in smaller western towns in the early 1990s (figure 5.5). Rutherford's twin statues borrowed iconography from many earlier Pioneer Mother statues. Like nearly every Pioneer Mother since Charles Grafly's model sparked protest in 1915 San Francisco, Rutherford's pioneer woman wears a wide-brimmed sunbonnet, prairie gown, and apron. But rather than emphasizing her reproductive role by holding an infant, Rutherford's pioneer woman performs productive field work, sowing wheat using the timeless broadcast method. By casting seed broadcast into soil, presumably prepared by her (unseen) frontiersman husband using a team of horses and steel equipment, symbolizing progress, she contributes to nourishing her family through work akin to feminine gardening and nurturance, rather than the male-dominated realm of field work. Moreover, sowing seeds from her apron, which is drawn up into a womb-like pouch, recasts her productive labor as symbolically reproducing white society. Metaphorically, she plants the seeds of white society deep into the waiting western soil.

Rutherford's 1992 pioneer woman appears right at home in grassy Pioneer Park, in central Worland, Wyoming, an overwhelmingly white town of about 5,500.[26] Taken together, the park's name and design, its statuary, and its dedicatory tablet tell a classic story of indigenous peoples and desert landscape yielding to Anglo-American hard work, ingenuity, and proper gender work roles. Peter Toth's enormous wooden Indian head,

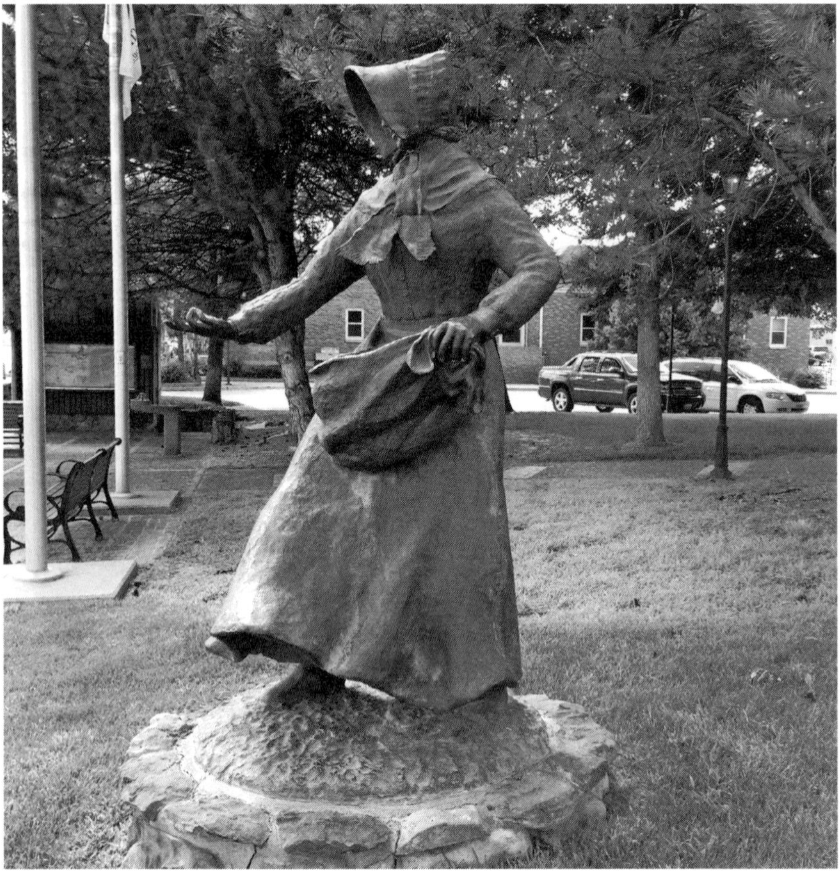

FIGURE 5.5. Burke Rutherford, *Pioneer Woman,* Worland, Wyoming, 1992. Photograph by Angela Harrison-Urlacher.

installed in 1980, memorializes the region's indigenous past. Lyndon Fayne Pomeroy's stylized 1989 steel sculpture depicts a white pioneer man using modern steel and irrigation technology to make the desert bloom, preparing the soil in which Burke Rutherford's *Pioneer Woman* plants the seed of white civilization. Large granite tablets dedicate the park "to those who came first" in the County of Washakie (named for Chief Washakie, the indigenous leader portrayed in Mahonri Young's *This Is the Place Monument*; see figure 4.3): "The Big Horn Basin for ten thousand Great Suns nurtured hunting tribes of Crow and Sioux, Arapahoe and Shoshone following *Pie Tanka,* the Buffalo." The Worland Pioneer Park tablet's version of local history—which as of 2018, also appeared on the town's official website—fit easily with a century of Turnerian frontier narratives, still dominant in the 1980s, and with the imagery Gordon Dingman used to celebrate peaceful coexistence in New Ulm, Minnesota, in the 1970s.[27] The tablet portrays the region's indigenes as children of nature who yielded their native lands to white trappers and gold miners, who in turn yielded the land to ranchers, farmers, and their "courageous wives . . . to weave a new civilization here in the wilderness." The settler colonialist language was even more clear on the tablet's reverse, where that same stone slab dedicated the park "to those who persevered and conquered . . . the desert" to establish the city of Worland. While the racial implications of Rutherford's pioneer woman statue were embraced in white Worland, Wyoming, they met with resistance on a predominantly Hispanic New Mexico college campus.

Burke Rutherford's other 1992 *Pioneer Mother* was cast by New Mexico Highlands University students and erected on the heavily Hispanic university campus near the Diversity Flagship circle, which displays flags representing the nations of current Highlands students. The sculptural design that fit in so well in Worland, Wyoming, sparked controversy in Las Vegas, New Mexico, where 82 percent identified as Hispanic.[28] Local resident Jean Hinkie told a Santa Fe newspaper that the statue "doesn't really represent the history of this area of New Mexico. It is not complete until a Hispanic and an American Indian woman are placed with their counterpart."[29] Similar calls for more inclusive monuments were heard—and occasionally realized—throughout the West in the years surrounding the Columbian quincentennial. But Hinkie's proposed trio of western women likely would not have pleased many in Hispanic Las Vegas—especially if, like Pat Mathiesen's *Spirit of the Frontier* in neighboring Arizona, it included a subtext celebrating white progress.

Local reactions to Rutherford's Pioneer Mother were mixed. Some Las Vegas residents were even more critical of the local Rutherford pioneer woman sculpture. For example, Anselmo Arellano, an oral history teacher and author of books and articles related to Hispanic New Mexicans, declared that "the female pioneers of Las Vegas were Hispanic. The Anglos did not arrive until after the Santa Fe Trail passed through the area," and that the sculpted figure should be wearing "tápalos or rebozos" rather than a prairie gown and sunbonnet. But not all Las Vegas residents shared Arellano's concerns. University spokesperson Benita

Budd responded to these critiques by claiming, "It was not intended to represent Anglo women, nor was there any effort to represent any ethnic group."[30] Of course, as this study has shown, pioneer women statues usually depicted a universal type, rather than a specific person. But most donors, sculptors, and viewers in Las Vegas and across the U.S. West recognized that type to be Anglo-American. While New Mexico had been settled in the seventeenth and eighteenth centuries by Spanish-speaking peoples who migrated north from Mexico, these Hispanos were rarely characterized as settlers, and certainly not as pioneers. As these southwestern monuments and the controversy surrounding David Manuel's contemporaneous statue for Portland, Oregon, demonstrate, true inclusivity is more challenging and complex than many people recognize.

THE PROMISED LAND?

Highly visible Hispanic and Native populations pushed for more ethnically diverse public monuments in the U.S. Southwest, but in the Pacific Northwest, where indigenous populations had been decimated by disease and forcibly removed to the arid interior by the 1850s, triumphal narratives about Anglo-American overland migrations predominated. While most Oregonians remain proud of their connection to the historic Oregon Trail, vocal protests to David Manuel's 1993 *The Promised Land* revealed the complexity of their relationship to pioneer memory. The racial politics of frontier memory was particularly complicated in relatively progressive Portland, even though it was among the least ethnically diverse metropolitan areas in the United States.[31] But in contrast to smaller inland towns and cities, many white Portlanders objected to the traditional pioneer family imagery promoted as part of Oregon Trail sesquicentennial celebrations.

The OTCC commissioned artist David Manuel to create a $200,000 sesquicentennial monument, which it envisioned as "a metaphor for all of us who have traveled one trail or another to Oregon."[32] Manuel's painted bronze *The Promised Land* (plate N), which resembled the nuclear family imagery appearing in several contemporaneous bronze statues erected elsewhere to generally favorable feedback, found widespread support in small towns across the Pacific Northwest. But because it reproduced the triumphalist narrative of white westward expansion, it met with both official and public resistance in cosmopolitan Portland, where pride in its frontier heritage collided with community demands that public art be culturally inclusive.

David Manuel's design aimed for historicity but did so while using iconography from a century-long tradition of historically inaccurate heroic pioneer statues. Like historians at colonial Williamsburg, Manuel pursued "credibility armor" by studying historic artifacts in museums and private collections.[33] In 1980 the artist explained to *Northwest Magazine*, "Even if it's just an Indian out in a meadow, it's still a *certain* Indian, of a *certain* tribe or a *certain* time in history, and he's there for a specific reason."[34] By the early 1990s, though, the Anglo-American artist was essentially a cowboy artist best known for works focusing on white men in the mythic Old West. These included statues of a generic frontier marshal and actor John Wayne playing the title role in the 1953 film *Hondo*. Manuel's piece intended for downtown Portland depicted generic white pioneer types upon their arrival in Oregon's Willamette Valley. A strong father points westward; his wife clings to "a flour-sack doll . . . that was once her daughter's, the child they buried far back on the Trail," and their son holds the family Bible; "[a] wagon's wheel, still sturdy yet worn, completes the story."[35] Only the substitution of a doll for a living baby strayed from the iconography similar to many other pioneer monuments. That substitution reminded viewers of hardships faced on the trail and reinforced the mother's nurturing role, rather than the productive one shown in Rutherford's pioneer women sculptures for Worland, Wyoming, and Las Vegas, New Mexico. By shifting the Bible from the mother to the son, Manuel echoed 1950s-era urban family monuments, emphasizing (male) youth as society's hope for the future. But the artist's reliance on nameless pioneer types and his use of religious symbolism—which were typical of the earlier Pioneer Mother movement and accepted in newer monuments elsewhere in the West—sparked controversy in 1990s Portland.

Concern about *The Promised Land*'s celebration of white westward expansion appeared as early as August 29, 1993, when the *Oregonian*'s Arts section featured a cover story titled "Art and Propaganda on the Oregon Trail: The Sesquicentennial Celebrates a Happy, Sanitized History at Odds with the Real Thing." In it, journalist Randy Gragg critiqued both Manuel's statue and official sesquicentennial souvenir kitsch, including machine-made "buffalo chips" and "covenant drums . . . designed by a white artist and based on an Iroquois belt pattern" that bore little connection to tribes over whose lands the Oregon Trail passed. The Oregon sesquicentennial was promoting exactly the kind of western myths that the New Western history sought to debunk. In 1991 the National Museum in Washington, D.C., mounted a provocative exhibition, *The West as America: Reinterpreting Images of the Frontier, 1820–1920*, which examined myths of the West through major works of art, emphasizing themes of imperialism, racism, and genocide.[36] Academics and Native activists managed to challenge and even—to a significant degree—rewrite the narratives told the following year at the five hundredth anniversary of Columbus's "discovery" of America. Meanwhile, the Maryhill Museum near Goldendale, Washington, mounted an exhibit curated by Oregon State University faculty that examined popular myths surrounding migration and westward expansion representing "the migration's transformation of the West to be equal parts commerce, religion, and male virility."[37] While the title of Manuel's work declared a divinely inspired white claim to indigenous lands, and was thus arguably more egregious than Jo Saylor's *This Land is Mine*, sculpted for Ponca City, Oklahoma, that same year, public debate in Portland centered on the statue's location, rather than its title.

Portlanders could not agree where to place the OTCC's gift. In March 1993, the statue was installed in a temporary location in front of the Oregon History Center, where it appeared right at home in front of Richard Haas's much-respected 1989 trompe l'oeil mural celebrating the Lewis and Clark expedition (which, in a manner typical of its time, achieved inclusivity by featuring Lewis, Clark, their African American slave York, Sacagawea, and her infant son). Yet, the History Center was hesitant to install the piece permanently. A site committee—including representatives of the OTCC, the Oregon History Center, Portland city agencies, and neighborhood associations—met biweekly for three months before unanimously approving a proposal to install *The Promised Land* in one of downtown Portland's North Park blocks, accompanied by quotes from Oregon Trail diaries and interpretive signage explaining the significance of the trail to modern visitors.

Strong opposition to siting the statue in the North Park blocks quickly arose. The Public Art Advisory Committee (PAAC) of Portland's Metropolitan Arts Commission (MAC) voted unanimously to reject the site proposal because "the depiction of subject matter was found to be

[an] inappropriate and inaccurate portrayal of the settlers of Oregon, excluding the many other races and religions of those who have come to call Oregon home. It is also insensitive to the history of the indigenous peoples of the area."[38]

Artists and art historians challenged the statue's artistic merit. Bob Hanson, a PAAC committee member and an instructor at the Pacific Northwest College of Art, judged it "mediocre." Another art historian likened it to "a Norman Rockwell cover for the Saturday Evening Post," and suggested that the monument should display a significant quantity of whiskey to balance the prominently displayed Bible.[39] According to a city official on the site committee, "The feeling among many of us . . . was this was really a dog of a piece and needs to be in the least conspicuous place possible."[40] But most of the controversy focused on the perceived cultural insensitivity of the monument during an era that favored racial diversity. One guest at a PAAC meeting declared that it "distorts historical facts and implies that only white Christians were involved in the settlement of Oregon."[41] Scholars and the general public both began to question the appropriateness of a statue celebrating white westward expansion. "A more appropriate statue might be called 'Receivers of Stolen Property,'" Art Alexander, an African American aide to the city commissioner, told the PAAC. Alexander suggested that this statue could "depict laughing European-American men standing on Native American corpses with torn up treaties scattered about, and a sign saying 'No N—Allowed.'"[42]

Opposition to the statue did not necessarily follow racial lines, however. Antone Minthorn, chairman of the general council of the Confederated Tribes of the Umatilla Indian Reservation and a member of the OTCC board, seemed unconcerned about erecting a monument that some perceived as celebrating the dispossession and genocide of Native peoples. Minthorn suggested that if people were unhappy with the sculpture, they should not simply reject it, and instead "do their own sculpture." But Henry Sayre, an Anglo-American art history professor at Oregon State University, believed that the statue was a "divisive gesture. . . . I'm not sure we need any more memorials to the dominant culture." Unlike Minthorn, Sayre expressed a legitimate concern that "other cultures just don't have the resources to match." Another expert found the statue "offensive," but argued that it was no more so than "other stuff around town."[43]

The PAAC appeared less concerned about the statue's failure to represent Oregon's ethnic diversity than its implied support for manifest destiny. An unpublished editorial, apparently drafted by MAC executive director William D. Bulick, declared that the "view that America and the West were given to white settlers by 'divine right,' regardless of the wishes of native settlers is a discredited one and offensive to many citizens," and compared the piece to public display of the Confederate flag at southern state capitals.[44] The MAC also collected newspaper articles related to other public depictions of crosses and Christian imagery in public sites.

Several outspoken Portlanders joined the PAAC and local academics in labeling the statue as politically incorrect. The story ultimately spread nationwide to the pages of *USA Today*, and conservative talk radio and television host Rush Limbaugh displayed a scale model of *The Promised Land* on his television show.[45] Yet, not all Portlanders opposed erection of the monument. According to an unscientific poll sponsored by Portland's ABC television affiliate, 94 percent of twelve thousand respondents believed that the city should accept the gift of the statue and install it in the North Park blocks.[46] A more reliable poll conducted by the *Oregonian* found that Portlanders supported placing the statue in a prominent downtown location by a two-to-one ratio.[47] Nonetheless, the controversy raged on in progressive Portland.

Tellingly, residents and city officials from smaller communities in the Pacific Northwest did not share Portlanders' angst about Manuel's design. Other Oregon towns that were heavily invested in remembering their frontier past likewise expressed a desire to own and display the statue, including Baker City, Echo, La Grande, Medford, Silverton, Springfield, and Tumwater. The mayor, the county's chief executive and sheriff, and the executive director for the Citizens for the Gorge Discovery Center all campaigned to bring the statue to The Dalles. "Being the end of the trail, I think it's only fitting" to bring the statue to Oregon City, that town's mayor insisted on a local radio show. "This is the promised land"—even if the supposed trail end had by that time become a landfill. Like their counterparts in small-town Kansas and Montana, these rural Oregonians wanted to identify their communities with the national narrative of westward migration. "We have been truly just flooded with phone calls from people all over the state, saying that they're outraged . . . [and] they'd be more than happy to take it," declared Joyce White, the OTCC's development director. "They can't understand what's wrong with these people in

Portland."[48] White refused to indicate a preference for any of the smaller towns staking a claim to the statue. "That would be like choosing among your children."[49] But even in these smaller towns, not all Oregonians embraced Manuel's monument. In fact, opinions of *The Promised Land* among the artist's neighbors in tiny Joseph, Oregon (population 1,500), reportedly "range[d] from 'wonderful' to 'wishy-washy' to 'crap.'"[50]

While many Portlanders appeared willing to accept the statue, the controversy about where to place it raged on. A second site committee, which included local community stakeholders as well as historians and members of the PAAC and MAC, ultimately rejected the OTCC's preferred location in the North Park blocks as being too prominent and beautiful, settling instead on Chapman Square as the statue's final destination. During construction on that downtown business district site, *The Promised Land* was moved to a second temporary location across the Willamette River in the Lloyd District, where it was placed on an existing pedestal overlooking a light-rail stop.[51] According to columnist Jonathan Nicholas, in that location "the pioneer family look[ed] a little nervous with the traffic zooming around and Pa pointing resolutely toward downtown."[52] The statue's opponents hoped that, after languishing in the Lloyd District several years, the piece would be forgotten and remain in that less noticeable location. But it was not to be. In fact, as the city prepared to move *The Promised Land* to its permanent home in Chapman Square in July 1996, the Lloyd District—led by Virgil Ovall of Ashforth Pacific, the powerful commercial real estate company that had recently purchased a significant portion of Lloyd District developments—expressed its determination to keep the statue. Joyce White, just as she had rejected smaller communities' claims on the statue, was not swayed by Lloyd District businesses' interest.[53] Meanwhile, popular opinion remained mixed: "Some people think it's a slice of Americana; others think it's a slice of baloney. Kind of a big version of a metal cowboy statue like you'd get from a Little America gift shop, next to the western knickknacks made out of driftwood and pine cones."[54]

The Site Committee II archives do not adequately explain why the committee selected a more central location than either the North Park blocks originally favored by the OTCC or the up-and-coming Lloyd District. By placing the monument in a less prominent location, the committee appears to have sought a compromise between the demands of the statue's donors and citizens who were strongly invested in Oregon's frontier heritage and those of outspoken critics of its cultural insensitivity. Ironically, over the next fifteen years, both the North Park blocks and Lloyd District would decline in importance, while the newly renovated Chapman Square flourished along with Portland's financial district.

If the site committee sought to hide the statue in plain sight because it celebrated white cultural dominance, then Chapman Square was an odd choice considering its long history of struggles over inclusivity and popular memory. It was home to anti-Chinese riots in the 1880s. By the 1920s, it was designated for the use of women only after working women complained of repeated sexual harassment in Portland's downtown parks. More recently, Asian women have collected nuts from the square's enormous trees, and the homeless have built protest camps in the square. In the 1990s, street people and businesspeople alike frequented its benches and grassy lawn.[55] The statue was installed near a monument to the imperialist Spanish-American War and a massive bronze elk celebrating the conquest of western lands. In its permanent location, *The Promised Land* is framed in the background by the city's modern Justice Center (a downtown jail).

The second site committee sought to make the monument more inclusive by installing bronze footprints and wagon wheel tracks crossing Chapman Square. Yet the discussion of this proposal revealed poorly masked racism among committee members. One suggested that some of the tracks end partway across the square, indicating that that person or animal had "died out."[56] Asked how bronze footprints were to represent the diverse Native peoples of Oregon, Parks Department project designer Jim Ringelberg cited western novels of questionable historical accuracy by Louis L'Amour, in which scouts identified different tribes by their tracks as if they were wild animals.[57] The final installation instead combined different sets of human prints—three sets of presumably Euro-American heeled shoe prints leading away from the statue, and another, less clearly defined set presumably intended to represent Indian moccasins—as well as what appear to be bear and dog paw prints, deer hoof prints, and duck foot prints. Eloise MacMurray, public art director from the Regional Arts and Culture Council, explained that the animal and Indian footprints were added to indicate that there was more to the story than just the pioneers depicted in Manuel's statue, but neither the final design nor MacMurray's explanation of it examined the devastation wreaked by white settlement on both indigenous peoples and native fauna.[58]

Members of the second site committee bemoaned the "baggage" associated with the name of the sculpture, but their supposed solution revealed the extent to which they were invested in the underlying logic of white dominance. One committee member expressed a hope that *The Promised Land* could "exist w[ith] mutual respect," and that they could "transform [the] title into something else" representing a "*mutual journey.*"[59] Toward that end, they replaced the OTCC's planned Oregon Trail diary excerpts with more inclusive-sounding lines supposedly spoken by Thomas Jefferson to Osage leaders on the eastern Great Plains to justify white expansion into Native lands. The committee thus sacrificed historical accuracy in favor of an appearance of mutuality, using a text that was in fact dedicated to white conquest to do so. And despite the brouhaha, the notion of Portland and the Willamette Valley as the promised land lived on in local culture and politics.[60]

But the public controversy surrounding Manuel's statue eventually died down. Even though the second site committee reached consensus on placing the statue in Chapman Square, members worried about the "irony of homeless people there" in the square.[61] Even more ironic, however, is the fact that by 2013, Chapman Square had been restored to its early twentieth-century status as a well-manicured location for picnic lunches by nearby businesspeople, while the North Park blocks—which the PAAC deemed too beautiful for a statue of questionable worth—languished. Large patches of dead grass marked the OTCC's desired location for Manuel's statue. In the blocks to the north of the Custom House, young men played basketball on a poorly maintained court. Although a well-maintained playground just south of the proposed site appeared popular with local residents, in the next block panhandlers congregated near a massive bronze elephant statue. While the North Park blocks were clearly being used by local residents, one Google reviewer complained, "Nothing. But. Junkies. Han[g] out. There."[62]

Meanwhile, sculptor David Manuel benefited immensely from the controversy surrounding his design, which amounted to significant free advertising for the artist. He received an offer of $250,000 for a copy of the much maligned statue. By August 1994, he and his wife had opened a new twelve-thousand-square-foot museum displaying his private collection of western memorabilia and a gallery of his artwork in the remote eastern

Oregon town of Joseph. Manuel placed a copy of *The Promised Land* out in front of the museum, where he claimed it was a "traffic-stopper."[63] Five years later, he told the *Oregonian* that he had learned from his experience with *The Promised Land.* When he depicted Nez Perce leader Chief Joseph in a long headdress adorned with "as many eagle feathers as I possibly could," though, Manuel failed to appreciate that his use of eagle feathers represented a betrayal of his supposed goal of authenticity and was an act of settler colonialism.[64] The artist next intended to create a sequel to *The Promised Land,* featuring the father plowing on their Willamette Valley farm, while his pregnant wife looks on and his son holds a handful of the rich soil. The artist anticipated complaints—"I know when they look at that they will say, where is the American Indian?"—but his solution suggested just how little others' critiques had affected the artist's imperialist conception of western history: "If they look real close, they will see the edge of an arrowhead sticking out of the dirt."[65]

Manuel's edge of an arrowhead seems grossly inadequate to address the cultural imperialism so vehemently opposed in *The Promised Land.* Nonetheless, most Portlanders appear willing to overlook the statue's shortcomings, and indeed to overlook the monument altogether. According to western historian Carl Abbott, "many Portlanders" in the early twenty-first century find *The Promised Land* "lacking in cultural inclusiveness and more than a bit sappy."[66] While they may still find the statue to be overly triumphalist and somewhat lacking in artistic merit, most seem content to simply ignore it as they go about their own business in Portland's business district. Significantly, even as Portlanders chose to forget the statue that sparked such controversy, both urban and rural Oklahoma residents chose to remember their frontier heritage. In that politically conservative state, pioneer commemoration enabled many to forget their homeland's complex racial history.

INDIAN TERRITORY OR COWBOY STATE?

Pioneer monuments became a popular way for Oklahomans to grapple with changing social norms and their state's multicultural history amid the culture wars of both the early and late twentieth century. Since E. W. Marland erected Ponca City's famous *Pioneer Woman* in 1929, Oklahoma has enthusiastically erected monuments and marked anniversaries using traditional pioneer imagery. Statues commemorating Anglo-American cowboys and white settlement were particularly popular in conservative Oklahoma, where many urban and rural whites remain eager to celebrate the region's transformation from a federally designated Indian Territory to a (white-dominated) American state. Comparing depictions of Indians and white settlers in Oklahoma's public statuary from the 1920s to the present highlights the ongoing tension between conservative and progressive representations of frontier life in the formerly Native lands.

Pioneer monuments erected between 1890 and 1915 explicitly celebrated the arrival of supposedly civilized white settlers and the resulting disappearance of indigenous peoples. Whites' interest in noble savage mythology then dwindled as they grew confident in their conquest of indigenous populations and western lands. Despite growing white dominance, indigenous peoples and their history remained more visible in Oklahoma because of its complex nineteenth-century racial history. After the American Revolutionary War, white settlers pushed west of the Appalachian Mountains. The federal government negotiated treaties and forcibly removed indigenous peoples from their homelands, pushing them west of the Mississippi River. The 1854 Kansas and Nebraska Act then opened those two areas to white settlement, and both Native and neo-local indigenous groups were pushed south into what became known as Indian Territory (present-day Oklahoma), where they competed for land and resources with indigenous groups, such as the Osage, and early nineteenth-century Indian settlers, including the Cherokee. White settlement then spread to central and western parts of Oklahoma beginning in 1889. In contrast to earlier frontiers that were claimed by white settlers over a span of months or years, large portions of Oklahoma Indian lands were opened to white settlement at a specific date and time. An estimated fifty thousand people from across the United States participated in Oklahoma's first land run on April 22, 1889. The sudden flood of white men (and much smaller numbers of African Americans) swiftly settled more than two million acres of land, enabling the rapid organization of Oklahoma Territory and statehood in 1907. Images of white horsemen and wagons racing to claim homesteads or town sites in 1889 and in subsequent land runs became a central part of popular memory in Oklahoma.[67]

At the height of the Pioneer Mother movement, and as Tulsa's African American community struggled to rebuild after the city's destructive 1921

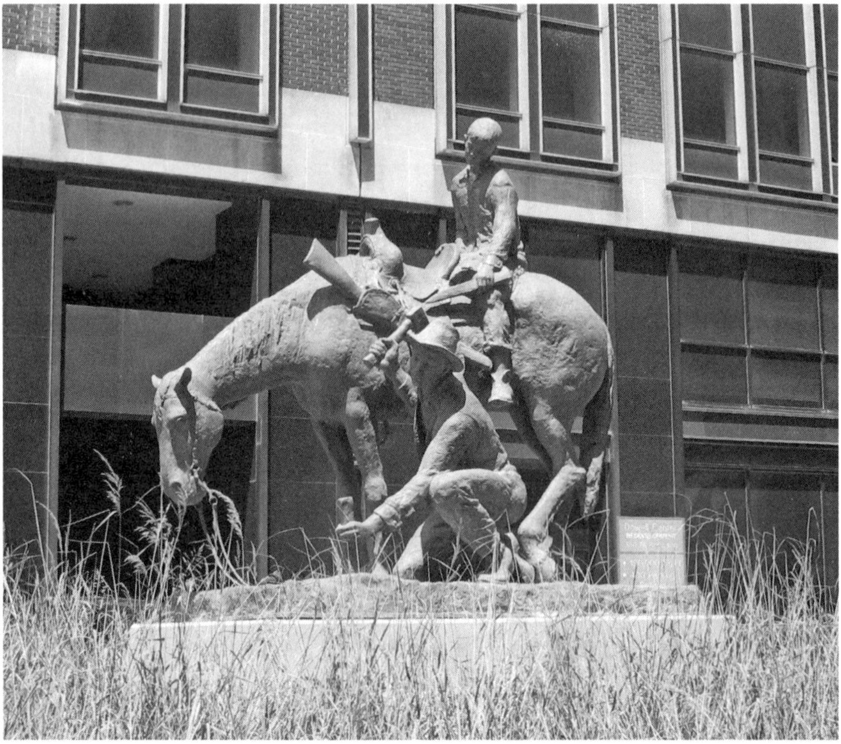

FIGURE 5.6. Leonard McMurry, *Pioneers of 1889*, Oklahoma City, Oklahoma, 1959. Photograph by David Prescott.

race riot, white oilman E. W. Marland erected a pioneer woman monument to commemorate the opening of the Cherokee Outlet (or Cherokee Strip) to white settlement, which was dedicated on the forty-first anniversary of Oklahoma's 1889 land run.[68] By commemorating white women carrying Christian civilization to the western frontier, that Ponca City *Pioneer Woman* statue (plate B) indirectly celebrated the conquest of diverse Indian groups, including the indigenous Osages; immigrant Cherokees, who had been forcibly removed from their homelands in Georgia and Tennessee to the Cherokee Outlet on land ceded by the Osages in the early nineteenth century; and the Poncas, who had been forcibly removed from their homelands when Kansas and Nebraska were opened for white settlement. Meanwhile, white Oklahomans also commemorated several prominent indigenous leaders in the 1920s and 1930s. Like the turn-of-the-century pioneer monuments that included Indian figures, these sculptures were intended as tributes to the noble Indian, marking the passing of not only these individual indigenous leaders, but also Indian dominance in Oklahoma.

No other monuments to white pioneers were erected in Oklahoma prior to World War II. But Oklahoma communities both large and small embraced land rush monuments in the postwar period that, rather than celebrating nuclear families, emphasized white masculine adventure and taking Indian territory. The first, Leonard McMurry's *Pioneers of 1889* (figure 5.6), marked the seventieth anniversary of the earliest land rush. Sculpted as African American activists held sit-ins at segregated lunch counters in Oklahoma City, Enid, and Stillwater, and dedicated in downtown Oklahoma City on '89ers Day, McMurry's statue depicted a kneeling white man driving a stake into the Oklahoma soil with his ax to stake his claim; his young son sits atop their horse, holding another stake.[69] Certainly, McMurry's choice not to depict a bonneted woman aligns with contemporaneous accounts that the land run was male dominated. Yet the accompanying plaque dedicates the statue to both male and female settlers, and McMurry's choice to include a young son, and to place the boy on horseback while his father kneels to stake his land claim, points to the importance that sculptors and the American public alike placed on sons as the hope for the future at a time of global uncertainty. From Tennessee to Oregon, postwar Americans pushed pioneer mothers to the shadows, and pioneer monuments focused on their hardy sons as the nation's hope for the future. Those settler families' whiteness—and fathers and sons' masculinity—took on special meaning in Oklahoma, where descendants of these turn-of-the-century settlers struggled with the region's complex indigenous history and persistent Indian populations.

In the 1970s, Guthrie, Oklahoma, joined communities across the nation in celebrating the nation's bicentennial by erecting a monument to local frontier history. Like New Ulm, Minnesota, Guthrie attempted to tell an inclusive frontier narrative in their bicentennial pioneer monument, but in conservative Oklahoma, what appeared on the surface to be culturally inclusive in fact reinforced long-held beliefs in white male authority. The town marked the U.S. bicentennial and the seventieth anniversary of statehood by erecting a pioneer monument in front of the Oklahoma Territorial Museum (which documents the history of the [white] homestead experience and territorial and state government),

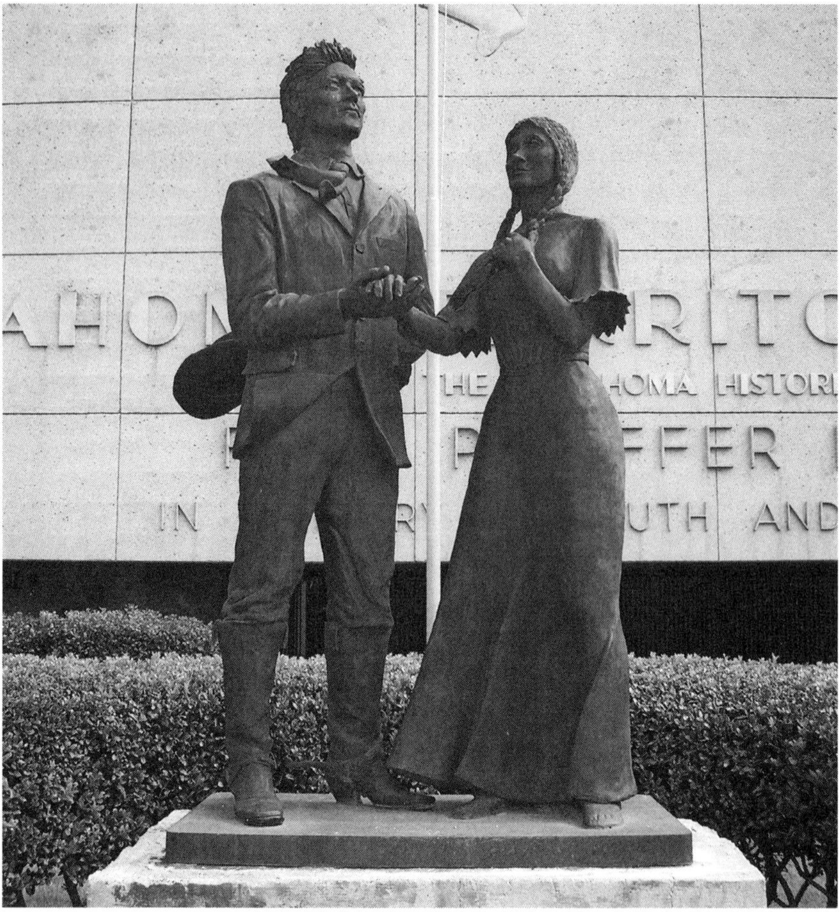

FIGURE 5.7. Frederick A. Olds, *Statehood*, Guthrie, Oklahoma, 1977. Photograph by author.

sculpted by a local artist who also served for fourteen years as director of that museum. In contrast to monuments that would soon appear in Kansas and Montana depicting young white settler couples, Frederick A. Olds's *Statehood* (figure 5.7) portrays a white cowboy and his indigenous bride. The local chamber of commerce's dedication plaque describes the statue as "the symbolic wedding uniting Miss Indian Territory and Mr. Cowboy Oklahoma." This "wedding" between a Native woman, wearing a simple floor-length gown with short sleeves and her hair in two long braids, and a young man dressed in a suit and tie, holding his cowboy hat behind his back—"symbolized the twin territories coming into the union as one state." Like nineteenth-century Canadian fiction about "a happy marriage of French and English who have freely chosen each other," Olds's monument declares the union of diverse indigenous and immigrant tribes of Indian Territory and the white settlers who staked claims to their lands to be a happy one.[70]

The choice to represent the state of Oklahoma as a marital union between an Indian maiden and an Anglo cowboy is telling in ways that the artist and donors likely did not fully recognize. First, the personification of Anglo-Oklahomans as cowboys reflected the influence of Hollywood's Cold War cowboys-and-Indians narrative and the lasting power of cowboy imagery in Oklahoma. By depicting a cowboy rather than a pioneer staking a farm claim, Olds erased the veneration of Pioneer Mothers that persisted in Ponca City. He also erased the role of the oil industry in building Oklahoma in the twentieth century (the very industry that financed Ponca City's beloved statue). And his embodiment of "Indian Territory" in one Indian maiden also hid the complex and often tense relations among the region's indigenous peoples and the Native tribes that had migrated or been forcibly relocated onto those indigenous groups' native ground.

Moreover, the sculpture's marriage metaphor subtly evokes the unequal power relations among those various groups. The active white cowboy is ready to conquer the open range; his more passive bride holds a gentle hand near her heart. But unlike Leo Friedlander's demure 1937 statue for Texas Woman's University (which replaced William Zorach's nude family grouping; see plates I and E), one of the Indian bride's long braids remains between her hand and her heart. Her ethnic traditions thus prevent her from fully becoming a Pioneer Mother yet leave her dependent on her bold white groom. At a time when American women were gaining rights within marriage—such as the right to control their own earnings—this monument drew on more traditional marital relations based in Common Law, in which a husband's rights took precedence over and superseded those of his bride. Likewise in the "marriage" of Native and Anglo-Oklahoma, indigenous peoples had ceded much of their identity and political authority to the Anglo government and business interests. Though Native activism persuaded Oklahomans to erect monuments to indigenous peoples as well as to white pioneers in subsequent decades, the matrimonial image promoted by the museum director and artist persisted in Guthrie. In fact, the town hosted a reenactment of the wedding between Mr. Cowboy Oklahoma and Miss Indian Territory, as well as a reenactment of the land run of 1889, as part of the state's centennial celebration in 2007.[71]

RURAL CONSERVATISM

Conservative cowboy and pioneer imagery also remain particularly powerful in Enid, Oklahoma, the hometown of Cowboy Artist of America Harold T. Holden. Holden sculpted several other heroic-sized western bronzes for towns across Oklahoma and surrounding states, but the greatest concentration of his monumental works are in Enid. In contrast to Leonard McMurry's 1959 Oklahoma City monument, which at a time of nationwide pioneer family commemoration presented land runs as an intergenerational project of laying down roots in the Oklahoma soil, Holden's 1987 *Boomer* depicted a solo man on horseback, racing to stake his claim. Holden's dramatic scene emphasized the land runs as masculine adventures. Of course, the statue also glorified the dispossession of Native peoples—albeit less directly than the social Darwinist monuments erected in California and Utah a century earlier.

While indigenous peoples struggling simply to survive had little recourse to such monuments in the late nineteenth century, local Native individuals offered competing imagery in 1990s Enid. But they did so by hiring the same local cowboy artist whose popular sculptures celebrated white settlement on Indian Territory. In 1994—just after Enid celebrated the centennial of the Cherokee Strip land run and as Portland, Oregon, debated the fate of its controversial *Promised Land* statue—Ponca Indian Isaiah Williams pushed Enid to erect Holden's *Keeper of the Plains* in an effort to balance the many local celebrations of white men claiming indigenous lands. Holden intended *Keeper of the Plains* to be a composite figure representing several Plains tribes.[72] Although that Indian figure was inspired by, dedicated to, and intended to benefit indigenous peoples, popular white conceptions of Indians clearly shaped the sculpture. In contrast to 1890s imagery of mounted horse nomads and more recent mounted Boomers, *Keeper of the Plains* stands tranquilly. Wearing a suit of fringed buckskin and kerchief, Holden's *Keeper of the Plains* wraps himself in a trade blanket and holds out a peace pipe. Both that pipe and his merging of indigenous and Euro-American attire signal his desire to coexist peacefully with white intruders bent on claiming and transforming his Native lands.

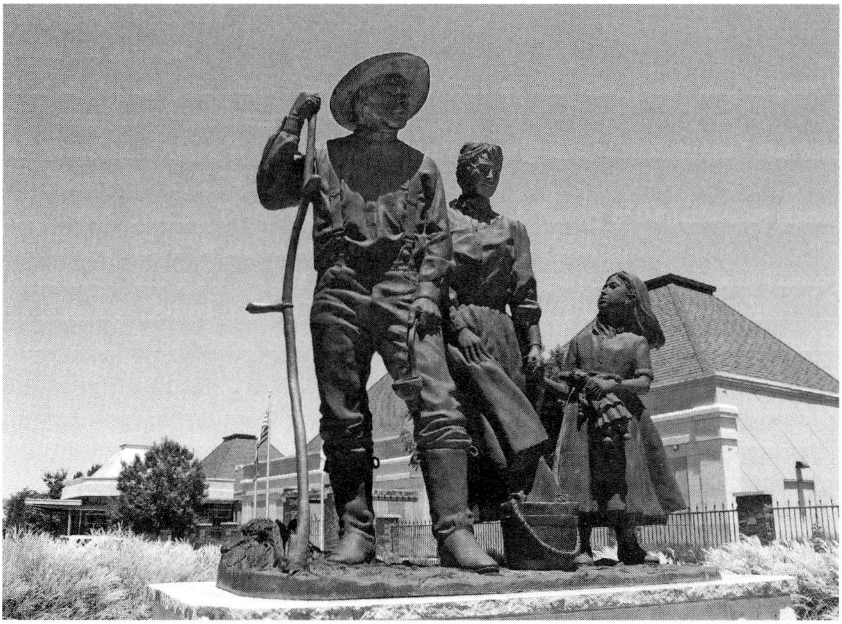

FIGURE 5.8. Harold T. Holden, *The Homesteaders*, Enid, Oklahoma, 2007. Photograph by author.

Two decades later, to celebrate Oklahoma's 2007 statehood centennial, Enid's Cherokee Strip Regional Heritage Center erected a bronze pioneer monument sculpted by the same popular local artist. Holden's *The Homesteaders* was featured—along with *Headin' to Market*, Holden's depiction of a cowboy herding a Texas longhorn—in a 2012 issue of *True West Magazine* highlighting the "53 Statues You Need to See Before You Die."[73] As one might expect from artwork highlighted in a magazine dedicated to the mythic West, Holden's *The Homesteaders* celebrates white settlement (figure 5.8). Like rural Kansas, Montana, and Wyoming pioneer monuments of the 1980s, it emphasizes settlers' hard work and persistence. Rather than emphasizing white men's use of horse-drawn technology, however, Enid's homesteaders labor with hand tools amid a presumably abundant harvest. Where 1950s pioneer family monuments emphasized strapping young sons, *The Homesteaders* highlights feminine nurturance and the persistence of family ties: the mother holds her young daughter's hand, who in turn grasps a rag doll. Although *The Homesteaders* suggests the hard work required to survive on the southern plains, like other western-themed artworks that appear throughout Enid, it also reassures viewers that—despite the diverse Indian tribes that persisted in Oklahoma—white cultural traditions are here to stay.

Enid was far from the only small town in Oklahoma determined to commemorate white settlement. In the two decades leading up to the state's centennial, Oklahoma towns and cities erected an impressive total of eleven monuments (one-fifth of all pioneer monuments erected during those years) commemorating their early white settlers, most of which included pioneer women. Like small towns in northwestern Kansas and eastern Montana a few years earlier, the northern Oklahoma towns of Perry and Newkirk erected monuments by local cowboy artists depicting married couples settling the land. But most white Oklahomans appear to have embraced more active imagery of masculine white Boomers at the turn of the twenty-first century. This was particularly true in Ponca City, home to Bryant Baker's famous *Pioneer Woman* statue.

INDIGENOUS ACTIVISM

Ponca City, Oklahoma, was and is immensely proud of its famous Bryant Baker statue (plate B). But local Native Americans fought efforts to erect a male counterpart to the town's bronze *Pioneer Woman*, and activists in Ponca City and elsewhere in the state erected their own monuments to Oklahoma Indians.

Ponca City residents commissioned a heroic-sized monument to mark the centennial of the Cherokee Outlet land opening, choosing a highly masculine scene to counterbalance its famous *Pioneer Woman*. Local artist Jo Saylor's ten-foot-tall bronze statue of a white cowboy preparing to jump off his rearing horse to stake his claim (figure 5.9) depicted the masculine excitement of the land rush even more dramatically than Enid's *Boomer*. Ponca City's Native American population vocally protested the erection of a statue commemorating white men staking claims to Indian lands. In Ponca City—as in Portland, Oregon, around the same time—protests focused on the artist's title for the work, *This Land Is Mine*, which blatantly ignored prior indigenous and immigrant Indian claims to local lands.

In protesting the monument, Native communities chose to overlook the complex history of intertribal tensions in the former Indian Territory and to embrace a pan-Indian tactic to fighting white incursion into Native lands. Intriguingly, the Poncas, who had been forcibly removed to the

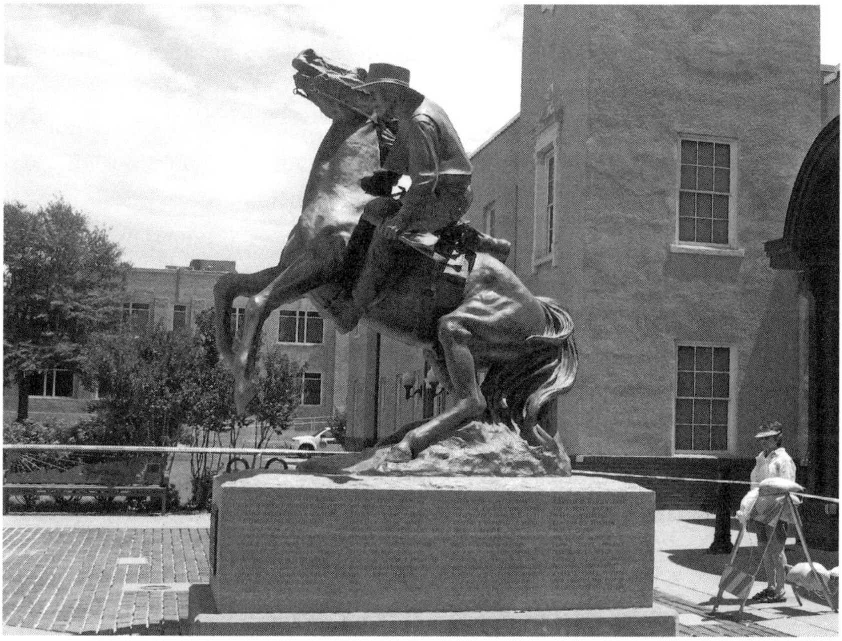

FIGURE 5.9. Jo Saylor, *This Land Is Mine (Centennial Statue)*, Ponca City, Oklahoma, 1993. Photograph by David Prescott.

region in the mid-nineteenth century (and who lent their name to the white town) led public opposition to the Cherokee Outlet land run monument. Ponca tribal member Ed Little Cook was not satisfied by the deletion of the offensive title. Instead, he argued for removal of the statue because it celebrated the theft of Indian lands. The official tribal statement about the statue, penned by Ponca administrative assistant Sherman Bo Warrior, labeled the land runs a form of genocide. The immigrant Cherokees and Ottawas soon joined the fight; tribes that lived in the area prior to forced relocations, who had the strongest historical claim to the area, including the Osages, Tonkawas, Kaws, Pawnees, and Otoe-Missourias, were far less vocal in protesting the land rush monument.[74]

Vocal protest from the local Indian community did persuade the city to remove the offensive title, and to place the statue in a slightly less prominent location. More than three hundred Native protestors sang, chanted, and beat a ceremonial drum nearby as the monument was dedicated without an official title before a crowd of 3,500 in September 1993. Ponca City's centennial committee chair declared flippantly in response to the protestors,

"This is one of the greatest honors. I've never had background music."[75]

Racial tensions surrounding the centennial commemoration persisted long after the statue's dedication. Frustrated with the many Ponca City residents who remained determined to celebrate their white pioneer forebears, the American Indian community chose to erect their own monument and memorial park in which to tell their perspective on local history. Two years after Ponca Isaiah Williams erected a white artist's composite, peaceful Indian figure in Enid, Poncas in Ponca City unveiled Southern Ute / Navajo Cowboy Artist of America Oreland C. Joe's twenty-two-foot-tall statue of Ponca Chief Standing Bear.[76] Standing Bear fought for the Ponca people—and by extension all Native Americans—through the United States legal system. In a landmark 1879 civil rights case in U.S. District Court, Standing Bear argued successfully that Native Americans are defined as persons in relation to federal law and entitled to citizenship rights.[77] Oreland Joe's statue became the centerpiece of sixty-three-acre Standing Bear Park, Museum, and Education Center, which seeks to educate visitors on the culture and history of Native Americans in Oklahoma. It also serves as a memorial to a former residential neighborhood that was razed after a Conoco oil leak contaminated the groundwater on that site.[78]

Other Oklahoma communities less wedded to the imagery of the Pioneer Mother movement also sought to commemorate indigenous peoples at the height of the culture wars. Indigenous activism inspired other Oklahoma communities to erect thirteen monuments to Oklahoma Indians between 1982 and 1996. Of these, seven were sculpted by prominent Native artists to celebrate indigenous cultures. Notably, two works by prominent Chiricahua Apache modernist artist Allan Houser (born Allan Haozous) were erected on the University of Oklahoma campus during this period, just a few years after another Houser depiction of an Indian man extending a peace pipe was placed at the United Nations building in New York City.[79] Two other public outdoor statues erected in Oklahoma during this period depict individuals of Native heritage succeeding in the white-dominated mainstream society. A pair of students at Northern Oklahoma College in Tonkawa sculpted a Native *Graduate* of their institution, wearing an academic cap and gown to symbolize educational opportunity for all people. And a composite figure honoring the state's five indigenous ballerinas was erected in Tulsa to mark the seventy-fifth anniversary of statehood.[80] While most Indian statuary tend to depict indigenous history, these statues declared the importance of Native people to Oklahoma's present and future.

Not all statues depicting Oklahoma Indians were so intentionally inclusive, though. White sculptors' depictions of indigenous leaders—whether produced in the 1920s or the 1990s—ring of tokenism. Efforts to commemorate arguably the most famous Native Oklahoman likewise suggest the limits of white cultural inclusion. Presumably some of the state's twenty-four public sculptures of Will Rogers, who was born in Oklahoma of Cherokee descent and publicly acknowledged his indigenous heritage, were intended to commemorate indigenous heritage as well as the famous actor and humorist. But he is arguably remembered more as a rural American social critic than as an indigenous Oklahoman. Moreover, not all Oklahoma artists even attempted to celebrate Native peoples. For example, Jim Powers's depiction of a local football team's mascot, the Indians, plays on long-held stereotypes. Many of these sculptures of Oklahoma Indians seem aimed at satisfying the mythical PC Police or even reinforcing racial divisions, rather than truly including and honoring indigenous peoples.

MONUMENT WARS

Indigenous figures were common in the earliest pioneer monuments, where noble savages appeared as foil to white civilization. As white westerners grew confident that they had vanquished those vanishing Indians, sculptors of pioneer monuments turned their attention almost exclusively to explicitly white settlers. Amid the culture wars of both the 1920s–1930s and the 1970s–1990s, white westerners erected pioneer monuments to reinforce their cultural dominance. Cold War celebrations of family togetherness and youth as hope for tomorrow fell out of favor as those youth began to protest racism, sexism, and U.S. imperialism. As we saw in this chapter, 1970s efforts at inclusivity soon yielded to highly traditional depictions of white pioneer women and couples persisting in the face of a farm crisis and rapid social change. At the turn of the twenty-first century, pioneer monuments sparked controversy in ethnically diverse and politically progressive communities, while more homogeneous and conservative communities clung to traditional forms of frontier commemoration. Loud protests in Portland and Ponca City challenged, but failed to defeat, determined efforts to erect monuments that enshrine white settler colonialism. Frontier commemoration largely shifted from small towns back to urban areas in the late 1990s, as rural outmigration continued and sprawling suburbs embraced pioneer monuments as a means to attract new visitors and residents—a phenomenon I explore in the next chapter.

CHAPTER 6

MEMORY MAKES MONEY, 1980–2005

Once an important camping site on the Chisholm Trail, the small town of Round Rock, Texas, was transformed by late twentieth-century urban growth into a rapidly growing bedroom community for Austin just twenty miles away. Its relatively abundant land and convenient location just off Interstate 35 made it a logical site for a vast outlet mall. Its chamber of commerce was determined to reinforce local history to attract tourists and homebuyers. Following the example of Dallas and other larger cities, Round Rock invested in an elaborate heroic-sized bronze sculptural installation depicting its cattle-driving history, which had all but been erased by strip malls and housing subdivisions. Sponsored by local families, the statues in *The Crossing* installed in Chisholm Trail Crossing Park honored specific individuals even as they depicted broader groups of white cowboys, pioneer women and children, and longhorn cattle (figure 6.1). By erecting an ever-growing assembly of bronze statues, Round Rock residents sought to inscribe local (white) history permanently on the landscape, with an eye toward shaping community identity and spurring economic growth.

As I have demonstrated, pioneer monuments consistently commemorate early white settlers, but other cultural needs typically provide the spark motivating communities to erect these public statues. Those local motivations varied over time and space, influencing the design of—and public reaction to—these memorials. While the Pioneer Mother movement had occurred primarily in urban centers, and pioneer monumentalization in the 1980s was focused in the rural Great Plains, since the 1990s, it has occurred primarily in suburban locales seeking to shape their community identity and spur further growth.

For the past century, and especially since the 1980s, smaller communities have tried to gain notoriety and attract tourism dollars by creating

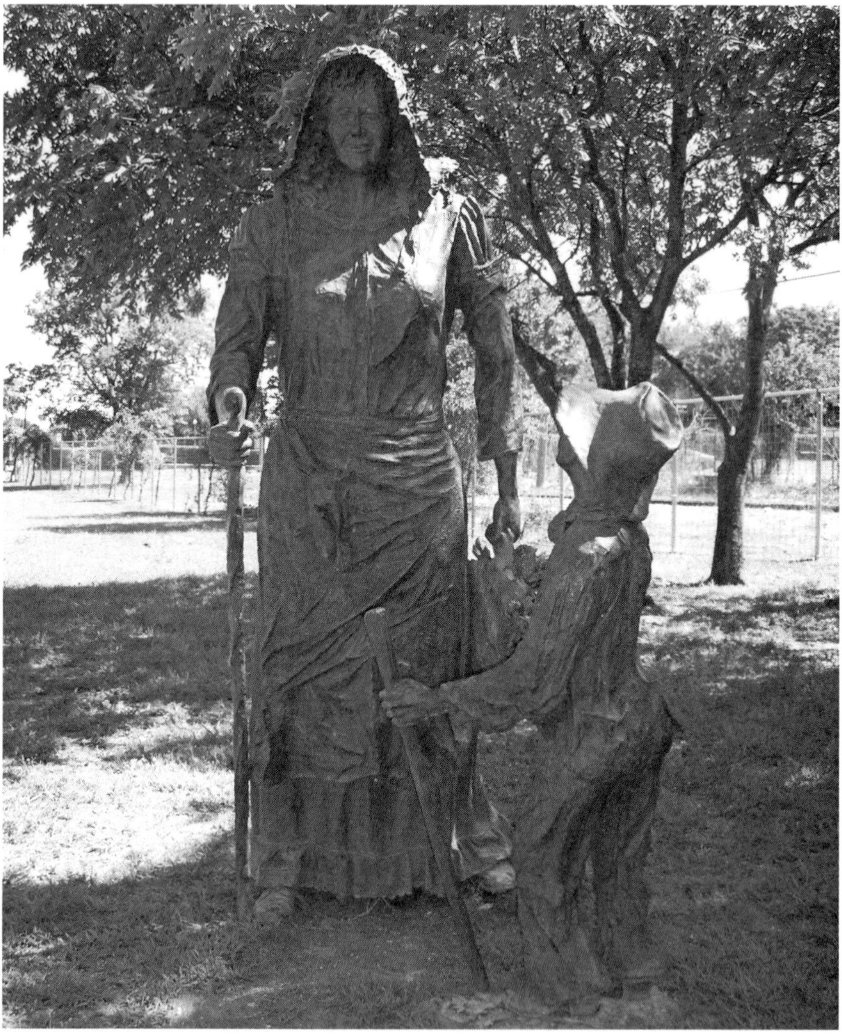

FIGURE 6.1. Jim Thomas, *The Pioneer Woman*. Detail of *The Crossing*, Round Rock, Texas, 2000. Photograph by author.

new *lieux de mémoire* (sites of memory) with an "illusion of authenticity."[1] In the absence of preserved historic structures, they erected reconstructed forts, history museums, and bronze monuments as heritage tourism sites. The National Trust for Historic Preservation defines heritage tourism as "traveling to experience the places, artifacts, and activities that authentically represent the stories and people of the past and present."[2] Where

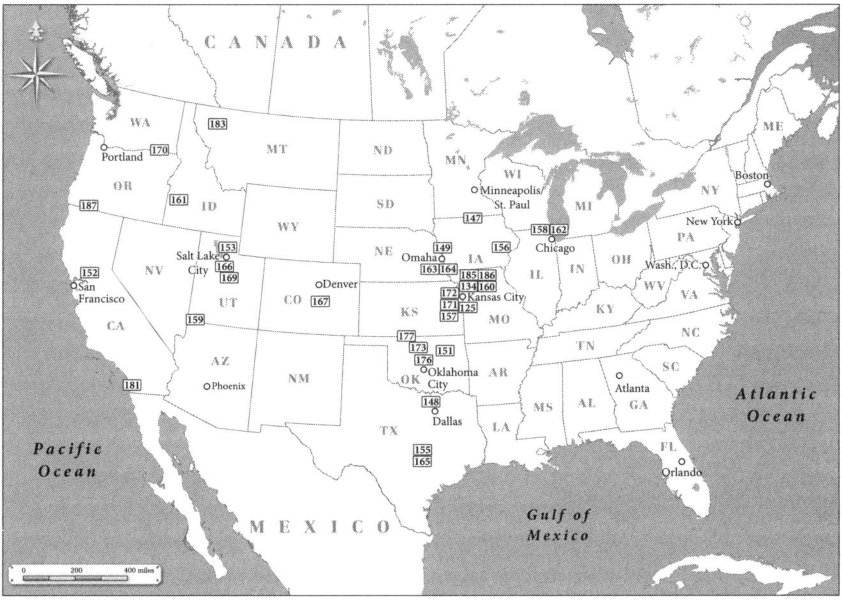

MAP 6. Pioneer Monuments Related to Heritage Tourism. Map by Gerry Krieg. Numbers on the map correspond with a chronological listing of monuments in the appendix.

twentieth-century urban growth had erased any physical evidence of frontier life, erecting pioneer monuments became a way to attract visitors to western locales and to represent local stories—albeit often with questionable authenticity. And in areas where pioneer monuments became common, communities sought to set themselves apart by stealing other communities' monuments or by simply building bigger ones.

Western communities have also embraced another aspect of heritage tourism: "raising awareness for and celebrating the distinct culture of your community."[3] Bronze statues created an illusion of authenticity not only for historic sites, but also new shopping districts and residential neighborhoods. Postwar suburbs embraced pioneer statuary as a means of inventing a distinct identity for communities that many cultural elites dismissed as being "cookie cutter" and soulless. New suburban communities claimed their historicity—and sought to increase property values—by erecting their own pioneer-themed statues, which mimicked those placed at historic sites and in historic downtown areas.

I thus argue that many recent monuments were erected primarily for pragmatic reasons, for towns to differentiate themselves from neighboring towns in order to attract commerce. Monuments attracted tourists interested in western stories and reinforced the historicity of newly constructed museums and suburban subdivisions. Once-bustling frontier towns that feared being swallowed up by sprawling metropolises erected pioneer-themed monuments to declare their historical importance to their region and their distinct identity. Some communities used pioneer monuments to reinforce Anglo-American cultural dominance, while in others, the pioneers' whiteness—like that of their affluent suburban residents—was taken for granted. In many cases, the design of the statue mattered less than its ability to attract visitor attention. In this chapter, I first explore the use of pioneer monuments at historic sites and museums throughout the twentieth century. Then I examine how rival communities vied for shoppers, tourists, and residents by erecting pioneer monuments beginning in the 1980s. Focusing on monuments erected in the Midwest (near Kansas City and Chicago), Texas, and Mormon sites in the Midwest and Utah reveals the many ways in which westerners used pioneer monuments to create a sense of place for the purpose of making money.

MUSEUMS AND MONUMENTS AS SITES OF MEMORY

Heritage tourism and historic preservation developed concurrent with the first Pioneer Mother movement. In the 1920s, prominent Americans like John D. Rockefeller Jr. and Henry Ford embraced efforts to preserve, restore, or reconstruct sites associated with the founding of American democracy and establishment of white American civilization. Efforts to preserve historic structures in Charleston, South Carolina, and to reconstruct colonial Williamsburg, Virginia, for instance, have been well documented.[4] Meanwhile, in the Southwest, as Phoebe Kropp and others have demonstrated, Anglo-American elites invented a Spanish fantasy past to justify their own cultural dominance, which they promoted through the preservation of the California missions and Santa Fe's distinctive architecture.[5] And from the Ohio Valley to the Great Basin, communities reconstructed frontier settlements, like Kentucky's Fort Harrod, or erected stone or bronze monuments to mark locations where forts or log cabins had disappeared in the face of so-called technological and cultural progress. Such reconstructions and associated museums worked together to instruct residents and visitors in local history and cultural values, to justify white settlement of indigenous lands, and, of course, to attract tourist dollars.

Heritage tourism sites—like pioneer monuments—taught visitors to view westward expansion as central to the American national story in a way that justified white dominance and reinforced traditional cultural values. Increasingly, however, those sites also became a means to compete with neighboring communities for commerce. The development of historic preservation aligned fortuitously with—and was spurred by—the rise of automobile tourism. Beginning in the 1920s, and escalating after World War II, communities throughout the West sought to attract automobile tourists and their money. Monuments—whether cast from bronze or, as with Mount Rushmore, literally blasted and carved into the landscape—and history museums could attract significant tourist dollars, particularly when the two appeared together. South Dakota state historian Doane Robinson initially proposed carving portraits of western heroes into the stone of the Black Hills in an effort to attract tourists. But artist Gutzon Borglum envisioned a monument to American imperialism at Mount Rushmore, and inside the mountain from which he carved busts of four American presidents, he planned to build a history museum as a shrine to democracy.[6] Similarly, Avard Fairbanks's proposed design for the *This Is the Place Monument* discussed in chapter 4 included a history museum beneath the base of the shaft. His son Eugene recognized the financial incentive behind this "very ambitious plan": "like all great masterpieces of Art [the artist believed that] it would in time more than pay for itself as a very attractive tourist point of interest."[7] Later preservation and commemoration efforts tended to place pioneer monuments at the entrance to reconstructed historic sites or museums. Regardless of the specific form they took, though, commemoration and economic development efforts were inextricably linked.

For example, local booster and entrepreneur James L. Isenberg drove the reproduction of Kentucky's Fort Harrod Pioneer Memorial State Park for financial gain. Beginning in the 1920s, as John D. Rockefeller reconstructed colonial Williamsburg and Henry Ford created Greenfield Village in Michigan to promote premodern values, Isenberg and several other prominent westerners embraced heritage tourism primarily as an economic strategy. Harrodsburg's claim to being the oldest permanent English settlement in Kentucky succeeded in attracting visitors: an elaborate statewide pageant celebrating its sesquicentennial attracted around twenty-five thousand people in 1924.[8] Isenberg's Kentucky Pioneer Memorial Association then cultivated public and private support from local ancestral organizations, women's clubs, and donors from across the state and beyond to construct a heritage tourism site in Harrodsburg. Like Ford's Greenfield Village, Fort Harrod became an assemblage of historic and reconstructed structures, including a reconstructed fort and a new brick Georgian colonial revival church built to house, protect, and consecrate as a sacred relic the reassembled cabin in which Abraham Lincoln's parents married. Isenberg even persuaded the U.S. Congress to appropriate one hundred thousand dollars at the height of the Great Depression for a large marble memorial by Ulric Ellerhusen (sculptor of the *Pioneer* atop Oregon's 1937 capitol) and for Francis Keally's monument to honor George Rogers Clark and early white settlers of Kentucky, incorporating the iconography of the Pioneer Mother movement.[9]

The pairing of pioneer monuments with historic sites or museums proved an effective way to boost visitation (and thus tourist income), particularly as family road trips became an iconic part of white middle-class life after World War II. In the 1950s, Ponca City, Oklahoma, sought to attract more families by constructing a Pioneer Woman Museum to accompany Bryant Baker's winning *Pioneer Woman* statue (plate B) as a literal reflection of that famous statue. Constructed directly behind the monument, the museum's entryway was lined with shiny copper to mimic the *Pioneer Woman*'s bronze sunbonnet, and the front door was made of mirrored glass to reflect the statue's image for approaching visitors. At the turn of the new millennium, amid renewed anxiety over changing gender roles and a heritage tourism boom, Ponca City greatly expanded the Pioneer Woman Museum. Yet the text of a publication celebrating the Pioneer Woman Museum's fortieth-anniversary grand reopening suggests that the expanded museum's purpose was not so much to curate the lived experiences of frontier women as to further the Pioneer Mother mythology that had grown synonymous with Ponca City. Removing actual frontier women from its narrative, that pamphlet instead animated a disembodied sunbonnet, crediting that article of clothing with bringing white civilization to a savage frontier: "The march of the sunbonnet into the new frontier . . . brought change. It spoke of permanence. . . . The sunbonnet brought fruit trees" and other signs of white civilization and progress.[10] While the museum's exhibits did in fact interpret frontier women's lives, the museum always played a supporting role to Baker's famous statue. Today, in the shadow of the statue stands a good-sized museum gift shop, where visitors can purchase models, postcards, and other souvenirs depicting the statue, and "a sunbonnet to reenact her."[11] Like many other heritage tourism sites, the Pioneer Woman Museum seeks to cash in on visitors to its famous statue as much as it seeks to educate the public or commemorate frontier women.

In nearby Enid, Oklahoma, and elsewhere in recent decades, historical groups have erected other bronze statues to enhance new or expanded history museums. But where the Ponca City museum will likely always play second fiddle to the monument that birthed it, museums like the one in Enid installed new monuments as design elements intended to attract visitation and reinforce the historicity of the museum's exhibits. Chasing heritage tourism dollars transformed Enid's small local museum into a Smithsonian-quality regional heritage center associated with the Oklahoma Historical Society. Once a watering hole on the Chisholm Trail, Enid was established by white settlers in the Cherokee Strip land rush of 1893. Shortly after Ponca City opened its Pioneer Woman Museum, the Sons and Daughters of the Cherokee Strip Pioneers Association established a Museum of the Cherokee Strip on the campus of Phillips University. A new building was constructed in time for the nation's bicentennial. Funded by a combination of state appropriations and private donations, Enid added a new five-thousand-square-foot museum wing and a living-history village featuring four historically significant buildings in time for the centennial of the land rush in 1993. Two decades later, a $10 million partnership with the Oklahoma Historical Society, Sons and Daughters of the Cherokee Strip Pioneers Association, and the Phillips University Legacy Foundation doubled the museum's size. The twenty-four-thousand-square-foot Cherokee Strip Regional Heritage Center now includes five exhibit galleries, a theater, a research center, and a visitor center and gift shop. Renowned Enid artist Harold Holden's heroic bronze *The Homesteaders* (see figure 5.8) stands in front of the expanded museum to lend historical authenticity.[12]

Since the 1990s, communities throughout the Midwest and West have embraced pioneer monuments as a means to enhance the historicity and public appeal of museums and historic sites. Erecting new bronze castings of old sculptures by Avard Fairbanks has become a popular way to attract attention to heritage museums and historic sites from Independence, Missouri, to Boise, Idaho. Similarly, in recent decades two Kansas City suburbs and two Mormon Trail sites constructed new museums related to westward migration that are accompanied by new pioneer monuments. And after Salt Lake City's This Is the Place Heritage Park's privatization, the owners built a new visitor's center, doubled the size of its reconstructed pioneer village, and added bronze monuments. Altogether, 25 of the 185 monuments included in this study (13.5 percent) were erected or now stand adjacent to historic sites or museums. And many more were erected at civic or religious sites that offer historic tours, such as the six pioneer monuments on or near Temple Square in Salt Lake City. Pioneer monuments enhance the credibility of sites where little evidence of local history remains. And while visitors are primarily attracted to the museum exhibits or genealogy research centers, bronze monuments out front declare these modern museums to be not just roadside stops but new lieux de mémoire.

STEALING A STATUE FOR WESTPORT, MISSOURI

Pioneer monuments also enhance towns' and cities' stature. Since the erection of Denver's *Pioneer Monument* in 1911 (see figure 1.2), which sparked controversy for placing a savage Indian above civilized whites, businesspeople have embraced public statues as a means to increase their own importance and to attract customers. Throughout the twentieth century, and especially in the 1980s, Westport, Missouri, sought to cash in on historic association with the Santa Fe and Oregon Trails. It repeatedly sought to boost its own importance and attract tourists by claiming a prominent existing pioneer monument from its much larger neighbor, Kansas City. When those efforts failed, the town became determined to erect a new bronze monument at the heart of its entertainment district but could not agree on the form that statue should take. Whether it commemorated the town's founder, its most famous son, or a victim of a recent tragedy was largely irrelevant, however. What mattered, Westport's residents believed, was that a bronze statue would attract tourist dollars.

When seeking a bronze statue to enhance its downtown business district, like many other midwestern and western towns, Westport instinctively turned to its frontier heritage. Westport is extremely proud of its role in white westward expansion. Established by Indian trader John Calvin McCoy in 1833, Westport was the eastern terminus of the Santa Fe Trail, which carried American freight to Mexico during the mid-nineteenth century, and later served as an outfitting location for the Oregon and California Trails. Its population peaked in 1858 at about two thousand. McCoy, along with thirteen investors, also founded the Town of Kansas at a nearby riverboat landing site; after the Civil War, that town grew dramatically, changing its name to Kansas City. By 1897 Kansas City had annexed the village of Westport, which it had eclipsed. But throughout the twentieth century, Westport residents were determined to maintain their village's distinct identity and insisted that Westport should receive credit as Kansas City's birthplace.[13]

When local resident Howard Vanderslice donated A. Phimister Proctor's larger-than-life bronze equestrian *Pioneer Mother* grouping (plate C) to Kansas City in 1927, Westport residents believed that the statue should be installed in their community. Seeing an opportunity to promote local commerce and their community's stature relative to its much larger neighbor, Westport business leaders and the Daughters of Old Westport urged Kansas City's park board to place the massive sculptural group on a minute trolley island at the heart of Westport's business district, which had been the site of their original town. Apparently dissatisfied with the bronze *Pioneer Mother* bas-relief by prominent artist Merrell Gage, which the Daughters of Old Westport had recently installed, the Westport groups were determined to also acquire the colossal equestrian group in lieu of the large stone tribute to the Santa Fe Trail that local businessmen had originally envisioned. They insisted that Westport's location on the old Santa Fe Trail (which was built for commercial traffic to Hispanic New Mexico, rather than Anglo-American overland migration) made it the most suitable location for Proctor's sculpture of a westering Anglo family.[14] In the end, though, the artist's and donor's preference that the statue be placed on a hilltop in the much larger Penn Valley Park closer to downtown Kansas City prevailed.

But the frontier trading post turned Kansas City suburb remained determined to claim its place in local history. In 1950, as Kansas City was preparing to celebrate its centennial, it asked Westport to contribute a western scene. As part of those commemoration efforts, the newly organized Westport Historical Society placed a permanent ox-yoke historical marker near the extant Daughters of Old Westport marker, on the small traffic island where Westport groups had sought to place Proctor's *Pioneer Mother* a quarter century earlier. Westport was largely overlooked as postwar Kansas City expanded rapidly around it, but a local real estate developer bought up old buildings in the area, eventually forming Westport Square surrounding the island, which became known as Heritage Park.[15]

In 1984—as communities in the rural West were staking claims to their westernness by erecting pioneer monuments, and urban and suburban areas were increasingly seeking to cash in on heritage tourism—Westport village merchants, led by advertising agent Tom Tupper, once again sought to claim Proctor's equestrian grouping for their business district. The Westport Tomorrow organization argued that the famous statue had been ignored by Kansas City residents for decades in the vast Penn Valley Park. Tupper declared that the "gigantic statue" was only viewed "by about 16 people a year—if they can find it."[16] Instead, the Westport business leaders proposed to move it to Heritage Park to commemorate Westport's 150th anniversary—and, opportunistically, in memory of a Westport resident and civic volunteer who had been among the 114 killed when the skywalk of Kansas City's Hyatt Regency hotel had collapsed near Proctor's *Pioneer Mother* monument in 1981. Paralleling Salem, Oregon, residents' proposals to build a golf course or purchase a new ambulance with Carroll Moores's bequest instead of erecting a pioneer monument, Tupper suggested that private donations to that victim's memorial fund should cover the estimated fifty-thousand-dollar cost to move the statue. Westport's business and political leaders endorsed the plan, but the Kansas City Parks and Recreation Board of Commissioners (and at least a few community members) seemed unconvinced by Westport's claims to greater historicity. The park board voted unanimously to leave the statue where Proctor had placed it a half century earlier, overlooking the 1926 Liberty Memorial (home to the National World War I Museum) and downtown Kansas City.[17]

Having failed once again to claim the Proctor *Pioneer Mother* grouping, many local residents supported erecting a new monument to attract visitors to the district's shops and restaurants. Pointing out that "most cities build tourism around their historic sites and buildings," one letter to the editor of the *Kansas City Times* proposed that Kansas City focus its tourism around "the jewel of historic 'Old Westport,'" insisting, "Promoting history for tourism could pay great dividends as well as boost civic pride."[18] The *Kansas City Star* agreed that creating a park on the narrow triangle of land in question would attract tourists, and historian and Westport Historical Society archivist Fred L. Lee insisted, "The eventual goal of that statuary is to promote tourism, a way to tell people and make them aware of our city's history."[19] But if Kansas City was unwilling to give up its long-forgotten *Pioneer Mother*, what form should Westport's new statue take?

Residents expressed competing visions for a new sculpture on the former trolley island. A small group seeking to commemorate prominent artist and former Westport resident Thomas Hart Benton raised one hundred thousand dollars in private donations to place a Benton statue in that location, and the Westport City Council added eighty thousand dollars in community development funds. Advertiser Tom Tupper and the Old Westport Improvement Association, which had initially sought to relocate the 1927 *Pioneer Mother*, quickly became strong proponents of the Benton statue. But Westport Historical Society members and other local western heritage societies remained committed to commemorating Westport's mid-nineteenth-century heyday. Rejecting the Benton statue proposal, they insisted that a monument to fur trader and Westport founder John Calvin McCoy should stand on the historic site. Many Westport residents seemed to view widely varied heroic statuary as broadly interchangeable. Kansas City's park board refused to be "the bad guys" by choosing between the Benton and McCoy camps. Park board president L. P. Cookingham, who was also a historical society member, finally brokered a compromise, recommending a different location several blocks away for the Benton statue, which cleared a path for erecting a monument to John C. McCoy and Westport's frontier past on the triangular traffic island.[20]

The completed pioneer statue by Kansas City cowboy artist Thomas L. Beard declared Westport's (and McCoy's) centrality to westward expansion by commemorating famous businessmen with ties to the area. As Patricia Limerick's *Legacy of Conquest* opened the public's eyes to New Western historians' darker perspective on the nineteenth-century West, Beard's statue was dedicated in October 1987 with elaborate pageantry evoking the Old West. Reflecting the influence of Westport's business community and contemporary culture's emphasis on promoting commerce, *Pioneer Square Monument* featured three prominent white businessmen who had connections to mid-nineteenth-century Westport: fur trader and Westport

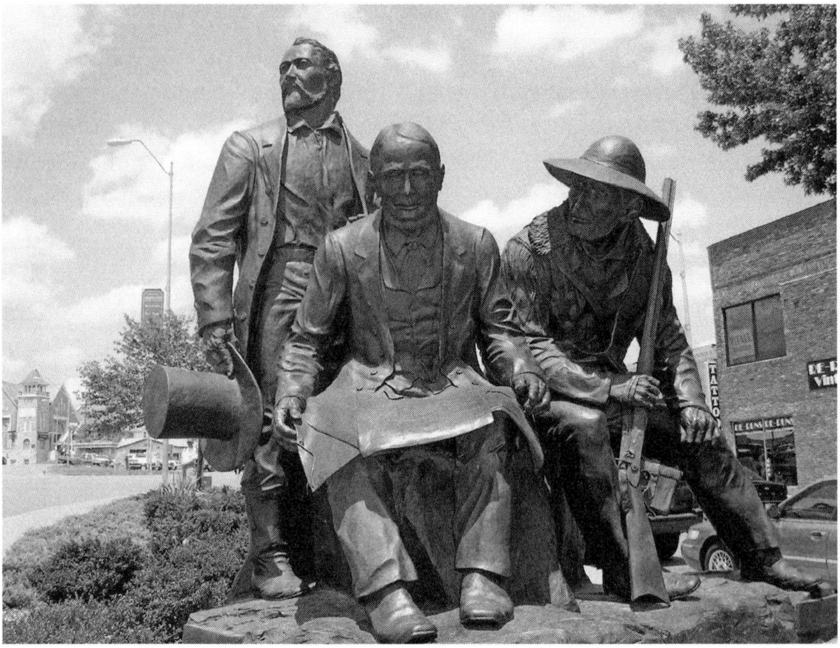

FIGURE 6.2. Thomas Beard, *Pioneer Square Monument,* Westport, Missouri, 1985. Photograph by author.

founder John C. McCoy (as initially proposed), plus Westport businessman and cofounder of the Pony Express Alexander Majors and western merchant and mountain man Jim Bridger, who retired to Westport in the 1850s (figure 6.2). Bridger's fringed buckskin coat and rifle mark him as a rugged frontiersman; an accompanying plaque identifies him as "an Indian fighter, fur trapper and trader, guide to the Far West, U.S. Army scout and explorer." He sits slightly behind McCoy, listening intently to the fur trader turned businessman. In contrast, Majors's upright posture, long coat, and top hat identify him as a successful businessman, but his informal work shirt reminds viewers of his earlier years hauling freight on the Santa Fe Trail. He gazes off into the distance, indicating his focus on future opportunities farther west. Central character John C. McCoy is dressed formally in a three-piece suit, thin neck bow, collared dress shirt, and pocket watch. His identifying plaque calls the surveyor "the father of Kansas City" and declares, "But always, he was a realtor and a builder." Although the three men were contemporaries, Thomas Beard's sculpture teaches that Bridger and Majors prepared the way for McCoy, just as white frontiersmen and traders—and, Westport residents insisted, the village of Westport—paved the road to urban development in Kansas City and throughout the West. The statue beautifies an awkward traffic island and enhances the village's claims to historical significance, competing for shoppers and diners against crosstown rivals such as Independence.

COMPETING CLAIMS TO HISTORICAL SIGNIFICANCE IN KANSAS CITY

Just as Westport competed with Kansas City for Proctor's famous *Pioneer Mother* grouping, Westport, Independence, and other Kansas City suburbs competed for regional stature and tourist income by erecting their own monuments to western trails, making them a particularly clear example of how midwestern and western towns competed as sites of frontier heritage. In the 1840s—while Kansas City was little more than a speculator's dream—Westport had competed with the nearby town of Independence for trade outfitting overlanders. Then as heritage tourism expanded dramatically in the 1980s, Westport and Independence once more competed for the title of Oregon Trail jumping-off point. But this time, instead of selling oxen and flour, the rival suburbs marketed historicity. Kansas City and its suburbs erected fourteen pioneer monuments altogether (7.6 percent of the 185 included in this study), ten of which were placed in suburban locations since 1985. As forced school desegregation and the 1980s drug wars fueled white flight from increasingly minority-dominated and presumably crime-ridden urban cores to wealthier—and lily white—suburbs, Kansas City's affluent suburbs erected monuments celebrating white pioneer settlement. Just a few years after Westport erected its *Pioneer Square Monument,* Independence, which called itself the Queen City of the Trails, built a five-thousand-square-foot National Frontier Trails Museum. Independence staked a claim to David Manuel's *The Promised Land* (plate N), which had sparked such controversy in Portland, Oregon, and placed the bronze *The Pioneer Woman* statue in its courtyard (figure 6.3).[21] When that monument was later stolen, Independence moved quickly to replace it (figure 6.4) *and* to erect its casting of Avard Fairbanks's popular 1924 *Old Oregon Trail* relief. Meanwhile, two other Kansas City suburbs erected monuments claiming their own connections to the western trails. The town of Olathe constructed a ten-thousand-square-foot heritage center to

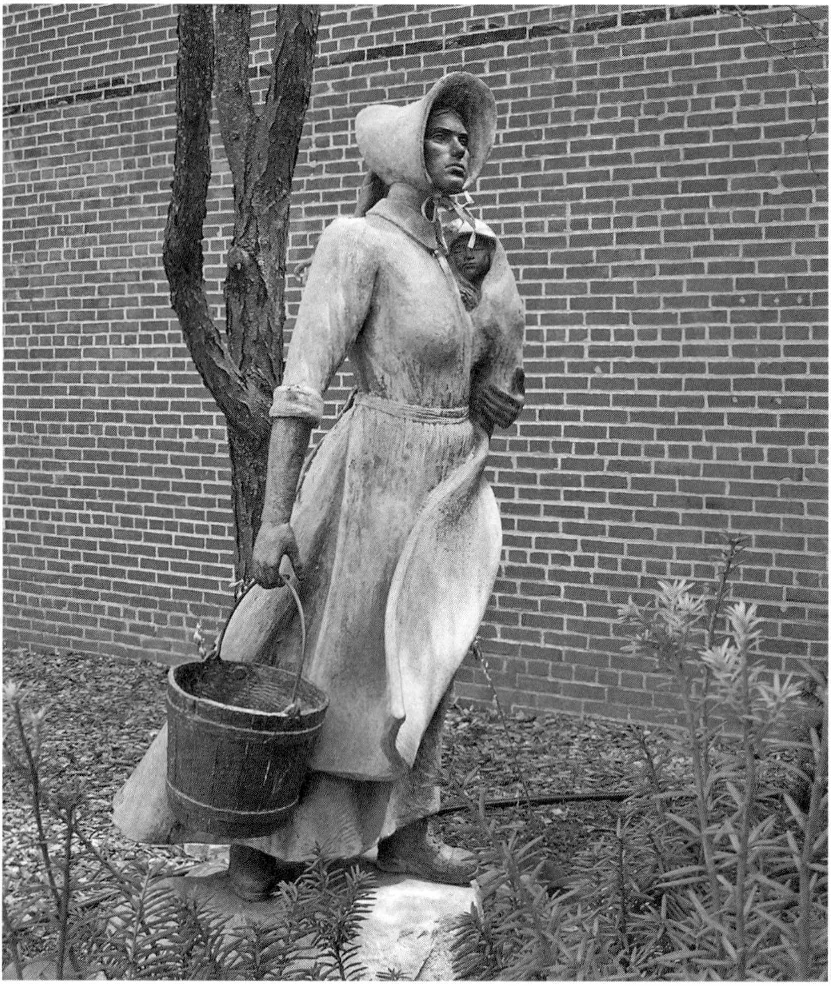

FIGURE 6.3. Juan Lombardo-Rivera, *The Pioneer Woman,* Independence, Missouri, 1990–2013. Photograph by author.

accompany the Mahaffie Stagecoach Stop and Farm historic site, erected a sixty-foot-long bronze stagecoach relief by local artist Kwan Wu (see figure 7.6), and installed metal cutouts of a farm wagon and covered wagon on a nearby overpass.

Nearby Shawnee, Kansas, followed suit, erecting an enormous sculpture of a wagon train. Some residents questioned spending nearly a million dollars to convert a used car lot into a 2.2-acre park featuring stone and bronze sculptures of a wagon master and wagon train along a

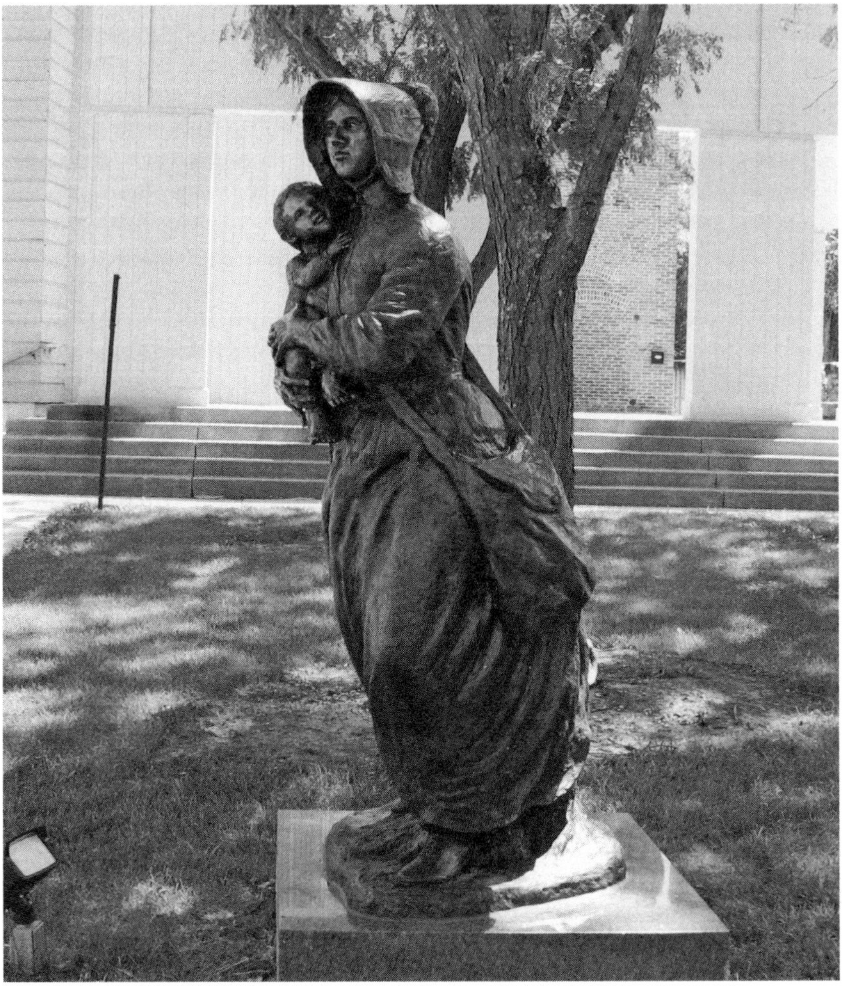

FIGURE 6.4. Charles Goslin, *Pioneer Woman*, Independence, Missouri, 2016. Photograph by David Prescott.

busy highway, but city leaders were determined to stake their own claim to historicity to mark the town's 2006 centennial. Viewed from automobiles speeding down Shawnee Mission Parkway to hop on I-35 into downtown Kansas City, the enormous installation lends both artistry and a sense of historicity—should drivers bother to take a look. While Westport's *Pioneer Square Monument* encourages shoppers and diners to linger, and Olathe's *Going West on the Old Santa Fe Trail* lends an air of permanence and historicity to its migration-themed museum and historic site, Shawnee's

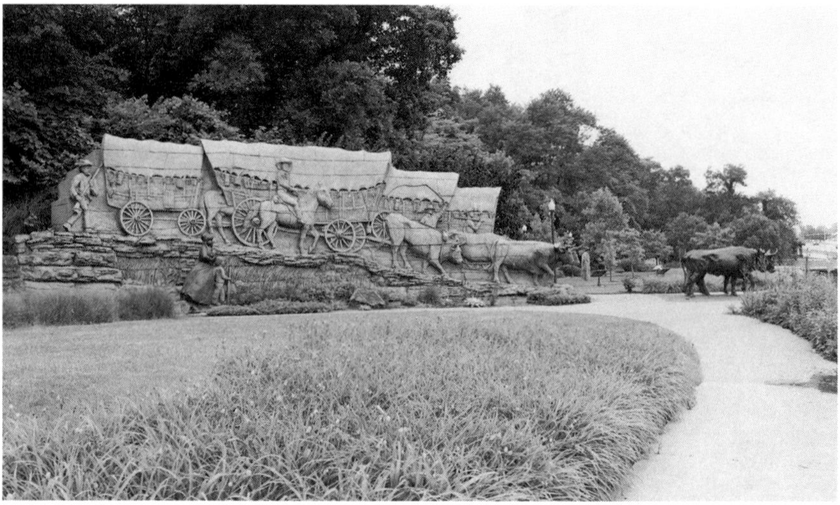

FIGURE 6.5. Charles Goslin, *Pioneer Crossing*, Shawnee, Kansas, 2006. Photograph by author.

much larger and more impressionistic Charles Goslin installation, *Pioneer Crossing*, seems out of place among surrounding office parks and fast food restaurants (figure 6.5). Shawnee's new park features a convenient parking lot adjacent to the monuments, but its excellent playground is accessible only by climbing a flight of fifty-seven stairs and appears to be used primarily by neighboring families who likely never descend to view the monuments. As of June 2017, the only consumer review the park had received on its 2009 *Yelp* page judged it worthy of 2.5 out of 5 possible stars, and noted, "A million for the sculptures? Hmmm."[22] While Goslin's outsized *Dick Williams, Wagon Master* and *Pioneer Crossing* monuments fit well with local white cultural identity, they do not appear to be competing successfully with more popular works in rival Kansas City suburbs. Meanwhile, the larger cities of Omaha and Oklahoma City competed to erect the largest bronze sculptural installation—monuments that dwarfed both Kansas City's alternately prized and forgotten *Pioneer Mother* equestrian group and Shawnee's large wagon train.

SIZE MATTERS

Just as Shawnee sought to outmuscle other Kansas City suburbs by building a bigger pioneer monument, sizable cities in neighboring

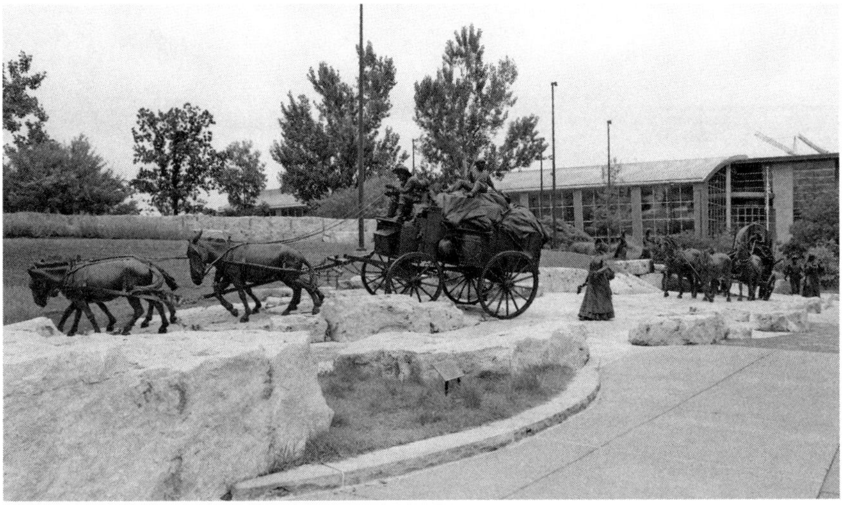

FIGURE 6.6. Blair Buswell and Edward Fraughton, detail of *Pioneer Courage*, Omaha, Nebraska, 2003. Photograph by author.

states seemed determined to out-monumentalize the entire Kansas City metropolitan area (and each other) by erecting even more enormous statues depicting westward migration amid this nationwide resurgence in pioneer commemoration. Two hundred miles north of Kansas City in Omaha, Nebraska, First National Bank chairman Bruce Lauritzen sought to honor the courage and determination of local pioneers (including his great-grandfather) and to add green space to the company's headquarters campus by turning five downtown city blocks into sculpture parks. A covered wagon train stretching the length of an American football field startles a herd of bison. The bison flee along downtown streets and through neighboring office buildings into another park, where they in turn frighten a flock of geese from a pond, which fly into the First National headquarters atrium. Utah sculptors Edward Fraughton (who studied art under traditionalist pioneer sculptor Avard Fairbanks) and Blair Buswell worked with landscape architects to design *Pioneer Courage* (figure 6.6), the heroic-sized bronze sculptures of an entire wagon company that fill an entire city block. Intended as a tribute to "the tenacity and the inventiveness of the pioneer spirit that opened the West" and to beautify the downtown area, Omahans immediately saw commercial opportunities serving tourists expected to visit the sculpture parks.[23]

Not to be outdone, Oklahoma City, Oklahoma, located 350 miles in

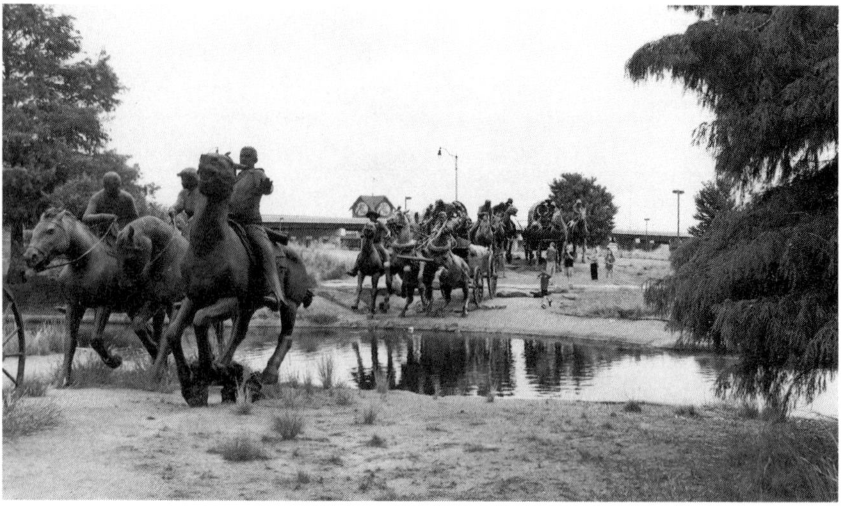

FIGURE 6.7. Paul Moore, detail of *Brand New State (Centennial Land Run Monument)*, Oklahoma City, Oklahoma, 2007. Photograph by Anna Prescott.

the opposite direction from Kansas City and increasingly surrounded by pioneer monuments in smaller, whiter Oklahoma towns, embarked on its own ambitious ten-year project. Apparently determined to outdo Omaha's 125 percent-sized wagon train and wildlife installations and to compete with suburban Kansas City for heritage tourism visitation, Oklahoma City erected forty-five 150 percent-sized bronze figures depicting Oklahoma's 1889 land run along the Bricktown Canal, which separates the redeveloped Bricktown entertainment district from downtown Oklahoma City (figure 6.7). Part of a major urban renewal effort, the $5.1 million public art project commemorated Oklahoma's statehood centennial and sought to attract tourists. Placed adjacent to Bricktown's high-density commercial zone, Paul Moore's *Brand New State (Centennial Land Run Monument)* declares that the 1889 land run and resulting white pioneer settlement formed the foundation for modern development. Tourists visiting the local hotels, shops, and restaurants can walk along the canal or ride in water taxis to the monument, which freezes the moment of initial white settlement of the Oklahoma prairie in bronze.[24] Some complain that it is too hidden to succeed in attracting tourists, but it—like Omaha's *Pioneer Courage*—has received primarily rave reviews on tourism websites. As of June 2017, it ranked 6th out of 126 things to do in Oklahoma City on TripAdvisor, receiving an average of 4.5 out of 5 stars in 328 consumer reviews.[25] Similar competitions for historic pride—and potential tourism dollars—occurred in smaller communities lying outside other bustling metropolises in the late twentieth century. In fact, tourism income enabled one community to erect a pioneer monument some seventy years in the making.

NEW MEANING FOR AN OLD MONUMENT

Elgin, Illinois, hoped to cash in on heritage tourism, but rather than competing in terms of size, it sought to resurrect the Pioneer Mother movement. In Elgin, failed 1920s efforts to enshrine pioneer values found new life—and new meaning—in the 1990s thanks to pseudo-historic entertainment tourism and efforts to grapple with the city's growing cultural diversity. In the late 1920s, Elgin's mayor had asked local sculptor Trygve Rovelstad to sculpt a pioneer family monument for the mill town turned manufacturing center located west of Chicago. But fundraising efforts languished during the Great Depression, and like most communities, Elgin lost interest in pioneer monuments after World War II. Yet Rovelstad and his supporters remained determined to see his vision to fruition. Rovelstad's dream of commemorating Elgin's early white settlers was finally realized after the sculptor's death amid a new wave of immigration to what had become a Chicagoland edge city. In the 1990s, income from gambling on a faux-historic riverboat permanently docked near the site of Elgin's former watch factory enabled the declining manufacturing center to transform itself into an entertainment tourism site. Rovelstad's long-forgotten *Pioneer Family Memorial* (plate G) became the centerpiece of urban renewal efforts aimed at luring riverboat gamblers to linger longer in the town. Combined with a sculpted American flag on nearby Walton Island, Rovelstad's statue declared the increasingly ethnically diverse city to be the modern realization of white settler values. Thus a Pioneer Mother movement statue was reinvented as the centerpiece of twenty-first-century urban renewal and a lesson in white American cultural values, as the Watch City sought to reinvent itself as the City in the Suburbs at the dawn of the new millennium.

Elgin's efforts to commemorate white settlers started as the town lost its nineteenth-century prominence. Founded by Yankee settlers in 1835 shortly after the Indian Removal Act of 1830 and the 1832 Black Hawk

Indian War expelled Native Americans from their homes in the area, by the early 1840s Elgin was a bustling mill town. The town enjoyed even greater prosperity during the 1850s, when it was temporarily the western terminus of the railroad, thirty-eight miles west of Chicago. Its wealth and influence peaked in the late nineteenth century, when a large watch factory thrived in Elgin, attracting relatively assimilable western European immigrant laborers, and two Elgin-based firms controlled creameries stretching from Wisconsin to Iowa.[26]

Elgin's regional influence was already in decline in the 1920s when the mayor approached Rovelstad—an Elgin artist who had studied under and worked for prominent Chicago artist Lorado Taft and would become an internationally known artist in his own right—to sculpt a portrait of the town's founder. Rovelstad, apparently inspired by the Pioneer Mother movement to which his mentor and many other prominent artists had contributed, instead envisioned a pioneer family group accompanied by an Indian scout to celebrate the pioneering spirit and white civilization. After commissioning Rovelstad to sculpt the pioneer monument in 1935, city officials changed their minds, opting instead to erect a log cabin replica similar to those erected at Harrodsburg, Kentucky, and other western communities. But Rovelstad remained determined to pursue his own vision for an Elgin pioneer monument.[27]

As his hometown struggled in the 1930s, Rovelstad's efforts to erect his pioneer monument also floundered. A Great Depression–era relief grant was later withdrawn, and amid widespread unemployment, sales of twenty-five thousand half-dollar coins commemorating Elgin's centennial proved limited.[28] Elgin's watch industry collapsed in the 1950s, furthering the town's decline even as new suburban development boomed in the surrounding area. Yet Trygve Rovelstad remained determined to complete his pioneer monument, forming the Pioneer Memorial Foundation (PMF) in 1957. The aging sculptor finally completed his masterpiece in gold-painted plaster of Paris with his daughter's assistance only five years before his death in 1990.[29] As suburban housing developments popped up seemingly overnight around Elgin after World War II, and despite receiving federal funding to help build a modern civic center in the 1960s, Elgin's businesses struggled to compete with nearby suburban malls. But shortly after Rovelstad's death, Elgin received aid from an unlikely source. In 1993 Elgin was selected as a riverboat gambling site by the Illinois Gaming Board. The *Grand Victoria* soon became the state's largest and most profitable riverboat, employing 1,600 people (many of them people of color), attracting 10,000 visitors per day, and generating $180 million dollars per year in revenue.[30]

Economic growth—fueled first by manufacturing in the 1880s and 1890s, and later by entertainment tourism in the 1990s—transformed the ethnic makeup of the city and fueled renewed interest in white pioneer commemoration. Elgin had remained over 95 percent white from the 1840s through the early 1960s.[31] Yet that statistic masks substantial ethnic diversity at the city's heyday. Manufacturing jobs attracted western European immigrants, roughly half of them from Germany. As of 1900, one-quarter of the city's 22,433 population were European immigrants, and another third were native-born children of immigrants.[32] But 1920s immigration restrictions combined with declining job opportunities discouraged further settlement. By the time the watch industry collapsed sixty years later, less than 6 percent of Elgin's population was foreign born. But the 1965 Immigration and Nationality Act soon abolished national origin quotas favoring western Europeans, and manufacturing jobs gradually returned to the city. While wealthier neighboring suburbs such as Schaumburg attracted white flight and remained predominantly Anglo-American, working-class Elgin grew more diverse beginning in the 1970s, attracting significant immigration from Mexico and Latin America, and smaller numbers of refugees from southeast Asia. *Money* magazine even selected Elgin as a "mirror of America" because of "its ethnic diversity and blend of urban, rural and suburban influences."[33] Whereas immigrants had once landed in Chicago and later moved to the suburbs, in the twenty-first century, suburbs like Elgin and neighbors Carpentersville and Aurora have become gateway communities for immigrants from Latin America.[34] By 2000 Elgin was only 70 percent white, and 34 percent identified as Hispanic or Latino; a decade later, it was 43.6 percent Hispanic or Latino.[35] In sharp contrast, nearby elite communities like Schaumburg largely remain bastions of wealthy white privilege.

The racial diversity attracted by industrial and tourism industry jobs appears to have fueled renewed interest in Trygve Rovelstad's tribute to white settler colonialism in Elgin. Rovelstad had long been associated with patriotism in the city. The artist sculpted an enormous concrete American flag and flagpole that stood on Elgin's Walton Island from the 1930s to the

1960s, declaring the community's patriotism even as the local economy failed to participate in the nation's economic growth. When Rovelstad's concrete flag was destroyed by high water in 1970, the city quickly replaced it with a giant painted steel American flag created by David Powers, reminding Elgin residents—and particularly newly arrived immigrants—of their place within the nation.[36] Then in the 1990s, riverboat gambling saved the city economically but seemingly challenged the traditional American value of hard work. While the casino fought a class-action lawsuit charging that it discriminated against African Americans when hiring relatively highly paid dealers, the city chose to make a heroic-sized bronze casting of Rovelstad's pioneer family grouping the visual centerpiece of its massive riverfront redevelopment project.[37] Replacing Rovelstad's Pioneer Mother movement–style bas reliefs of pioneer life with a simple landscaped base, and moving the statue from the site of Elgin's first log cabin to an urban plaza overlooking a giant American flag, shifted the monument's emphasis from 1920s local frontier memory to celebrating the increasingly diverse city as a hardworking all-American community with traditional (white, middle-class) family values.

The intervening decades' changing attitudes toward western history inspired the public to interpret the finished statue (plate G) in ways that were at odds with Rovelstad's intended meaning. Rovelstad gave his "scout" a beard, fringed buckskin suit, moccasins, and bowie knife to distinguish him from the clean-shaven male settler dressed in broadcloth and boots. Ignoring the scout's Anglo-American features, twenty-first-century viewers accustomed to multiculturalism interpreted the bearded man as honoring indigenous knowledge of their lands as well as the settlers who claimed the land as their own. A *Chicago Tribune* article characterized the statue as depicting "three phases of pioneer America": a scout representing the Indian past, followed by a pioneer man with his wife and baby, and a pioneer youth representing the future.[38] And the PMF president's interpretation seemed informed by postwar pioneer family monuments: "The mother, holding her baby, looks on with love, and the scout bravely looks to the unknown territories. The youth looks to the knowledge of the past to prepare for the future."[39] Rovelstad's design did not change substantially in the seventy years between its conception and erection, but it allowed space for more recent viewers to read into it assurance of their own cultural values.

Some local residents cheered the much-belated completion and installation of the statue. An acquaintance of the late artist declared, "I thank God for this every day when I come to take the train to Chicago."[40] But even individuals not acquainted with the late artist seemed to appreciate the statue. An Elgin journalist—and relative newcomer to the community—described it as "a powerful symbol of Elgin's past" that "is the centerpiece of the city's rebirth along the riverfront."[41]

With the help of gambling income, Rovelstad's statue became a centerpiece of Elgin's rebirth as the City in the Suburbs. While the city's promotional materials today celebrate Elgin's status as the second most diverse city in Illinois, unease over that growing diversity appears to have helped fuel local residents' support for erecting the monument.[42] Installing Rovelstad's 1930s monument to white settler colonialism overlooking a steel American flag provided a way for Elgin to promote white American culture amid the city's growing ethnic diversity. And placing the early twentieth-century statue amid an early twenty-first-century urban greenway enabled Elgin to celebrate its nineteenth-century regional dominance while luring Chicagoland gamblers coming to its faux-historic riverboat to linger and perhaps even settle onshore in the edge city. While Elgin celebrated and reinvented its long history with a resurrected pioneer monument by its famous local artist, neighboring Schaumburg sought to invent history where there was none by buying generic cowboy art.

NEW (SUB)URBANISM

After decades of decline, Elgin now actively seeks to portray itself as a historic City in the Suburbs to set itself apart from the many postwar housing developments in Chicago's northwest suburbs. But only one year after Elgin finally erected Rovelstad's *Pioneer Family Memorial*, the neighboring postwar Chicago suburb of Schaumburg dedicated its own bronze pioneer grouping as part of a concerted effort to prove that it was not the epitome of suburban sprawl, as it was rapidly becoming known. Where Elgin had fought long and hard to erect a monument to pioneer values, Schaumburg's frontier-themed statues were selected as one relatively minor piece of a larger public art project that conveniently contributed to the village's invented history. Just as vacation destinations such as Southern California and Colorado's high country "packaged" their leisure attractions for tourists, Schaumburg and other midwestern suburbs marketed a careful merging of urban, suburban, and rural life, and of past and present that disguised parallels between suburbanization and settler colonialism.[43] Indeed, Lorenzo Veracini argues that suburbia reenacts settlement.[44] And much of American suburban growth since the 1970s has been fueled by white flight. I argue that, like many other bedroom communities surrounding western metropoles, Schaumburg embraced pioneer monuments in the late twentieth century to enhance the town's historicity to attract tourists and increase the appeal of modern subdivisions. But even its efforts to invent a unique history ultimately relied on reproducing forms and imagery borrowed from elsewhere.

Located just east of Elgin and thirty miles from Chicago, the village of Schaumburg was also settled in the mid-nineteenth century. Because it was bypassed by the railroad line that caused Elgin to boom, however, Schaumburg remained a small farming village for more than a century. When it finally incorporated in 1956, the village still claimed only 130 residents. But the expansion of Chicago's O'Hare Field into a major airport midway between Schaumburg and downtown Chicago and the construction of the Northwest Tollway in the mid-1950s transformed Schaumburg into a desirable suburban area. After a second expressway linked Schaumburg to Chicago and to other suburbs in 1970, Schaumburg became Illinois's second largest retailer center and an edge node encouraging further suburban sprawl.[45] By 1980, Schaumburg's population exceeded 50,000, nearly all of them white, and the village boasted several major shopping centers—including Woodfield Mall, which for a time was the world's largest enclosed shopping mall—and lots of office space.[46] Efforts to resettle African American households from the notorious Cabrini Green housing projects near downtown Chicago to the job-rich suburb elicited anxiety among the far wealthier and whiter population of Schaumburg, but did little to affect its ethnic makeup. A few years later, Schaumburg's leaders announced proudly on the village's website that their residents were "more racially homogeneous" and "better educated" than those of the region overall.[47]

In many ways, Schaumburg is the epitome of a postwar suburb. As American cities grew in the late twentieth century, they sprawled out into ever larger and more distant single-family tract homes erected on former farmland. Previously isolated small towns and villages—many of them originally farming communities—were transformed into bedroom communities or edge nodes populated almost entirely by commuters. Suburbs constructed in the late 1940s and 1950s—like New York's famous Levittown—typically featured grid patterns of practically identical homes. Vast shopping plazas and climate-controlled shopping malls replaced downtown department stores and corner markets.[48] But by the late twentieth century, American suburbanites had begun to rebel against cookie-cutter suburbs. They increasingly embraced "new urbanism," which sought to reinvent city life by building vibrant urban, exurban, or edge node communities. New urbanist housing developments and shopping plazas sought to replicate desirable aspects of the nineteenth-century downtown areas that these suburban shopping districts had supplanted. In their efforts to combat suburban sameness, many of these new urbanist communities came to closely resemble one another.[49] This was particularly true in Schaumburg, which became so closely associated with suburban placelessness that people in other places even began to use the suburb's name as a verb: "We don't want to Schaumburgize our town."[50] Schaumburg soon turned to cowboy art as a means to differentiate itself from its neighbors and to shed its vanilla reputation.

Schaumburg's residents became determined to set their town apart from neighboring bedroom communities by inventing a fictional historic character for their community. The Schaumburg Village Board established the Olde Schaumburg Centre Overlay District in 1978 to "preserve the character of the area" located near the intersection of Schaumburg and Roselle Roads. The Olde Schaumburg Centre Commission was established at the same time to review new development and "restoration" projects in the Overlay District "to ensure the continued historic appeal of the area." In 1995 the village purchased and began redeveloping a twenty-seven-acre site that was supposed to "respect the historic character of the Olde Schaumburg Centre," using turn-of-the-century architectural design "and a park to entice residents to casually walk the area and stop at the various establishments."[51]

Schaumburg thus sought to invent a historic core modeled on a fictional fin de siècle town center far larger than its actual history as a country crossroads with a couple of businesses, a scattering of houses, and a school. "We have to create a downtown area, something that hasn't really existed, and the older[-looking] buildings help give the village some charm," the chair of the Olde Schaumburg Centre Commission's economic development subcommittee told the *Chicago Tribune* in 1987. "Schaumburg has more going for it than most communities in the country, but we lack warmth, a heart, a place for people to walk and talk."[52] Like Easton Town Center outside Columbus, Ohio, Olde Schaumburg Centre took its design inspiration not from local vernacular architecture—such as that located in the nearby manufacturing center of Elgin—but from a romanticized version of a New England town square.[53] Whereas Easton was in fact a shopping and entertainment mecca built to resemble a nineteenth-century town center, Schaumburg worked hard to bring public life into its "olde centre." It built a large, modern public library overlooking a park with a pond and outdoor amphitheater. But in the end the faux historicity of Olde Schaumburg, like Easton, was just window dressing. Local residents parked in front of the sizable grocery store and other commercial amenities, just as they would at strip malls outside Schaumburg's historic district. For most Chicago-area residents, the name Schaumburg remains synonymous with its enormous indoor mall and IKEA superstore, rather than its quaint town center.[54]

As part of their efforts to build civic pride, beauty, and historicity—and escape its placeless reputation—Schaumburg committed to spending 1 percent of its capital improvement budget each year.[55] One of its first projects was to select a piece of art for town square. The One Percent Committee—which included the mayor, a trustee, and several nonelected officials—judged some seventy entries and made a decision "based on technical merit, aesthetic value and durability."[56] The committee greatly admired Chicago artist Christine Rojek's *Ecce Hora*, a colorful twelve-foot-tall sundial, but decided that Wyoming cowboy artist David Alan Clark's *Spirit of the Prairie* (figure 6.8)—a life-size bronze pioneer man and woman—was better suited to their intended location and would "serve as a reminder of Schaumburg's agrarian past." In contrast to neighboring Elgin's small but committed PMF, which sought to erect a native son's life's work within their community, Schaumburg chose to erect bronze pioneers by an outside artist primarily for aesthetic reasons. But the One Percent Committee also purchased Rojek's giant sundial for a more visible spot on the modern municipal center grounds on heavily traveled Schaumburg Road.[57] By contrast, Clark's far more conventional *Spirit of the Prairie* was tucked into a picturesque corner overlooking the town square pond and

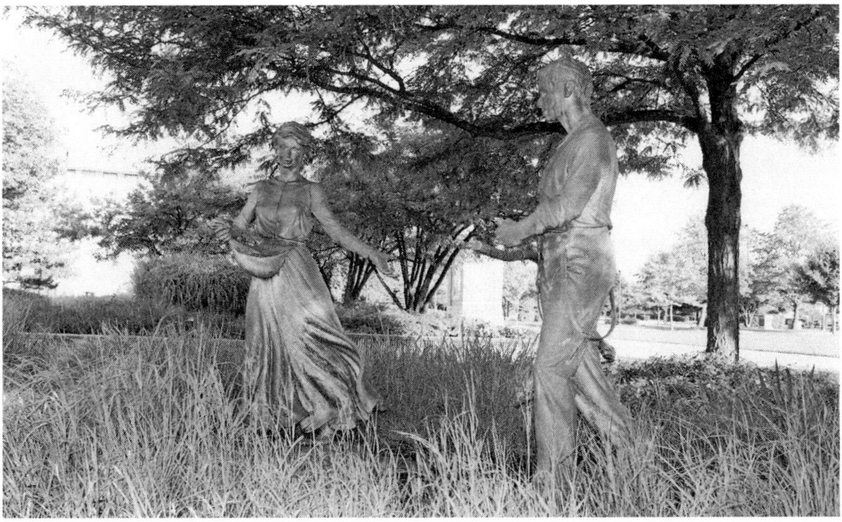

FIGURE 6.8. David Alan Clark, *Spirit of the Prairie*, Schaumburg, Illinois, 2002. Photograph by author.

amphitheater, where it is easily missed. Perhaps not surprisingly, *Ecce Hora* received far more attention in the *Daily Herald* and on local websites than did Clark's more traditional *Spirit of the Prairie.*

The strong young man and feminine wife clad in prairie-style gown that David Alan Clark sculpted to represent the *Spirit of the Prairie* in many ways resembles pioneer monuments erected for small western towns' centennial celebrations in the 1980s and 1990s. Where pioneer mothers nurtured their offspring, however, the Schaumburg farm woman feeds Illinois's fertile soil. Like the subject of Burke Rutherford's *Pioneer Woman* in Worland, Wyoming, and Las Vegas, New Mexico, she uses the apron covering her prairie-style gown as a womb-like sack from which she sows seed broadcast. Her husband works beside her, harvesting their abundant crop with a scythe. This depiction is surprisingly fitting for Schaumburg, given that the German immigrant women who settled near Schaumburg in the mid-nineteenth century were likely more willing to do field labor than their Anglo-American neighbors, for whom such field work challenged their highly desired domesticity.[58] But this historically accurate element of the Schaumburg statues appears to have been accidental. Just as the faux-historic architectural elements of both Schaumburg's new urbanist "olde town centre" and its cookie-cutter McMansions are essentially interchangeable, so are the pioneer-themed sculptures erected to historicize the manufactured heart of Schaumburg. Indeed, sculptor David Alan Clark also sells the two figures separately as a *Next Winter's Bread* and *The Haymaker.*[59] It appears that the cowboy artist—like the Schaumburg leaders who selected his work—was less concerned with historical accuracy and specificity than with creating an *appearance* of historicity that would appeal to white suburban residents. Many visitors question the value of all this faux historicity. Travel blogger Dave Seminara queried about his visit to what he described as "America's least impressive historic district, . . . [W]hat's the point of trying to market a thoroughly modern suburb as a historic place?"[60] The point, it seems, is to make money. Pioneer-themed statues can lend a historic aura, but their ability to create a site of memory is limited. Yet as Schaumburg selected appealing art, other suburban communities have likewise embraced pioneer statuary to promote commerce and heritage tourism.

HISTORICIZING TEXAS SPRAWL

Like Elgin and Schaumburg, small nineteenth-century towns throughout the West that now serve as bedroom communities or weekend destinations outside major urban centers have been particularly active in erecting pioneer monuments in search of heritage tourism dollars—monuments that ultimately reinforce white dominance. This process is particularly pronounced in Texas. For example, in 1996, Grapevine, Texas, erected a pioneer family monument as the first of several public statues in its historic downtown area. First settled by whites in the mid-nineteenth century, Grapevine remained a small agricultural town outside Dallas and Fort Worth until after World War II. The construction of Dallas–Fort Worth International Airport adjacent to Grapevine transformed it into a bedroom community and tourist destination. Although most tourists stay in Grapevine hotels because of their proximity to the gargantuan DFW airport, the town has worked hard to persuade tourists to linger for a day or a weekend. The town invented a wine industry to align with its name (which was actually inspired by local wild mustang grapevines) and, like Round Rock outside Austin, constructed a vast outlet mall. Tax revenue from DFW helped fund the revitalization of the town's historic downtown.[61]

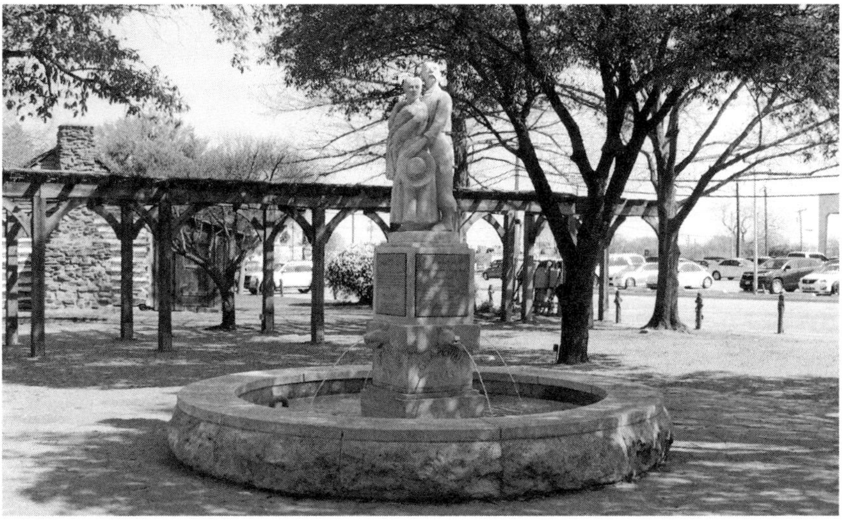

FIGURE 6.9. Mike Cunningham, *Walking to Texas*, Grapevine, Texas, 1996. Photograph by Anna Prescott.

As in Schaumburg, Illinois, according to travel writer Syd Kearney, "Residents in this little, tax-rich city make up the hometown image and ambience as they go along. . . . In Grapevine, if it cannot be restored, it is replicated."[62] Local artist Mike Cunningham's 1996 limestone sculpture of a pioneer man, woman, and infant is a centerpiece of Grapevine's new historic district. Although Cunningham is primarily an abstract sculptor, his piece for Grapevine imitates the Pioneer Mother movement—except that, despite being called *Walking to Texas*, the characters in it stand still rather than striding purposely westward (figure 6.9). Presumably, Cunningham and the city of Grapevine hoped that the monument would become a "mecca for tourists," like the 1971 *Pioneer Family* in Oberlin, Kansas.[63]

In a nod toward cultural inclusivity, Cunningham placed horse head fountains on the square base "represent[ing] the Four Directions and the spirit of the American Indians."[64] But its dedication reproduced less inclusive earlier narratives of Anglo-American settlement with even less attention to historical accuracy. The town's mayor grew a beard, and he and other city staffers wore "period" clothing. "Comanche Indians" were invited to participate. Executive director of the Grapevine Convention and Visitor Bureau P. W. McCallum told the *Fort Worth Star-Telegram*, "We're going to try to create the sense of the early 18th century when people first arrived on the Grapevine prairie."[65] McCallum's reference to the wrong century aligned with the town's general looseness with historical detail. Presumably the period they actually sought to replicate was the 1840s, when a treaty signed by General Sam Houston, other Republic of Texas commissioners, and ten Native nations opened the region to white settlement. Though the veracity of details in the lively historical narrative that the town's mayor told at the monument's dedication could not be verified, Grapevine residents insisted that his depiction of local customs and traditions was authentic.[66] While Grapevine did not completely invent its heritage as Schaumburg did, the resulting tourist destination relied more on reproducing old western myths than on accurately depicting local history.

A different form of faux diversity was erected 150 miles away in the Austin bedroom community of Round Rock. In its efforts to compete for tourism dollars, as we saw in the opening of this chapter, Round Rock—population forty-four thousand—modeled its pioneer commemoration after the enormous installations going up in much larger cities.[67] Round Rock traces its origins to a stream crossing on the Chisholm Trail, which was an important route for driving Texas longhorn cattle to central Kansas railroad towns en route to market from 1867 until 1884, when barbed-wire fences and cattle disease quarantine laws ended the long cattle drives. While locals insist that wheel ruts left by wagons lumbering along the Chisholm remained visible, by the early twenty-first century, they were difficult to find amid flourishing local flora on the few acres that remained undeveloped, and local leaders sought more striking ways of marking the historic site.[68]

In the mid-1990s, the tourism committee of the Round Rock Chamber of Commerce turned to bronze public sculpture to attract historical tourism. It was a potentially lucrative effort. Texas had 110 million leisure travelers in 1998, about 17 percent of whom included visiting historical sites and museums among the major activities of their trips. Seeking a share of the estimated $18 billion spent by those tourists, Round Rock became determined to bolster the importance of their Chisholm Trail site by erecting bronze statuary modeled after those in other Texas cities.[69]

Round Rock's tourism committee was particularly interested in sculptor Robert Summers's Texas-sized bronze art installation featuring three life-sized cowboys driving forty longhorn cattle in Dallas's 4.2-acre

Pioneer Plaza, which by 2000 was a must-see for visitors. Round Rock chamber officials sought to make *The Crossing* a similarly popular tourist destination, including it as a stop on paid tours of the city, which could also include a new shopping center and a Round Rock Express baseball game.[70] Tourist visitation was expected to generate revenue through increased sales taxes; the chamber also sought to increase revenue for local businesses and to promote local real estate sales in the fast-growing suburb. Chamber operations manager and tourism director Michelle Rackley insisted, "The statues would not only pull tourists to the area, it would be a claim for Round Rock pride. . . . This will be something original. It will be ours."[71] But, like many other pioneer statues erected to attract tourists, the Round Rock installation borrowed heavily from other communities' monuments—recent cowboy artwork as well as the Pioneer Mother movement canon.

Initial plans for a life-size statue of a cowboy and three steers crossing Brushy Creek near I-35 soon hit a snag. The chamber's tourism committee worried that flooding in the creek could cause major damage to the proposed one-hundred-thousand-dollar statue. A revised plan placed the bronze cattle in a parklike setting with convenient adjacent landscaped parking, likely to appeal to the outlet mall shoppers and suburban residents Round Rock sought to attract. From there, plans for bronze work expanded dramatically. By September 1996, chamber members envisioned a bronze cattle drive featuring some twenty steers, and perhaps a stagecoach and horses, that would rival Dallas's Pioneer Plaza installation (but that appears modest in comparison to Omaha's and Oklahoma City's enormous monuments erected a decade later). The chamber commissioned local cowboy art sculptor Jim Thomas to erect a series of 150 percent-sized bronze statues of pioneer figures and livestock as part of a $3 million art and landscape project on some six acres of land along Brushy Creek. Thomas had worked in ranching, advertising, and earth sciences before pursuing art professionally. He had sold his tabletop western-themed sculptures at about fifty art shows per year until the recession of the mid-1980s persuaded him to focus on heroic-sized public art, for which projects like Round Rock's were driving demand despite hard economic times. Though informed by local historical research on the Chisholm Trail, Thomas's designs did not stray far from his earlier tabletop works, other than their scale.[72]

As Omaha and Oklahoma City did with their football-field-sized bronze monuments, the Round Rock chamber erected its large bronze pioneer-themed installation in several distinct phases. By 2008, Red Rock had installed *The Pioneer Woman* (see figure 6.1), *Pioneer Boy*, and four longhorn steers. Although referred to under generic titles, Jim Thomas's figures were intended to depict Harriet "Hattie" Cluck, the first woman to travel the Chisholm Trail, and her five-year-old son, Emmett. Donor Sissy Peckham was a face model for the 1,200-pound statue, suggesting that it serves as a monument to Peckham as much as it does to generic pioneer womanhood.[73] The unusually styled depiction of a sunbonneted Pioneer Mother and her young son stand facing each other, leaning on matching walking sticks. She carries a small tote of foodstuffs, while her son shows off a frog he has caught in the streambed. Longhorn steers lounge nearby. In an odd form of twenty-first-century ethnic inclusiveness, two of those steers commemorated Swedish and Mexican immigrants to the region. Apparently, their descendants valued the project and their ethnic heritage enough to donate bronze statues as tributes to their immigrant forebearers, but the artist and community did not value those donors enough to use them as models for other human characters, which, in contrast to the Dallas Pioneer Park installation that had inspired them, remained entirely Anglo-American. Area businesspeople saw a different kind of value in the installation: local developers sought to create what Judy Mattivi Morley calls an "illusion of authenticity" by naming nearby streets and housing subdivisions to emphasize Round Rock's location on the old Chisholm Trail—a strategy that appears to have been successful.[74]

MODERN MORMON MEMORY

Such efforts to historicize sprawling suburbs are also common in Utah, where pioneer memory remains at the center of Mormon cultural identity. I argue in chapter 4 that LDS pioneer monuments became a means for Mormons to negotiate competing demands for exceptionalism and assimilation into mainstream American culture. In recent decades, LDS church and Mormon groups have embraced sesquicentennial commemorations to reinforce LDS identity and to educate non-Mormons about their faith. And in Utah, as in other midwestern and western states, they offer a veneer of historicity to suburban subdivisions.

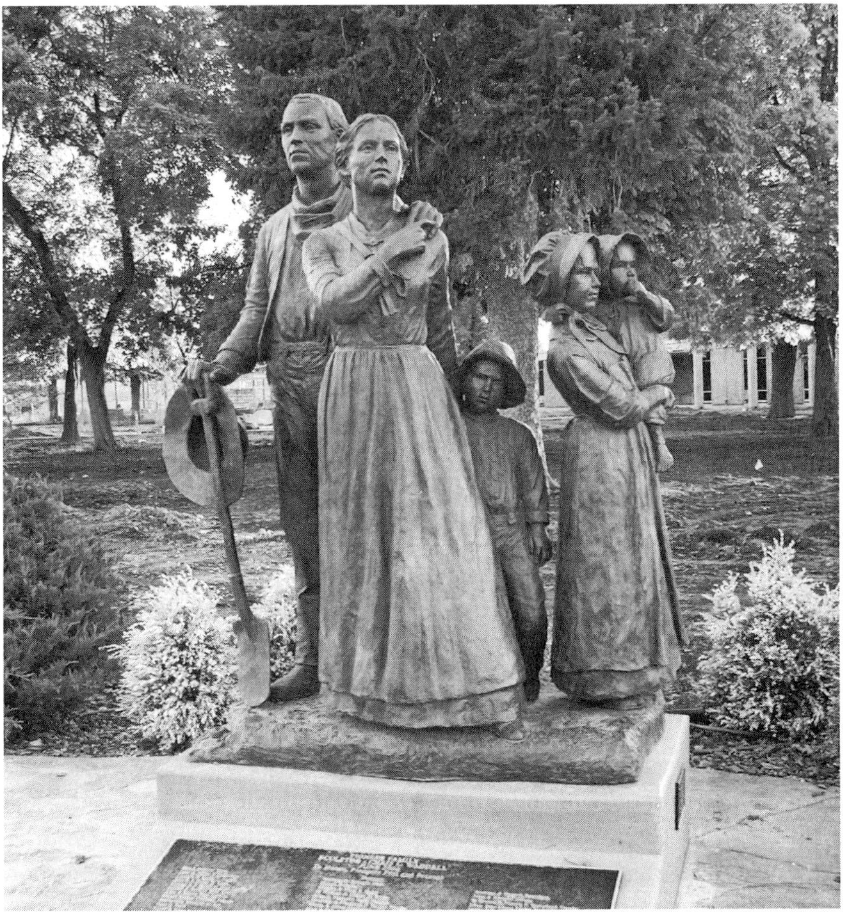

FIGURE 6.10. Chris L. Waddell, *Pioneer Family*, Springville, Utah, 2006. Photograph by author.

Herriman, Utah, is typical. Herriman was founded in 1849 but remained a small town for the next 150 years, before being transformed into a bedroom community for Salt Lake City. As recently as 2000, its population was just 1,500; ten years later it had ballooned to more than 20,000.[75] The edge city placed Chris L. Waddell's bronze 2005 *Pioneer Family* (figure 6.10) in a plaza on the edge of the city cemetery. Like many late twentieth-century monuments, it emphasizes the relationship between the pioneer man and woman. He places his left hand authoritatively on the bare-headed woman's shoulder; in his right are a wide-brimmed hat and a shovel, indicating his hard work. The woman's left arm rests in a feminine touch on her young son, who stands partially hidden by her long skirts. To his left, gazing seriously off in a different direction, an older sister holds their younger sister, a barefooted toddler, who sucks her thumb. In some ways, Waddell's work depicted Mormon pioneer families more accurately than had many other Utah statues. The artist's inclusion of three children suggests the large families that remain a hallmark of Mormon culture. The positioning of the figures hints at continuing patriarchal Mormon values: producing a separation between the parents and son as the primary unit (that in some ways resembles non-Mormon nuclear family monuments) and the two daughters as a supporting unit. While Waddell freed the mother of the burden of nursing an infant, he passed the burden of domestic drudgery onto her eldest daughter. Although the mother stands nearest to the viewer and at the apex of the triangular grouping, the positioning of her right arm across her chest, grasping the ends of her husband's fingers just above her heart, subtly directs attention away from her and toward her continued dependence on her husband, further reinforcing the authority of the Mormon patriarch in ways similar to that of Avard Fairbanks's works of the 1930s and 1940s. That Waddell's sculpture was soon copied for Springville, Utah, Memorial Park, adjacent to Cyrus Dallin's 1930s *Pioneer Mother* bust (see figure 4.2), indicates the appeal of Waddell's Mormon family imagery.

When the population and coffers of the city of Lehi (located halfway between Salt Lake City and Provo) exploded in the 1990s as a result of the area's technology boom, Lehi—jealous of Springville's identity as Art City—joined nearby Herriman in eagerly embracing public art. But where vanilla Schaumburg, Illinois, had purchased art haphazardly, based on aesthetics and the personal taste of its public art committee, Lehi's art acquisitions had a strong Mormon frontier bent. The Historic Preservation Commission requested a statue representing "the challenges and struggles endured and the faith and optimism shown by the [Lehi] pioneers."[76] Scott Streadbeck's proposed composition features a grizzled man in a wide-brimmed hat, with a broadax on his left shoulder. His wife cradles their infant son between them and holds a basket of vegetables. In front of them stands a young girl with her hair in twin braids, grasping a small bunch of flowers in both hands and smiling. Her short, puffed sleeves emphasize her innocence and femininity, while her mother's rolled-up sleeves reinforce the hard work involved in her dual burdens of gardening and child care. Mid-nineteenth-century Utah frontier girls would not have worn such decorative elements on their simple dresses, nor would girls her age have worn the long skirts of womanhood that Streadbeck depicted. But such historical anachronisms did not bother Lehi civic leaders. City councilmen quickly settled on Streadbeck's ninety-thousand-dollar proposal, only debating whether to pay an additional ten thousand dollars to include a wagon wheel in the final monument.[77] Ultimately, financial calculations motivated and underpinned the decision to erect these pioneer monuments in Utah and throughout the American West. Meanwhile, Mormon memory increasingly shifted to emphasize one aspect of the westward migration that the LDS church had long desired to forget: the handcart companies of the 1850s.

HANDCARTS AND HERITAGE TOURISM

In recent decades, both Mormons and non-Mormons have recognized pioneer commemoration's commercial potential. Ironically, Mormon efforts to capitalize on heritage tourism have emphasized the experiences of the most impoverished and long-suffering Mormon settlers: the handcart migrants. Mormons at the height of the late nineteenth-century polygamy crisis generally sought to avoid the taint of the impoverished—and in some cases doomed—handcart migrants. But attitudes toward handcarts have changed as Mormons have become increasingly assimilated into mainstream culture, as the Church of Jesus Christ of Latter-day Saints seeks new ways to promote Mormon heritage, and as Mormon businesspeople seek to cash in on heritage tourism. Once a symbol of suffering and failed autocratic church leadership, at the dawn of the new millennium, handcarts were reinvented as proud symbols of Mormon hard work, thrift, and family unity. If Mormons were the most American of Americans, then handcarts could become the embodiment of those model Mormon citizens.

Embracing this transformation, a new handcart monument helped to reinvent an infamous site of Mormon suffering. The LDS church had marked the site of the Winter Quarters cemetery in Florence, Nebraska, with an Avard T. Fairbanks bronze statue in 1936. A half century later, a small visitor's center appeared in a renovated home near the cemetery. Then in the mid-1990s, the LDS church undertook a reimagining of

Mormon historic sites, combining a "site-specific story" with their "sacred purpose . . . to witness and to remember" LDS history.[78] As part of that massive project, the church constructed a new visitor's center at Winter Quarters with more than seven thousand square feet of exhibit space.[79] The Mormon Trail Center at Winter Quarters was dedicated in 1997 to mark the sesquicentennial of the Mormon migration, and soon attracted sixty thousand to eighty thousand visitors annually, nearly all of whom were Mormons from outside Nebraska.[80] While the museum told the specific history of Winter Quarters, it deemphasized the suffering of Mormon migrants who camped—and died—there. Instead, it framed the historic cemetery now surrounded by an Omaha suburb both as a site of Mormon community formation and as a principal point in the mid-nineteenth-century overland migrations, on par with Kansas City's Westport and Independence.

Like the Cherokee Strip Regional Heritage Center's *Homesteaders* monument (see figure 5.8), the LDS church erected a heroic-sized bronze pioneer family monument in front of the Mormon Trail Center. But where Harold Holden had sculpted a farm family typical to the region surrounding Enid, Oklahoma, to mark the sesquicentennial of the Mormon Trail, LDS sculptor Franz Johansen and his son Nathan sidestepped the tragic story of Winter Quarters by substituting another tragedy-rimmed narrative, which had become a sculptural shorthand for a uniquely Mormon migration: the LDS handcart companies of the 1850s. Utah Pioneer Day parades included handcarts as early as 1869, but early Mormon monuments had glorified Brigham Young's triumphant first pioneer company. The notable exception was Torleif Knaphus's beloved monument, which was first displayed at Temple Square in 1926 and enlarged to heroic size for the centennial of the first pioneer company's journey in 1947 (plate M). At a time of Mormon cultural assimilation, that influential monument encouraged many to embrace handcarts as a uniquely LDS aspect of the Mormon migration.

Like Knaphus's design, the Johansens' 1997 sculpture for Winter Quarters, *Handcart Pioneer Monument* (figure 6.11), commemorates the faith that sustained handcart pioneers on the long journey, favoring religious virtue and idealized gender roles over historical reality. The Johansens' men and boys perform physical labor, while women and girls do "emotional pulling."[81] The father pulls the handcart, while the

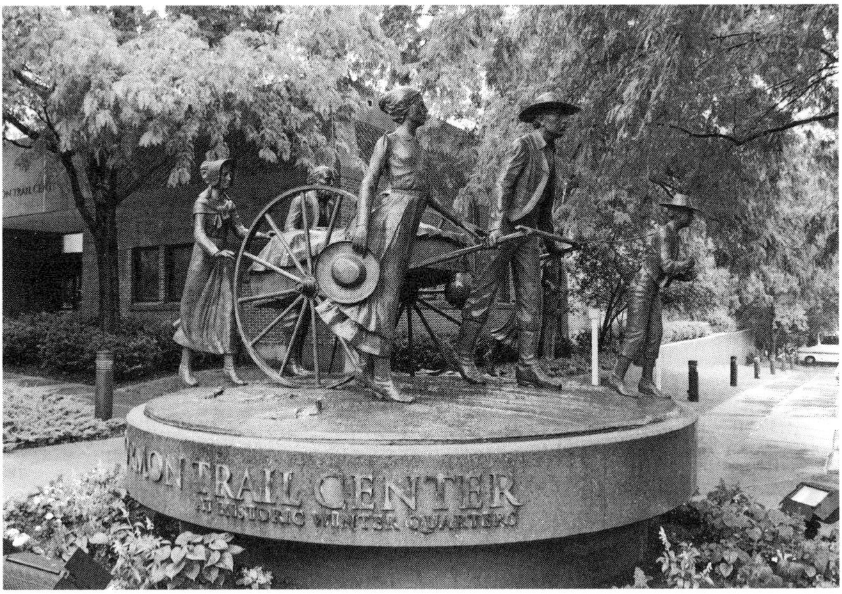

FIGURE 6.11. Franz Johansen and Nathan Johansen, *Handcart Pioneer Monument*, Florence, Nebraska, 1997. Photograph by author.

mother walks beside him, carrying her straw hat (*not* a sunbonnet) in her hand. A son mimics his father's actual work pulling the cart. A toddler boy takes the place of Knaphus's young girl riding inside the cart among the family's belongings. A bearded grandfather and sunbonneted grandmother walk behind the cart. The grandfather leans on his walking stick, echoing the way the father leans into the cart's pull bar. The grandmother walks upright as the mother and daughter do, stretching out both her hands to steady the precious cargo in the cart. The sculpture's bronze base shows the tracks of the settlers who went before them. But the feet of the Johansens' family members barely touch the ground in their sturdy boots, emphasizing their faith and anticipation of the promised land, rather than the determination required for the long, difficult journey. Their hopeful journey amid the particularly trying work of migration by handcart stands as an uplifting counterpoint to Avard Fairbanks's grim 1936 tribute to the suffering that migrants endured at Winter Quarters (see figure 4.4). In place of Winter Quarters misery, the Johansens offer hopeful overland migrants on the trail. In place of LDS guilt and embarrassment over the suffering of the handcart companies, they offer handcarts as a symbol of Mormons' hard work and unwavering faith.

Sculptural tributes to the handcart brigades make more sense in Iowa, where the handcarts' distinct history set Mormon Trail communities apart from other overland trail jumping-off points, such as Independence and Westport, Missouri. In 1856, 1,300 Mormons who had ridden the railroad to its western terminus at Iowa City camped at nearby Coralville to build handcarts before setting off across the plains. The Daughters of the American Revolution erected a commemorative plaque at Iowa City on the eightieth anniversary of that first handcart migration in 1936. Although the plaque gives an accurate brief history, an unrealistic bas-relief depiction of the handcart company downplays their Mormonness. Tall, rounded covers more characteristic of ox-pulled wagons partially hide those laboring to pull the carts. Instead of rolling toward the viewer, as was typical of Oregon Trail reliefs, the handcarts are pulled away. The only figure who faces the viewer is a young child peeking through the parted wagon cover at the rear of the cart. In contrast to later Mormon-sponsored commemorations, the relief's design suggests that it was intended to identify Iowa City as an important jumping-off point for the overland trails. Indeed, local newspaper coverage paid little attention to the religious identity of the handcart migrants, instead emphasizing the hardships that they faced on the journey westward.[82]

As interest in heritage tourism grew, so did Iowans' efforts to commemorate the handcart migration, and their willingness to tell a distinctly Mormon story. The Mormon Trek Memorial Foundation was established in 1967, later broadening its scope to become the Johnson County Historical Society. In conjunction with the U.S. bicentennial, the University of Iowa and the LDS Church created Mormon Handcart Park to preserve and commemorate the handcart campsite. Then to mark the sesquicentennial of the handcart migration, the county historical society worked with the Salt Lake City–based Mormon Historic Site Foundation and local LDS church members to erect a new museum. Its centerpiece was a twelve-thousand-dollar life-size diorama of a handcart family. Handcart- and pioneer-themed festivals in Coralville and in Kearney, Nebraska, were supported, though not officially sponsored, by the LDS church.[83]

The Mormon Historic Site Foundation (a nonprofit organization independent from the LDS church that raises funds to commemorate church history sites throughout the United States) also erected a bronze replica of Torleif Knaphus's handcart family monument near the new Johnson County Historical Museum.[84] Rather than placing the life-sized monument on the grounds of the county museum, though, as Winter Quarters had done, or along the picturesque Iowa River Landing wetland walkway at the nearby Coralville Conference Center, the foundation placed it on the plaza in front of the Marriott hotel (a hospitality company with Mormon roots), and directly next to a four-story red brick new urbanist mixed-use commercial development. A bronze plaque briefly recounts the history of the handcart companies and declares that the monument honors the "dedicated families who sacrificed homelands, possessions, and in some instances even their lives for their faith." That plaque does not identify artist Stanley J. Watts, who created the close reproduction of the Knaphus monument at Temple Square. The new work invites tourists and locals alike to remember the handcart pioneers as the LDS church had remembered them for decades.

Handcarts have become increasingly central to Mormon memory in Utah in recent decades. What had once been a depressing and slightly embarrassing episode in LDS history has been reimagined as a point of pride. Focusing on handcart pioneers became an effective way to emphasize LDS cultural values of hard work and determination. Abandoning the double speak of Avard Fairbanks's *American Family* (plate J), Mormons have embraced handcarts as an emblem embodying their identity as the most American of Americans. It is perhaps not surprising, then, that LDS church member and Utah resident Lewis D. Bowerman became concerned that This Is the Place Heritage Park in Emigration Canyon lacked a handcart memorial. That former state park was privatized in 1998 and is now administered by a foundation that actively seeks tourist visitation by offering an array of nineteenth-century Mormon stories. Besides Mahonri Young's 1947 *This Is the Place Monument* (see figure 4.3), the park features the 1921 historical marker that it replaced; an Avard Fairbanks Pony Express monument; a sesquicentennial Mormon Trail wagon train marker; and a replica of prominent LDS sculptor Dee Jay Bawden's *Eyes Westward,* depicting Joseph Smith and Brigham Young.[85] The Utah Statehood Centennial Commission built a visitors' center in the park in 1996

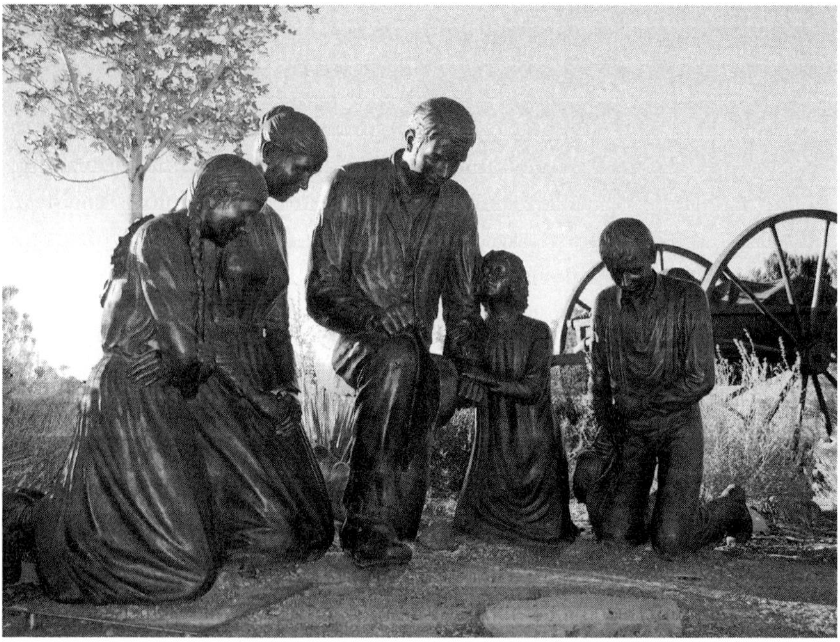

FIGURE 6.12. Stanley J. Watts, *Journey's End (Mormon Trail Monument; Handcart Monument)*, Salt Lake City, Utah, 1999. Photograph by author.

and doubled the size of Old Deseret Village, a living-history attraction of restored and reconstructed buildings, which *LDS News* likened to colonial Williamsburg and historic Nauvoo.[86] In addition to ghost tours and other events marketed as very American pioneer experiences, the park also offers LDS-focused handcart day treks, in which youth reenact the handcart migration. A Mormon handcart monument would thus attract new visitors while also reinforcing the message that Mormon settlers were the most hardworking and moral of Americans. With encouragement from LDS Elder M. Russell Ballard of the Quorum of the Twelve and park officials' approval, Bowerman commissioned Stanley J. Watts—who also copied Torleif Knaphus's famous depiction of a family migrating westward by handcart for Coralville, Iowa—to sculpt a handcart family kneeling together in prayer.[87]

Watts's 1999 *Journey's End* depicted a handcart family "offering a humble prayer of gratitude" for arriving safely in Zion (figure 6.12). The accompanying text-heavy plaque describes the handcart pioneers' arduous journey and commemorates "these noble pioneers . . . who exemplified sacrifice, courage, determination and unwavering faith." Prominent church and government leaders attended its dedication, including LDS president Gordon B. Hinckley, who claimed a connection to the handcart companies because his wife's grandmother had traveled to Utah in a wagon company that was assigned to travel with the Martin handcart company. Hinckley recounted the hardships of the trail, including the death of some two hundred handcart migrants. He insisted that "Everybody who lives in Utah, be he Mormon, non-Mormon, Jew, Gentile, whatever, owes a debt of obligation to those who paid so great a price for the comforts which we enjoy this day."[88] Dedicated on Pioneer Day in 1999, Watts's bronze monument declared handcart pioneers—and by extension all Mormon settlers—to have been particularly dedicated pioneers. In other words, the Mormon handcart pioneers were the most American of all white settlers. Both Mormon and non-Mormon residents presumably hoped that the sculpture would attract more visitors to the park's other pioneer-themed attractions.

MEMORY MAKES MONEY

In conclusion, since the rise of heritage tourism in the 1920s, western communities have erected pioneer monuments not only to commemorate local histories but to present those local histories to visitors. Pioneer statuary declared a community's historicity and promised to promote commerce by attracting tourists, shoppers, or new residents. Beginning in the 1990s, new urbanism and a desire for historical authenticity inspired a number of exurbs outside large cities to erect pioneer monuments. Elgin, Illinois, sought to erect Trygve Rovelstad's pioneer family monument at times of significant social upheaval and economic hardship: during the Great Depression, in the 1950s as the Watch City's leading industry collapsed while surrounding suburbs boomed, and again in the 1990s, amid continued economic struggles and increasing ethnic diversity. Ultimately, gaming industry income enabled the city to erect Rovelstad's sculpture as part of a larger riverfront redevelopment project, which sought to set Elgin apart as a historic city amid suburban sprawl. At nearly the same time, nearby Schaumburg—which had successfully competed with Elgin for population and economic growth since the mid-1950s—chose to devote a portion of its capital improvement budget to purchase statues of a pioneer man and woman as part of a broader beautification project. Similarly, rural communities turned suburbs in Texas, Utah, and throughout the West embraced pioneer statuary as a means to promote local pride, increase property values, and attract shoppers. Those statues borrowed liberally from the iconography of the Pioneer Mother movement. Yet even as these suburbs embraced pioneer statuary, nearby urban centers rediscovered, and some came to challenge, their own pioneer mothers.

INCLUSIVITY AND THE LIMITS OF PIONEER MEMORY, 1990–2020

In 1997, the El Paso County Pioneers' Association proposed to erect a monument to early white settlers of Colorado Springs, Colorado. Predictably, club members anticipated a pioneer monument that closely resembled those that had been erected across the country since the 1920s, and that continued to appear in other conservative communities in the Midwest and West. But as the late twentieth-century culture wars faded elsewhere in the United States, progressive voices rang out even in that bastion of cultural and political conservatism, insisting that Colorado Springs's new monument should *not* be just another covered wagon. Bowing to public pressure, the pioneer association abandoned the type of representative bronze sculpture that had been the norm for nearly a century. Instead, in *Follow the Setting Sun*, local artist Harriet Lee imprinted scenes of local history—from Native Americans to cell phones—into a stainless steel pyramid evoking the sun setting in the Rocky Mountains (plate F). Yet this design still represented a compromise between conservative commemoration and progressive visions for innovative public art. Moreover, even Lee's efforts to include diverse stories ultimately reinforced late nineteenth-century narratives of progress from untamed Indians to the triumph of white technology. Examining Americans' varied efforts to remember—or forget—early white settlers reveals the limits of inclusivity in pioneer commemoration and the persistence of U.S. settler colonialism.

Americans' attitudes toward and uses of pioneer monuments have fragmented in recent decades. Scholars have critiqued the cultural imperialism inherent in traditional frontier narratives. Even the general public began to recognize that Hollywood's popular "cowboys and Indians" version of western history was inherently racist and historically inaccurate. By the late twentieth century, many communities had allowed their

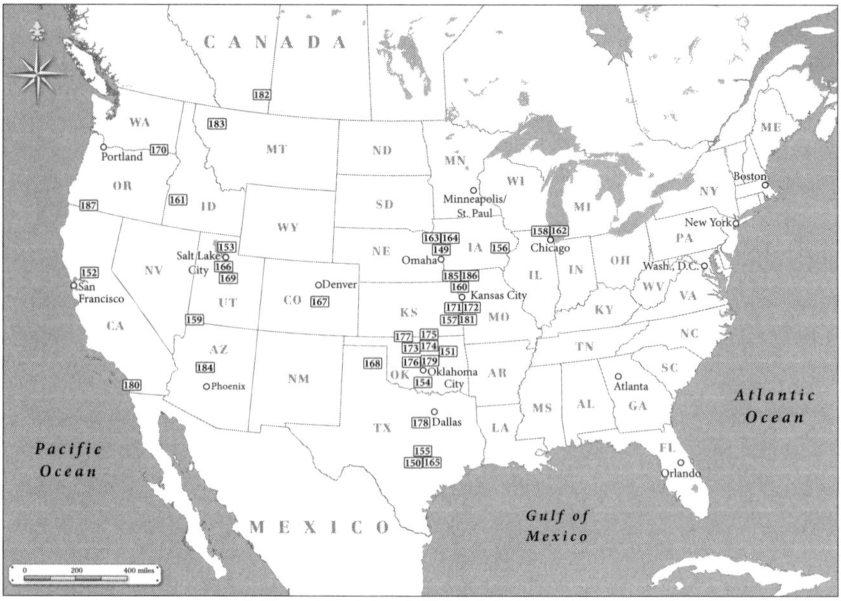

MAP 7. Pioneer Monuments Erected 1996–2016. Map by Gerry Krieg. Numbers on the map correspond with a chronological listing of monuments in the appendix.

monuments to become overgrown, or had moved them aside to make room for the wider roads and new buildings suited to a postindustrial economy. Erected to enshrine and instruct viewers in specific cultural values, many communities chose to forget these statues when they no longer matched widely held values. Statues created to serve as a valued lieux de mémoire soon became just more pieces of public art to be reinterpreted or outright neglected by successive generations of residents and visitors. As Brian Black and Bryn Varley argue, communities "seeking to maintain a sacred site must constantly reaffirm [their] attitudes toward the past."[1] Rather than reaffirming their allegiance toward old notions of white dominance and maternalism, residents of western cities increasingly sought instead to distance themselves from sites that celebrated exclusionary historical memory. But some city leaders rediscovered long-forgotten statues and sought to use them in new ways. At the same time, new pioneer monuments have been welcomed with open arms in several smaller western communities seeking to profit from their connection—however tenuous—to the mythic Old West, just as similar towns did during the culture wars of the 1980s. In the face of urban memory erasure—what Alfredo González-Ruibal calls "oblivion"—these smaller towns are creating a new "topography of remembering" to promote both heritage tourism and their own sense of place.[2]

The United States at the dawn of the twenty-first century was a heterogeneous culture struggling to redefine itself. Examining the varied uses of pioneer monuments in recent decades reveals the variety of American cultural perspectives and the multiple forms "the work of memory" surrounding America's frontier past has taken since the supposed close of the culture wars.[3] As city leaders sought to resurrect long-forgotten statues in the name of urban renewal, some citizens ascribed new meanings to old statues or erected new variations on old themes. Yet other viewers rejected both old and new tributes to pioneer motherhood, choosing to forget or even deface existing statues. A handful of western communities embraced new pioneer-themed memorials that critiqued the iconography that dominated twentieth-century western monuments, incorporating somewhat greater ethnic diversity, using humor to gently challenge the traditional depiction of white settler women as saintly Prairie Madonnas, or even rejecting representational sculpture altogether. But even these newest pioneer statues ultimately celebrate narratives about civilizing the frontier quite similar to those that dominated public commemoration in the American West throughout the twentieth century. As such, even these seemingly inclusive stories reinforce settler colonialism and national foundation myths centered on the frontier. In this final chapter, I explore the range of recent popular reactions to older pioneer monuments erected from the 1880s through the 1980s, before turning attention to the various forms that new pioneer monuments have taken since the 1990s and exploring the limits of inclusivity in the new millennium.

THE FATE OF OLDER PIONEER MOTHER MONUMENTS

Many statues erected at the height of the Pioneer Mother movement to commemorate frontier women's sacrifices and to declare a town's urban sophistication were soon forgotten by local residents. In some cases, cities forgot that they had once-famous statues until other communities sought to claim them. After decades of neglect, as suburban communities increasingly erected their own pioneer statues to attract commerce and increase real estate values, some of these 1920s statues have been rediscovered by city leaders seeking to attract people back to downtown areas. Yet public reactions to these rediscovered statues vary widely. While a few historic monuments have become centerpieces of local culture, other statues' original meaning has been forgotten or abandoned by the publics they were intended to serve.

FORGETTING PIONEER MOTHERS

New public monuments are consistently erected to great fanfare, but many of those discussed in this book were soon forgotten by communities who were no longer motivated to emphasize the cultural values enshrined in those statues. Perhaps the best example of a city actively forgetting a monument—and, by extension, that city's role in western history—comes from Kansas City, Missouri. While surrounding communities emphasize their role as jumping-off points for the mid-nineteenth-century western trails, Kansas City's tourism bureau works hard to promote itself as a hip urban center, emphasizing its thriving arts scene. It directs visitors to the National World War I Museum at Liberty Memorial but ignores what Donald Reynolds calls one of "the best-known monuments in the nation" a short distance away.[4] Like Pioneer Mother monuments in other western cities, although A. Phimister Proctor's *Pioneer Mother* was received gleefully by Kansas City residents in 1927 (plate C), with nearly thirty thousand reportedly attending its dedication, interest in the statue quickly waned.[5] By the 1980s, residents and city leaders had chosen to forget the statue that glorified westward expansion and depicted women as meekly submitting to their husbands. But Westport, Missouri, business interests still viewed the statue as a desirable symbol of their glory days in the Old West. They appealed to have Proctor's statue moved to a small park in their historic downtown in 1984, as we saw in chapter 6, arguing that it was neglected in its location on a winding, hilly road through Penn Valley Park. But the park board unanimously voted to leave the statue where Proctor had placed it a half century earlier. By 2007, the *Kansas City Star* decried the "embarrassing weedy mess" that surrounded the "icon of KC's frontier past," opining that it "should be a place for peaceful contemplation and beauty"—apparently unconcerned about the darker aspects of that frontier past. Tellingly, city officials only discovered the neglect of the statue (and, it appears, its very existence) while surveying potential light-rail routes through the park.

The following summer I spent several frustrating hours scouring the vast urban park in search of this massive bronze pioneer family grouping. Local residents who played softball in Penn Valley Park every week within one hundred yards of the statue had never heard of it. Only with the assistance of Google's satellite imagery did I manage to locate the 16,000-pound monument atop a tall hill at the center of the park. While the statue itself and the immediate surroundings by then were carefully manicured, the parking lot and hiking trail that provided access to the statue remained neglected, and the massive statue was hidden behind mature trees. By 2016, the trees ringing the statue on its less accessible southern side had been cut down, but those hiding it from view of an adjacent playground remained in place. Hundreds of visitors filled its parking lot to attend ceremonies at the nearby World War I memorial and to watch Independence Day fireworks over downtown Kansas City and surrounding communities, but few saw the monument. Proctor's supposedly well-known *Pioneer Mother* may still gaze out over the heart of Penn Valley Park and downtown Kansas City beyond, but she clearly has been forgotten by the people working and playing at her feet.

LOST AND FOUND STATUES

While many monuments dating from the Pioneer Mother movement have been forgotten by the communities that erected them, city leaders have recently rediscovered a number of these lost or neglected statues. Comparing the fate of the twelve identical August Leimbach *Madonna of the Trail* statues (plate D) erected in 1928 and 1929 by the DAR to mark prominent nineteenth-century westward migration routes—and to enshrine their vision of white womanhood—demonstrates the various ways in which early twentieth-century monuments have been forgotten, rediscovered, relocated, and reinterpreted. Half of the twelve *Madonna of the Trail* statues have been moved at least once to accommodate urban growth. Smaller towns have simply pushed their statues out of the way. As Ponca City, Oklahoma, was building a museum to accompany and to attract visitors to its nationally renowned Pioneer Mother movement–era *Pioneer Woman*, in 1956, Springfield, Ohio, moved its contemporaneous *Madonna of the Trail* from the Ohio Masonic Home grounds to a carefully landscaped alcove in Snyder Park, slightly farther west on U.S. Highway 40, to make room for a new highway bypass around downtown. While the

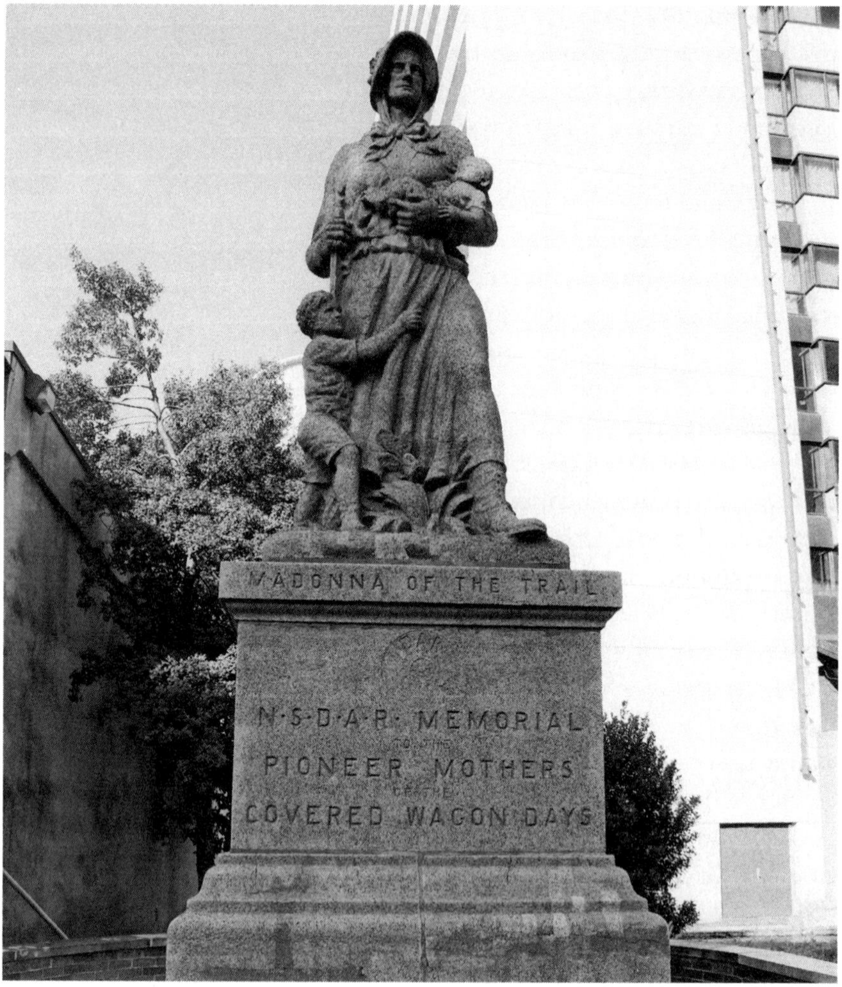

FIGURE 7.1. August Leimbach, *Madonna of the Trail*, Bethesda, Maryland, 1928. Photograph by author.

new park location might sound idyllic, it was largely inaccessible, with no parking available. Visitors therefore had to brave a busy four-lane highway with no sidewalk and then jump a guardrail to access the statue.[6]

Smaller mid-Atlantic and midwestern communities have begun to rediscover their August Leimbach *Madonnas* as potentially valuable destinations for heritage tourism. After languishing for half a century at an inaccessible site, Springfield's *Madonna* was moved again in 2011 to a more prominent downtown location, where she became the centerpiece of a new downtown park, National Road Commons, that replaced a vacant lot (plate D).[7] The city leaders who embrace these *Madonnas* as a means to attract tourism and promote local pride appear unconcerned that the statues also teach outdated gender norms and celebrate white cultural imperialism. And local residents' attitudes toward these and other Pioneer Mother statues remain mixed, as some embrace them, while many more seem content to forget them, and a few actively seek to damage or destroy them.

While city leaders increasingly seek to profit from historic *Madonna of the Trail* statues, popular responses to these statues are shaped by local concerns. Many local residents have questioned the placement of a *Madonna of the Trail* in urban Bethesda, Maryland, and she seems to garner little attention except when threatening to fall onto passing commuters (figure 7.1).[8] Even an editorial in the *Washington Times* celebrating her seventieth birthday seemed more interested in marking Bethesda's transformation "from a farming community and streetcar suburb to a vibrant urban center" than it was in celebrating the statue itself.[9] Nonetheless, city leaders remain committed to maintaining the statue within their community's business district. In a move reminiscent of Westport's repeated attempts to claim Kansas City's *Pioneer Mother*, Cumberland, Maryland, sought to raise its own visibility as the easternmost point on the Old National Road by adopting Bethesda's *Madonna of the Trail*. "Not in my lifetime," responded Bethesda Chamber of Commerce president Jack Alexander. "'You all are welcome to come look at it,' he said, 'but you're not leaving with our madonna.'" Bethesda city officials clung to the largely forgotten statue, which is one of the few historic items left in what is now a new urbanist Washington, D.C., suburb. The Leimbach *Madonna* is even featured in the city's logo, though few Bethesda residents seem to know about either the statue or the city logo.[10]

Greater local ethnic diversity influenced public reception of southwestern *Madonna of the Trail* statues in different ways. Although Albuquerque, New Mexico was a major city on Route 66, it received its *Madonna* only after the DAR met resistance to placing a Leimbach statue at the terminus of the historic Santa Fe Trail: prominent Anglo-American Santa Fe residents rejected the statue for not aligning with the Spanish fantasy past they had constructed for their adopted hometown.[11] Today, Albuquerque—a metropolitan area of nearly one million that is nearly half Hispanic or Latino—seems content to shove the once-controversial statue aside.[12] The city recently moved the monument about one hundred feet to accommodate the construction of a new federal courthouse. One blogger opined, "For decades, Albuquerque's Madonna of the Trail was ensconced in a pretty neighborhood park; unfortunately the park was destroyed around the sculpture to make way for a public building—an architectural monstrosity of which [Adolf Hitler's lead architect] Albert Speer would have been proud. The sculpture is sadly diminished by such surroundings."[13] Of course, whether Albuquerque's *Madonna* and the eleven others like it deserve to be celebrated remains open to debate—a question to which I return in the conclusion.

Like Chicago's edge city of Elgin, the more diverse the population of suburban Upland, California, became, the stronger that community's investment grew in their Pioneer Mother movement–era statue. Established in the 1880s, postwar interstate highway construction transformed agrarian Upland into a bedroom community for burgeoning Ontario. Whites, African Americans, and Latinos escaping nearby Los Angeles's rapid growth and urban unrest converged with immigration from Latin America and Asia. By the early twenty-first century, Upland's population—like that of Southern California overall—grew quite diverse. Upland's foreign-born population swelled from 5 percent in 1970 to 19 percent in 2010.[14] But it remained much more Anglo than neighboring Ontario, which was 69 percent Hispanic or Latino, and only 18 percent non-Hispanic white.[15] As Anglo-Americans lost their majority status, Uplanders embraced their *Madonna of the Trail* as an emblem of Anglo middle-class cultural norms. One Upland resident proclaimed in 2011 that the *Madonna* was crying because she—along with her community—had recently discovered the size of city manager Robb Quincey's annual salary.[16] Similarly, that same year a local columnist likened a coming Shakespeare production to seeing "a full frontal nude Madonna of the Trail in the middle of Euclid Avenue."[17] In general, Upland's seventy-five thousand residents appear less interested in attracting tourists to their portion of Route 66 than to promoting their community as a particularly peaceful Los Angeles suburb, in sharp contrast to the larger, more industrial, and more brown Ontario. Uplanders' devotion to the postwar middle-class American dream may help explain their continued embrace of their *Madonna*'s maternal ideology, while their efforts to come to terms with their community's growing ethnic diversity no doubt increases the appeal of the *Madonna*'s whiteness.

PUBLIC RESPONSES TO PIONEER MOTHERS

The range of public responses to long-forgotten *Madonna of the Trail* statues suggests the various ways in which pioneer monuments' changing physical context shapes public reception. While city leaders sometimes seek to revive the symbolic power of forgotten monuments, more often they view these statues as parts of broader urban renewal campaigns. But moving monuments alters both their geographic and their cultural context. Moreover, whether statues are relocated or remain in their original locations, urban growth, decay, and renewal have transformed the physical context of many once-prominent statues. Changes to the American urban landscape have altered once-important—and often long-forgotten—monuments to white civilization into just another piece of public art open to popular interpretation.

While relocating a statue can attract attention (as it has for Springfield's *Madonna of the Trail*), it can also make the statue easier for residents to forget. Urban renewal motivated both the erection of John K. Daniels's 1936 *Pioneers' Monument* (figure 7.2) in downtown Minneapolis and its removal. Daniels's *Pioneers' Monument* was erected as part of a project to replace a block of brothels and other dilapidated buildings in downtown Minneapolis with a new main post office building and public park called Pioneer Square. But the Minneapolis Planning Commission's vision of an entire government district floundered at the height of the Great Depression. Three decades later, a massive freeway construction project spurred another round of redevelopment, placing an apartment tower on Pioneer Square. The fourteen-ton granite monument was moved to a "temporary" location in the St. Anthony West neighborhood, on a tiny triangle of land beside a split-level home, where it "served as a Jersey barrier for errant drivers."[18] After languishing in that location for another forty years, a local neighborhood association raised funds to move the statue across Main Street to the newly created B. F. Nelson Park. While the new location is far more safe and accessible, footprints in the snow surrounding the statue in March 2013 suggest that it is of greater interest to local dogs marking their territory than to their human companions.[19] Visitors to the Minnesota State Fair in Minneapolis's sister city St. Paul often notice and

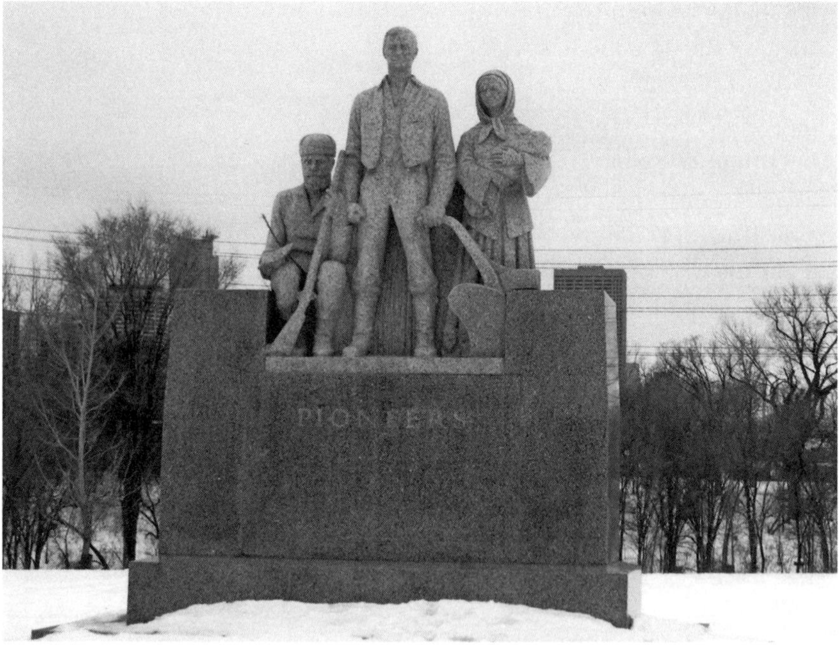

FIGURE 7.2. John K. Daniels, *Pioneers' Monument*, Minneapolis, Minnesota, 1936. Photograph by author.

photograph the 1958 gold fiberglass *Pioneer Woman* statue standing near Pioneer Portrait Hall, which likewise celebrates the state's frontier past (see figure 3.1). But local residents experience Daniels's twice-relocated *Pioneers' Monument* primarily as an obstacle on their daily walks, and tourist visitation in its current residential neighborhood seems unlikely.

Even when city leaders relocate forgotten statues to more prominent locations, the public can be slow to embrace these monuments' celebration of pioneer mothers. In 1928, Vancouver, Washington, declared its urban sophistication—and its continuing cultural significance as rapidly growing sister city Portland, Oregon, threatened to eclipse the former fur trading fort—by erecting renowned sculptor Avard Fairbanks's bronze *Pioneer Mother* in historic Esther Short Park (see figure 2.2). Established in 1853, Esther Short Park had become a center of civic life by the early twentieth century, hosting the county fair, big band concerts, and baseball games. But like many American cities, Vancouver's downtown area was abandoned by the growing middle class amid suburbanization in the postwar era. By the mid-1970s, Esther Short Park was primarily frequented by vagrants and panhandlers. The park became so overgrown that visitors would have to climb through the surrounding shrubs to see the *Pioneer Mother* statue.[20]

Then in the late 1990s, as David Manuel's once-controversial *The Promised Land* statue (plate N) was gradually forgotten across the river in Portland, Vancouver's massive downtown revitalization effort succeeded in transforming Esther Short Park into a town plaza. As part of those renovations, Fairbanks's *Pioneer Mother* was relocated to a far less tranquil site, facing a busy downtown street that made the statue more visible to passing motorists. Vancouver residents have reclaimed the renovated park, but many reject Fairbanks's shrine to white civilization. The historic statue has become an obstacle to park visitors rather than a centerpiece of modern urban planning. On a sunny summer Sunday in 2008, access to the statue was blocked because parents of young ballerinas performing on a nearby outdoor stage turned its plaza into an impromptu parking lot. And while Vancouver resident Heather Baron tried to use the statue to teach her sons the meaning of the term *pioneer*, her young sons were more interested in hiding from pretend bears than in learning about the sacrifices of frontier women. Visiting Seattle resident Holly Burpo told the *Vancouver (Wash.) Columbian* in 2012 that she found the statue "creepy. . . . Her, with the kids. I don't know, the meaning is unclear."[21] The city's tribute to pioneer motherhood has become at best confusing, and at worst an impediment to Vancouverites' enthusiastic return to the once dangerous downtown park.

NEGLECT, VANDALISM, AND PROTEST

Many pioneer monuments erected from the 1880s to the 1980s have been forgotten, and communities' neglect has taken a physical toll on once-proud monuments. Save Outdoor Sculpture!—a joint program of the Smithsonian American Art Museum and Heritage Preservation—determined that many of the statues included in this study were in need of repair. Outright vandalism and even theft have also taken a toll on several monuments. Unfortunately, individuals' motivations for vandalizing monuments are often difficult to uncover. While some are clearly politically motivated, in other cases, the attacker's intent is less clear. Are they making a political statement? Or simply targeting what they perceive to be an outdated piece of public art? Because such actions typically are

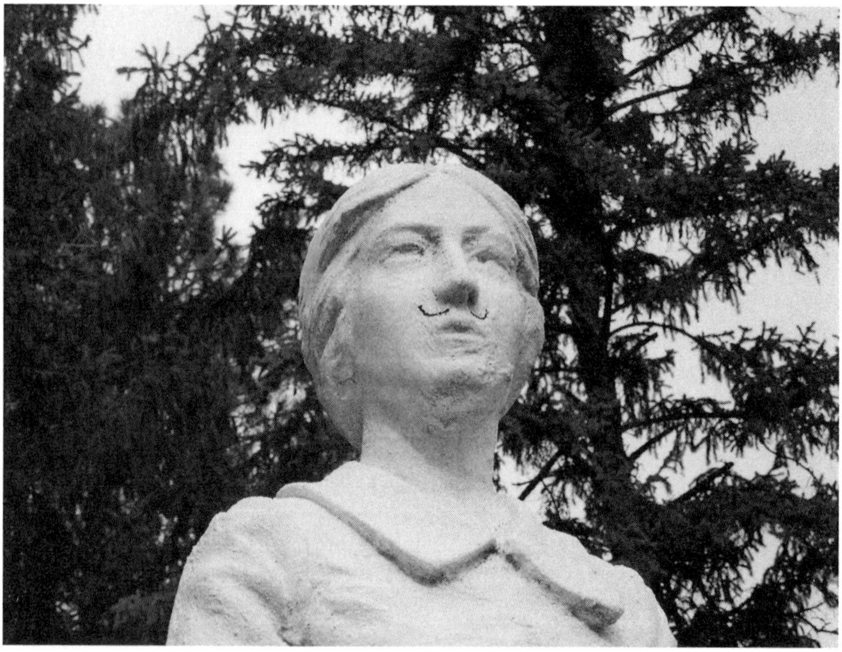

FIGURE 7.3. Ellis Luis Burman, detail of *The Pioneer Woman*, Lincoln, Nebraska, 1935. Photograph by author.

done in secret, their intended meaning can be difficult to parse. Whether motivated by politics or personal gain, however, attacks on pioneer statuary make clear that not all westerners embrace the racial and gender ideology those statues promote.

When residents neglect or choose to forget public statuary, once-celebrated monuments can become a target for pranks or theft. For example, Ellis Luis Burman's *The Pioneer Woman* commemorated Nebraska frontierswomen's sacrifices and symbolized the sophistication of the Lincoln Woman's Club members who donated the statue at the height of the Great Depression. Although the Lincoln Arts Council and Lincoln Woman's Club received a Save Outdoor Sculpture! Assessment Award in 1997 to assess the condition of this and other area statues, and the monument is now included on the Lincoln Arts Council's list of public art, the work has largely been forgotten. Few current Lincoln residents know the statue exists. Presumably, it was local youth who mocked Burman's depiction of respectable western motherhood by adding a comic mustache (figure 7.3).

Edgier monuments can motivate more dramatic damage. Richard Bergen's nude *Heritage Woman* was enthusiastically received by Wichita, Kansas, arts and heritage leaders in 1976 (see figure 3.6). But over time Kansans came to question the appropriateness of the nude figure. While Wichitans apparently appreciated Dorothy L. Koelling's more traditional 1994 *Hardship and Dreams*, which stood determinedly on Wichita's greenway, vandals targeted Bergen's nude statue in a park behind the county historical society museum in 2005, 2006, and 2013, causing increasingly severe damage.[22] But far more traditional depictions of pioneer women are not immune from vandalism and outright theft.

At least two Pioneer Mother monuments have been stolen in apparent efforts to monetize their value: Nancy Coonsman Hahn's 1929 Pioneer Mother statue was pried from its 3.5-foot-tall granite base and stolen in 1969 but soon recovered. Today it sits largely forgotten in the Missouri Historical Society's locked storage facility.[23] And Juan Lombardo-Rivera's *The Pioneer Woman* statue (see figure 6.3) was stolen from the Independence, Missouri, National Frontier Trails museum courtyard in summer 2013 and delivered in pieces to a local recycling center. While the thieves stood trial, donors worked quickly to replace the destroyed statue with another pioneer woman sculpted by local artist Charles Goslin (see figure 6.4). And Independence also erected its casting of Avard Fairbanks's 1924 *Old Oregon Trail* medallion about a mile away. But the heist, along with recent acts of vandalism against historic markers displaying Independence's importance to nineteenth-century overland trails, indicate that some local residents do not want to remember the town's frontier history.[24]

NEW PIONEER MOTHERS

As the twenty-first century dawned, two very different types of new pioneer monuments appeared on the landscape. Several western communities erected new Pioneer Mother monuments that, like the 2004 World War II Memorial in Washington, D.C., suggest a return to the reactionary motivations of the Pioneer Mother movement and a reengagement with the late twentieth-century culture wars. Meanwhile, other western cities began to stray significantly from the tried-and-true iconography and artistic style of the Pioneer Mother movement. Like the Martin Luther King Jr. monument in Washington, D.C., these western monuments broke from long-established Beaux-Arts commemorative traditions. Yet whether these innovative pioneer monuments poked fun at the gender norms depicted in more traditional statues or included other western stories, even they ultimately celebrated white cultural imperialism.

In recent years a few western communities have embraced more light-hearted portrayals of western life that challenge twentieth-century monuments' Prairie Madonna imagery. For example, Tom Otterness created cartoonish knee-high bronze figures depicting the California gold rush for the federal courthouse plaza in Sacramento, California. Larger versions of one of those pieces, *The Covered Wagon* (plate O), Otterness's whimsical sculpture of a woman driving a covered wagon pulled by a bull, were later installed in Pioneer Park in Walla Walla, Washington, and at Joslyn Art Museum, in Omaha, Nebraska, and toured the country from New York City to Beverly Hills, with stops in Indianapolis and Grand Rapids, Michigan. Otterness's depiction of a covered wagon differs from traditional renditions not only in its cartoonish style, but also in challenging traditional gender norms and blending periods. Otterness placed a smiling sunbonneted woman in the driver's seat, a pipe in her mouth. Meanwhile, a girl dressed in a modern sleeveless top leans out the back of the wagon, holding on to a boy who is plunging headfirst out of the wagon onto the hard earth below. "When I conceived Covered Wagon, I saw the pioneers as your typical family—Dad is the bull, Mom is driving and the kids are fighting in the back," the artist explained.[25] Yet his interpretation of the nation's mid-nineteenth-century frontier is filtered through an icon of mid-twentieth-century American life: "It's that classic cross-country station wagon trip we all took as kids."[26] By conflating the two supposed golden ages of American family life, Otterness offered a critique of white family norms in both eras. This is the closest that any pioneer monument has come to actually questioning white cultural dominance.

Humor also provided a way for Prescott Valley, Arizona, to celebrate its foremothers' feistiness as well as their supposedly civilizing influence—just down the road from Pat Mathiesen's 1990 attempt at ethnic inclusivity, *Spirit of the Frontier* (see figure 5.4). Artist and executive editor of *True West Magazine* Bob Boze Bell offered a somewhat updated version of the nearly century-old Pioneer Mother in a painting to honor Prescott Valley's centennial. "Whether they were wrangling ornery kids or dispatching hogs, chickens, scorpions and rattlesnakes, the women who lived in the Arizona

Territory had to be tough."[27] Or, as he explained more colorfully in his *True West Magazine* blog, "That was the point of the whole deal, to honor the brave and tenacious women of Arizona who tamed the West AND the men."[28] While the title and image directly challenge mid-twentieth-century depictions of western women, its creator, Bob Boze Bell, made clear that he was gently challenging the "gentle" label, but not the bigger message that women did indeed "tame" the West and its supposedly wild men.

So eagerly did Prescott Valley residents embrace Bell's image that they installed a monumental bronze based on it in front of the Prescott Valley Civic Center to honor their white foremothers' grit (plate P).[29] Deb Gessner's 2013 *Not-So-Gentle Tamer* "pays tribute to the brave pioneer women who helped tame and settle the west."[30] This pioneer woman, holding a rattlesnake whose head she has just removed with a shovel, presents a more active female role than had been typical of the Pioneer Mother movement. Vicky O'Hara, president of the local League of Women Voters, said that American women "have fought for equal rights and women's issues throughout our history. The statue exemplifies this spirit. . . . The women who built the West were fighting for a better life for their families and equal rights and an equal voice."[31] While some Arizonans have complained about the *Not-So-Gentle Tamer*'s attack on local wildlife, most appear to embrace Bell and Gessner's depiction of white pioneer women's tenacity. They are far less interested in celebrating the tenacity of indigenous and Spanish-speaking peoples who lived in the area for centuries before the arrival of white Americans, as did the largely forgotten 1990 monument to both white settler and indigenous motherhood in neighboring Prescott. While Latinas and indigenous women remain widely excluded from celebrations of pioneer womanhood, though, some recent monuments do seek to expand the boundaries of pioneer whiteness.

WHITENESS AND THE LIMITS OF INCLUSIVITY

Throughout the past 125 years, pioneer monuments have been erected to express and reinforce the whiteness of western settlers. Heritage groups' erection of ethnically identified statues that adapted conventions from Anglo pioneer monuments declared their part in the broader national story of western settlement. But other racial and ethnic groups—particularly American Indians, but also Hispanics, Asians, and African

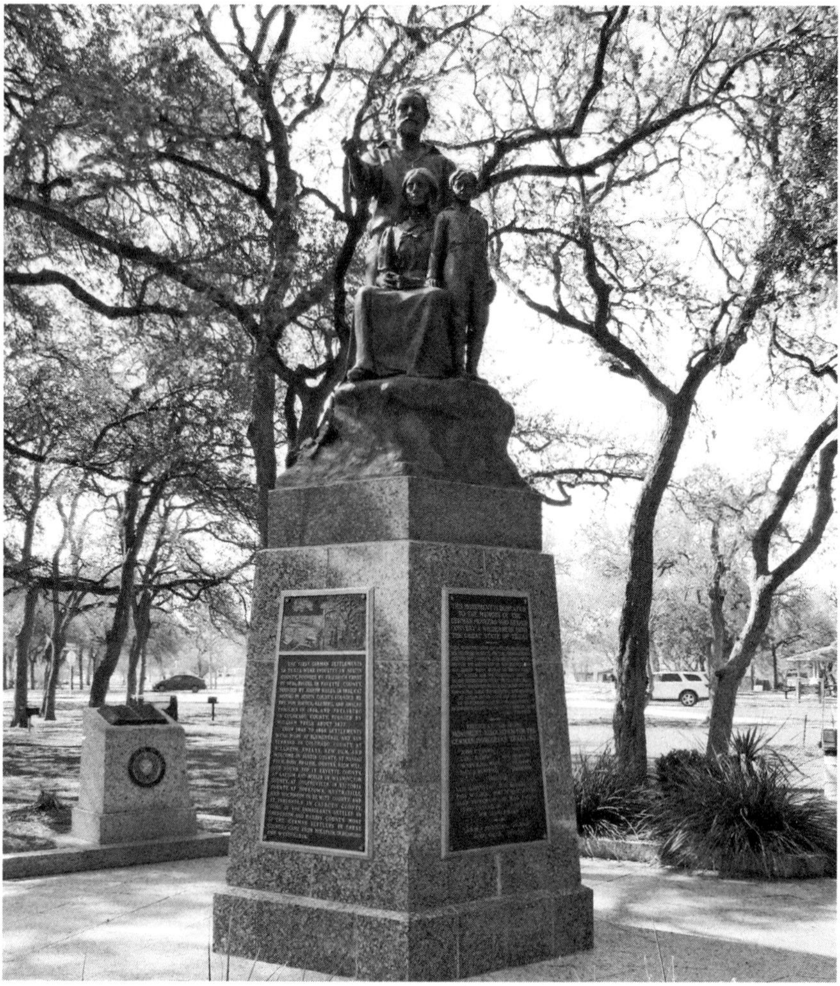

FIGURE 7.4. Hugo Villa, *German Pioneers of Texas*, New Braunfels, Texas, 1938. Photograph by author.

Americans—continue to serve as foils to heroic white frontiersmen as they did in the nineteenth century.[32] Considering who *cannot* cast their ancestors as iconic American pioneers reveals the limits of inclusivity in the new millennium.

IMMIGRANT PIONEERS

Over the course of the twentieth century, descendants of immigrants from several European nations erected monuments that claimed their ancestors to be part of the American national story of westward expansion. As anti-German sentiment reached a fevered pitch throughout the United States on the eve of World War I, German Americans in Texas pursued a monument celebrating early German settlers' whiteness and Americanness. Despite raising a reported $81,000 ($1.5 million in 2015 dollars) in Germany, that project soon stalled amid war and anti-immigrant attitudes; it was resurrected as Adolf Hitler spouted racist ideology and German Jews fled Nazi persecution.[33] Texans of German descent sought to educate the larger public about German contributions to Texas society, and to claim their place in American pioneer memory, by erecting Hugo Villa's *German Pioneers of Texas* in New Braunfels, a predominantly German community between Austin and San Antonio, as part of Texas's lavish 1936 centennial celebration of its brief independence. Employing a combination of Pioneer Mother movement iconography and extensive explanatory text, *German Pioneers of Texas* (figure 7.4) declared German immigrants to be true white pioneers. A seated woman, with a book resting in her lap, and her young son look into the future as the patriarch stands behind them, gesturing forward. In place of the covered wagon imagery typical of the Pioneer Mother movement, four large plaques on the monument's base depict an immigrant family arriving by ship and celebrate German pioneers' contributions to the political, economic, and cultural life of Texas. The extensive use of German and English text on these plaques reflects and celebrates the richness of German literary culture. But when compared to other pioneer monuments of the Pioneer Mother movement, the inclusion of long explanatory texts appears highly defensive. As the United States geared up for a second global war against their German homeland, German Texans struggled to convince their Anglo neighbors of their devotion to the American nation.

Attitudes toward ethnic diversity changed in the second half of the twentieth century. Cold War anxieties helped fuel the 1950s' emphasis on white middle-class suburban conformity, but the civil rights movement and 1970s identity politics soon encouraged Americans to embrace cultural diversity. New Ulm, Minnesota, rejected stereotypes such as German beer wagons in favor of a more inclusive whiteness, and even attempted to include indigenous peoples in their celebration of peaceful coexistence. But while midwestern communities grew increasingly willing to accept nineteenth-century northern European immigrants as white pioneers, other non-Anglo groups

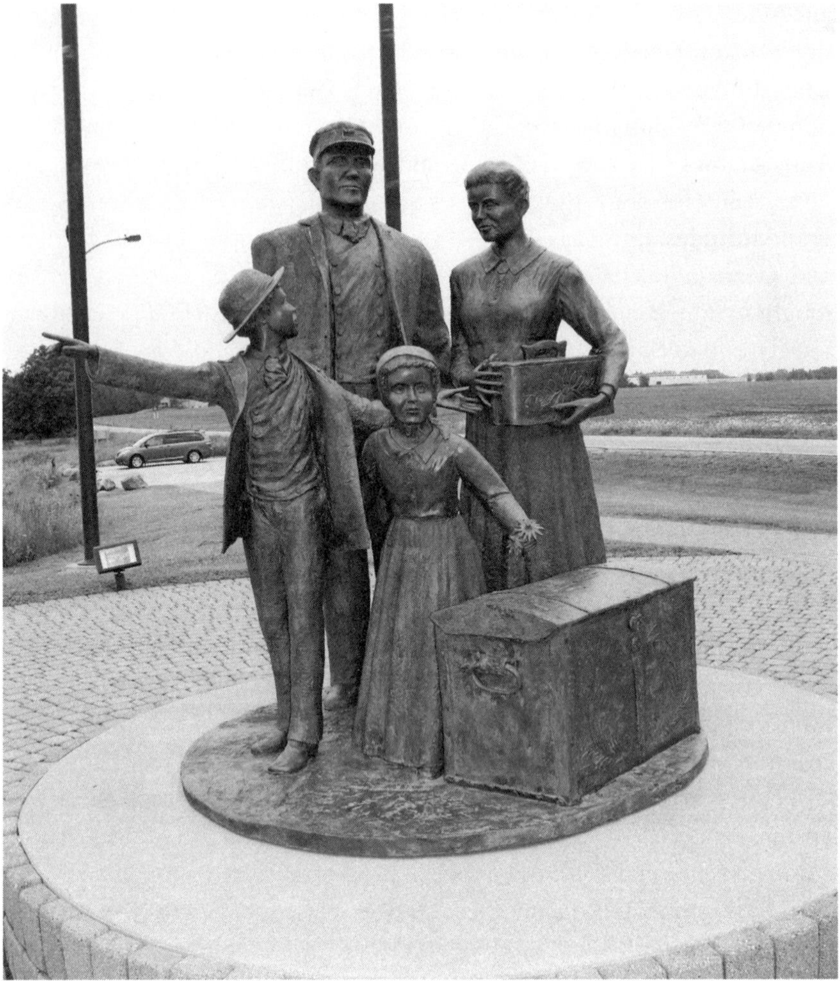

FIGURE 7.5. Clifford J. Carlson, *The Promise of America,* Lake Mills, Iowa, 1995. Photograph by author.

were beyond the reach of even twenty-first-century inclusivity.

Since the rise of multiculturalism, ethnic heritage societies have erected monuments in the Upper Midwest that—like *German Pioneers of Texas*—present their immigrant forefathers and foremothers as iconic white American pioneers. For example, local artist Clifford J. Carlson's 1995 bronze Norwegian immigrant grouping for Lake Mills, Iowa, *The Promise of America,* echoed the imagery of pioneer family monuments (figure 7.5). But where the *German Pioneers of Texas* statue was accompanied by extensive interpretive text, Carlson assumed that residents of the Upper Midwest (many of whom are descended from turn-of-the-twentieth-century Scandinavian immigrants) would readily accept his claim that Norwegian immigrants counted as American pioneers. *The Promise of America* both played to the America-as-melting-pot trope and interjected the Norwegian immigrant experience into narratives celebrating white settlement of the West. Carlson's sculpture features a husband and wife standing behind their two school-aged children. In place of an ax or a rifle, the father holds a suitcase and stares stoically forward, pondering the new land, while his son points excitedly out over the Iowa prairie, leading their family westward as Yankee pioneer sons had done for half a century. The mother clings to a treasured rosemaling box and a similarly decorated shipping trunk, emphasizing her as a keeper of Norwegian culture rather than the enthusiastic bearer of white civilization characteristic of 1920s pioneer mothers. Her daughter clasps local wildflowers in her hand like young girls in many pioneer family monuments, but her Norwegian-style cap and wide-eyed expression likewise reflect her uncertainty about their new home. A welcome center was built seven miles away on I-35, suggesting that Lake Mills residents believed that the statue could attract Norwegian American heritage tourism. But while European immigrant groups are increasingly accepted as contributors to the national project of westward expansion, people of color remain beyond the pale of whiteness.

THE LIMITS OF WHITENESS

Explicit references to white cultural superiority and disappearing Indians—a hallmark of pioneer monuments a century ago—today spark controversy. But more recent pioneer monuments, whether they simply copy earlier Pioneer Mother statues, portray spunkier pioneer women, or present European immigrants as pioneers, likewise reinforce the notion that Indians belong in the past. And the New Western history's insistence that the West was a particularly diverse place has failed to transform most Americans' mental image of a pioneer.

Who else remains excluded from whiteness and full participation in American nationhood? The United States has long debated the racial identity of Spanish-speaking peoples. While in many ways Cuernavaca, Mexico, sculptor Juan Lombardo-Rivera's 1990 *Pioneer Woman* (see figure 6.3) for Independence, Missouri, closely resembled Anglo-American artists'

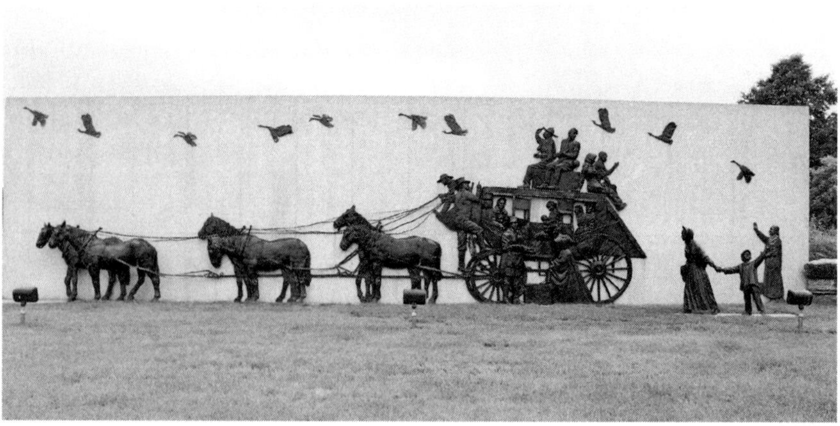

FIGURE 7.6. Kwan Wu, *Going West on the Old Santa Fe Trail (Two Trails)*, Olathe, Kansas, 2008. Photograph by author.

depictions of Anglo pioneer women, several members of the heavily Anglo monument committee were "totally spastic" about Lombardo-Rivera's application of a bold blue patina, which suggested Hispanic cultural influences.[34] That Hispanic groups have not erected comparable monuments may suggest that these groups have not yet achieved whiteness. Or perhaps, like Native Americans, Hispanos and Latinos are more interested in protesting Anglo-American land theft in the U.S.-Mexican borderlands than in attempting to depict themselves as white American pioneers.

There appears even less space in American frontier memory for peoples of African or Asian descent. In April 2016, the Cherry County Historical Society and the Nebraska State Historical Society dedicated a historical marker to the town of DeWitty, one of Nebraska's largest rural African American homesteading communities, but the only sculptural depiction of African Americans that I have identified among 185 pioneer monuments is part of Kwan Wu's unusually diverse depiction of the westward migration for Olathe, Kansas.[35] And even that Chinese immigrant only dared incorporate Asian influences far more subtly. Kwan Wu's *Going West on the Old Santa Fe Trail* (which was erected amid the Kansas City suburbs' competition for heritage tourism; figure 7.6) depicts diverse stagecoach passengers: an Anglo mother cradling a sleeping infant, an older gentleman, and a grandmother with her young granddaughter ride inside the Overland Mail Company coach; another Anglo mother and son wait to board the coach. A Latino man, an Anglo soldier, and an African

American couple perch on the roof, indicating their poverty and lower social status. An indigenous woman waves farewell to the travelers—and perhaps also her peoples' land. The only Asian cultural presence visible in Wu's ethnically diverse scene is the origami crane that the Anglo boy holds aloft toward the waterfowl flying overhead. Apparently this artist born and trained in China dared not depict Chinese immigrants as American pioneers. While they participated in the iconic California gold rush in substantial numbers and contributed crucial labor to constructing the transcontinental railroad, Chinese immigrants' Otherness persists in American memory. It is hardly coincidental that pioneer monument construction began just as Chinese immigrants were excluded and American Indians were forced onto reservations. That Asian and African Americans' presence in the West has been largely forgotten, and that Hispanic and Indian stories have been told only as a foil against which American pioneer heritage can be highlighted, suggests the continuing limits of American inclusivity.

THE LIMITS OF INCLUSIVITY

Cultural diversity and pioneer memory interacted in particularly complex ways in Oklahoma. The Oklahoma Centennial Commission's work to erect several new monuments to mark the state's 2007 centennial further demonstrate the limits of Oklahoma inclusivity and the persistence of pioneer mythology.

In preparation for its 2007 statehood centennial, Oklahoma chose to celebrate its American Indian heritage atop the capitol's new dome. In a statewide competition, the Oklahoma Arts Council selected *The Guardian*, a male Indian figure sculpted by an Oklahoma politician and Seminole tribal leader who is also an internationally recognized artist. While serving as a state senator and running for governor, Enoch Kelly Haney sculpted a bronze warrior thrusting his spear into the ground, indicating his refusal to bow in the face of overwhelming odds. At its 2002 dedication, Haney explained that he intended it to represent *all* Oklahomans: it honors Native peoples who were forced from their homes in the nineteenth century, but also Oklahomans of all ethnicities who overcame adversity such as the dust bowl of the 1930s and the 1995 bombing of the Murrah Federal Building in Oklahoma City.[36] In an award-winning essay, Choctaw Lindsey Hancock agreed that *The Guardian* "represents a common bond that unites us with people of other cultures," but asserted that the statue is also a symbol of Native pride, "strength and longsuffering and endurance."[37] Some non-Native Oklahomans apparently objected to placing an Indian atop the capitol building, but their complaints received little attention in generally positive press coverage of the statue.[38]

The capitol dome and statue kicked off a series of public projects designed to mark the state's centennial. University of Oklahoma art professor Paul Moore sculpted what he described as "the largest bronze monument in the world" to commemorate white settlement of Indian lands.[39] Erected on a newly constructed canal, *Brand New State* (see figure 6.7) incorporates a total of forty-five statues depicting Anglo men and women participating in the 1889 unassigned lands run. Moore's massive installation, which stretches the length of an American football field, features land run participants in wagons, on horseback, and on foot rushing to claim free land; soldiers armed with a cannon mark the starting line for the rush. In contrast to earlier monuments that focused on land runs as male-dominated events, *Brand New State* showcases the age and gender diversity of individuals who participated in the run: men, women, and children of all ages, including single men and an unaccompanied woman riding sidesaddle. But as with most other pioneer monuments in Oklahoma and across the country, it includes only Anglo actors and depicts indigenous peoples only through their absence as white people rush to claim their lands.[40]

Debate over Moore's massive land run sculpture highlighted the complexity of ethnic interaction and land ownership in the region. Indigenous activists protested the monument, arguing that the white settlement of Indian lands was not something to celebrate. Cherokee Nation spokesperson Mike Miller declared, "I wouldn't find fault with the individuals involved [in the land run], but the actual event is criminal." But many Oklahomans continue to embrace the romance and excitement of the land runs. Centennial commission executive director J. Blake Wade insisted *Brand New State* was being sculpted "by a Native American, so what is wrong with doing this project?" In fact, the sculptor's heritage reflects the complexity of racial identity in the former Indian Territory: Paul Moore is indeed of Creek (Muscogee) descent, but he inherited land from his white great-grandfather, who participated in the land run that settled two million acres of the former Indian Territory. Moore insisted that he did not wish to speak for any ethnic group in the monument.

Centennial commission director Wade pointed out that many non-Natives had opposed the placement of an American Indian bronze atop the Oklahoma State Capitol dome: "The same way Indians are against the land rush—I don't know why."[41] Like Wade, many white Oklahomans seemed unwilling even to attempt to unpack their state's persistent tensions surrounding land ownership and ethnic identity.

Yet both white and indigenous individuals did critique Moore's enormous bronze installation. A local white artist mounted a highly visible protest against the monument. Geoffrey Krawczyk scattered thirty-nine cast-iron human skulls, some with fake blood, among the monument's bronze figures to protest the state's celebration of the land runs. He explained, "As a white Oklahoman, it has always bothered me how ready the state is to claim its native culture while blatantly whitewashing the actual history of the place." An Indian woman who helped Krawczyk place the skulls at the land rush monument argued that it presented "a silent but powerful message." Police quickly removed the skulls but did not press charges, and *Brand New State* sculptor Moore defended Krawczyk's and others' "right to feel however they want and to protest however they want to." Oklahoma Historical Society executive director Bob Blackburn defended the monument, pointing out that contested land claims were not limited to white-Indian relations: "Indian tribes fought each other, and as one tribe would grow and [become] more prosperous they would expand," taking land from another tribe even before the arrival of Europeans.[42] While Blackburn's statement was accurate, like Director Wade, he pointedly refused to acknowledge the differential power relations involved in Oklahoma's racial strife. While some challenged the motivation behind *Brand New State*, most agreed that the massive work was attractive and historically accurate. Public protests in Oklahoma City—which despite the region's indigenous heritage and a century-long trend of indigenous migration to urban areas was 68.4 percent white, 15.4 percent black or African American, and only 3.5 percent American Indian in 2000—never reached the fever pitch seen in more progressive Portland, Oregon, a decade earlier.[43]

DIVERSITY AS NARRATIVE THERAPY

In the aftermath of the late twentieth-century culture wars, several communities erected more ethnically inclusive monuments. While some sculptors and donors may still be seeking to escape the PC Police, others have sincerely sought to honor the West's cultural diversity. Moving well beyond David Manuel's arrowhead in the dirt, they seek to honor Native Americans or Hispanic peoples through their monument designs. But however well-intentioned these statues may be, by celebrating American westward expansion and white settlement, they still ultimately reinforce white cultural dominance. Some, in fact, serve as a form of narrative therapy, telling stories that include local peoples of color but—like the explicitly social Darwinist monuments of a century earlier—portray white society as the pinnacle of regional development, or Anglo-American settlers as the saviors of local indigenes.

In recent years, larger cities with vibrant civic life have seen lively debates about proper commemoration of their frontier past. In Colorado Springs in 1997, progressive civic groups persuaded the El Paso County Pioneers' Association to abandon their plans to commission "a rather traditional piece, featuring a family portrayed next to a prairie schooner" cast from concrete.[44] Colorado Springs is perhaps best known as the home of the United States Air Force Academy and evangelical Christian groups such as Focus on the Family, and the previous year, the pioneer association had gathered signatures to prevent the local history and art museum from removing the word "Pioneers" from its title.[45] But input from local experts and at public meetings convinced the pioneer association to abandon its vision of a traditional pioneer family statue in favor of something more symbolic. The association's special projects committee received input from "various boards and commissions" and held a series of public meetings before selecting a final design from among thirty submissions that explored "the spirit of pioneerism."[46] They chose a local artist's design, *Follow the Setting Sun*, featuring a sixteen-foot-tall stainless steel pyramid imprinted with a series of images telling the history of the Pike's Peak region (plate F). "I wanted to capture the pioneer spirit, but I wanted a more contemporary piece as opposed to a Conestoga wagon," artist Harriet Lee said.[47]

Although Lee incorporated images of indigenous peoples, the Air Force Academy, and cell phones, the primary message of the pyramid that was erected in front of the Colorado Springs Pioneers Museum in 2005 celebrates "Horace Greeley's famous urging: 'Go West, young man.'"[48] A member of the Art Commission of the Pikes Peak Region called the piece "daring" and "inspiring" and commended the Pioneers Association's "courageous" decision to support a piece that diverged so much from their original idea.[49] But others in the arts community saw the piece as a compromise that pleased no one.[50]

Reading Colorado Springs's *Follow the Setting Sun* against other recent attempts to tell multicultural stories reveals just how far these works fall short of telling a truly inclusive western history. Small Texas towns have placed greater value on specific local stories. The town of Glen Rose, which sits fifty-five miles southwest of Fort Worth, erected a bronze tribute to its local founding couple in 2007 in a similar effort to tell an inclusive local history. Yet like Colorado Springs's *Follow the Setting Sun, Barnards of the Brazos: First Family of Glen Rose* ultimately reinforces white dominance more than it celebrates ethnic diversity (figure 7.7). Glen Rose artist Robert Summers (who is better known for the enormous bronze cattle drive installed about seventy-five miles away in Dallas's Pioneer Plaza) sculpted his hometown's founder. Like many other recent pioneer monuments—particularly those depicting non-Anglos—the Glen Rose statue is accompanied by a lengthy interpretive plaque explaining the figures' historical significance. According to that plaque, Charles Barnard, a white New Englander who came to the Republic of Texas in 1843 to establish Indian trading posts, ransomed and then fell in love with Juana Cavasos, the daughter of a wealthy family, rescuing her from the Comanches who had held her captive. Upon her ransom from that widely feared Indian tribe, the "spirited, intelligent young captive . . . proved to be . . . an outstanding mother, horsewoman, herbal doctor, and neighborhood midwife." By choosing to commemorate this couple and to tell this story, the Somervell History Foundation and those who spoke at the monument's dedication appear to celebrate the town's cultural diversity and to write strong women back into Texas history. Yet the story of Glen Rose's "first family" actually reinforces traditional racial and gender ideologies embodied in Turnerian frontier narratives and the Spanish fantasy past: A white settler came to profit off local Indians. In the absence of Anglo-American women, he "bartered successfully" for and married the Mexican-born daughter of a large "Spanish" landholder, simultaneously saving her from barbarous Indian captivity—and gained access to a large Mexican land grant on which his African American slaves labored.[51] And like the cowboy marrying Miss Indian Territory in Guthrie's *Statehood*

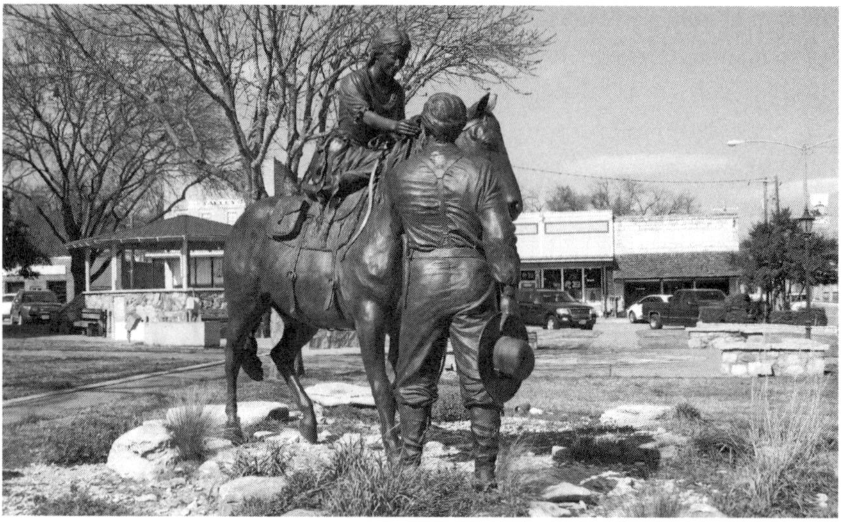

FIGURE 7.7. Robert Summers, *Barnards of the Brazos: First Family of Glen Rose*, Glen Rose, Texas, 2007. Photograph by Anna Prescott.

(see figure 5.7), Glen Rose's monument depicts the literal and figurative marriage of different ethnic groups to form a supposedly united society. Seeking reflected fame from Dallas's heavily visited Pioneer Plaza installation, Glen Rose hired its native son Robert Summers to produce this impressive form of narrative therapy.

PIONEER MOTHERS AT THE NEW MILLENNIUM

In the late 1920s, growing cities throughout the western United States declared their arrival on the national scene by erecting monuments that memorialized the sacrifices of settler women and enshrined nineteenth-century gender norms and white cultural superiority. After World War II, pioneer monuments increasingly glorified the supposedly traditional nuclear family, but continued to silence the Native peoples displaced by white westward expansion. Over time, Pioneer Mother monuments in larger cities have been forgotten, if not actively rejected, by local residents. Meanwhile, smaller towns seeking to attract tourists and new residents by promoting their locations on bygone migration routes have rediscovered forgotten statues and embraced a new pioneer monument movement that celebrates traditionalist cultural values. As the new millennium dawned, a few western communities erected monuments that strayed from the standard iconography established during the Pioneer Mother movement nearly a century earlier. While they employed humor to challenge the outdated gender norms of older Pioneer Mother statues or embraced more abstract forms, even these new monuments silence Native voices and celebrate white settler colonialism. It is not sufficient for us to forget historic statues or to insert a few western European immigrants and feisty women. It is time to reimagine the future of the pioneer monuments erected over the past 125 years and to begin frank public discussions about how they reinforce misogyny and white cultural dominance.

CONCLUSION

Public Perceptions of the American Pioneer Past

In 1992, as the United States celebrated—and protested—the five hundredth anniversary of Christopher Columbus's arrival in the western hemisphere, Portland, Oregon, debated the appropriateness of commemorating the Oregon Trail sesquicentennial by erecting David Manuel's *Promised Land* statue. Meanwhile, plans to move the hundred-year-old *James Lick Pioneer Monument*—an elaborately decorated pillar constructed in front of the San Francisco city hall in 1894 that told a story of white American civilization coming to California (plate A)—to accommodate a new public library also sparked controversy. Twenty-five years later, as Americans debated the removal of Confederate monuments across the country, San Francisco's Art Commission voted to remove the controversial *Early Days* bronze grouping, depicting a Mexican vaquero and a Spanish Franciscan missionary towering over an indigenous Californian seated submissively at their feet (see figure 1.1), from that massive monument. I am returning to the Lick monument—whose story opened the introduction and which I analyze in more depth in chapter 1—because it exemplifies how monuments as objects of public art can evolve. Constructed to meet particular cultural needs in a specific time and place, they tend to be forgotten when a community's identity changes. Yet long-forgotten statues can be rediscovered and become lightning rods for debating cultural issues well removed from the artist's and erectors' original intent. In this conclusion, I compare recent controversies surrounding frontier and Confederate memory, such as the debate over the future of the Lick monument, and explore ways forward for the two hundred pioneer-themed monuments erected in the United States over the past 125 years.

For decades Californians vehemently disagreed over the Lick monument's value and appropriateness. Over the years, activists had repeatedly targeted that portion of the monument for graffiti and vandalism. Native

Americans offended by the statue's demeaning portrayal of indigenous Californians splashed gallons of red paint onto the monument—which they argued "symbolizes the humiliation, degradation, genocide and sorrow inflicted upon this country's indigenous people by a foreign invader"—and called for its removal.[1] But preservationists objected to removing the only physical evidence remaining of San Francisco's old city hall, which had been destroyed by the great 1906 earthquake and fire, to accommodate the library construction. To answer these competing interests, in the 1990s the city chose to move the monument and to erect three interpretive plaques around its base commemorating the old city hall, explaining the monument's origin and symbolism, and describing missionaries' and settlers' mistreatment of indigenous Californians. As with recent decisions to erect interpretive plaques for Confederate lost cause monuments, the compromise satisfied no one: Indian groups, San Francisco's Catholic Archdiocese, and the Spanish government all complained for different reasons. Mayor Willie Brown suggested "that the troubles of these times cannot be corrected by a single plaque."[2] Neither, it seems, can the debate surrounding this historic monument be quelled by a single interpretive sign. But while cities across the nation have debated the fate of Confederate monuments in recent years, and San Francisco has begun the process of removing the most controversial portion of the Lick monument, most American pioneer monuments have been embraced or benignly forgotten.[3] Because this comparison between Confederate statues and pioneer monuments illustrates the shifting racial politics of commemoration with such clarity, in this conclusion I examine twenty-first-century debates over both pioneer and Confederate monuments to consider just how far American society has come from the racial and gender anxieties that motivated their erection in the United States' first golden age of commemoration. I then assess the current state of frontier memory, some four decades into a second age of commemoration. I then close this book by considering lessons learned from this book's history of frontier commemoration and suggesting ways for communities to reconsider the pioneer monuments in their midst.

DEBATING THE FUTURE OF PROBLEMATIC MONUMENTS

Debates surrounding historical commemoration have become heated in recent years. The June 2015 shooting of nine African American worshippers at Emanuel African Methodist Episcopal Church in Charleston, South Carolina, by a white supremacist sparked many calls to retire use of Confederate flags throughout the American South. Outrage over those killings and well-publicized killings of unarmed black civilians by white police officers galvanized public opinion in many parts of the United States against the display of the Confederate battle flag. Activists have also worked to remove or relocate Confederate monuments that were erected during the late nineteenth and early twentieth centuries. But far less public attention has been paid to pioneer monuments that, while celebrating the laudable attributes of fortitude, adventurousness, and family unity, also enshrined white supremacy.

Both the best-known pioneer monuments and monuments to the "lost cause" of the Confederacy were erected in the decades following the U.S. Civil War in response to rapid social change. While white political leaders labored to "redeem" the South from what they perceived as the excesses of Reconstruction, heritage organizations and other powerful groups commissioned monuments to commemorate the sacrifices of Confederate soldiers and citizens. These monuments worked with new segregation laws to reinforce white supremacy just as pioneer monuments celebrated the coming of white civilization to the savage West.[4] Confederate and pioneer monuments drew on a common French Beaux-Arts artistic tradition. Indeed, A. Phimister Proctor sculpted an equestrian monument of Robert E. Lee and a young Confederate soldier as well as famous tributes to pioneer men and women. And today, both Confederate memorials and pioneer monuments continue to be constructed, even as activists have challenged the values enshrined in them.

CONFEDERATE MONUMENTS

The recent debates surrounding Confederate memory suggest the power of a century of a certain form of historical memory; comparing the fate of historic Confederate monuments to that of pioneer monuments highlights how race and gender interact in both lost cause and frontier cultural memory.

Lost cause ideology remains powerful in the former Confederacy. Efforts to remove Confederate monuments have generated backlash. In late 2015, New Orleans city councilors voted six-to-one to remove four Confederate monuments, but Louisiana governor Bobby Jindal denounced the move, protestors armed with Confederate flags and firearms traveled from as far away as Oklahoma to resist their removal, and the company contracted to remove the statues received death threats and its CEO's Lamborghini was torched.[5] A 2017 Alabama law bars the removal, renaming, and alteration of all monuments, memorial streets, memorial buildings, and architecturally significant public buildings for at least forty years.[6] Incredibly, even as communities and institutions across Texas are debating the removal of memorials that many Texans find offensive, the Texas chapter of the Sons of Confederate Veterans is erecting the largest Confederate monument to be built in a century in Orange, a small city near Texas's Louisiana border.[7] And in a move reminiscent of offers to accept Portland's controversial *Promissed Land* statue, The Woodlands Township Board chairman Gordy Bunch proposed moving any Confederate monuments removed from other towns to that young bedroom community outside Houston.[8]

Statues honoring Confederate women have been far less controversial. In part, this is no doubt because far fewer monuments to Confederate women were erected than to Confederate soldiers and statesmen. But it also indicates the different ways in which race and gender identity have been negotiated in recent decades. Many people now critique statues of Confederate leaders for symbolizing precisely the values that they were erected to promote—namely, white male dominance. But while twenty-first-century feminists protest assumptions that women belong only within the domestic sphere, they are less likely to contest the values of grace amid suffering and reconciliation that monuments to Confederate women celebrated.[9]

MASSACRES AND CONTESTED PIONEER MONUMENTS

Though in many ways erected with a similar ethos, pioneer monuments have generally been less controversial than Confederate monuments. A few, like San Francisco's 1894 *James Lick Pioneer Monument* (plate A) and Portland's 1993 *The Promised Land* (plate N), have sparked controversy in recent decades because of their depictions of race. But, paralleling recent discussions of Confederate monuments, very few people have questioned pioneer statues' depictions of gender. For decades, as we saw in the opening to this conclusion, activists have challenged Frank Happersberger's depiction of subservient indigenous peoples in San Francisco's 1894 pioneer monument but accepted its portrayal of specific male heroes and female allegories. More recent depictions of white manhood and womanhood have likewise been challenged on the basis of race, as we will see in this section, but very few have questioned their repetition of early twentieth-century gender norms.

Pioneer commemoration—including lavish Pioneer Day celebrations and old and new pioneer monuments—remains central in Mormon-dominated Utah. But a recent effort to commemorate particular early white settlers in Washington City in southwestern Utah sparked controversy because of its association with the Mountain Meadows Massacre. In 1857, after years of disagreement between the U.S. federal government and the LDS church, the federal government sent troops to Mormon Utah. Tensions poured over into Mormon settlers' interactions with California-bound overland emigrants passing through Utah settlements. A Mormon militia dressed as Paiute Indians attacked a wagon train from Arkansas at Mountain Meadows, killing 120. Most agree that white Mormons were primarily responsible for the bloodshed but sought to blame it on their Paiute allies.[10]

Public memory of the events at Mountain Meadows have been contested for 150 years. John Doyle Lee was the only man tried, convicted, and executed for his role in the attack. As historian Douglas Seefeldt detailed, the Utah Pioneer Trails and Landmarks Association erected a monument at the site of the massacre on the seventy-fifth anniversary of the event. Then, in the mid-twentieth century, the Church of Jesus Christ of Latter-day Saints sought to uncover the truth surrounding the massacre, and reinstated John D. Lee's church membership.[11] In 1989, as groups across the United States challenged monuments celebrating white conquest of indigenous peoples, descendants of Lee and of wagon train victims formed the Mountain Meadows Association (MMA) to commemorate the lives lost and to "come together for understanding and forgiveness."[12] The following year, the LDS church replaced a plaque that had singled out Lee and worked with the MMA to erect a new monument inspired by Maya Lin's Vietnam War memorial in Washington, D.C., but some descendants of the massacre victims were openly critical of the new monument's placement and the church's failure to apologize for the massacre.[13] Vandals soon defaced the new monument, blaming white Mormons for the massacre. The LDS church then rebuilt the 1932 monument and improved access to the burial site, then worked with the MMA to add two new interpretive plaques to the hillside monument.[14]

Shortly after these 1999 efforts to reinterpret Mountain Meadows, nearby Washington City commissioned a statue of John D. Lee to appear alongside monuments to other prominent pioneers in Washington City's Pioneer Memorial Park. But descendants of those killed at Mountain Meadows loudly protested commemorating the scapegoated Lee. Local heritage society officials insisted that they were not condoning his part in the massacre but were honoring him as a local pioneer. While Lee's significance as one of the region's earliest Mormon settlers was not disputed, many believed that Lee's role in Mountain Meadows outweighed the good he had done: "He did many fine things for this community, but he also committed [premeditated] mass murder," statue opponent Bill Stolz said. "I'm amazed this is even up for discussion."[15] Lee remains a divisive figure, but more generic depictions of pioneers remain popular in the early twenty-first century. And while Lee may well have been "a good family man," as one statue defender insisted, Americans remain unwilling to challenge the gender ideology underpinning such claims.[16]

Residents of Washington City and throughout much of the United States continue to embrace century-old notions of ideal Pioneer Mothers. One of the Lee statue's most ardent supporters became determined to commemorate the women who had struggled to survive in the desert settlement by erecting another Jerry Anderson sculpture. Borrowing from Ponca City's 1929 scripture-wielding pioneer woman, Washington City's larger-than-life pioneer woman holds her baby in one arm and scriptures in the other. But Washington City sought to frame its Pioneer Mother as standing in for all Mormon mothers regardless of ethnic background or how recently they arrived in Utah. A speech at the dedication ceremony by the first nonwhite general president of an LDS church auxiliary organization, Chieko Okazaki, emphasized that universality. For Okazaki, who had converted from Buddhism to the LDS faith as a teenager, the monument symbolized the Mormon mothers who raised faithful sons to become global missionaries and to bring the LDS gospel to her Japanese-Hawaiian family.[17] Anderson and Okazaki—like many twenty-first century Americans—embraced Pioneer Mother monuments' timeless celebration of maternalism while choosing to ignore the racial implications of those statues.

Racial tension was arguably unavoidable when marking the 150th anniversary of the U.S.-Dakota War, which had pitted indigenous Dakota warriors against Anglo and German immigrant settlers, culminating in the nation's largest mass execution. The decades following the 1862 conflict saw at least thirty-four monuments and memorial plaques erected in memory of the white settlers and soldiers killed in the conflict, including New Ulm's 1891 *Defenders* monument, and two monuments to "friendly" Indians.[18] Only since the advent of Native activism, like what inspired New Ulm's 1974 mural depicting Indian-settler peaceful coexistence, has Minnesota's memorial landscape begun to include Natives. For the 150th anniversary in 2012, state and county heritage organizations sought to produce more evenhanded histories and to engage with public memory of the conflict and its aftermath. Mankato, site of the largest mass execution in United States history, dedicated a $110,000 memorial on the spot where thirty-eight Dakota men had been hanged—a site now designated Reconciliation Park.[19] But not all Minnesotans joined reconciliation efforts. Some wrote to local newspapers memorializing their settler ancestors killed during the 1862 conflict. And a Mankato third-grade teacher explained to her students that "the only way [the Dakota Indians] knew how to solve their disagreements was to fight. . . . And so then the white settlers needed to fight back to protect themselves."[20] While that teacher's desire to teach her students to "use our words" to settle conflicts was admirable, her lesson ultimately reinforced cultural stereotypes depicting all Dakota people as warlike.

Native activists insist that white settler descendants' good intentions are not sufficient. As Minnesotans marked the 150th anniversary of the U.S.-Dakota War, California artist Sam Durant exhibited a wood and steel sculpture at The Hague and other prominent European sites titled *Scaffold.* The piece was a composite of seven historical gallows used in U.S. state-sanctioned executions by hanging between 1859 and 2006, including those of abolitionist John Brown, individuals accused in the 1886 Haymarket labor uprising, and the thirty-eight Dakotas executed at Mankato in 1862. Through this piece, Durant sought to critique capital punishment and to draw attention to the "racial dimension of the criminal justice system in the United States," including the dispossession and killing of Native Americans.[21] Five years later, as I wrote this book, the Walker Art Center installed Durant's *Scaffold* in the newly revamped Minneapolis

Sculpture Garden as one of several works that "explore complex questions about the times in which we live."[22] The placement of the work in the highly visible "crown jewel of the city's park system" and just eighty miles from Mankato's Reconciliation Park sparked protests by Native activists, who argued that it trivialized Dakota history and genocide—particularly when placed alongside sculptures of an enormous spoon holding a cherry, a giant blue rooster, and a miniature golf course.[23] Both the artist and Walker executive director Olga Viso publicly apologized for the pain caused by the work's display in Minneapolis, and expressed regret that they had not invited Native perspectives prior to its installation. The artist later agreed to permit Native people to dismantle and symbolically burn his work.[24] This incident raises the question, Just how far has American frontier commemoration come in the past 125 years?

PIONEER MEMORY AT THE NEW MILLENNIUM

Where does American pioneer memory stand in 2019? To be certain, much progress has been made. Professional and amateur athletic teams have abandoned the use of Indian nicknames and imagery for their teams, and a few—including Lewis and Clark College—have stepped away from pioneer mascots.[25] And attitudes toward pioneer monuments have changed significantly from memorialization's golden age in the early twentieth century. In the 1910s, white viewers protested monuments such as Charles Grafly's buckskin-clad *Pioneer Mother* for San Francisco and Frederick MacMonnies's placement of an Indian warrior atop a social Darwinist pillar for failing to adequately celebrate white civilization. A century later, Native activists achieved the removal of a Minnesota art installation intended to protest the execution of indigenous warriors resisting their extermination. San Francisco's 1894 *James Lick Pioneer Monument* is accompanied by interpretive plaques—albeit plaques that are hidden by the landscaping surrounding the pillar, hiding their controversial text from all but the most vigilant observer—and may soon remove its depiction of Indian submission to white civilization. But the example of Sam Durant's *Scaffold* also highlights that much work still needs to be done. Minnesota leaders speak of genocide and seek reconciliation with the Dakota nation yet fail to include Native voices in their selection of art addressing the mass execution of Dakota people. Most Americans no longer boast about the superiority of white civilization, and many sincerely desire to build a more inclusive society. White civic leaders and artists seek to critique the nation's racist past and to celebrate diversity yet continue to believe that they can and ought to do so on behalf of underrepresented minorities. Not surprisingly, resulting monuments that stray from traditional iconography still fall short of true inclusivity.

While a few western communities have challenged monuments to white dominance embodied in pioneer-themed sculptures in recent years, even those statues seeking to be more inclusive ultimately commemorate settler colonialism, and monuments to generic Pioneer Mothers are still widely revered. Portland sought to make David Manuel's *Promised Land* statue (plate N) more inclusive by replacing excerpts from Oregon Trail diaries with an inclusive-sounding quotation credited to Thomas Jefferson. Critics attacked the statue as racist and as ugly, but no one publicly questioned its depiction of a strong, forward-looking pioneer father and son, docile mother, and deceased daughter. And a statue of Mountain Meadows leader John D. Lee has proved as controversial as those of Confederate general Robert E. Lee, but one of a generic Mormon woman devoted to family and faith has been well received. Instead of a classic Pioneer Mother, Glen Rose, Texas, commemorated a story that included indigenous, Hispanic, and Anglo actors, as well as both men and women, but that story actually reinforced multiple stereotypical depictions: Indian captivity narratives, a Spanish fantasy past, and white male savior.

Perhaps the closest that any of the two hundred monuments included in this study came to critiquing traditional depictions of pioneer womanhood was Prescott Valley's *Not-So-Gentle Tamer* (plate P). *Not-So-Gentle Tamer* did grant white women more active roles on the frontier, albeit in comedic fashion and in extremely limited form. Yet even this work was intended to reinforce the notion that western women's proper role was to protect their families and to tame western lands and western men. Tom Otterness portrayed a cartoonish pioneer woman actively driving a covered wagon (plate O), but rather than empowering her, this depiction evokes sympathy for her husband (in the form of a bull) who is the target of her harping. In each of these works, the artist mocks traditional depictions of pioneer mothers in ways that ultimately reinforce rather than challenge all the other pioneer monuments' depictions of frontier gender roles.

Moreover, traditional Pioneer Mother imagery remains powerful. Communities continue to erect Pioneer Mother statues that closely resemble those of the Pioneer Mother movement. Oklahomans remain so devoted to Bryant Baker's Ponca City *Pioneer Woman* that the bronze statue (plate B) actually inspired the construction of a companion Pioneer Woman Museum, which first opened during the heyday of the TV western in 1958 and tripled in size amid competition for heritage tourism in 1998. So popular had the statue become that its image came into widespread use throughout the region. In 1958, the sculptor sued National Bank of Tulsa and the Petroleum Publishing Company for copyright infringement, but a U.S. District Court judge ruled that the image was in the public domain and available to anyone for use as a logo, and images of the statue have been widely reproduced ever since.[26] And in 2007, as Oklahoma celebrated its centennial and communities throughout the state erected monuments to late nineteenth-century land rushes, Baker's *Pioneer Woman* was featured in four of the five top design narratives for Oklahoma's state quarter, alongside oil derricks, an Indian peace pipe, and outlines of the state. Intriguingly, the only one of the top entries *not* incorporating some version of the Ponca City monument was overwhelmingly selected by the voting public: a rendering of Oklahoma's state bird, which conveniently avoided debates over historical memory. But the presence of Baker's iconic image on four out of five finalists suggests the Oklahomans' continuing embrace of this imagery.

Almost a century after Baker's statue design was overwhelmingly picked by the American public, some twenty-first-century Oklahomans vocally defend the popular statue's celebration of white civilization. Although it bears no marking in the completed sculpture, both the artist and the donor indicated that the book was intended to be a Christian Bible.[27] U.S. Mint artists' exclusion of that Bible in their proposed designs for Oklahoma's 2007 quarter elicited some two dozen phone calls and letters to Oklahoma governor Brad Henry, as well as several letters to the *Tulsa World*, bemoaning the mint's decision to excise a more subtle reference to Christianity and manifest destiny than that which elicited such controversy in Portland more than a decade earlier.[28]

Americans remain hesitant to question national mythology centered on westward expansion. Controversy surrounding San Francisco's pioneer monument focused on the most explicitly racist sculptural groupings at the base of the enormous monument. Modern viewers seem far less inclined to challenge Happersberger's hierarchical honor roll of famous white men; the bas-reliefs depicting California's Spanish, Mexican, and early American periods; and his allegorical female figures embodying the state's prosperity. In contrast, several southern communities have singled out monuments to famous Confederate leaders as being particularly problematic and candidates for reinterpretation or removal. Perhaps this discrepancy is because these less controversial aspects of San Francisco's monument require careful study and significant knowledge of California history and neoclassical sculpture to interpret, whereas Americans are expected to know about Robert E. Lee. But perhaps more important, despite the Texas state legislature's success recasting the Civil War around the notion of state's rights in history textbooks, beginning in elementary school Americans must grapple with the legacy of race-based slavery in relation to the Civil War. In contrast, many Americans refuse to challenge or even acknowledge the racial underpinnings of the national story of westward expansion. While "cowboys and Indians" history may be passé, tales of (white) men conquering untamed wilderness remain very much in vogue, and few challenge the notion of American manifest destiny.

Even 125 years after the U.S. Census Bureau declared the frontier to be "closed," historical memory of the frontier remains central to American identity. *Little House on the Prairie* reruns and the juvenile novel series on which that television show was based still have faithful followings—so much so that a Wilder Trail links eight heritage tourism sites in six states, marking the former homes of the books' author.[29] The vintage *Oregon Trail* computer game continues to be played online via Internet Archive, even generating a new card game adaptation.[30] Although a few schools' athletic programs are moving away from pioneer mascots, frontier imagery remains powerful and widely accepted. Malone University unveiled a new pioneer mascot in 2011.[31] Four years later, the University of Oregon Ducks football team partnered with sporting goods titan Nike to don uniforms commemorating the Oregon Trail and Lewis and Clark expedition.[32] Pioneer Day remains an important civic and religious holiday in Utah. Frontier-oriented historic sites have a strong following, and cowboy art and poetry remain extremely popular. And, as this study reveals, communities continue to erect monuments to white pioneers.

American memory of the frontier was and is overwhelmingly white.

At the turn of the twentieth century, Americans were deeply invested in establishing the whiteness of the men and women who settled supposedly empty, virgin lands. They believed that those white settlers carried the blessings of Euro-American civilization to untamed lands and savage indigenous peoples who were destined to disappear. By midcentury, so convinced were they that the West was settled by civilized whites, Americans felt little need to discuss the racial identity of the pioneers. Battles for control of western land and culture were no longer fought with guns and arrows, or even through the design of commemorative statues, but on screen in western films and television shows. Only at the turn of the twenty-first century did mainstream white culture hear critiques of this white-dominated frontier narrative. And those critiques were soon forgotten, as more and more western communities declared their place in the national narrative of westward expansion. Few efforts have been made to tell more inclusive histories of the West.

PUBLIC PERCEPTION AND POPULAR MEMORY

As this study has shown, memorialization of pioneers has varied over time and space as the culture has evolved and changed. The earliest pioneer monuments celebrated white men who conquered the West and paid tribute to supposedly vanishing American Indians. In the 1920s and 1930s, amid anxieties about urbanization, new immigration, and new roles for women, communities across the United States erected monuments to a generic sunbonneted Pioneer Mother. Interest in erecting new monuments and maintaining old ones declined in the postwar period. Yet even as larger cities chose to forget the pioneer monuments in their midst, a new wave of monuments to pioneer women and families appeared in smaller and more conservative communities that clung to their pioneer heritage in the face of rapid cultural changes and sought to cash in on heritage tourism.

How much does all this remembering and forgetting actually matter to the average American? Very few actively seek out these statues, and most remain unaware of the prominent statues in their midst. Yet many people will pause to glance at a statue, and when they are visiting an unfamiliar place, they might read the accompanying plaque or even snap a photo. It is extremely challenging to measure the impact of such casual viewing of public monuments on individuals' understanding of the past. How does visiting a statue as a tourist stop or destination differ from walking past the same statue regularly? How can we unpack the influence of viewing a statue on our conception of the history depicted in that statue many days, or even years later? This study provides several insights that help to answer these challenging questions.

First, and perhaps most obviously, statue design matters. Although the monuments used similar imagery, how frontier women and men were depicted in Pioneer Mother statues varied by artist and audience in important ways. Moreover, changes in pioneer monument design reflected and helped reinforce changing American racial and religious identities and gender norms. As we have seen, early monuments' elaborate iconography and emphasis on social Darwinism soon yielded to simpler designs. The 1920s monuments typically featured a sunbonneted Pioneer Mother striding westward with a young child, armed with a Bible or rifle. After World War II, pioneer monuments usually represented a frontier family, emphasizing the role of the patriarch or adolescent son, with the Pioneer Mother playing a supporting role in the background. While that nuclear family imagery remains common, a handful of monuments erected since 2000 have struck out in new artistic directions. These artistic decisions have a profound influence on how viewers experience these monuments.

The design of the statue's base and its interpretive signage (or lack thereof) also make a difference. Older pioneer monuments typically have minimal or no interpretive signage but sometimes include supporting bas-reliefs depicting frontier scenes. The DAR selected local historic events to highlight on the base of each *Madonna of the Trail* monument but did not comment on August Leimbach's statue design. This reliance on visual images rather than text represented a conscious choice by donors and city leaders, who assumed that they and the statue's viewers could agree on the meaning of their frontier past. Yet that lack of signage left viewers free to interpret the monuments in their own way, or it left them adrift, wondering why the statue existed at all. Interpretive signage for pioneer monuments has become more extensive because the meaning of American westward expansion has become more publicly contested over the past twenty-five years. Ironically, the typical amount of interpretive text has increased dramatically even as Americans' willingness to read lengthy text has decreased dramatically in an age dominated by internet memes and 140-character tweets. Committees painstakingly produce interpretive signs that place pioneer monuments in historical context of the era in which they were erected, but that cannot satisfy every perspective, and most viewers do not bother to read them.

Second, the statue's physical context matters. The placement of a monument has a significant effect on how it is perceived by its viewers. A lone white stone pioneer woman standing in an out-of-the-way cemetery outside Ellis, Kansas, sends a very different message than a similar statue placed in a prominent location on a college campus quadrangle. Placing a pioneer woman monument in front of a county courthouse or statehouse suggests a greater political role for women than does one placed in a community park or near a commercial structure. A monument that stands alone encourages viewers to contemplate what it commemorates, while several standing together that employ similar iconography can reinforce one another, as do the Confederate monuments on Monument Avenue in Richmond, Virginia.[33] Placing a monument among other, seemingly unrelated sculptures can strike a discordant note that challenges viewers to ponder its significance (as does the Arthur Ashe statue on Monument Avenue), but in other circumstances, it can encourage the public to approach it as one of many pieces of public art without commemorative power. Presumably, most people who view the bronze pioneer family in Portland's Chapman Square (plate N) see it as just another piece of the city's public sculpture collection, and do not recognize that *The Promised Land* and two nearby sculptures—a bronze elk and stone Spanish-American War memorial—all celebrate different aspects of nineteenth-century white conquest.

Over time, even monuments placed in prominent locations can be forgotten. Trees and shrubbery planted to attract visitors to the statue grow large enough to hide it from view, as with Kansas City's 16,000-pound A. Phimister Proctor *Pioneer Mother* grouping (plate C). Urban centers decay and new construction bypasses or eliminates older thoroughfares. These changes to the surrounding landscape influence the ways in which viewers experience and interpret public monuments.

Third, the viewer's reason for viewing the monument matters. Even those monuments that have become important tourist destinations can become an unremarkable piece of the local landscape for people who walk or drive past them every day. The traditional imagery of a Pioneer

Mother still resonates with the white population of Oklahoma, a culturally conservative state that still struggles to come to terms with its past as Indian Territory. While most of the other Pioneer Mother statues erected in the late 1920s have been forgotten, Ponca City, Oklahoma, promoted its massive *Pioneer Woman* statue in 1929 (plate B) as a symbol of their community and an important tourist destination in its own right. Like Wall Drug in tiny Wall, South Dakota, which became a nationally known roadside attraction thanks to clever billboards offering a free drink of ice water to travelers en route to Mount Rushmore's shrine of democracy, Ponca City leaders promoted their community by turning their pioneer monument into a memorable wayside attraction.[34] Their promotion of the statue encouraged Oklahomans and visitors to notice the statue and to remember it, thus helping to shape how those locals and tourists thought about Oklahoma and its history.

Yet viewers' personal priorities trump the best-laid plans of sculptors and community leaders. Vancouver, Washington, moved its 1928 *Pioneer Mother* statue (see figure 2.2) from a hidden, garden-like setting to a busy city street as part of a massive urban renewal project. While they apparently sought to increase the monument's visual—and thus cultural—impact, many local residents view the statue primarily as an obstacle to their return to Esther Short Park.

Fourth, viewers use and abuse statues to fulfill their own purposes. A few pioneer monuments have been targeted by individuals seeking to make a political point. In 2011, students at the University of Oregon adorned the 1918 A. Phimister Proctor *Pioneer* statue (see figure 1.4)—but, significantly, not Proctor's 1928 *Pioneer Mother*—with a rainbow-colored balloon arch to mark National Coming Out Day, which encourages students and others to identify publicly as homosexual, bisexual, or transgender. Apparently the university administration did not want the "Pioneer Father" to be associated with homosexuality, because the balloons were removed from the statue within forty-five minutes.[35] Like the more blatant (and physically damaging) painting of pioneer and Confederate monuments, these individuals challenged local residents to see these gender and racial symbols in new ways.

A few pioneer monuments have been severely damaged or destroyed in recent years. Apparently in protest to her nudity, unidentified individuals attacked and severely damaged Wichita's *Heritage Woman* (see figure

3.6) three times in eight years. And in 2013 a trio of local residents stole a pioneer woman monument (see figure 6.3) from the courtyard of the National Frontier Trails Museum in Independence, Missouri, and tore apart the bronze statue before attempting to sell it for scrap.[36] Whether the perpetrators sought to make a political statement or to personally profit from civic investments, these acts of vandalism ultimately failed to remove these Pioneer Mothers from the public eye. Instead, the attacks galvanized both communities to repair or replace the statues and, in the process, to more thoroughly enshrine the symbols of frontier maternalism.

Fifth, the viewer's cultural identity affects their perception of the monument. A Native American whose ancestors lost their land, and perhaps their lives, to white westward expansion is likely to view a Pioneer Mother statue differently than would a white descendant of western homesteaders. And a member of the Church of Jesus Christ of Latter-day Saints is likely to find greater resonance in a monument to Mormon handcart pioneers than would a non-Mormon viewer. But ethnic and cultural identity can operate in complex ways. One of the most outspoken critics of Portland's *Promised Land* monument was an African American man who felt that the statue celebrated whites' mistreatment of peoples of color. Yet a local indigenous leader—whose ancestors were far more directly affected by white settlement of the region—actually supported the monument, arguing that other ethnic groups were free to erect their own statues. While ethnic identity may not be as simple as black (or red) and white, it clearly affects individuals' reactions to pioneer monuments.

Sixth, novelty matters. Statues tend to garner attention when they are erected, and then that attention dwindles over time. In some cases, being inundated with a certain image can cause it to have a greater influence on us. Many Americans picture frontier women in sunbonnets or with wagon-cover halos, although most likely could not identify where they have learned these traits or seen such images. Prominent sculptors like A. Phimister Proctor and Avard Fairbanks consciously sought to balance artistic traditions, historical accuracy, popular memory, and aesthetics when they designed pioneer monuments; they and their viewers were also influenced at a more subconscious level by the images they encountered every day. Yet regular exposure to something can also cause us to take it for granted, or even to ignore it. In the case of public monuments, regular viewing seems to cause us to pass the statue without actually *seeing* it. Indeed, even scholars trained to examine and question the historical memory of the American West apparently pay little attention to the pioneer statues in their own backyards. A 2007 query posted on H-West, the primary online discussion board for historians of the American West, yielded only a handful of references to the same few monuments. But I have since identified a total of 185 pioneer-themed monuments located throughout the United States.

Changing the context in which one views a monument can create novelty. Most commuters who walk by the *Madonna of the Trail* statue outside the Metro station in downtown Bethesda, Maryland (see figure 7.1), barely notice that the statue is there. Even the statue's presence on the city's logo did not lead Bethesda residents to notice the statue that seemed at odds with their urban existence—until a sinkhole caused her to tip sideways like the Leaning Tower of Pisa.[37] In recent years, several communities have relocated Pioneer Mother statues to novel settings to *increase* their visibility. Springfield, Ohio, even created a new downtown park with their *Madonna of the Trail* monument as its centerpiece and namesake. Nonetheless, though news stories draw public attention to these statues when they are relocated, their presence in their new location soon becomes part of the familiar—and thus little noticed—landscape, unless something new occurs to once again create novelty. In the 1990s, David Manuel's *Promised Land* monument sparked such controversy when it was erected in Portland, Oregon, that the city moved it *twice.* Today that statue is barely noticed by businesspeople bustling at its feet. When I discussed that statue in a presentation at a history conference in Portland, several conference participants reported taking a break from attending conference sessions to visit the statue for the first time, or to view it in a new way.

THE FUTURE OF PIONEER MEMORY

What, then, have we learned? Assessing the impact of a monument on American society is extremely challenging, because many factors influence the ways in which individuals—let alone entire communities—view these statues. Unpacking how our viewing of these monuments has shaped our understanding of western history is even more complex. It is influenced by our formal education, popular culture, and many other factors. But studying 185 pioneer-themed monuments erected over some 125 years makes clear that the design of pioneer monuments changed over time, and that those changes both reflected and helped reinforce changing popular memory of western history, race, religion, gender, and individuals' place within the American nation.

Are all pioneer monuments necessarily offensive and problematic? Should we tear them down or move them to museums, as some communities have done with Confederate monuments? Or is it better to leave them in place and erect interpretive plaques that explain the historical context for their erection and intended meaning? There are no easy answers to these questions. But as we have seen, design and context matter. To move forward, then, we will need to consider the specific design and the physical and social contexts of each monument. A rarely noticed pioneer woman statue in a rural cemetery might rightfully be forgotten. Monuments that are rediscovered amid urban renewal might wisely be relocated to a museum, where they could be reinterpreted regarding their contribution to western mythology. In most cases, however, pioneer monuments should remain in place. After all, removing a statue is itself a form of erasure. And because there are few monuments of other kinds to western women, removing pioneer woman monuments—however problematic their depiction may be—would contribute to women's underrepresentation.

In some cases, interpretive signs could significantly influence how viewers think about a statue. For example, a series of carefully worded interpretive signs could guide viewers to examine the cultural imperialism inherent in Portland's *Promised Land* statue, along with the nearby bronze elk and Spanish-American War monuments. Providing a brief history of gender and ethnic inclusion and exclusion in Chapman Square would challenge both tourists and local residents to ponder the ways in which social power are carved into Portland's urban landscape.

But a series of interpretive signs would be insufficient to override the symbolic power of a monument like Ponca City's *Pioneer Woman*. State leaders have erected a new, more inclusive centennial memorial nearby. While that is a good first step, there is much more work to do. Even that more inclusive monument implies that indigenous peoples represent the region's past, while descendants of white settlers will lead the state into the future. Standing Bear Park, Museum, and Education Center outside

Ponca City counters with indigenous perspectives but is largely ignored by visitors and residents. The Pioneer Woman Museum that accompanies Bryant Baker's famous statue does a fairly good job of depicting the realities of frontier women's lives. That museum should expand its scope to critique the white dominance and patriarchal social structure that the massive statue embodies. But as we have seen, Bryant Baker's depiction of white womanhood is not only a popular tourist destination. It also remains a powerful symbol of (white) Oklahoma identity. Even a well-curated exhibit in the Pioneer Woman Museum will not reach many of those who remain invested in its pioneer imagery. And its celebration of settler colonialism and patriarchy continue to be reinforced with new monuments across the state.

Instead, it will take a much broader public discussion to influence popular ideas. Historical museums, heritage societies, and schools across the state should teach both Oklahomans and visitors a more complex history of the area. While it is appropriate to teach people about the realities of frontier life, that history must acknowledge that Oklahoma land was neither empty nor free. Exhibits and lesson plans representing Native Americans both as indigenous to the region and as settlers in Indian Territory would complicate popular understandings of Oklahoma frontiers. Histories of local women should show their ethnic diversity and narrate their participation in all aspects of Oklahoma society, rather than reinforcing tired tropes. And patrons and students should be encouraged to explore how such tropes and the logic of settler colonialism permeate myths of the West. Such an endeavor would require broad cooperation among public and private entities. The broader the reach of such public reinterpretation, the greater its potential influence on popular opinion.

There is no one-size-fits-all solution to the challenge presented by our nation's pioneer monuments. Western communities need to discuss and together decide the future of their tributes to our frontier past. It is time for us to begin these difficult conversations, so that future generations will learn not only from what happened in the past, but from how our memories of the past have changed over time and can build a more inclusive future.

APPENDIX
Monuments Keyed to Maps in This Study

Monument numbers correspond with numbered locations on maps throughout this volume.

1. Unknown, *Pioneer Monument (Centennial Monument).* Granite. Diamond Park, Meadville, Pa. 1888.
2. Karl Gerhardt, *Pioneer Statuary Group.* Bronze. Capitol, Des Moines, Iowa. 1892.
3. Frank Happersberger, *James Lick Pioneer Monument.* Bronze and granite. Main Library, San Francisco Public Library, San Francisco, Calif. 1894.
4. Cyrus Edwin Dallin, *Brigham Young Pioneer Monument.* Bronze. Temple Square, Salt Lake City, Utah. 1897.
5. Allen G. Newman, *Pioneer.* Zinc. Near capitol, Salem, Ore. 1903–1917.
6. Hermon MacNeil, *Coming of the White Man.* Bronze. Washington Park, Portland, Ore. 1904.
7. Alice Cooper, *Sacajawea.* Bronze. Washington Park, Portland, Ore. 1905.
8. Frederick MacMonnies, *Pioneer Monument.* Bronze. Civic Center Park, Denver, Colo. 1911.
9. Allen G. Newman, *Pioneer Mike (Carter Memorial Fountain; Iron Mike).* Zinc. Ashland Plaza, Ashland, Ore. 1910–2014.
10. Allen G. Newman, *Minuteman.* Zinc. University of Northern Colorado campus, Greeley, Colo. 1911–1938.
11. Allen G. Newman, *Pioneer.* Zinc. Lake Avenue and Lakeshore Drive, Storm Lake, Iowa. 1912–1972.
12. Mahonri M. Young, *Seagull Monument.* Bronze. Temple Square, Salt Lake City, Utah. 1913.
13. Charles Grafly, *Pioneer Mother.* Bronze. Golden Gate Park, San Francisco, Calif. 1915.
14. James Earle Fraser, *The End of the Trail.* Plaster. Panama-Pacific International Exposition, San Francisco, Calif. [1915?]
15. Solon Borglum, *The American Pioneer (Pioneer).* Plaster. Panama-Pacific International Exposition, San Francisco, Calif. 1915.
16. Frederick Hibbard, *Pioneer (Corn Planter).* Bronze. University of Kansas campus, Lawrence, Kans. 1904; erected 1916.

17. A. Phimister Proctor, *The Pioneer.* Bronze. University of Oregon campus, Eugene, Ore. 1918.
18. John McQuarrie, *Pioneer Family (Donner) Monument.* Bronze. Donner State Park, Truckee, Calif. 1918.
19. Paul Fjelde, *Mormon Trail Memorial.* Bronze. Bayliss Park, Council Bluffs, Iowa. 1918.
20. James Earle Fraser., *The End of the Trail.* Bronze copy of original plaster. Mooney Grove Park, Visalia, Calif. 1919.
21. Solon Borglum, *The American Pioneer (Pioneer).* Plaster. Mooney Grove Park, Visalia, Calif. 1919–1980.
22. Robert Merrell Gage, *Daughters of Old Westport Memorial.* Bronze. Near Pioneer Park, Westport, Mo. 1920.
23. A. Phimister Proctor, *The Circuit Rider.* Bronze. Capitol Park, Salem, Ore. 1924.
24. Avard T. Fairbanks, *Old Oregon Trail.* Bronze. Broadway Bridge, Seaside, Ore. 1924.
25. Avard T. Fairbanks, *Old Oregon Trail.* Bronze. Oregon Trail Interpretive Center, Baker City, Ore. 1924.
26. Myra Reynolds Richards, *Pioneer Family.* Limestone. Fountain Square, Indianapolis, Ind. 1924.
27. Robert Garrison, *Covered Wagon Frieze.* Terra cotta with patina. Denver Botanical Gardens, Denver, Colo. 1925.
28. Avard T. Fairbanks, *U.S. Bank Doors.* Bronze. U.S. Bank Building, Portland, Ore. 1926.
29. Torleif S. Knaphus, *Handcart Pioneer Monument.* Bronze. Original, smaller version. LDS Temple Square, Salt Lake City, Utah. 1926.
30. A. Phimister Proctor, *Pioneer Mother.* Bronze. Penn Valley Park, Kansas City, Mo. 1927.
31. A. Phimister Proctor, *Pioneer Mother.* Bronze. University of Oregon campus, Eugene, Ore. 1928.
32. Avard T. Fairbanks, *Pioneer Mother.* Bronze. Esther Short Park, Vancouver, Wash. 1928.
33. Avard T. Fairbanks, *The Pioneer Mothers.* Bronze. Esther Short Park, Vancouver, Wash. 1928.
34. August Leimbach, *Madonna of the Trail.* Poured algonite stone. Old Post Office, Bethesda, Md. 1928.
35. August Leimbach, *Madonna of the Trail.* Poured algonite stone. Madonna of the Trail Park, Beallsville, Pa. 1928.
36. August Leimbach, *Madonna of the Trail.* Poured algonite stone. Wheeling Park, facing National Road, Wheeling, W.Va. 1928.
37. August Leimbach, *Madonna of the Trail.* Poured algonite stone. National Road Commons Park, Springfield, Ohio. 1928.
38. August Leimbach, *Madonna of the Trail.* Poured algonite stone. Glen Miller Park, Richmond, Ind. 1928.

39. August Leimbach, *Madonna of the Trail.* Poured algonite stone. Old State House, Vandalia, Ill. 1928.

40. August Leimbach, *Madonna of the Trail.* Poured algonite stone. Above Missouri River, downtown Lexington, Mo. 1928.

41. August Leimbach, *Madonna of the Trail.* Poured algonite stone. Corner of Main St. (U.S. 56) and N. Union St. (KS 177), Council Grove, Kans. 1928.

42. August Leimbach, *Madonna of the Trail.* Poured algonite stone. Colorado Welcome Center, Lamar, Colo. 1928.

43. August Leimbach, *Madonna of the Trail.* Poured algonite stone. Corner of Marble Ave. and Fourth St., Albuquerque, N.Mex. 1928.

44. August Leimbach, *Madonna of the Trail.* Poured algonite stone. 318 E Main St., next to McDonald's, Springerville, Ariz. 1928.

45. August Leimbach, *Madonna of the Trail.* Poured algonite stone. Euclid Ave. at Foothill Blvd (Route 66), Upland, Calif. 1928.

46. Nancy Coonsman Hahn, *Memorial to Pioneer Women (The Colonial Mother).* Bronze. Forest Park, St. Louis, Mo. 1929.

47. Lorado Taft, *The Pioneers.* Bronze. Central Park, Elmwood, Ill. 1928.

48. Bryant Baker, *Pioneer Woman.* Bronze. Pioneer Woman Museum, Ponca City, Okla. 1929.

49. Maurice Sterne, *The Settlers of New England (The Monument to Our Pioneers; Rogers–Kennedy Memorial).* Stone and bronze. Elm Park, Worcester, Mass. 1929.

50. James Earle Fraser, *The End of the Trail.* Bronze. Shaler Park, Waupun, Wisc. 1915; erected 1929.

51. James Earle Fraser, *The Pioneers.* Limestone. Michigan Ave. Bridge (DuSable Bridge), Chicago, Ill. 1930.

52. Cyrus Edwin Dallin, *Pioneer Mother (End of the Trail).* Bronze. City Park, Springville, Utah. 1931.

53. Unknown, *The Pioneers Who Founded Topeka.* Bronze or copper. Gage Park, Topeka, Kans. 1931.

54. Ulric Ellerhusen, *George Rogers Clark Memorial (The First Permanent Settlement of the West; Settlers of the West).* Granite. Fort Harrod State Park, Harrodsburg, Ky. 1932.

55. Julius Loester, *Pioneers Monument (Benediction).* Bronze. Kingsborough Cemetery, Gloversville, N.Y. 1932.

56. Unknown, *Untitled (Pioneer Woman).* Marble. Mount Hope Cemetery, Ellis, Kans. 1933.

57. William Zorach, *Pioneer Family Group* (later cast as *The Family*). Model. Texas Centennial Commission, Austin, Tex. 1935.

58. Ellis Luis Burman, *The Pioneer Woman.* Bronze. Antelope Park, Lincoln, Neb. Commissioned 1925; erected 1935.

59. Leo Friedlander, *Pioneer Woman.* Marble. Texas Woman's University, Denton, Tex. 1936.

60. Avard T. Fairbanks, *Tragedy at Winter Quarters.* Bronze. Pioneer Mormon Cemetery, Florence, Neb. 1936.
61. Ulric Ellerhusen, *Pioneer.* Gold-gilded bronze. Oregon Capitol dome, Salem, Ore. 1936.
62. John K. Daniels, *Pioneers' Monument.* Granite. B. F. Nelson Park, Minneapolis, Minn. 1936.
63. Unknown, *Mormon Handcart Brigade Camp Marker.* Bronze. S. T. Morrison Park, Coralville, Iowa. 1936.
64. Frank A. Teich, *Pioneer Memorial Obelisk.* Granite. Hermann Park, Houston, Tex. 1936.
65. Robert Neely, *The Pioneer Family.* Cement. Grinnell Community Center, Grinnell, Iowa. 1937.
66. Unknown, *Massengil Memorial Monument.* Winged Deer Park, Johnson City, Tenn. 1937.
67. Leo Friedlander, *The Covered Wagon.* Marble. Capitol, Salem, Ore. Ca. 1937.
68. Avard T. Fairbanks, *New Frontiers.* Bronze. LDS Conference Center, Temple Square, Salt Lake City, Utah. 1937.
69. Robert Merrell Gage, *Pioneer Women of Kansas.* Bronze. Capitol, Topeka, Kans. 1937.
70. Hugo Villa, *German Pioneers of Texas.* Bronze. Landa Park, New Braunfels, Tex. 1938.
71. Samuel Cashwan, *Pioneer Mother.* Stone. Clare Middle School, Clare, Mich. 1938.
72. Gabriel Lavare, *Pioneer Woman Reading to Child.* Marble. Oregon State Library, Salem, Ore. Ca. 1939.
73. Byron S. Johnson, *Humanity.* Bronze. Pioneer Center, Reno, Nev. 1939.
74. Elbert Porter, *Swiss Colony Daughters of Utah Pioneers Historical Marker.* Plaster and concrete. Church of Jesus Christ of Latter-day Saints, Santa Clara, Utah. 1939.
75. Clarence Addison Shaler, *Pioneers of Wisconsin.* Bronze. Wilcox Park, Waupun, Wisc. 1939.
76. Alfonso Iannelli, *Fountain of the Pioneers.* Concrete. Bronson Park, Kalamazoo, Mich. Dedicated 1940; relocated 2018.
77. Avard T. Fairbanks, *Pioneering.* Bronze. Temple Square, Salt Lake City, Utah. 1942.
78. Avard T. Fairbanks, *Pioneer Family Group.* Bronze. Capitol, Bismarck, N.Dak. 1946.
79. Torleif S. Knaphus, *Handcart Pioneer Monument.* Bronze. LDS Temple Square, Salt Lake City, Utah. 1947.
80. Mahonri M. Young, *This Is the Place Monument.* Bronze. This Is the Place Park, Salt Lake City, Utah. 1947.
81. Marshall M. Fredericks, *Early Kentucky Settlers.* Bronze. Courier-Journal Building, Louisville, Ky. 1948.

82. Alonzo Victor Lewis, *The Prospector.* Bronze. Pioneers Home, Sitka, Alaska. Commissioned 1926; erected 1949.

83. Unknown, *Pioneer Memorial Obelisk.* Quartzite. Hilltop overlooking Sioux Falls, S.Dak. 1949.

84. Anna Belle Campbell, *Prairie Family (The Homesteaders).* Composite of concrete and stone. Mission Road traffic circle, Prairie Village, Kans. 1951.

85. (Thomas) Puryear Mims, *Mountain Group (Pioneer Family).* Bronze. Cordell Hull State Office Building, Nashville, Tenn. 1951.

86. Unknown, *Pioneer Mothers' Memorial.* Stone. Pioneer Mothers Memorial Forest, Paoli, Ind. 1951.

87. Jo Davidson, *Pioneer Woman.* Bronze. Pioneer Pipe Line Company, Woods Cross, Utah. 1953.

88. George Bauwens, *Glendale Pioneers.* Bronze. Church of Jesus Christ of Latter-day Saints, Glendale, Utah. 1955.

89. Francis Minturn Sedgwick and Vladimir Oslou, *Laurel Hill Pioneer Monument.* Bronze, marble, and concrete. Cypress Lawn Memorial Park, Colma, Calif. 1955.

90. Frederic Littman, *Pioneer Woman (Joy; Young Pioneer Woman; Laberee Memorial Fountain; Mother/Child).* Bronze. Council Crest Park, Portland, Ore. 1956.

91. Avard T. Fairbanks, *Guidance of Youth.* Bronze. Bush's Pasture Park, Salem, Ore. 1958.

92. Avard T. Fairbanks, *Oregon Centennial Medallion.* Bronze. Bush's Pasture Park, Salem, Ore. 1958.

93. Gordon Shumaker, *Pioneer Woman.* Fiberglass. Pioneer Portrait Hall, Minnesota State Fairgrounds, St. Paul, Minn. 1958.

94. Leonard McMurry, *Pioneers of 1889.* Bronze. Kerr Couch Park, Oklahoma City, Okla. 1959.

95. Unknown, *Pioneer Woman and Child.* Painted concrete. Western Savings Bank Building, Mesa, Ariz. Ca. 1960.

96. Wheeler Williams, *Pioneer Mother of Kansas.* Bronze. Public Library, Cooper Park, Liberal, Kans. Designed 1927; erected 1961.

97. William Zorach, *The Family.* Bronze. Columbia Savings Bank, Colorado Springs, Colo. 1964; relocated 1990s.

98. William Zorach, *The Family.* Bronze. Columbia Savings Bank, Pueblo, Colo. 1964; relocated 1994.

99. Susan M. Pogzeba, *Homage to the Pioneer.* Bronze. Zeckendorf Park, Denver, Colo. 1968.

100. Charles B. Martin, *Arizona's Pioneer Women.* Copper. Wesley Bolin Plaza, Phoenix, Ariz. 1968.

101. Pete Felten Jr., *Pioneer Family Statue.* Limestone. North Penn Avenue, Oberlin, Kans. 1971.

102. James Earle Fraser, *The End of the Trail.* Plaster. National Cowboy and Western Heritage Museum, Oklahoma City, Okla. 1971.

103. Granville W. Carter, *West Texas Pioneer Family*. Bronze. Avenue Q at 13th St., Lubbock, Tex. 1971.

104. Gus Shafer, *The Wagon Master*. Bronze. Intercontinental Hotel, Kansas City, Mo. 1973.

105. Pete Felten Jr., *Boot Hill Cowboy (The Homesteader)*. Limestone. Boot Hill Cemetery, Hays, Kans. 1973.

106. Gordan Dingman, *Life Sketches*. Brick. 16 N Minnesota St., New Ulm, Minn. 1974.

107. Edward J. Fraughton. *Mormon Pioneer Memorial Monument ("All is Well")*. Bronze. Brigham Young Family Memorial Cemetery, Salt Lake City, Utah. 1974.

108. Allen G. Newman, *Pioneer*. Bronze. Lake Ave. and Lakeshore Dr., Storm Lake, Iowa. 1974.

109. Pete Felten Jr., *Pioneer Family (Volga German Immigrant Family)*. Limestone. Corner of 19th and Cathedral, Victoria, Kans. 1976.

110. Ann Opgenorth and Donna Marihar, *Five Figures for Five Flags (Pioneers Sculpture)*. Bronze. Cathedral Square, Dubuque, Iowa. 1976.

111. Richard Bergen, *Heritage Woman*. Bronze. Heritage Park, Wichita, Kans. 1976.

112. W. Walter Campbell, *Pioneer Family*. Limestone. Blair County Courthouse, Hollidaysburg, Pa. 1976.

113. Rich Muno, *Pioneer Man*. Bronze. City Hall, Clinton, Okla. 1976.

114. Frederick A. Olds, *Statehood*. Bronze. Oklahoma Territorial Museum, Guthrie, Okla. 1977.

115. George Bassett, *Delavan Pioneers (Land is Our Heritage)*. Bronze. 2nd St. park. Delavan, Minn. 1977.

116. Avard T. Fairbanks, *The American Family*. Bronze. Utah County Courthouse, Provo, Utah. 1978.

117. Avard T. Fairbanks, *American Motherhood*. Marble. Utah County Courthouse, Provo, Utah. 1979.

118. Pershing Geiger, *The Homesteader*. Bronze. Homesteader Plaza, Casper, Wyo. 1979.

119. Christian Petersen, *Madonna of the Prairie (Prairie Woman)*. Limestone. Iowa State University College of Education, Ames, Iowa. Ca. 1940; erected 1982.

120. Steve Shields, *Pioneer*. Copper. Pioneer Cemetery, Hopkinsville, Ky. 1984.

121. Jack Cartlidge, *Pioneer Family (Pioneer Family Hears a Sound Is It Bears or Billy Bowlegs?)*. Copper. City Hall, Sarasota, Fla. 1984.

122. Charlie Norton, *Spirit of the Prairie*. Bronze. Thomas County Courthouse, Colby, Kans. 1985.

123. Mike Capser, *Pioneer's Vision*. Bronze with patina. First Interstate Bank Building, Billings, Mont. 1985.

124. Bill Nebeker, *Early Settlers*. Bronze. Memorial Island Park, Prescott, Ariz. 1985.

125. Thomas L. Beard, *Pioneer Square Monument*. Bronze. Pioneer Square, Westport, Mo. 1986.

126. Greg Todd, *They Came to Stay*. Bronze. Sherman County Courthouse, Goodland, Kans. 1987.

127. Harold T. Holden, *Boomer.* Bronze. Cherokee Strip Conference Center, Enid, Okla. 1987.

128. Claude H. Pomeroy, *Mesa Pioneer Monument (Pioneer Park Statue).* Bronze. Pioneer Park, Mesa, Ariz. 1988.

129. Orville Quick, *Pioneer Woman and Child.* Concrete. McCone County Museum, Circle, Mont. 1989.

130. Lyndon Fayne Pomeroy, *Pioneer Canal Digger.* Steel. Pioneer Park, Worland, Wyo. 1989.

131. Michael Westergard, *With Courage They Came.* Bronze. Sheridan County Civic Center, Plentywood, Mont. 1989.

132. George O. Cornish, *Pioneer Gratitude.* Bronze. Hurricane Valley Heritage Park, Hurricane, Utah. 1989.

133. Dee Jay Bawden, *Sons of Utah Pioneers Pioneer Monument.* Bronze. Founders Park, Centerville City, Utah. 1990.

134. Juan Lombardo-Rivera, *The Pioneer Woman.* Bronze. National Frontier Trails Museum, Independence, Mo. 1990–2013.

135. Pat Mathiesen, *Spirit of the Frontier.* Bronze. Frontier Village shopping center, Prescott, Ariz. 1990.

136. Burke Rutherford, *Pioneer Woman.* Bronze with patina. Pioneer Park, Worland, Wyo. 1992.

137. David Manuel, *The Promised Land.* Painted bronze. Chapman Square, Portland, Ore. 1993.

138. George Wayne Lundeen, *Promise of the Prairie.* Bronze. Lincoln Park, Greeley, Colo. 1993.

139. George Wayne Lundeen, *Promise of the Prairie.* Bronze. City Hall, Westminster, Colo. 1993.

140. Bill Bennett, *Hopes and Dreams.* Bronze. Noble County Courthouse, Perry, Okla. 1993.

141. Harold T. Holden, *Holding the Claim.* Bronze. Government Springs Park, Enid, Okla. 1993.

142. Jo Saylor, *This Land Is Mine (Centennial Statue).* Bronze. City Hall, Ponca City, Okla. 1993.

143. Dorothy L. Koelling. *Hardship and Dreams.* Bronze. A. Price Woodard Park, Wichita, Kans. 1994.

144. Bernadette Hess Carman, *Land of Hope.* Bronze. Kay County Courthouse, Newkirk, Okla. 1994.

145. Scott Stearman, *Harvest Prayer.* Bronze. MidAmerica Nazarene College campus, Olathe, Kans. 1994.

146. Burke Rutherford, *Pioneer Woman.* Bronze with patina. New Mexico Highlands University, Las Vegas, N.Mex. 1995.

147. Clifford J. Carlson, *The Promise of America (Norwegian-American Immigrant Family Monument)*. Bronze. N 3rd Ave. E near Hwy 971, Lake Mills, Iowa. 1995.
148. Mike Cunningham, *Walking to Texas*. Limestone. Liberty Plaza Park, Grapevine, Tex. 1996.
149. Franz Johansen and Nathan Johansen, *Handcart Pioneer Monument*. Bronze. Mormon Trail Center at Winter Quarters, Florence, Neb. 1997.
150. Linda Sioux Henley, *Texas Pioneer Woman*. Bronze. Capitol, Austin, Tex. 1998.
151. Jay O'Meilia, *Frontier Woman*. Bronze. Gilcrease Museum, Tulsa, Okla. 1998.
152. Tom Otterness, *Gold Rush*. Bronze. Robert T. Matsui U.S. Courthouse, Sacramento, Calif. 1999.
153. Stanley J. Watts, *Journey's End (Mormon Trail Monument; Handcart Monument)*. Bronze. This Is the Place Park, Salt Lake City, Utah. 1999.
154. L'Deane Trueblood, *Pioneer Classroom*. Bronze. Legacy Trail Park, Norman, Okla. 1999.
155. Jim Thomas, *The Crossing*. Bronze. Chisholm Trail Crossing Park, Round Rock, Tex. 2000.
156. Stanley J. Watts, *Handcart Pioneers*. Bronze. Coralville Marriott, Coralville, Iowa. Ca. 2000.
157. Kwan Wu, *Children of the Trails*. Bronze. Johnson County Courthouse, Olathe, Kans. 2000.
158. Trygve A. Rovelstad, *Pioneer Family Memorial*. Bronze. Kimball St. Bridge, Elgin, Ill. Designed 1935; erected 2001.
159. Jerry Anderson, *Pioneer Mother Monument*. Bronze. Historic Relief Society Hall, Washington, Utah. 2001.
160. Mischell Riley, *Stella at the Spring*. Bronze. Roger T. Sermon Community Center, Independence, Mo. 2001.
161. Avard T. Fairbanks, *Old Oregon Trail*. Bronze. Oregon Trail Historic Reserve Park, Boise, Idaho. 1924; erected 2002.
162. David Alan Clark, *Spirit of the Prairie*. Bronze. Town Square, Schaumburg, Ill. 2002.
163. Blair Buswell and Edward Fraughton, *Pioneer Courage*. Bronze. Pioneer Courage Park, Omaha, Neb. 2003.
164. Tom Otterness, *Large Covered Wagon*. Bronze. Joslyn Art Museum. Omaha, Neb. 2004.
165. Patrick Oliphant, *Angelina Eberly*. Bronze. Downtown Austin, Tex. 2004.
166. Chris L. Waddell, *Pioneer Family*. Bronze. Herriman City Cemetery, Herriman, Utah. 2005.
167. Harriet Lee, *Follow the Setting Sun*. Stainless steel. Pioneer Museum, Colorado Springs, Colo. 2005.
168. David Frech, *Pioneer Woman and Child*. Bronze. Lovett Memorial Library, Pampa, Tex. 2005.
169. Chris L. Waddell, *Pioneer Family*. Bronze. City Park, Springville, Utah. 2006.

170. Tom Otterness, *Large Covered Wagon.* Bronze. Pioneer Park, Walla Walla, Wash. 2006.

171. Charles Goslin, *Dick Williams, Wagon Master.* Concrete and bronze. Pioneer Crossing Park, Shawnee, Kans. 2006.

172. Charles Goslin, *Pioneer Crossing.* Brick and bronze with patina. Pioneer Crossing Park, Shawnee, Kans. 2006.

173. Harold T. Holden, *The Homesteaders.* Bronze. Cherokee Strip Regional Heritage Center, Enid, Okla. 2007.

174. [Jim Dodson?], *Oklahoma Centennial.* Pioneer Park, Ponca City, Okla. 2007.

175. [Jim Dodson?], *Oklahoma Centennial.* Eastman National Bank, Newkirk, Okla. 2007.

176. Paul Moore, *Brand New State (Centennial Land Run Monument).* Bronze. Bricktown Canal, Oklahoma City, Okla. 2007.

177. Calvin L. Graybill, *Pioneer Man and Woman.* Granite. Courthouse Square Park, Alva, Okla. 2007.

178. Robert Summers, *Barnards of the Brazos—First Family of Glen Rose.* Bronze. Historic Courthouse Square, Glen Rose, Tex. 2007.

179. Mary Lou Gresham, *Leaping into History.* Bronze. Festival Market Place Plaza, Edmond, Okla. 2007.

180. Richard Becker, *The Pioneers.* Bronze. Old Poway Park, Poway, Calif. 2007.

181. Kwan Wu, *Going West on the Old Santa Fe Trail (Two Trails).* Bronze. Mahaffie Stagecoach Stop and Farm, Olathe, Kans. 2008.

182. Jim Hauser, *Germans from Russia.* Bronze. Esplanade Arts and Heritage Centre, Medicine Hat, Alberta, Canada. 2011.

183. Ron Adamson, *Pioneer Woman.* Bronze. Everit L. Sliter Memorial Park, Bigfork, Mont. 2011.

184. Debbie Gessner after Bob Boze Bell, *Not-So-Gentle Tamer.* Bronze. Prescott Valley Civic Center, Prescott Valley, Ariz. 2013.

185. Avard T. Fairbanks, *Old Oregon Trail.* Bronze. Historic Truman Courthouse. Independence, Mo. 1924; erected 2016.

186. Charles Goslin, *Pioneer Woman.* Bronze with patina. National Frontier Trails Museum, Independence, Mo. 2016.

187. Allen G. Newman, *Pioneer Mike (Carter Memorial Fountain; Iron Mike).* Bronze. Ashland Plaza, Ashland, Ore. 2016.

NOTES

PREFACE

1. Laura Ingalls Wilder, *Pioneer Girl: The Annotated Autobiography*, ed. Pamela Smith Hill (Pierre: South Dakota Historical Society Press, 2014).

INTRODUCTION

1. Frederick Jackson Turner and John Mack Faragher, *Rereading Frederick Jackson Turner: The Significance of the Frontier in American History, and Other Essays* (New York: Holt, 1994).

2. Patricia Nelson Limerick, *The Legacy of Conquest: The Unbroken Past of the American West* (New York: Norton, 1987); Richard White, *"It's Your Misfortune and None of My Own": A History of the American West* (Norman: University of Oklahoma Press, 1991); William Cronon, George A. Miles, and Jay Gitlin, *Under an Open Sky: Rethinking America's Western Past* (New York: Norton, 1992); Donald Worster, *Under Western Skies: Nature and History in the American West* (New York: Oxford University Press, 1992).

3. A rich body of literature explores the myth of the Old West and its place in popular culture. See, for example, Richard White and Patricia Nelson Limerick, *The Frontier in American Culture: An Exhibition at the Newberry Library, August 26, 1994–January 7, 1995*, ed. James R. Grossman (Berkeley: University of California Press, 1994); Beverly J. Stoeltje, "Making the Frontier Myth: Folklore Process in a Modern Nation," *Western Folklore* 46, no. 4 (Fall 1987): 235–54; John Springhall, "Have Gun, Will Travel: The Myth of the Frontier in the Hollywood Western," *Historian* 112 (Winter 2011): 20–24; Ted Amley, "The Visual Politics of the Myth of the Frontier," *Midwest Review* 14 (1992): 71–90; Lee Clark Mitchell, "Whose West Is It Anyway? Or, What's Myth Got to Do with It? The Role of 'America' in the Creation of the Myth of the West," *American Review of Canadian Studies* 33, no. 4 (December 2003): 497–508.

4. Lorenzo Veracini, *Settler Colonialism: A Theoretical Overview* (New York: Palgrave Macmillan, 2010); Lorenzo Veracini, "Introducing," *Settler Colonial Studies* 1, no. 1 (January 1, 2011): 1–12; Lorenzo Veracini, *The Settler Colonial Present* (New: Palgrave Macmillan, 2015); Patrick Wolfe, "Settler Colonialism and the Elimination of the Native," *Journal of Genocide Research* 8, no. 4 (December 2006): 387–409.

5. Wolfe, "Settler Colonialism."

6. Kirk Savage, *Standing Soldiers, Kneeling Slaves: Race, War, and Monument in Nineteenth-Century America* (Princeton, N.J.: Princeton University Press, 1997), 4.

7. Janet Galligani Casey, "The American Pioneer Woman circa 1930: Cultural Debates and the Role of Public Art," *American Studies* 51, no. 3 (2010): 85–107.

8. Marianne Hirsch and Valerie Smith, "Feminism and Cultural Memory: An Introduction," *Signs* 28, no. 1 (Autumn 2002): 5.

9. See, for example, Michael Kammen, *Mystic Chords of Memory: The Transformation of Tradition in American Culture* (New York: Knopf, 1991); Michael Kammen, *Visual Shock: A History of Art Controversies in American Culture* (New York: Vintage Books, 2006); Kirk Savage, *Monument Wars: Washington, D.C., the National Mall, and the Transformation of the Memorial Landscape* (Berkeley: University of California Press, 2009); Marita Sturken, *Tourists of History: Memory, Kitsch, and Consumerism from Oklahoma City to Ground Zero* (Durham, N.C.: Duke University Press, 2007); Karen L. Cox, *Dixie's Daughters: The United Daughters of the Confederacy and the Preservation of Confederate Culture* (Gainesville: University Press of Florida, 2003).

10. Paul Connerton, *How Modernity Forgets* (New York: Cambridge University Press, 2009), 99. See also Paul Connerton, *How Societies Remember*, Themes in the Social Sciences (New York: Cambridge University Press, 1989); Michel-Rolph Trouillot, *Silencing the Past: Power and the Production of History* (Boston: Beacon Press, 1995).

11. Savage, *Standing Soldiers, Kneeling Slaves*, 182.

12. Savage, *Monument Wars*. See also Teresa Bergman, *Exhibiting Patriotism: Creating and Contesting Interpretations of American Historic Sites* (Walnut Creek, Calif.: Left Coast Press, 2013), chap. 4.

13. Savage, *Standing Soldiers, Kneeling Slaves*; Cynthia J. Mills and Pamela H. Simpson, eds., *Monuments to the Lost Cause: Women, Art, and the Landscapes of Southern Memory* (Knoxville: University of Tennessee Press, 2003); Paul A. Shackel, *Memory in Black and White: Race, Commemoration, and the Post-Bellum Landscape* (Walnut Creek, Calif.: Altamira Press, 2003); Catherine W. Bishir, "Landmarks of Power: Building a Southern Past, 1885–1915," *Southern Cultures*, December 2, 1993, 5–45.

14. See, for example, Sabine Marschall, "Transforming the Landscape of Memory: The South African Commemorative Effort in International Perspective," *South African Historical Journal* 55 (2006): 165–85; Alta Steenkamp, "Apartheid to Democracy: Representation and Politics in the Voortrekker Monument and Red Location Museum," *Architectural Research Quarterly* 10, nos. 3–4 (2006): 249–54.

15. Savage, *Monument Wars*, 21.

16. Jason E. Pierce, *Making the White Man's West: Whiteness and the Creation of the American West* (Boulder: University Press of Colorado, 2016), chap. 8; Susan Lee Johnson, *Roaring Camp: The Social World of the California Gold Rush* (repr., New York: Norton, 2000).

17. Anne McClintock, *Imperial Leather: Race, Gender, and Sexuality in the Colonial Contest* (New York: Routledge, 1995), 378–79.

18. Rebecca Weaver-Hightower, "'Before God This Was Their Country': History and Guilt in Stuart Cloete's Turning Wheels and the Voortrekker Monument, Pretoria," *English in Africa* 40, no. 2 (October 2013): 101–20; Rebecca Weaver-Hightower, "'Do We Reverse the Medal?': Settler Guilt, the Indian Speech, and the Untold Side of the Story," *Journal of Settler Colonial Studies* 52, no. 1 (2017): 25–53; Rebecca Weaver-Hightower, "The Frontier Landscape and Guilty Settler in Nineteenth Century Colonial Literature," in *Geocritical Explorations: Space, Place, and Mapping in Literary and Cultural Studies*, ed. Robert Tally (New York: Palgrave Macmillan, 2011), 123–38.

19. Among the best works in this vein are William H. Goetzmann and William N. Goetzmann, *The West of the Imagination* (Norman: University of Oklahoma Press, 2009); and William H. Truettner, ed., *The West as America: Reinterpreting Images of the Frontier, 1820–1920* (Washington, D.C.: Smithsonian Institution Press, 1991).

20. Jeffrey Sanders, "Public Art, Memory, and Mobility in 1920s New Mexico," in *City Dreams, Country Schemes: Community and Identity in the American West*, ed. Kathleen A. Brosnan and Amy Louise Scott (Reno: University of Nevada Press, 2011), 178–95; Brenda D. Frink, "San Francisco's Pioneer Mother Monument: Maternalism, Racial Order, and the Politics of Memorialization, 1907–1915," *American Quarterly* 64, no. 1 (2012): 85–113; Casey, "American Pioneer Woman"; Rebecca Solnit, "The Struggle of Dawning Intelligence: Creating, Revising, and Recognizing Native American Monuments," in *Storming the Gates of Paradise: Landscapes for Politics* (University of California Press, 2007), 40–50; Patricia Vettel-Becker, "Sacagawea and Son: The Visual Construction of America's Maternal Feminine," *American Studies* 50, no. 1 (2011): 27–50; Deborah M. Olsen, "Fair Connections: Women's Separatism and the Lewis and Clark Exposition of 1905," *Oregon Historical Quarterly* 109, no. 2 (2008): 174–203; Gail H. Landsman, "The 'Other' as Political Symbol: Images of Indians in the Woman Suffrage Movement," *Ethnohistory* 39, no. 3 (1992): 247–84; Jan C. Dawson, "Sacagawea: Pilot or Pioneer Mother?," *Pacific Northwest Quarterly* 83, no. 1 (Spring 1992): 22–28; Lisa Blee, "Completing Lewis and Clark's Westward March," *Oregon Historical Quarterly* 106, no. 2 (Summer 2005): 232–53; Kent Ahrens, "Avard T. Fairbanks and the Winter Quarters Monument," *Nebraska History* 95, no. 3 (Fall 2014): 176–85; Richard Holzapfel and J. Michael Hunter, "New Photograph of the Granite Shaft for the Brigham Young Monument," *All Faculty Publications* 1396 (2000), http://scholarsarchive.byu.edu/facpub/1396; J. Michael Hunter, "The Monument to Brigham Young and the Pioneers: One Hundred Years of Controversy," *Utah Historical Quarterly* 68, no. 4 (Fall 2000): 332–50; Sara M. Patterson, "The Plymouth Rock of the American West: Remembering, Forgetting, and Becoming American in Utah," *Material Religion: The Journal of Objects, Art and Belief* 11, no. 3 (2015): 329–53.

21. Paul Scolari, "Indian Warriors and Pioneer Mothers: American Identity and the Closing of the Frontier in Public Monuments, 1890–1930" (PhD diss., University of Pittsburgh, 2005).

22. Annette Stott, "Prairie Madonnas and Pioneer Women: Images of Emigrant Women in the Art of the Old West," *Prospects* 21 (October 1996): 299–325. A few other formal studies of western art include pioneer-themed monuments: Patricia J. Broder, "The Pioneer Woman, Image in Bronze," *American Art Review* 2, no. 5 (1975): 127–34; Patricia Janis Broder, *Bronzes of the American West* (New York: Abrams, 1975); Pamela H. Simpson, "Pioneer Mother Monuments, 1914–1930: Images of Western Expansion," *Southeastern College Art Conference Review* 13, no. 5 (2000): 435–43. See also Greg Esser, "Hazardous Trail to a Lasting Legacy," *Public Art Review* 13, no. 1 (Fall/Winter 2001): 29–33; Solnit, "Struggle of Dawning Intelligence."

23. Michael Rowlands, "Remembering to Forget: Sublimation as Sacrifice in War Memorials," in *The Art of Forgetting*, ed. Adrian Forty and Susanne Küchler (New York: Berg, 1999), 129–45.

24. Barbara Berglund, *Making San Francisco American: Cultural Frontiers in the Urban West, 1846–1906* (Lawrence: University Press of Kansas, 2007).

25. Yannis Hamilakis and Jo Labanyi, "Time, Materiality, and the Work of Memory," *History and Memory: Studies in Representation of the Past* 20, no. 2 (Fall/Winter 2008): 5–17. See also Barbara J. Mills and William H. Walker, eds., *Memory Work: Archaeologies of Material Practices*, School for Advanced Research Advanced Seminar Series (Santa Fe, N.Mex.: School for Advanced Research Press, 2008). On remembering and forgetting, see Connerton, *How Modernity Forgets*; Connerton, *How Societies Remember*; Pierre Nora, "Between Memory and History: Les Lieux de Mémoire," *Representations*, no. 26 (April 1, 1989): 7–24; Trouillot, *Silencing the Past*; Rowlands, "Remembering to Forget"; Alfredo González-Ruibal, "Time to Destroy: An Archaeology of Supermodernity," *Current Anthropology* 49, no. 2 (April 1, 2008): 247–79.

26. Hirsch and Smith, "Feminism and Cultural Memory," 8.

27. Erving Goffman, *Gender Advertisements* (Cambridge, Mass.: Harvard University Press, 1979), 25.

28. Fredric Jameson, "Third-World Literature in the Era of Multinational Capital," *Social Text* 15 (Autumn 1986): 65–88; Anne McClintock, "Family Feuds: Gender, Nationalism and the Family," *Feminist Review* 44 (Summer 1993): 61–80; Aijaz Ahmad, "Jameson's Rhetoric of Otherness and the 'National Allegory,'" *Social Text* 17 (Autumn 1987): 3–25.

29. Connerton, *How Modernity Forgets*.

CHAPTER 1. ENSHRINING WHITE CIVILIZATION

1. Savage, *Standing Soldiers, Kneeling Slaves*; Bishir, "Landmarks of Power," 5–45; Mills and Simpson, *Monuments to the Lost Cause*.

2. W. Lair Hill, "Annual Address," *Transactions of the Eleventh Annual Re-union of the Oregon Pioneer Association for 1883* (Salem, Ore.: E. M. Waite, 1884), 21.

3. Tom Brokaw, *The Greatest Generation* (New York: Random House, 2001); Nora, "Between Memory and History," 7–24.

4. Cynthia Culver Prescott, *Gender and Generation on the Far Western Frontier* (Tucson: University of Arizona Press, 2007), chap. 6.

5. Sergiusz Michalski, *Public Monuments: Art in Political Bondage, 1870–1997* (London: Reaktion Books, 1998), 44.

6. U.S. Commission of Fine Arts, *Annual Report* (Washington, D.C.: U.S. Government Printing Office, 1920), 55–72; Savage, *Monument Wars*, 19–20; Savage, *Standing Soldiers, Kneeling Slaves*; Mills and Simpson, *Monuments to the Lost Cause*; Bishir, "Landmarks of Power."

7. Gail Bederman, *Manliness and Civilization: A Cultural History of Gender and Race in the United States, 1880–1917*, Women in Culture and Society (Chicago: University of Chicago Press, 1996), 25.

8. Philip J. Deloria, *Playing Indian* (New Haven, Conn.: Yale University Press, 1998), chap. 4; Shari M. Huhndorf, *Going Native: Indians in the American Cultural Imagination* (Ithaca, N.Y.: Cornell University Press, 2001), chap. 1. See also Alan Trachtenberg, *Shades of Hiawatha: Staging Indians, Making Americans, 1880–1930* (New York: Hill and Wang, 2004), chap. 4; Sherry L. Smith, *Reimagining Indians: Native Americans through Anglo Eyes, 1880–1940* (Oxford: Oxford University Press, 2000).

9. On white settler guilt, see Weaver-Hightower, "Frontier Landscape and Guilty Settler," 123–38.

10. Andrea G. Radke-Moss, "Mormon Women, Suffrage, and Citizenship at the 1893 Chicago World's Fair," in *Gendering the Fair: Histories of Women and Gender at World's Fairs*, ed. T. J. Boisseau and Abigail M. Markwyn (Urbana: University of Illinois Press, 2010), 97–112; Erika Doss, *Twentieth-Century American Art* (New York: Oxford University Press, 2002).

11. Helen Wright, *James Lick's Monument: The Saga of Captain Richard Floyd and the Building of the Lick Observatory* (New York: Cambridge University Press, 1987).

12. Frank Happersberger, *The Pioneers Monument* database entry, *Inventories of American Painting and Sculpture* [online catalog], Smithsonian American Art Museum, http://siris-artinventories.si.edu/ (accessed April 22, 2018). Relative value estimations are based on a simple purchasing power calculator. By other methods, the value of $100,000 in 2015 dollars could be as high as $126 million. Samuel H. Williamson, "Seven Ways to Compute the Relative Value of a U.S. Dollar Amount—1774 to Present," *Measuring Worth*, https://www.measuringworth.com/uscompare/ (accessed September 27, 2016).

13. The *Mission Play*, which romanticized the rise and fall of California's mission system, shattered the American theater record. William Deverell, *Whitewashed Adobe: The Rise of Los Angeles and the Remaking of Its Mexican Past* (Berkeley: University of California Press, 2004), 216. See also Phoebe S. Kropp, *California Vieja: Culture and Memory in a Modern American Place* (Berkeley: University of California Press, 2006).

14. "Lick Statuary," *San Francisco Evening Bulletin*, September 11, 1894, 6, in Happersberger, *Pioneers Monument* database entry.

15. Veracini, *Settler Colonialism*, 90.

16. "Gossip from Paris," *Brooklyn (N.Y.) Daily Eagle*, May 21, 1911; "Fine Arts," *Brooklyn (N.Y.) Daily Eagle*, October 8, 1907; "MacMonnies Now to Start Denver Pioneers' Statue," *Washington Times*, August 30, 1907.

17. Quoted in Scolari, "Indian Warriors and Pioneer Mothers," 114.

18. "Change Pioneers' Statue," undated *Rocky Mountain News* (Denver) clipping in Printed Material: Clippings, 1907–1909, Frederick William MacMonnies Papers, Archives of American Art, Smithsonian Institution, Washington, D.C.

19. Veracini, *Settler Colonialism*, 81–83.

20. "Haywood's Mind, on Eve of Trial, Wanders to the Pioneers' Monument, and He Suggests Pony Rider," *Rocky Mountain News* (Denver), May 12, 1907.

21. Ibid.; Emma Bullett, "The News and Views of Paris," *Brooklyn (N.Y.) Daily Eagle*, December 22, 1907; "A New Colorado Movement," *Nebraska State Journal* (Lincoln), July 17, 1909, Printed Material: Clippings, 1907–1909, MacMonnies Papers.

22. "Art in Denver," *Art and Progress* 2, no. 10 (August 1, 1911): 306.

23. "Kit Carson Pioneer Monument," *Daily Ardmoreite* (Ardmore, Okla.), June 25, 1911.

24. Vettel-Becker, "Sacagawea and Son," 27–50; Olsen, "Fair Connections," 174–203; Landsman, "The 'Other' as Political Symbol," 247–84; Dawson, "Sacagawea," 22–28; Blee, "Completing Lewis and Clark's Westward March," 232–53.

25. Cynthia J. Mills, "Gratitude and Gender Wars: Monuments to the Women of the Sixties," in Mills and Simpson, *Monuments to the Lost Cause*, 183–200.

26. Wanda M. Corn, *Women Building History: Public Art at the 1893 Columbian Exposition* (Berkeley: University of California Press, 2011), 64.

27. Maureen Reed, "How Sacagawea Became a Pioneer Mother: Statues, Ethnicity, and Controversy in Portland and Santa Fe," in *Public Memory, Race, and Ethnicity*, ed. G. Mitchell Reyes (Cambridge: Cambridge Scholars Publishing, 2010), 39.

28. Olsen, "Fair Connections."

29. "Ten Reasons Why Women of the Northwest Should Erect a Statue to Sacajawea," quoted in Dawson, "Sacagawea," 27.

30. Dawson, "Sacagawea."

31. "Interest in Pioneer Mothers' Fund Will Have Monument at Exposition," *San Francisco Examiner*, April 19, 1914.

32. Sarah J. Moore, *Empire on Display: San Francisco's Panama-Pacific International Exposition of 1915* (Norman: University of Oklahoma Press, 2013).

33. Ibid.

34. Frank Morton Todd, *The Story of the Exposition: Being the Official History of the International Celebration Held at San Francisco in 1915 to Commemorate the Discovery of*

the Pacific Ocean and the Construction of the Panama Canal, vol. 2 (New York: Putnam, for the Panama-Pacific International Exposition Company, 1921).

35. Juliet Helena Lumbard James, *Sculpture of the Exposition Palaces and Courts: Descriptive Notes on the Art of the Statuary at the Panama-Pacific International Exposition, San Francisco* (San Francisco: H. S. Crocker, 1915).

36. Moore, *Empire on Display*; Burton Benedict, *The Anthropology of World's Fairs: San Francisco's Panama Pacific International Exposition of 1915* (Berkeley, Calif.: Scolar Press, 1983).

37. Quoted in Todd, *Story of the Exposition*, 269–70.

38. Ibid., 334.

39. Broder, *Bronzes of the American West*, 180.

40. Shannon Vittoria, "*End of the Trail*, Then and Now," *The Metropolitan Museum of Art*, February 19, 2014, http://www.metmuseum.org/exhibitions/listings/2013/the-american-west-in-bronze/blog/posts/end-of-the-trail.

41. Julie Schimmel, "Inventing 'the Indian,'" in Truettner, *The West as America*, 172–74; A. L. Freundlich, *The Sculpture of James Earle Fraser* (n.p.: self-pub., 2001), 5–12, http://www.bookpump.com/upb/pdf-b/1127103b.pdf.

42. Renato Rosaldo, "Imperialist Nostalgia," *Representations*, no. 26 (April 1, 1989): 107–22.

43. James, *Sculpture of the Exposition Palaces and Courts*, 34.

44. Elizabeth Gordon, *What We Saw at Madame World's Fair: A Series of Letters from the Twins at the Panama-Pacific International Exposition to Their Cousins at Home* (San Francisco: Levinson, 1915); Douglas Cazaux Sackman, *Wild Men: Ishi and Kroeber in the Wilderness of Modern America*, New Narratives in American History (New York: Oxford University Press, 2010); Elizabeth Clendenning Ring, *San Francisco: Glimpses of the Fairy Palaces of the Great Panama-Pacific International Exposition* (Philadelphia: Book News Monthly, 1915).

45. Frink, "San Francisco's Pioneer Mother Monument."

46. J. Rush Bronson and Clarence M. Hunt, "Generous Offer for Boys and Girls," *Grizzly Bear* (Los Angeles, Calif.), September 1916.

47. "Motherhood Monument," *Journal of Education* 80, no. 9 (1914): 240.

48. Trask considered four artists to be qualified for this major commission: Daniel C. French, Paul Bartlett, Hermon MacNeil (sculptor of Portland's *Coming of the White Man*), and Charles Grafly. Others on the art committee suggested Frederick MacMonnies and Andrew O'Connor. Trask believed that only MacNeil and Grafly would be willing to undertake the work, and he reached out to Grafly confidentially to urge him to consider the commission. John Trask to Charles Grafly, May 13, 1913, folder 22, box 7, Charles Grafly Papers, Special Collections, Wichita State University Libraries.

49. Trask to Grafly, May 13, 1913.

50. Deloria, *Playing Indian*, chap. 4.

51. "Pioneer Mother Draped Like a Sioux Squaw," undated *San Francisco Chronicle* clipping, Special Collections, Wichita State University Libraries.

52. Laurel Thatcher Ulrich, *The Age of Homespun: Objects and Stories in the Creation of an American Myth* (New York: Vintage, 2002).

53. Telegram from Helen P. Sanborn to John Hays Hammond, October 29, 1914, folder 17, box 7; night letter from Helen P. Sanborn to Charles Grafly, October 28, 1914, folder 22, box 7; John Trask to Charles Grafly, July 20, 1914, folder 23, box 7; telegram from Phoebe A. Hearst to Charles Grafly, December 31, 1914, folder 20, box 7, Grafly Papers, Special Collections, Wichita State University Libraries.

54. "Viewed Sculptor's Masterpiece: Thousands Impressed With 'Pioneer Mother' at the Grafly Studio," *Gloucester (Mass.) Daily Times*, October 19, 1914.

55. Letters from schoolchildren to Mr. Putney, October 1914, folder 50, box 2, Grafly Papers, Special Collections, Wichita State University Libraries. (Mr. Putney appears to have been their teacher, and these letters to have been composed as a class assignment. One is dated Oct. 18, 1914. The rest are dated Oct. 21, 1914.)

56. James, *Sculpture of the Exposition Palaces and Courts.*

57. Benedict, *Anthropology of World's Fairs*; Freundlich, *Sculpture of James Earle Fraser*, 47–49.

58. "End of the Trail: Introduction," *National Cowboy and Western Heritage Museum*, http://nationalcowboymuseum.org/learn-discover/online-unit-studies/end-of-the-trail-introduction/ (accessed June 1, 2015); Vittoria, "*End of the Trail*, Then and Now"; "Quake Shakes Visalia Statue Apart," *Visalia Times-Delta*, May 27, 1980.

59. Rebecca Weaver-Hightower, "Frontier Fictions: Settler Stories and the Origins of White Guilt," unpublished manuscript, n.d., in possession of Weaver-Hightower.

60. Alexander Phimister Proctor, *Sculptor in Buckskin: The Autobiography of Alexander Phimister Proctor*, ed. Katharine C. Ebner, 2nd ed. (Norman: University of Oklahoma Press, 2009); Peter H. Hassrick, *Wildlife and Western Heroes: Alexander Phimister Proctor, Sculptor*, 1st ed. (Fort Worth, Tex: Amon Carter Museum, 2003).

61. "Bronze to Perpetuate Pioneer; University to Have Sculpture," *Oregon Daily Journal* (Portland), January 30, 1917; "Subject for Statue of 'Pioneer' Found After Long Years of Search," *Oregon Daily Journal* (Portland), May 18, 1919.

62. Frederick V. Holman, "Qualities of the Oregon Pioneers," *Quarterly of the Oregon Historical Society* 20, no. 3 (September 1919): 235–42.

63. Bederman, *Manliness and Civilization*, chap. 5.

64. Quoted in Doris Foley, *The Pioneer (Donner) Monument: The Origin of a Statue* (Nevada City, Calif.: Nevada County Historical Society, 2000), 11.

65. "Shaft to Pioneers: Donner Lake Site: Statewide Subscription Aims to Keep Tragic Memory in Stone," *San Francisco Call*, July 11, 1910.

66. "Historic Statue Far Afield," *San Francisco Chronicle*, January 24, 1915; "Survivors of Donner Party Recall Perils," *San Francisco Call*, June 11, 1910; "For Donner Monument," *Santa Cruz (Calif.) Sentinel*, May 15, 1910; "Will Commemorate the Ill Fated Donner Party: Native Sons Will Lay Cornerstone of Monument,"

San Francisco Call, March 27, 1910; "In Honor of Donner Party: Native Sons Visit Historic Spot and Will Raise Monument," *Bakersfield Californian,* June 10, 1910; "Cornerstone of Pioneer Donner Monument Laid: Three Survivors of Party Hear an Address Made by Past President Kronland," *Los Angeles Herald,* June 11, 1910.

67. "Grand Parlor to Open Tomorrow: Native Sons Are Going to Truckee," *Oakland (Calif.) Tribune,* June 2, 1918.

68. "Shaft Raised for Pioneers Is Dedicated," *Oakland (Calif.) Tribune,* June 6, 1918.

69. "A Monument to the Pioneer Men and Women," *Santa Cruz (Calif.) Evening News,* June 3, 1918.

CHAPTER 2. BIBLES, RIFLES, AND SUNBONNETS

1. John Joseph Mathews, *Life and Death of an Oilman: The Career of E. W. Marland* (Norman: University of Oklahoma Press, 1951), 179–80. See also Alison Fields, "Memory, Reenactment, and Oklahoma's Pioneer Woman Statue," *Journal of the West* 52, no. 1 (Winter 2013): 31.

2. Broder, *Bronzes of the American West,* 276.

3. Rebecca Jo Plant, *Mom: The Transformation of Motherhood in Modern America* (Chicago: University of Chicago Press, 2010).

4. Laura L. Lovett, *Conceiving the Future: Pronatalism, Reproduction, and the Family in the United States, 1890–1938* (Chapel Hill: University of North Carolina Press, 2007).

5. Janet Galligani Casey, *A New Heartland: Women, Modernity, and the Agrarian Ideal in America* (New York: Oxford University Press, 2009).

6. Veracini, *Settler Colonialism,* 99–104; John Mack Faragher, "Americans, Mexicans, Métis: A Community Approach to the Comparative Study of North American Frontiers," in Cronon, Miles, and Gitlin, *Under an Open Sky,* 90–109.

7. Veracini, *Settler Colonialism.* This differential treatment of southern mammies and western Indian mothers parallels distinctions between occupation and settler colonies discussed in Wolfe, "Settler Colonialism."

8. Mick McElya, "Commemorating the Color Line: The National Mammy Monument Controversy of the 1920s," in Mills and Simpson, *Monuments to the Lost Cause,* 203–18.

9. Stott, "Prairie Madonnas and Pioneer Women" 299–325.

10. On the power of Marian imagery, see Elizabeth Hayes Alvarez, *The Valiant Woman: The Virgin Mary in Nineteenth-Century American Culture* (Chapel Hill: University of North Carolina Press, 2016).

11. A. Joan Saab, *For the Millions: American Art and Culture Between the Wars* (Philadelphia: University of Pennsylvania Press, 2004), 4.

12. Goetzmann and Goetzmann, *The West of the Imagination*; Jimmy L. Bryan Jr., "The Weary West," in *Branding the American West: Paintings and Films, 1900–1950,* ed. Marian Wardle and Sarah E. Boehme (Norman: University of Oklahoma Press, 2016), 88–113.

13. Walt Reed, *Harvey Dunn: Illustrator and Painter of the Pioneer West* (Santa Cruz, Calif.: Flesk, 2010); W. H. Hutchinson, *The World, The Work, and the West of W. H. D. Koerner* (Norman: University of Oklahoma Press, 1978); *Harvey Dunn: Feminine Images,* "Past Exhibitions," *South Dakota Art Museum,* http://www.sdstate .edu/southdakotaartmuseum/explore/Exhibitions/past-exhibits.cfm (September 7, 2012), some images viewable in "An Evening with Harvey Dunn's Feminine Images 2015 performance (SDPB version)," video, 56:46, Yeager Media Center, December 23, 2015, https://www.youtube.com/watch?v=Vp_l2fx3OUA; *Howard Pyle and Harvey Dunn: Teacher and Student, April 8, 2014–August 3, 2014* (Brookings: South Dakota Art Museum, 2014), exhibition brochure, http://www.sdstate.edu /sites/default/files/southdakotaartmuseum/exhibitions/upload/Howard-Pyle-and-Dunn.pdf.

14. Hassrick, *Wildlife and Western Heroes.*

15. Donald Martin Reynolds, *Masters of American Sculpture: The Figurative Tradition from the American Renaissance to the Millennium* (New York: Abbeville Press, 1994), 220.

16. Hutchinson, *The World, The Work, and the West,* 144.

17. Ibid.

18. Quoted in Hassrick, *Wildlife and Western Heroes,* 211.

19. Proctor, *Sculptor in Buckskin,* 193.

20. Ibid.

21. Hassrick, *Wildlife and Western Heroes,* 86–91.

22. Wardle and Boehme, *Branding the American West,* 5–7; Broder, *Bronzes of the American West,* 107–77; Hassrick, *Wildlife and Western Heroes.*

23. Williamson, "Seven Ways to Compute"; Walton Ralph Edmonds to Gifford Proctor, February 7, 1955, Papers Concerning Alexander Phimister Proctor's *The Pioneer Mother,* 1924–1950, Archives of American Art, Smithsonian Institution, Washington, D.C.

24. "As Those of Their Blood: Kansas Citians View the 'Pioneer Mother' and Reminisce," *Kansas City Star,* November 13, 1927.

25. Hassrick, *Wildlife and Western Heroes,* 89.

26. Quoted in "Vice-President Barker Gives Statue of Pioneer Mother," Alexander Phimister Proctor, Pioneer Mother sculpture file, *Inventories of American Painting and Sculpture,* Smithsonian American Art Museum; see also Peter H. Hassrick, "The Oregon Art of Alexander Phimister Proctor," *Oregon Historical Quarterly* 104, no. 3 (Fall 2003): 412.

27. Eugene F. Fairbanks, "Competition for This Is the Place Monument," May 10, 1989, Avard T. Fairbanks Papers, accession no. 1336, J. Willard Marriott Library, University of Utah, Salt Lake City.

28. Prescott, *Gender and Generation.*

29. Goffman, *Gender Advertisements.*

30. "Vancouver Unveils Fountain Memorial," *Morning Oregonian,* n.d., Avard T. Fairbanks vertical file, Oregon Historical Society Research Library, Portland.

31. Plant, *Mom.*

32. Personal correspondence with Grey Osterud, October 20, 2009.

33. Sandra Haarsager, *Organized Womanhood: Cultural Politics in the Pacific Northwest, 1840–1920* (Norman: University of Oklahoma Press, 1997).

34. Westport Improvement Association, *Westport, 1812–1912* (Kansas City, Mo.: Franklin Hudson, 1912), 9, http://archive.org/details/westport1812191200west.

35. "About Town," *Kansas City Times*, September 29, 1960.

36. Kropp, *California Vieja*, 47–102.

37. Elizabeth Butler Gentry, "National Old Trails Road Committee: An Open Letter to Every Daughter from Elizabeth Butler Gentry, Chairman," *Daughters of the American Revolution Magazine* 43 (July–December 1913): 531.

38. "Madonna of the Trail Golden Anniversary, 1929–1979," n.d., Statues—Madonna of the Trail vertical file, Missouri Valley Special Collections, Kansas City Public Library, Kansas City, Missouri; "The Madonna of the Trail," *Daughters of the American Revolution Magazine* 63, no. 6 (1929): 402.

39. Gentry, "National Old Trail Roads Committee"; "Madonna of the Trail," *DAR Magazine.*

40. Fern Ioula Bauer, *The Historic Treasure Chest of the Madonna of the Trail Monuments* (Springfield, Ohio: John McEnaney, 1984); "Madonna of the Trail Golden Anniversary"; Carol Medlicott and Michael Heffernan, "'Autograph of a Nation': The Daughters of the American Revolution and the National Old Trails Road, 1910–1927," *National Identities* 6, no. 3 (2004): 233–60.

41. "Madonna of the Trail," *DAR Magazine*, 129.

42. Casey, "American Pioneer Woman"; Fields, "Memory, Reenactment"; Hirsch and Smith, "Feminism and Cultural Memory."

43. Williamson, "Seven Ways to Compute."

44. "State to Get Memorial for Plains Woman," *Daily Oklahoman* (Oklahoma City), October 22, 1926; Elmo Scott Watson, "The Pioneer Mother," *Waterloo (Ind.) Press*, July 24, 1927; "Baker's Pioneer Woman Model Is Choice of Public," *Pittsburgh (Pa.) Post-Gazette*, April 25, 1927; Casey, "American Pioneer Woman," 94.

45. "Pioneer Woman Seen in Bronze: Twelve Sculptors Show Their Models for the Proposed Monumental Statue to Be Erected in Oklahoma—Other States to See Them," *New York Times*, March 20, 1927.

46. Ibid.

47. "State to Get Memorial for Plains Woman."

48. "Pioneer Woman Seen in Bronze."

49. Casey, "American Pioneer Woman."

50. Bryant Baker, "Pioneer Woman" art file 1927, Missouri Valley Special Collections, Kansas City Public Library; "Pioneers (Arts)," *Time* 11, no. 1 (1928): 20.

51. Quoted in Casey, "American Pioneer Woman," 89.

52. Quoted in "The Pioneer Woman," *New York Art Digest*, November 1, 1927.

53. "Vote on 'Pioneer Woman': Bryant Baker's Statue in the Lead—H. A. MacNeil's Second," *New York Times*, March 20, 1927.

54. "Sugar?," *New York Art Digest*, n.d. See also Paul S. Leeper, quoted in "The Pioneer Woman."

55. "Pupils Analyze Pioneer Women," *New York Times*, April 3, 1927, sec. 8.

56. "Picks Baker Statue of 'Pioneer Woman': Marland Names Winner among 12 Sculptors for Monument in Oklahoma," *New York Times*, December 21, 1927; "Texans Choose Gregory's 'Pioneer Woman,'" *New York Art Digest*, December 1, 1927.

57. August Leimbach, quoted in Bauer, *Historic Treasure Chest*, 18.

58. "The Kansas Pioneer Woman's Memorial Association," *Kansas Womans Journal: The Western Womans Forum* [*sic*], May 1927.

59. Kansas Pioneer Woman's Memorial Association clippings file, Kansas State Historical Society, Topeka, Kansas; "Merrill [*sic*] Gage Designs Work for State Grounds," *Kansas Business*, December 1935; Mae C. Patrick, "Kansas Pioneer Woman's Memorial," *Jayhawk: The Magazine of Kansas*, February 1929, n.p.; "To Be No Change in Kansas Pioneer Woman's Memorial Monument," *Jayhawk: The Magazine of Kansas*, September 1929, 272.

60. "The Woman with the Gun," unidentified, undated clipping, Robert Merrell Gage Papers, 1911–1982, Archives of American Art, Smithsonian Institution.

61. Paula S. Fass, *The Damned and the Beautiful* (New York: Oxford University Press, 1977).

62. Saab, *For the Millions*, 16.

63. Paul S. Wingert, *The Sculpture of William Zorach* (New York: Pitman, 1938), 38–39.

64. John I. H. Baur, *William Zorach* (New York: Praeger, 1959), 133.

65. Leo Friedlander, The Pioneer Woman, (sculpture) file, *Inventories of American Painting and Sculpture*, Smithsonian American Art Museum.

66. Quoted in Nita Thurman, "Original TWU Pioneer Statue Caused a Statewide Hoopla," *Denton (Tex.) Record-Chronicle*, February 15, 2006.

67. Telegram to Governor James V. Allred from Mrs. Herman Hirsch, April 12, 1936, box 1985/024–34, Records of Texas Governor James V. Allred, Archives and Information Services Division, Texas State Library and Archives Commission.

68. Tom Kirland, "The Nude Woman Who Shocked Denton," *Denton (Tex.) Record Chronicle* undated clipping [1958], "Pioneer Woman" clippings file, University Archives, Blagg-Huey Library, Texas Woman's University, Denton, Texas.

69. "Pioneer Woman Sculpture Narrative," Friedlander, Pioneer Woman file, *Inventories of American Painting and Sculpture*, Smithsonian American Art Museum.

CHAPTER 3. MEMORY AND MODERNITY IN POSTWAR FAMILY MONUMENTS

1. Anne M. Butler, "Selling the Popular Myth," in *The Oxford History of the American West*, ed. Clyde A. Milner II, Carol A. O'Connor, and Martha A. Sandweiss (New York: Oxford University Press, 1994), 771–801; Mitchell, "Whose West Is It Anyway?"

2. Dolores Hayden, *Building Suburbia: Green Fields and Urban Growth, 1820–2000* (New York: Vintage Books, 2003), chap. 7.

3. Doss, *Twentieth-Century American Art.*

4. Natasha Zaretsky, *No Direction Home: The American Family and the Fear of National Decline, 1968–1980* (Chapel Hill: University of Chapel Hill Press, 2007), 4.

5. On changing conceptions of the American family in the twentieth century, see Stephanie Coontz, *The Way We Never Were: American Families and the Nostalgia Trap* (New York: Basic Books, 1993); David Peterson del Mar, *The American Family: From Obligation to Freedom* (New York: Palgrave McMillan, 2011); Stephanie Coontz, *Marriage, a History: From Obedience to Intimacy, or How Love Conquered Marriage* (New York: Viking, 2005). On conservative visions of gender and the American family, see Catherine E. Rymph, *Republican Women: Feminism and Conservatism from Suffrage through the Rise of the New Right* (Chapel Hill: University of North Carolina Press, 2006); Kirsten Marie Delegard, *Battling Miss Bolsheviki: The Origins of Female Conservatism in the United States* (Philadelphia: University of Pennsylvania Press, 2012); Donald T. Critchlow, *Phyllis Schlafly and Grassroots Conservatism: A Woman's Crusade* (Princeton, N.J.: Princeton University Press, 2005).

6. John E. Bodnar, *Remaking America: Public Memory, Commemoration, and Patriotism in the Twentieth Century* (Princeton, N.J.: Princeton University Press, 1991), chap. 6.

7. Mrs. Avard Fairbanks to George Putnam, October 11, 1954, folder 8, box 1, Fairbanks Papers.

8. Barbara Flanagan, "State Bids Fair to Honor Its 100th Birthday," *Minneapolis (Minn.) Morning Tribune,* August 23, 1958.

9. Doss, *Twentieth-Century American Art,* chap. 7.

10. Barbara Flanagan, "Fair Begins, Meets a New Princess Kay," *Minneapolis (Minn.) Morning Tribune,* August 24, 1958; Flanagan, "State Bids Fair to Honor Its 100th Birthday."

11. Rowlands, "Remembering to Forget," 129–45.

12. "Sculptor Enlists Students' Aid in Picking 20 Great Illinoisans," *Bloomington (Ill.) Pantagraph,* October 12, 1958; "Nine of Ten Figures to Be Carved in Granite," *Freeport (Ill.) Journal-Standard,* September 8, 1958; "Free: Your Sesquicentennial Medallion," *Chicago Daily Herald,* October 25, 1968; "State History Told on Medal," *Chicago Daily Herald,* May 22, 1968.

13. "Student to Design New Liberal Statue," *Hutchinson (Kans.) News,* December 27, 1959. See also "Statue to Be Built in Liberal City Park," *Amarillo (Tex.) Daily News,* December 24, 1959.

14. "Monument to Pioneer Mothers Dedicated," *Amarillo (Tex.) Daily News,* June 2, 1961.

15. "Pioneer Woman Statue Finds Home," *Provo (Utah) Sunday Herald,* November 10, 1953.

16. "Pioneer Statue to Be Dedicated at Liberal," *Hutchinson (Kans.) News,* May 29, 1961.

17. "Monument to Pioneer Mothers Dedicated."

18. Mrs. Samuel M. Ralston, ed., *The Memorial to the Pioneer Mother of Indiana* (Indianapolis: Hollenbeck Press, 1916), 3.

19. "Reviews and Notes," *Indiana Magazine of History* 12, no. 3 (September 1916): 285.

20. Ralston, *Memorial to the Pioneer Mother of Indiana,* 19.

21. Ibid., 20.

22. McElya, "Commemorating the Color Line," 203–18.

23. Ibid., 21.

24. "Historical News," *Indiana Magazine of History* 17, no. 3 (September 1921): 298–309; "Weddings of Three Periods to Be Centennial Party Features," *Indianapolis News,* May 29, 1920; "Club Programs to Take up Many Civic Affairs," *Indianapolis News,* June 18, 1921; "Clubwomen Plan Service to Welcome Home Guests," *Indianapolis News,* May 3, 1919; "Committees Named for Mothers' Memorial Fund," *Indianapolis News,* March 8, 1917; "Society," *Indianapolis News,* February 21, 1917; "Pioneer Mothers Will Give Party Wednesday," *Indianapolis Star,* May 30, 1920.

25. L. E. M., "'Pioneer Mothers' of Indiana to Have Striking Monument," *American Art News,* September 17, 1921; "Mrs. J. N. Carey Named to Head Memorial Society," *Indianapolis News,* March 13, 1926.

26. Ulrich, *Age of Homespun.*

27. "Sparing the Trees," *Franklin (Ind.) Evening Star,* November 17, 1941.

28. "Mothers' Memorial Forest Dedicated," *Terre Haute (Ind.) Tribune,* September 7, 1955; Carol Kugler, "Love of Woods Leads to Celebration," *Bloomington (Ind.) Herald Times,* n.d.

29. Quoted in "View with Pride," *Tipton (Ind.) Daily Tribune,* September 6, 1955.

30. Elaine Tyler May, *Homeward Bound: American Families in the Cold War Era* (New York: Basic Books, 1988), chaps. 1, 8; Patricia Nelson Limerick, "The Adventures of the Frontier in the Twentieth Century," in White and Limerick, *Frontier in American Culture,* 66–102; Susan J. Douglas, *Where the Girls Are: Growing up Female with the Mass Media* (New York: Times Books, 1995), chaps. 2–3.

31. Coontz, *The Way We Never Were*; May, *Homeward Bound,* chap. 6; Douglas, *Where the Girls Are,* chap. 2; Viviana A. Rotman Zelizer, *Pricing the Priceless Child: The Changing Social Value of Children* (New York: Basic Books, 1985), chap. 6; Steven Mintz, *Huck's Raft: A History of American Childhood* (Cambridge, Mass.: Belknap Press of Harvard University Press, 2004), chap. 14.

32. Stephanie Coontz, *A Strange Stirring: The Feminine Mystique and American Women at the Dawn of the 1960s* (New York: Basic Books, 2011), 75. However, Coontz made clear, this ideology was not embraced by all women, particularly working-class women and women of color.

33. Joanne J. Meyerowitz, ed., *Not June Cleaver: Women and Gender in Postwar America, 1945–1960* (Philadelphia: Temple University Press, 1994); Joanne

Meyerowitz, "Beyond the Feminine Mystique: A Reassessment of Postwar Mass Culture," *Journal of American History* 79 (1993): 1455–83; Jessica Weiss, *To Have and to Hold: Marriage, the Baby Boom, and Social Change* (Chicago: University of Chicago Press, 2000).

34. Catherine McNicol Stock, *Main Street in Crisis: The Great Depression and the Old Middle Class on the Northern Plains* (Chapel Hill: University of North Carolina Press, 1992), chap. 8.

35. Avard Fairbanks [hereafter AF] to Governor C. A. Robbins, September 3, 1948, folder 2, box 11, Fairbanks Papers.

36. "New Monument is Completed," *Bismarck (N.Dak.) Capitol Journal*, August 22, 1947.

37. Francis Breidenbach, "Master of Bronze," folder 21, box 12, Fairbanks Papers; "New Monument is Completed," *Bismarck (N.Dak.) Capitol Journal* August 22, 1947; AF to Robbins, September 3, 1948, Fairbanks Papers; AF to Russell Reid, October 13, 1947, folder 4, box 6, Fairbanks Papers; George F. Will to AF, May 9, 1947, folder 5, box 6, Fairbanks Papers; William B. Falconer to AF, May 1, 1947, folder 9, box 8, Fairbanks Papers.

38. The *Courier-Journal* Building with "Spirit of Kentucky," June 1948, folder 35, box 20, series V, Marshall M. Fredericks Papers, *Marshall M. Fredericks Sculpture Museum Digital Archives and Objects Collection*, http://omeka.svsu.edu/items/show/3030 (accessed April 27, 2018).

39. "Puryear Mims: General Practitioner of Sculpture," *Southeast Missourian* (Cape Girardeau, Mo.), April 4, 1975.

40. Francis Keally, "Oregon State Capitol," 5, Capitol Reconstruction Commission (CRC) Papers, Oregon State Archives, Salem.

41. "Description of State Library, Salem, Oregon," CRC Papers.

42. Doris Smith to Robert W. Sawyer, April 25, 1938, CRC Papers.

43. Walter E. Meacham to George Marshall, April 23, 1937, CRC Papers.

44. CRC meeting transcript, September 1, 1937, CRC Papers.

45. Will of Carroll Moores, quoted in "Living Memorial for Pioneers Proposed," *Salem (Ore.) Daily Capital Journal*, December 21, 1950.

46. Ibid.

47. "Greider Has Suggestion for Use of Moores Fund," *Salem (Ore.) Daily Capital Journal*, January 27, 1951; "Public Hearing Dated on Pioneer Memorial," *Salem (Ore.) Daily Capital Journal*, July 27, 1951; "Asks How to Spend Fund," *Oregon Statesman* (Salem), May 31, 1951; Charles A. Sprague, "It Seems to Me," *Oregon Statesman* (Salem), April 9, 1951.

48. "Council to Act on New 'Nuisance' Taxes," *Salem (Ore.) Daily Capital Journal*, December 27, 1951.

49. Francis M. Howell, Willis I. Ray, and Glen L. Vernon, "Church Board Enters Protest, Venus Statue," *Salem (Ore.) Daily Capital Journal*, June 20, 1953; R. S. Brady, "Salem Garden Club Enters Its Protest," *Salem (Ore.) Daily Capital Journal*, June 20, 1953; Maude Porter Boone, "Wouldn't Have Venus in Her Backyard,"

Salem (Ore.) Daily Capital Journal, June 20, 1953; E. D. Caswell, "Roman Goddess Not Anything to Inspire," *Salem (Ore.) Daily Capital Journal,* June 20, 1953; Opal Baker and nine co-signers, "Venus Belongs Only in Art Galleries," *Salem (Ore.) Daily Capital Journal,* June 20, 1953; Mary Bello, "Christian Pioneers in Place of Venus," *Salem (Ore.) Daily Capital Journal,* June 20, 1953; "Memorializing Our Pioneers," *Salem (Ore.) Daily Capital Journal,* June 15, 1953.

50. "Venus Observed," *Time,* July 6, 1953, http://www.time.com/time/magazine/article/0,9171,822851,00.html.

51. Quoted in "Venus or Old Pioneer: Salem Council to Decide on Nude," *Klamath Falls (Ore.) Herald and News,* June 19, 1953.

52. "Nude Venus Will Not Stand for Pioneers," *Council Bluffs (Iowa) Nonpareil,* June 21, 1953.

53. "Memorial Committee Sets up Rules," *Oregon Statesman* (Salem), February 19, 1954.

54. "Avard Fairbanks' North Dakota Pioneer Monument," *Salem (Ore.) Daily Capital Journal,* May 5, 1954.

55. "Suggestions for Pioneer Memorial," *Salem (Ore.) Daily Capital Journal,* October 19, 1954; "Marble Group Proposed by Dr. Fairbanks," *Oregon Statesman* (Salem), May 19, 1955.

56. "Interest High in Sculptures at Bush House: Public Opinion Running in Favor of Work by Frances MacCollin," *Salem (Ore.) Daily Capital Journal,* February 7, 1956; Calvin D. Johnson, "Sketches, Pictures of Proposed Moores Memorial on Display," *Oregon Statesman* (Salem), February 17, 1956, sec. 3; "Art Group Backs MacCollin's Work for Memorial," *Oregon Statesman* (Salem), February 14, 1956; "Bush House to Get Paint Job During Spring: Art Association Board Takes Poll on Bids for Memorial," *Salem (Ore.) Daily Capital Journal,* February 14, 1956.

57. "Wants a Real Memorial to the Oregon Pioneers," *Salem (Ore.) Daily Capital Journal,* February 16, 1956.

58. "Moores Statue Chosen: Trick Photo Shows It in Bush Park," *Oregon Statesman* (Salem), May 9, 1956.

59. Charles A. Sprague, "It Seems to Me," *Oregon Statesman* (Salem), July 5, 1959.

60. Mrs. Avard Fairbanks to George Putnam, October 11, 1954, folder 8, box 1, Fairbanks Papers.

61. AF to Barbara Cross, May 22, 1956, folder 6, box 4, Fairbanks Papers.

62. *Oregonian* (Portland), reprinted as "Sub for Venus," *Salem (Ore.) Daily Capital Journal,* May 12, 1956.

63. Quoted in "Guidance of Youth," *Salem (Ore.) Capital Journal,* undated clipping, folder 22, box 12, Fairbanks Papers.

64. Quoted in "Moores Sculptor: City Okay Condition for Pick," *Capital Journal,* May 8, 1956, 1, 5.

65. "Guidance of Youth."

66. Weiss, *To Have and to Hold.*

67. Plant, *Mom.*

68. Mary Trapp, "Proposed Sculpture Draws Criticism, Praise, and Dismay," *Dakota Student* (University of North Dakota, Grand Forks), September 27, 1966; William Borden, "Alma Mater: Art or Good Art?," *Dakota Student* (University of North Dakota, Grand Forks), October 11, 1966.

69. Letter from "We have spoken" to President Starcher, April 25, 1966, George Starcher Papers, 1927–1979, Elwyn B. Robinson Department of Special Collections, Chester Fritz Library, University of North Dakota, Grand Forks.

70. William Zeckendorf quoted in "Zeckendorf Unit to Give Donation," *Rocky Mountain News* (Denver), April 2, 1966.

71. "How Prize Is Picked," *Colorado Springs Gazette*, April 6, 1968.

72. Doss, *Twentieth-Century American Art*, chaps. 6, 8.

73. "Housewife, Artist, Sculptor, Winner," *Rocky Mountain News* (Denver), November 6, 1966.

74. "We Don't Like It," *Kenosha (Wisc.) News*, April 3, 1968; "Unveiling," *Kingston (N.Y.) Daily Freeman*, April 3, 1968.

75. Emily Toman, "For a Major Piece of Public Art at White Rock Lake, the Future Is Uncertain," *Lakewood/East Dallas Advocate*, January 21, 2014, http://lakewood.advocatemag.com/2014/01/21/white-rock-lake-water-theater-removal/.

76. Gil Asakawa, "Party Arty: When the Depot Arts District Celebrates, Everyone Is Invited," *Colorado Springs Gazette-Telegraph*, July 21, 1995, sec. Go!; D'Arcy Fallon, "'The Family' Finds Happy Home at Fine Arts Center, Statue Doesn't Stand Still," *Colorado Springs Gazette-Telegraph*, December 22, 1993; Greg Pitts, "Columbia Savings Celebrates 50 Years in Pueblo," *Pueblo (Colo.) Chieftain*, March 1, 1992, sec. Bus.

77. Joanne Ditmer, "Will Denver Lose Its Prized Sculpture?," *Denver Post*, December 7, 1990.

78. "'Deep Fund of Humanity' Enriches Zorach's Work," *Colorado Springs Gazette-Telegraph*, December 12, 1964.

79. "The Beautiful Difference in Savings," *Colorado Springs Gazette-Telegraph*, September 8, 1968, sec. B.

80. Personal correspondence with Saskia Kesners, January 16, 2009.

81. Mella Rothwell Harmon, National Register of Historic Places Registration Form, "Pioneer Theater-Auditorium," Reno, Nevada, August 31, 2004, http://focus.nps.gov/pdfhost/docs/NRHP/Text/04001528.pdf; "New Fountain Due June 1st; Price Memorial Will Be Installed," *Nevada State Journal* (Reno), May 6, 1939; "New Fountain Is Installed: Price Memorial Is Put in Place," *Nevada State Journal* (Reno), May 17, 1939; "Price Fountain Now Installed; Bronze Statute [*sic*] Put in Place Tuesday," *Nevada State Journal* (Reno), August 23, 1939; "William E. Price Will Contest Filed in Court," *Nevada State Journal* (Reno), September 26, 1937; Alicia Marie Barber, "Living It Up, Living It Down: Civic Reputation, Tourism and Urban Development in Reno, Nevada" (PhD diss., University of Texas at Austin, 2003); Mella Harmon, "Pioneer Theater-Auditorium," *Reno Historical*, http://renohistorical.org/items/show/70 (accessed November 2, 2015).

82. Pat Gaston, "Work Underway on Trifinity's Sister," *Salina (Kans.) Journal*, May 19, 1976.

83. "Bergen Sculpture Okayed by Wichita," *Salina (Kans.) Journal*, June 23, 1976.

CHAPTER 4. MORMON EXCEPTIONALISM, ASSIMILATION, AND AMERICANNESS

1. James L. Haseltine, "Mormons and the Visual Arts," *Dialogue: A Journal of Mormon Thought* 1, no. 2 (Summer 1966): 17–29; Terryl Givens, *People of Paradox: A History of Mormon Culture* (New York: Oxford University Press, 2007), chaps. 7, 13.

2. Giles H. Florence Jr., "Harvesting the Light: The 1890 Paris Art Mission," *Ensign*, October 1988, https://www.lds.org/ensign/1988/10/harvesting-the-light-the-1890-paris-art-mission?lang=eng; Jeffrey D. Andersen, "Portrait of the 1890–1892 LDS Paris Art Mission: An Andragogical Perspective" (PhD diss., University of Idaho, Moscow, 2006).

3. Steven L. Olsen, "Pioneer Day," *Utah History Encyclopedia*, http://www.uen.org/utah_history_encyclopedia/p/PIONEER_DAY.shtml (accessed March 2, 2016); "A Look Back at Pioneer Day," *Utah Department of Heritage and Arts*, July 19, 2013, https://heritage.utah.gov/history/pioneerday.

4. Armand L. Mauss, "The Mormon Struggle with Assimilation and Identity: Trends and Developments Since Midcentury," *Dialogue: A Journal of Mormon Thought* 27, no. 1 (Spring 1994): 129–49; O. Kendall White and Daryl White, "Polygamy and Mormon Identity," *Journal of American Culture* 28, no. 2 (June 2005): 165–77; Ethan R. Yorgason, *Transformation of the Mormon Culture Region* (Urbana: University of Illinois Press, 2010); David L. Bigler, *Forgotten Kingdom: The Mormon Theocracy in the American West, 1847–1896* (Logan: Utah State University Press, 1998); Scott C. Esplin and E. Vance Randall, "Living in Two Worlds: The Development and Transition of Mormon Education in American Society," *History of Education* 43, no. 1 (2014): 3–30; Greg (Fritz) Umbach, "Learning to Shop in Zion: The Consumer Revolution in Great Basin Mormon Culture, 1847–1910," *Journal of Social History* 38, no. 1 (Fall 2004): 29–61; Brent Corcoran, *Multiply and Replenish: Mormon Essays on Sex and Family* (Salt Lake City: Signature Books, 1994); Givens, *People of Paradox*, pt. 3.

5. Stephen Prothero, *Why Liberals Win (Even When They Lose Elections): How America's Raucous, Nasty, and Mean "Culture Wars" Make for a More Inclusive Nation* (New York: HarperCollins, 2016), 136.

6. Nathaniel Smith Kogan, "The Mormon Pavilion: Mainstreaming the Saints at the New York World's Fair, 1964–65," *Journal of Mormon History* 35, no. 4 (Fall 2009): 36–37. See also Paul F. Starrs, "Meetinghouses in the Mormon Mind: Ideology, Architecture, and Turbulent Streams of an Expanding Church," *Geographical Review* 99, no. 3 (July 2009): 323–55.

7. Armand L. Mauss, *The Angel and the Beehive: The Mormon Struggle with Assimilation* (Urbana: University of Illinois Press, 1994); Armand L. Mauss, "Rethinking Retrenchment: Course Corrections in the Ongoing Campaign for Respectability,"

Dialogue: A Journal of Mormon Thought 44, no. 4 (2011): 1–42; Jan Shipps, "From Peoplehood to Church Membership: Mormonism's Trajectory since World War II," *Church History* 76, no. 2 (June 2007): 241–61; Gregory A. Prince and William Robert Wright, *David O. McKay and the Rise of Modern Mormonism* (Salt Lake City: University of Utah Press, 2005).

8. W. Paul Reeve, *Religion of a Different Color: Race and the Mormon Struggle for Whiteness* (New York: Oxford University Press, 2015).

9. Holzapfel and Hunter, "New Photograph of the Granite Shaft"; Wendell B. Wheeler Johnson and Rell G. Francis, *Frontier to Fame: Cyrus E. Dallin, Sculptor,* ed. Denice Dallin Wheeler ([Mass.]: self-pub., 2005).

10. Johnson and Francis, *Frontier to Fame.*

11. Ibid., 24.

12. Quoted in Johnson and Francis, *Frontier to Fame,* 78.

13. "The Brigham Young Memorial," *Contributor,* June 1892; Johnson and Francis, *Frontier to Fame.*

14. "Brigham Young Memorial."

15. Johnson and Francis, *Frontier to Fame*; Holzapfel and Hunter, "New Photograph of the Granite Shaft."

16. Thomas G. Alexander, *Mormonism in Transition: A History of the Latter-Day Saints, 1890–1930* (Urbana: University of Illinois Press, 1996), chap. 1; Mormon Church v. United States 136 U.S. 1 (1890), *Justia Law,* https://supreme.justia.com/cases/federal/us/136/1/ (accessed October 17, 2016).

17. "The Pioneers' Monument: A Matter of Interest to All Utah," *Salt Lake Tribune,* January 7, 1895.

18. Quoted in Hunter, "Monument to Brigham Young and the Pioneers," 332–50.

19. Reeve, *Religion of a Different Color.*

20. "The Pioneers' Monument."

21. Barry Laga, "In Lieu of History: Mormon Monuments and the Shaping of Memory," *Dialogue: A Journal of Mormon Thought* 43, no. 4 (Winter 2010): 131–53; Kathleen Flake, "Re-Placing Memory: Latter-Day Saint Use of Historical Monuments and Narrative in the Early Twentieth Century," *Religion and American Culture* 13, no. 1 (Winter 2003): 69; Eric A. Eliason, "The Cultural Dynamics of Historical Self-Fashioning: Mormon Pioneer Nostalgia, American Culture, and the International Church," *Journal of Mormon History* 28, no. 2 (April 2002): 139–73; Yorgason, *Transformation of the Mormon Culture Region,* chap. 4.

22. Daughters of the American Revolution, *Twenty-Second Report of the National Society of the Daughters of the American Revolution: March 1, 1918, to March 1, 1919* (Washington, D.C.: U.S. Government Printing Office, 1921), 146.

23. William G. Hartley, "Torleif Knaphus, Sculptor Saint," *Ensign,* July 1980, https://www.lds.org/ensign/1980/07/torleif-knaphus-sculptor-saint.

24. Elizabeth Cannon Porter, "A Monument to the Handcart Pioneers," *Improvement Era,* July 1925, 834–37; LaRene Porter Gaunt and Linda Dekker, "Go

and Bring Them In," *Ensign*, December 2006; Lyndia McDowell Carter, "The Mormon Handcart Companies," *Overland Journal* 13, no. 1 (1995): 2–18; William G. Hartley, "The Place of Mormon Handcart Companies in America's Westward Migration Story," *Annals of Iowa* 65 (Spring/Summer 2006): 101–23; Don H. Smith, "Leadership, Planning, and Management of the 1856 Mormon Handcart Emigration," *Annals of Iowa* 65 (Spring/Summer 2006): 124–61.

25. "Handcart Bronze Shown to Public," *Ogden (Utah) Standard-Examiner*, September 26, 1926.

26. "Crew Lays Base for Statue of Utah Handcart Group," *Salt Lake Tribune*, September 20, 1947; "Interesting Personalities Attending Semiannual Conference," *Salt Lake Tribune*, October 26, 1934; "Monument Ready for Dedication," *Ogden (Utah) Standard-Examiner*, September 23, 1926; "Camera Looks In . . . ," *Salt Lake Tribune*, April 10, 1961; "Timber Base Holds Monument To Utah's Handcart Pioneers," *Ogden (Utah) Standard-Examiner*, April 16, 1966; "Missionary Reunions," *Ogden (Utah) Standard-Examiner*, April 3, 1970; "LDS Missionary Reunions Scheduled: Locations Given," *Ogden (Utah) Standard-Examiner*, October 4, 1973, sec. B.

27. David Hall, "New Identities for a New Century: Shifting Gender Roles for Mormon Women in the Early Twentieth Century" (paper presented at the Western History Association Annual Conference, St. Paul, Minnesota, October 20–23, 2016).

28. Pierce, *Making the White Man's West*, chap. 7.

29. Rebecca Mead, *How the Vote Was Won: Woman Suffrage in the Western United States, 1868–1914* (New York: NYU Press, 2006), chap. 3; Yorgason, *Transformation of the Mormon Culture Region*, chap. 2; Suzanne M. Stauffer, "A Good Social Work: Women's Clubs, Libraries, and the Construction of a Secular Society in Utah, 1890–1920," *Libraries and the Cultural Record* 46, no. 2 (2011): 135–55.

30. Quoted in Johnson and Francis, *Frontier to Fame*, 155.

31. Quoted ibid., 156.

32. "Springville Plans Monument Ceremony," *Salt Lake Telegram*, May 27, 1932.

33. Johnson and Francis, *Frontier to Fame*.

34. "Plans for Pioneer Day at Springville Progress," *Salt Lake Telegram*, July 15, 1932; "Ivins Will Speak at Monument Rites," *Salt Lake Telegram*, June 21, 1932; "Contest for Queen Plans Announced," *Salt Lake Telegram*, June 30, 1932; Johnson and Francis, *Frontier to Fame*; "Springville Ready for Monument Fete," *Salt Lake Telegram*, July 23, 1932.

35. E. F. Fairbanks, "Competition for This Is the Place Monument."

36. W. Douglas Seefeldt, "Constructing Western Pasts: Place and Public Memory in the Twentieth-Century American West" (PhD diss., Arizona State University, Tempe, 2001), 300.

37. "Sons of Pioneers Reelect Officers and Adopt 12-Year Plan of President Morris," *Salt Lake Tribune*, August 12, 1935.

38. "Utahn to Design Pioneer Monument," *Provo (Utah) Daily Herald*, February 1, 1938; "'This Is the Place' Mahonri Young's Tribute," *Salt Lake Tribune*, March 6,

1945; Wayne K. Hinton, "Mahonri Young and the Church: A View of Mormonism and Art," *Dialogue: A Journal of Mormon Thought* 7, no. 4 (1972): 35–43.

39. Eugene F. Fairbanks, *A Sculptor's Testimony in Bronze and Stone: The Sacred Sculpture of Avard T. Fairbanks* ([Salt Lake City], [Publishers Press], 1972).

40. E. F. Fairbanks, "Competition for This Is the Place Monument."

41. Mahonri Young, "'This is the Place' Monument," n.d., sec. L, Mahonri M. Young Papers, Tom Perry Special Collections, Harold B. Lee Library, Brigham Young University, Provo, Utah.

42. "Sculptor Tells Plans for Young Monument," *Ogden (Utah) Standard-Examiner,* May 31, 1944.

43. M. Young, "'This is the Place' Monument," Young Papers.

44. Quoted in Hinton, "Mahonri Young and the Church," 40.

45. M. Young, "'This is the Place' Monument," Young Papers.

46. Hinton, "Mahonri Young and the Church," 40.

47. "Pioneer Monument Contract Awarded to Mahonri M. Young," *Salt Lake Tribune,* January 8, 1939.

48. "Young—Marriott Library—The University of Utah," accessed March 7, 2016, http://www.lib.utah.edu/collections/utah-artists/UAP-Mahonri-Young.php; "Famous Artist Predicts End of Modernism," *Salt Lake Tribune,* May 3, 1936, sec. B; Hinton, "Mahonri Young and the Church."

49. M. Young, "'This is the Place' Monument," Young Papers.

50. "Sculptor Tells Plans for Young Monument."

51. Yorgason, *Transformation of the Mormon Culture Region*; Alexander, *Mormonism in Transition*; Jan Shipps, "Difference and Otherness: Mormonism and the American Religious Mainstream," in *Minority Faiths and the American Protestant Mainstream,* ed. Jonathan D. Sarna (University of Illinois Press, 1998), 81–109.

52. "Houses View Model of Pioneer Shaft," *Salt Lake Telegram,* March 2, 1939.

53. "Church Lays Monument Stone Today," *Salt Lake Tribune,* July 24, 1946; "Lessons to Learn from Utah's Pioneers by Beneficiaries of Their Struggle," *Salt Lake Tribune,* July 24, 1945.

54. Barbara Kirshenblatt-Gimblett, *Destination Culture: Tourism, Museums, and Heritage* (Berkeley: University of California Press, 1998), 125.

55. E. F. Fairbanks, *A Sculptor's Testimony,* 78–83, 146–47.

56. Avard Fairbanks, "New Frontiers," 1, undated typescript, folder 6, box 4, Fairbanks Papers.

57. Ibid.; "New Frontiers," *Relief Society Magazine* 28, no. 7 (July 1941): 1.

58. *Relief Society* adapted language from Fairbanks, "New Frontiers."

59. "Pioneering," *Relief Society Magazine* 29, no. 9 (September 1942): 1.

60. Givens, *People of Paradox,* 331–35; White and White, "Polygamy and Mormon Identity"; Mauss, *The Angel and the Beehive*; D. Michael Quinn, "LDS 'Headquarters Culture' and the Rest of Mormonism: Past and Present," *Dialogue: A Journal of Mormon Thought* 34, nos. 3–4 (Fall 2001): 135–64; Armand L. Mauss, "Assimilation and Ambivalence: The Mormon Reaction to Americanization,"

Dialogue: A Journal of Mormon Thought 22, no. 1 (Spring 1989): 30–67; Prince and Wright, *David O. McKay*; Martha Sonntag Bradley, *Pedestals and Podiums: Utah Women, Religious Authority, and Equal Rights* (Salt Lake City: Signature Books, 2005); Jenny Lynn Mcgee Harris, "The Silent Majority: Conservative Perception, Mobilization, and Rhetoric at the Utah State International Women's Year Conference" (master's thesis, Brigham Young University, 2005); Lisa McGirr, *Suburban Warriors: The Origins of the New American Right* (Princeton, N.J.: Princeton University Press, 2001).

61. Avard Fairbanks to the First Presidency of the Church of Jesus Christ of Latter-day Saints, , March 18, 1941, Fairbanks Papers.

62. "Family Monument Fund Drive to Open across Utah County," *Provo (Utah) Herald*, September 3, 1978; "Garage Sale and Flea Market to Help Finance American Family Monument," *Spanish Fork (Utah) Press*, undated clipping, folder 2, box 13, Fairbanks Papers; donor plaque on Fairbanks, *American Family*.

63. Avard Fairbanks to the First Presidency, March 18, 1941; "Garage Sale and Flea Market."

64. "The American Family," *Daily Herald: Women Today*, November 11, 1979, 41.

65. "Eternal Family Monument Unveiled at Provo Ceremony," *Deseret News* (Salt Lake City), September 15, 1979.

66. E. F. Fairbanks, *A Sculptor's Testimony*, 96.

67. Kathryn M. Daynes, *More Wives Than One: Transformation of the Mormon Marriage System, 1840–1910* (Urbana: University of Illinois Press, 2001); Eugene E. Campbell and Bruce L. Campbell, "Divorce among Mormon Polygamists: Extent and Explanations," in *The New Mormon History: Revisionist Essays on the Past*, ed. D. Michael Quinn (Salt Lake City: Signature Books, 1992): 181–200; Neil J. Young, "'The ERA Is a Moral Issue': The Mormon Church, LDS Women, and the Defeat of the Equal Rights Amendment," *American Quarterly* 59, no. 3 (September 2007): 623–44; Prince and Wright, *David O. McKay*; Bradley, *Pedestals and Podiums.*

68. "Family Monument Fund Drive to Open Across Utah County," *Provo (Utah) Herald*, September 3, 1978, folder 2, box 13, Fairbanks Papers.

69. "Eternal Family Monument Unveiled at Provo Ceremony." On the dominance of conservative Mormon culture in Utah County, see Jared Farmer, *On Zion's Mount: Mormons, Indians, and the American Landscape* (Cambridge, Mass.: Harvard University Press, 2008).

CHAPTER 5. CONSERVATIVE COMMEMORATION AND PROGRESSIVE PROTEST

1. Minutes of the Promised Land Memorial Committee Meeting, June 19, 1994, "The Promised Land," North Park Blocks folder, Oregon Trail Coordinating Council Papers, City of Portland Archives and Records Center, Portland, Oregon (hereafter PARC).

2. Hamilakis and Labanyi, "Time, Materiality, and the Work of Memory," 5–17. See also Mills and Walker, *Memory Work*.

3. Goetzmann and Goetzmann, *The West of the Imagination*, chap. 29.

4. Pierce, *Making the White Man's West*, xii.

5. Connerton, *How Modernity Forgets*, 99. See also Connerton, *How Societies Remember*; Trouillot, *Silencing the Past*.

6. Andrew Hartman, *A War for the Soul of America: A History of the Culture Wars* (Chicago: University of Chicago Press, 2015); Steven P. Miller, *The Age of Evangelicalism: America's Born-Again Years* (New York: Oxford University Press, 2014).

7. Coontz, *Marriage, a History*, chaps. 15–16; Coontz, *The Way We Never Were*; Meyerowitz, *Not June Cleaver*.

8. Bodnar, *Remaking America*, 234–37.

9. Laura Barraclough, "The Western Spirit of '76: The American Bicentennial and the Making of Conservative Multiculturalism in the Mountain West," *Western Historical Quarterly* 47, no. 2 (Summer 2016): 176.

10. Karl Jakob Skarstein, Richard Rothaus, and Dakota Goodhouse, *The War with the Sioux: Norwegians against Indians, 1862–1863*, trans. Melissa Gjellstad and Danielle Mead Skjelver (Grand Forks: University of North Dakota Digital Press, 2015); Kenneth Carley, *The Dakota War of 1862: Minnesota's Other Civil War*, 2nd ed. (St. Paul: Minnesota Historical Society Press, 2001); *The U.S.-Dakota War of 1862*, Minnesota Historical Society, http://usdakotawar.org/ (accessed February 17, 2017).

11. "New Ulm's Defenders," n.d., Defenders Monument vertical file, Brown County Historical Society Archives, New Ulm, Minnesota.

12. "Changing Memorials," *The U.S.-Dakota War of 1862*, Minnesota Historical Society, http://usdakotawar.org/history/today-memory-commemoration/changing-memorials (accessed February 17, 2017).

13. On the historical accuracy of Catlin, Eastman, and Bodmer, see Goetzmann and Goetzmann, *The West of the Imagination*, chaps. 2–4.

14. Gordon Dingman, text for sculpture brochure, 1974, Dingman Brick Sculpture vertical file, Brown County Historical Society Archives, New Ulm, Minnesota.

15. Cj Carmichael Braun, comp., *Marking Time: An Illustrated Guide to Brown County's Sites of Historical Interest* (New Ulm, Minn.: Brown County Historical Society, 2006), http://www.browncountyhistorymn.org/uploads/2/1/9/9/21990898/marking_time__current.pdf.

16. Dingman, "Life Sketches: New Ulm 1850's," 1–2, Dingman Brick Sculpture vertical file.

17. "Felten at Work on Oberlin's Statue," *Oberlin (Kans.) Herald*, June 24, 1971.

18. Quoted in Chris Cioffi, "Timeless Design," *Billings (Mont.) Gazette*, January 17, 2015.

19. On cowboy poetry, see David Stanley, "Cowboy Poetry Then and Now: An Overview," in *Cowboy Poets and Cowboy Poetry*, ed. David Stanley and Elaine Thatcher (Urbana, Ill.: University of Illinois Press, 2000), 1–18.

20. Jaci Webb, "Artistic Celebration," *Billings (Mont.) Gazette*, December 12, 2003; Jaci Webb, "Billings Artist Mike Caper Marks 25th Anniversary of Career," *Billings (Mont.) Gazette*, December 11, 2003.

21. M. Solberg, "Pioneer's Vision Statues at the 1st Interstate Bank in Billings, Montana by Mike Capser," *dcMemorials*, last updated April 20, 2013, http://www.dcmemorials.com/index_indiv0006601.htm.

22. Limerick, *Legacy of Conquest.*

23. Rowlands, "Remembering to Forget," 129–45.

24. U.S. Census Bureau, *1990 Census of Population: General Population Characteristics, Arizona*, 20, May 1992, http://azmemory.azlibrary.gov/cdm/ref/collection/feddocs/id/43.

25. "Things to Do in Prescott, Arizona," *Visit Prescott*, City of Prescott, Office of Tourism, http://www.visit-prescott.com/visit-prescott-arizona (accessed May 9, 2017).

26. As of 2010, Worland was 90 percent white, and 80 percent non-Hispanic white. U.S. Census Bureau, "Population Estimates, July 1, 2015" (V2015) *QuickFacts: Worland city, Wyoming*, http://www.census.gov/quickfacts/table/PST045215/5684925 (accessed September 29, 2016).

27. "History of Worland," About Us page, *City of Worland*, http://www.cityofworland.org (accessed January 17, 2018).

28. U.S. Census Bureau, *1990 Census of Population: General Population Characteristics, New Mexico* (Washington, D.C.: U.S. Government Printing Office, 1992), 15.

29. H. L. Lavato, *New Mexican*, June 8, 1995, quoted in Einar [Kvaran], "Las Vegas, New Mexico Pioneer Woman," *Pioneer Women in Sculpture* (blog), September 28, 2011, http://pioneerwomen.blogspot.com/2011/09/las-vegas-new-mexico-pioneer-woman.html.

30. Ibid.

31. Carl Abbott, *Ethnic Minorities in Portland: A 1990 Census Profile* (Portland, Ore.: Center for Urban Studies, Portland State University, September 1991), 2, 13, https://www.pdx.edu/sites/www.pdx.edu.cus/files/SR021.pdf.

32. "Project Summary," MAC Promised Land Statue folder, OTCC Papers.

33. Eric Gable and Richard Handler, "After Authenticity at an American Heritage Site," *American Anthropologist* 98, no. 3 (1996): 568–78.

34. Marcia L. Mitchell, "David Manuel: Sculpting the Old West," *Northwest Magazine*, November 20, 1980.

35. *The Promised Land*, Oregon Artists vertical file, Oregon Historical Society Research Library, Portland, Oregon.

36. Randy Gragg, "Art and Propaganda on the Oregon Trail: The Sesquicentennial Celebrates a Happy, Sanitized History at Odds with the Real Thing," *Oregonian* (Portland), August 29, 1993; Kammen, *Visual Shock.*

37. Gragg, "Art and Propaganda on the Oregon Trail."

38. "Report on Site Committee I Process," n.d., Metropolitan Arts Commission Special Arts Project Files—Promised Land Move (hereafter MAC Promised Land Move), PARC.

39. "A Tarnished Sculpture? Portland Rejects Oregon Trail Statue," n.d., *The Promised Land*, Portland Sculpture vertical file, Oregon Historical Society Research Library, Portland, Oregon.

40. Randy Gragg, "Bronze Brouhaha," *Oregonian* (Portland), March 4, 1994.

41. "Report on Site Committee I Process," MAC Promised Land Move, PARC.

42. "A Tarnished Sculpture?" *The Promised Land,* Portland, Sculpture vertical file.

43. All quoted ibid.

44. William D. Bulick, draft editorial, n.d., Metropolitan Arts Commission Special Arts Project Files—Promised Land Statue, PARC.

45. Richard Conkle, "Artist Knows Danger of Immortalizing a Legend," *Oregonian* (Portland), August 1, 1999.

46. Ned Look, Site Committee II draft document with handwritten edits, August 12, 1994, MAC Promised Land Sculpture folder, MAC Papers, PARC; Randy Gragg, "Decision on Politically Hot Statue of Oregon Pioneers Delayed Again," *Oregonian* (Portland), April 16, 1994, C8.

47. Ben Whiteley to Mary Anne Cassin, September 20, 1994, *The Promised Land,* North Park blocks, Oregon Trail Coordinating Council Papers, PARC.

48. Jeanie Senior, "The Statue Scramble," *Oregonian* (Portland), March 11, 1994, C01.

49. Dan McCue, "Bronze's Backers to Appeal," *Oregonian* (Portland), March 11, 1994, C08.

50. R. Gregory Nokes, "Thriving on Controversy," *Oregonian* (Portland), August 22, 1994, B8.

51. Portland, Oregon, City Ordinance 168299 (1994); "Temporary Siting of 'Promised Land' Sculpture," memorandum from Eloise MacMurray to Ron Kleinschmidt, November 1, 1994, MAC Promised Land Statue, PARC; Randy Gragg, "Her Art Is a Blast from the Past," *Oregonian* (Portland), May 18, 1997.

52. Jonathan Nicholas, "Promises, Promises," *Oregonian* (Portland), February 8, 1995.

53. Bill B. to Eloise [MacMurray], July 15, 1996, MAC Promised Land Move, PARC; Elliot Njus, "Ashforth Pacific CEP Scott Langley to Buy Company as Ashforth Bows Out," *Oregonian* (Portland), September 26, 2011; Brian K. Miller, "Liberty Centre Went Up in Near Record Time," *Portland Business Journal,* August 23, 2013.

54. John Snell, "'Promised Land' Not All Milk and Honey," *Oregonian* (Portland), October 2, 1996.

55. R. Gregory Nokes, "Eastward Ho! 'The Promised Land,'" *Oregonian* (Portland), August 25, 1994.

56. Handwritten meeting notes dated April 1 [1997?], MAC Promised Land Move, PARC.

57. Gragg, "Her Art Is a Blast from the Past."

58. Chris Kenning, "City Reopens Renovated Plaza Blocks," *Oregonian* (Portland), October 19, 1998.

59. Handwritten meeting notes, December 18 [1996?], 3, MAC Promised Land Move, PARC (emphasis in original).

60. Vera Katz, "1997 State of the City Address," January 17, 1996 [*sic*], MAC Promised Land Move, PARC.

61. Handwritten meeting notes dated December 18 [1996?], 3, MAC Promised Land Move, PARC.

62. Anonymous Google Plus Review of North Park Blocks, *Google Maps*, https://plus.google.com/117769637945176466867/ (accessed July 3, 2013).

63. Nokes, "Thriving on Controversy."

64. Conkle, "Artist Knows Danger of Immortalizing a Legend."

65. Ibid.

66. Carl Abbott, "Pioneer Monuments," H-West electronic discussion network, November 30, 2007.

67. Stan Hoig, "Land Run of 1889," *The Encyclopedia of Oklahoma History and Culture*, Oklahoma Historical Society, http://www.okhistory.org/publications/enc/entry.php?entry=LA014 (accessed August 28, 2015); William Willard Howard, "The Rush to Oklahoma," *Harper's Weekly*, May 18, 1889; Dianna Everett, "Land Openings," *The Encyclopedia of Oklahoma History and Culture*, http://www.okhistory.org/publications/enc/entry.php?entry=LA016 (accessed February 28, 2017).

68. Fields, "Memory, Reenactment," 26.

69. "Sooners Observe Holiday: Guthrie Expecting 50,000," *Miamii (Okla.) Daily News-Record*, April 22, 1960; "State Notes Run of 1889," *Lawton Constitution*, April 22, 1960.

70. Carl Murphy, "The Marriage Metaphor in Nineteenth-Century English Canadian Fiction," *Studies in Canadian Literature / Études En Littérature Canadienne* 13, no. 1 (January 1, 1988), https://journals.lib.unb.ca/index.php/scl/article/view/8073/9130.

71. Jeremy Adam Carey, "Celebrating Memory and Space: Three Case Studies of Centennial Projects to Commemorate Oklahoma's History" (master's thesis, University of Central Oklahoma, Edmond. 2013), 79.

72. Michael McNutt, "Indian Statue Proposal Gains Support in Enid," *Sunday Oklahoman*, December 20, 1992; Michael McNutt, "Statue Honoring Indian Heritage Unveiled in Enid," *Sunday Oklahoman*, April 17, 1994, sec. A.

73. "Enid Statue Featured in True West Magazine," *Cherokee Strip Regional Heritage Center*, August 27, 2012, http://www.csrhc.org/press-homesteaderintruewestmag.html.

74. Joseph Benjamin Norris Swain, "Claims to History: Commemorating Progress in Oklahoma Territory, 1989–2007" (PhD diss., University of Oklahoma, Norman, 2008), 120–23.

75. Michael McNutt, "Ponca City Remembers Settlers Indians Protest Statue Dedication," *NewsOK*, September 17, 1993, http://newsok.com/ponca-city-remembers-settlers-indians-protest-statue-dedication/article/2442217.

76. Michael McNutt, "Standing Bear Statue Leading Tribe's Influence in Ponca City," *NewsOK*, June 9, 1996, http://newsok.com/article/2543064; Swain, "Claims to History," 181–88.

77. Dennis J. Smith, "Trial of Standing Bear," *Encyclopedia of the Great Plains*, http://plainshumanities.unl.edu/encyclopedia/doc/egp.pd.053 (accessed June 16, 2017).

78. Swain, "Claims to History," 186–87.

79. "Allan Houser, 80, a Sculptor Known for Apache Themes," *New York Times*, August 25, 1994, sec. Obituaries; Allan Houser, *May We Have Peace* (1992); "Native American Sculptor Casts Tribute to Heritage," *Chicago Tribune*, April 12, 1985.

80. Jennifer Dunning, "Tulsa Salutes Five Indian Ballerinas," *New York Times*, November 15, 1982, sec. Arts.

CHAPTER 6. MEMORY MAKES MONEY

1. Nora, "Between Memory and History," 7–24; Judy Mattivi Morley, *Historic Preservation and the Imagined West: Albuquerque, Denver, and Seattle* (Lawrence: University Press of Kansas, 2006), 10.

2. Jamesha Gibson, "[Preservation Glossary] Today's Word: Heritage Tourism," *National Trust for Historic Preservation*, June 17, 2015, https://savingplaces.org/stories/preservation-glossary-todays-word-heritage-tourism.

3. Ibid.

4. Stephanie E. Yuhl, *A Golden Haze of Memory: The Making of Historic Charleston* (Chapel Hill: University of North Carolina Press, 2005); Eric Gable and Richard Handler, *The New History in an Old Museum: Creating the Past at Colonial Williamsburg* (Durham, N.C.: Duke University Press, 1997); Gable and Handler, "After Authenticity at an American Heritage Site," 568–78.

5. Kropp, *California Vieja*; Deverell, *Whitewashed Adobe*; Chris Wilson, *The Myth of Santa Fe: Creating a Modern Regional Tradition* (Albuquerque: University of New Mexico Press, 1997).

6. Bergman, *Exhibiting Patriotism*, chap. 5; Justin J. Mayer, "Historical Memory of Mount Rushmore" (master's thesis, University of North Dakota, Grand Forks, 2010).

7. E. F. Fairbanks, "Competition for This Is the Place Monument."

8. William D. Moore, "'United We Commemorate': The Kentucky Pioneer Memorial Association, James Isenberg, and Early Twentieth-Century Heritage Tourism," *Public Historian* 30, no. 3 (2008): 62.

9. "Hoover Invited to Visit Centre College," *Danville (Ky.) Advocate-Messenger*, March 5, 1931; Gable and Handler, *New History in an Old Museum*; Gable and Handler, "After Authenticity at an American Heritage Site"; Geoffrey C. Upward, *A Home for Our Heritage: The Building and Growth of Greenfield Village and Henry Ford Museum, 1929–1979* (Dearborn, Mich.: Henry Ford Museum Press, 1979); Jessie Swigger, *"History Is Bunk": Assembling the Past at Henry Ford's Greenfield Village* (Amherst: University of Massachusetts Press, 2014); Hal Rothman, *Devil's Bargains: Tourism in the Twentieth-Century American West* (Lawrence: University Press of Kansas, 1998); Moore, "United We Commemorate."

10. Quoted in Fields, "Memory, Reenactment," 31.

11. Ibid.

12. Cherokee Strip Regional Heritage Center home page, http://www.csrhc.org/ (accessed May 25, 2016); David Page, "Cherokee Strip Regional Heritage Center Opens in Enid, Oklahoma," *Oklahoma City Journal Record*, April 4, 2011; "Cherokee Strip Regional Heritage Center," Oklahoma Historical Society, http://www.okhistory.org/sites/csrhc (accessed May 25, 2016); Max Nichols, "Cherokee Strip Centennial Yields Benefits for Enid," *Oklahoma City Journal Record*, September 25, 1993.

13. "The History Westport: Where the West Began," *Westport Historical Society*, http://westporthistorical.com/westport-history/ (accessed May 18, 2016); Jason Roe, "In For the Landing," *This Week in Kansas City History* (blog), Kansas City Public Library, http://www.kclibrary.org/blog/week-kansas-city-history/landing (accessed May 18, 2016); "Westport: Where The West Began," *Experience Kansas City*, http://www.experiencekc.com/westport.html (accessed May 18, 2016); "A Brief History of Westport," *WestportKC*, http://www.westportkc.com/history.php (accessed May 18, 2016).

14. John N. Booth to Members of the Park Board, June 24, 1925, microfilm PA-78, Kansas City Parks and Recreation Department Archives, Kansas City, Missouri.

15. Lucille B. Bettis, "Background Story of Pioneer Park," *Weekly Westport (Mo.) Reporter*, September 30, 1987.

16. "Will Pioneers Find a Home in Westport?," *Kansas City Star*, January 12, 1983.

17. Statues—Pioneer Mother vertical file, Missouri Valley Special Collections, Kansas City Public Library, Kansas City, Missouri.

18. Laurance C. Phister, "Build on History," *Kansas City Times*, May 5, 1984.

19. "An Instant Oasis in Old Westport," *Kansas City Star*, June 14, 1983, sec. A; Michelle T. Johnson, "Groups Pick KC Artist for Westport Sculpture," *Kansas City Star*, January 8, 1985, sec. A.

20. Fred L. Lee to John Lucas, December 6, 1983, Pioneer Park Committee Records, SC 12, Missouri Valley Special Collections, Kansas City Public Library, Kansas City, Missouri; Subject Files of Parks Board President LAP Cookingham, Board of Parks and Recreation Commissioners, , Kansas City Parks and Recreation Department Archives, Kansas City, Missouri; Lisa Massoth, "Group Again Pushes for Statue of Benton," *Kansas City Times*, May 9, 1984, sec. B; Lisa Massoth, "Island Is Focus of New Battle of Westport," *Kansas City Times*, April 20, 1984, sec. B; Lisa Massoth, "Park Board Defers Action on Statues," *Kansas City Times*, May 16, 1984, sec. B; James Kuhnhenn, "Commissioner Suggests New Site for Benton Statue to Solve Dispute," *Kansas City Times*, July 11, 1984, sec. B.

21. Andrew Waters, "'Bah, Humbug' Greets Statue Depicting Pioneer Family," *Los Angeles Times*, April 3, 1994.

22. Ken L., Pioneer Crossing Park—Shawnee, Kans., review, *Yelp*, August 29, 2009, https://www.yelp.com/biz/pioneer-crossing-park-shawnee.

23. Steve Jordon, "Bison Herd Grows Again," *Omaha (Neb.) World-Herald*, August 12, 2009; Ashley Hassebroek, "Development Project in Omaha, Neb., Will Depict Bronze Monument of Wagon Train," *Omaha (Neb.) World-Herald*, June 27, 2003; Judy Magid, "'Eastward, Ho!' For This Wagon Train," *Salt Lake Tribune*, August 31, 2005; Steve Jordon, "First National Bank Opens New Park in Omaha, Neb.," *Omaha (Neb.) World-Herald*, September 24, 2002; Steve Jordon, "If Hoofing It in Downtown Omaha, Neb., You Won't Be Alone," *Omaha (Neb.) World-Herald*, August 18, 2005; Carma Wadley, "Larger-than-Life Sculptures Are Monumental Undertaking," *Deseret News* (Salt Lake City), September 18, 2005, sec. Arts; Ashley Hassebroek, "Wagon Master Marks Project's Halfway Point," *Omaha (Neb.) World-Herald*, December 5, 2006; John D. Linford, "Sculptor's Works Bigger Than Life," *Salt Lake Tribune*, October 21, 2005; Casey R. Basden, "Sculptor Shapes His Own Philosophy," *Salt Lake Tribune*, January 29, 2009; "Signature Art in Omaha—Scene Is Ideal for Walking Tour. Next, How About Tourist-Oriented Shopping?," *Omaha (Neb.) World-Herald*, September 28, 2005, sec. Editorial.

24. Swain, "Claims to History," 109.

25. "Centennial Land Run Monument," *TripAdvisor*, https://www.tripadvisor.com/Attraction_Review-g51560-d2322328-Reviews-Centennial_Land_Run_Monument-Oklahoma_City_Oklahoma.html (accessed June 29, 2017).

26. E. C. Alft, *Elgin: An American History* (Elgin, Ill.: Daily Courier-News, ElginHistory.com, 1984), chaps. 1 and 6, http://www.elginhistory.com/eaah/.

27. Jennifer Patterson, "Fulfilling an Artist's Dream," *Chicago Daily Herald*, October 9, 1999, sec. F; Melissa Ramsdell, "Elgin's Arts Fest Has Growing Attraction," *Chicago Daily Herald*, August 24, 1997, sec. 1.

28. E. C. Alft, *Elgin: Days Gone By* (Carpentersville, Ill.: Crossroads Communications, 1992), chap. 14, http://www.elginhistory.com/dgb/; "Local Trivia," *Chicago Daily Herald*, November 26, 2009, sec. F.

29. Danelle Wozniak, "Pioneers Come Home to Elgin," *Chicago Daily Herald*, November 11, 2001, sec. 5; Ramsdell, "Elgins Arts Fest Has Growing Attraction."

30. Alft, *Elgin: An American History*, sec. Special Update.

31. Ibid., chap. 10.

32. Only 187 persons (0.8 percent) were classified as Negro, and 8 persons (less than 0.1 percent) were of Asian descent. U.S. Census Bureau, *Twelfth Census of the United States—1900, Census Reports*, vol. 1, *Population*, part 1, chap. 10 (Washington, D.C.: U.S. Government Printing Office, 1901), https://www.census.gov/prod/www/decennial.html; Alft, *Elgin: An American History*, chap. 4.

33. Alft, *Elgin: An American History*, sec. Special Update.

34. Odette Yousef, "Elgin Latinos: Big in Number but Not in Representation," *Race: Out Loud*, WBEZ, June 26, 2012, https://www.wbez.org/shows/race-out-loud/elgin-latinos-big-in-number-but-not-in-representation/f1104972-d22c-4415-936d-10fd816ca4f0.

35. David Buisseret, "Elgin, IL," *Encyclopedia of Chicago*, http://www.encyclopedia.chicagohistory.org/pages/420.html (accessed December 14,

2015); U.S. Census Bureau, "Population estimates, July 1, 2017 (V2017)," *QuickFacts: Elgin city, Illinois*, accessed May 15, 2017, http://www.census.gov/quickfacts/table/AGE275210/1723074.

36. "Walton Island," *Historic Elgin*, Elgin Heritage Commission, http://historicelgin.com/walton-island/ (accessed July 28, 2016); Alft, *Elgin: Days Gone By*, chap. 24; "Trygve A. Rovelstad," *Fox Valley Arts Hall of Fame*, http://www.foxvalleyarts.org/rovelstad.htm (accessed December 17, 2015).

37. Michael Higgins, "Judge Permits Class-Action Suit Against Casino," *Chicago Tribune*, April 1, 2000.

38. "Elgin To Actualize Deceased Artist's Decades-Long Work," *Chicago Tribune*, August 5, 2000, http://articles.chicagotribune.com/2000-08-05/news/0008050246_1_sculpture-pioneer-youth-works-project-administration.

39. "Statue Stands for Elgin's Past and Future," *Chicago Daily Herald*, November 12, 2001, sec. Elgin and Fox Valley.

40. Quoted in Elena Ferrarin, "Elgin Community Gathers to Celebrate Memorial," *Chicago Daily Herald*, November 13, 2011.

41. "Pioneer Sculpture Finally Erected After 70 Years," *Chicago Daily Herald*, November 14, 2001, sec. 5.

42. "Elgin Listed in National Rankings," *Elgin Neighbor*, no. 3 (2015): 1.

43. William Philpott, *Vacationland: Tourism and Environment in the Colorado High Country* (Seattle: University of Washington Press, 2014), 131, 301–2.

44. Lorenzo Veracini, "Suburbia, Settler Colonialism and the World Turned Inside Out," *Housing, Theory and Society* 29, no. 4 (December 1, 2012): 339–57.

45. "Schaumburg's History," *Village of Schaumburg*, http://www.ci.schaumburg.il.us/offic/history/Pages/default.aspx (accessed December 14, 2015).

46. Hayden, *Building Suburbia*, 181.

47. David Fleming, *City of Rhetoric: Revitalizing the Public Sphere in Metropolitan America* (Albany: SUNY Press, 2008), 108.

48. Kenneth T. Jackson, *Crabgrass Frontier: The Suburbanization of the United States* (New York: Oxford University Press, 1987), chaps. 13–15; Hayden, *Building Suburbia*, chaps. 7–8; Lizabeth Cohen, *A Consumers' Republic: The Politics of Mass Consumption in Postwar America* (New York: Knopf, 2003), chap. 6; Bob Thall, *The New American Village* (Baltimore, Md.: Johns Hopkins University Press, 1999).

49. Joel Kotkin, *The New Suburbanism: A Realist's Guide to the American Future* (Costa Mesa, Calif.: Planning Center, 2005); Meredith Marsh, "Striking the Balance: Finding a Place for New Urbanism on Main Street" (master's thesis, University of Pennsylvania, Philadelphia, 2009), http://repository.upenn.edu/hp_theses/122; Charles C. Bohl, "The Social, Civic and Symbolic Functions of the Public Realm: A Comparative Analysis of New Urbanist Town Centers and Conventional Shopping Centers" (PhD diss., University of North Carolina at Chapel Hill, 2004); Easton L. Branam, "Spanning the Rural Urban Divide: Toward an Expanded Theory of Landscape Architecture" (master's thesis, University of Washington, Seattle, 2012); Brenda Case Scheer and Mintcho Petkov, "Edge City Morphology: A Comparison

of Commercial Centers," *Journal of the American Planning Association* 64, no. 3 (September 30, 1998): 298–310; Jackson, *Crabgrass Frontier.*

50. Hayden, *Building Suburbia*, 181.

51. "Schaumburg's History."

52. Jennifer Stoffel, "Downtown Is Taking New Shape Around Olde Schaumburg Centre," *Chicago Tribune*, February 18, 1987, http://articles.chicagotribune.com/1987-02-18/news/8701130314_1_downtown-village-town-center.

53. John Michael Ryan, "Easton: A 21st Century (R)Evolution in Consumption, Community, Urbanism, and Space" (master's thesis, University of Maryland, College Park, 2005), http://drum.lib.umd.edu/handle/1903/2493; Bohl, "Social, Civic and Symbolic Functions of the Public Realm."

54. Dave Seminara, "Olde Schaumburg Centre: America's Least Impressive Historic District?," *Gadling*, August 4, 2012, http://gadling.com/2012/08/04/olde-schaumburg-centre-americas-least-impressive-historic-dist/.

55. "Mayor Aims to Put Art in Eyes of Schaumburg," *Chicago Tribune*, December 26, 1999, http://articles.chicagotribune.com/1999-12-26/news/9912260134_1_art-teacher-culture-commission-art-bug.

56. Natasha Korecki, "Sculpture to Depict Old Farms," *Daily Herald Suburban Chicago*, August 24, 2001.

57. Chad Brooks, "Schaumburg Picks Sundial Sculpture for Village Hall," *Daily Herald Suburban Chicago*, October 17, 2001.

58. Prescott, *Gender and Generation*, chap. 1.

59. David Alan Clark, *Next Winter's Bread*, David Alan Clark Sculpture, http://davidalanclark.com/my-work/public-art/spirit-of-the-prairie/next-winters-bread-2.html (accessed March 17, 2016).

60. Seminara, "Olde Schaumburg Centre."

61. Syd Kearney, "Grapevine by Design," *Houston Chronicle*, September 7, 1997, 2 Star Zone edition, sec. Texas Magazine.

62. Ibid.

63. Pete Felten Jr., "Pioneer Family," n.d., *Inventories of American Painting and Sculpture*, Smithsonian American Art Museum.

64. "Walking to Texas," Grapevine, Texas, Convention and Visitor Bureau, http://www.grapevinetexasusa.com/listings/Walking-to-Texas/112/?fromMenu=727 (accessed June 30, 2016).

65. Andrew Backover, "Grapevine to Dedicate Statue of Pioneer Family," *Fort Worth (Tex.) Star-Telegram*, December 2, 1996, sec. Metro.

66. William D. Tate, "Toasting the Trailblazers," *Fort Worth (Tex.) Star-Telegram*, December 8, 1996, sec. Zone NE.

67. Cara Tanamachi, "Tourist Roundup for Round Rock? Officials Hope Planned Chisholm Trail Statue Will Bring in Visitors," *Austin (Tex.) American Statesman*, May 7, 1996.

68. Pamela LebLanc, "The Hoofbeats of Herds Echo at Brushy Creek," *Austin (Tex.) American Statesman*, November 21, 2002.

69. Michelle M. Martinez, "Down History's Trail: Round Rock Chamber Shapes Park into a Piece of the Past," *Austin (Tex.) American Statesman*, May 18, 2000.

70. Ibid.

71. Tanamachi, "Tourist Roundup for Round Rock?"

72. Pamela Ward, "Plan for Cattle Statues Now a Bronzed Bonanza of Steer," *Austin (Tex.) American Statesman*, September 12, 1996; Tanamachi, "Tourist Roundup for Round Rock?"; Camille Wheeler, "Blazing an Art Trail: First Phase of City's Chisholm Trail Park Project Unveiled with 3 Larger-than-Life Bronzes," *Austin (Tex.) American Statesman*, September 11, 2003; Elizabeth McGuire, "Carving Out a Sculpting Career," *Austin (Tex.) American Statesman*, May 1, 1999.

73. Wheeler, "Blazing an Art Trail."

74. Morley, *Historic Preservation and the Imagined West*, 10.

75. U. S. Census Bureau, "American FactFinder—Community Facts," http://factfinder.census.gov/faces/nav/jsf/pages/community_facts.xhtml (accessed May 24, 2016).

76. Lehi City Corporation Administrative Services Department, "Legacy Park Sculpture—Request for Qualifications" (Lehi City, Utah), June 30, 2015, http://www.lehi-ut.gov/wp-content/uploads/2013/09/2015–05_Legacy-Park-Sculpture.pdf.

77. Cathy Allred, "One More Year, One More Statue: Lehi Commissions for Pioneer Family Bronze," *Provo (Utah) Daily Herald*, September 10, 2015.

78. Peggy Fletcher Stack, "New Mormon Winter Quarters Center Helps Visitors Understand. . . ; Zion in the Wilderness: Winter Quarters Is Site of New Visitors Center," *Salt Lake Tribune*, April 19, 1997, sec. Nation-World.

79. "Mormon Pioneers to Be Commemorated at Nebraska Center," *Salt Lake Tribune*, July 22, 1995, sec. Religion.

80. Karen Sloan, "Florence Revitalization Plan Unveiled," *Omaha (Neb.) World-Herald*, September 20, 2007.

81. Jeffrey P. Haney, "New Statue Portrays Struggle of LDS Pioneers," *Deseret News* (Salt Lake City), April 20, 1998, http://www.deseretnews.com/article/625423/New-statue-portrays-struggle-of-LDS-pioneers.html?pg=all.

82. "Marking the Site of a Mormon Camp," *Fayette County (Iowa) Leader*, January 14, 1937; "Marking Site of Mormon Camp Close to Iowa City," *Postville (Iowa) Herald*, February 4, 1937; "D. A. R. Dedicates Camp Site Marker," *Carroll (Iowa) Daily Herald*, December 22, 1936; "Mormon Camp to Be Marked," *Mason City (Iowa) Globe-Gazette*, December 17, 1936; "Marking Site of Old Mormon Camp on Highway No. 6," *Humboldt (Iowa) Republican*, January 8, 1937.

83. Carrie A. Moore, "Pres. Hinckley to Honor Handcart Pioneers," *Deseret News* (Salt Lake City), June 9, 2006, http://www.deseretnews.com/article/640185613/Pres-Hinckley-to-honor-handcart-pioneers.html?pg=all; R. Scott Lloyd, "Celebrations Recall Handcart Pioneer Era," *Deseret Morning News*, May 20, 2006, http://mormonhistoricsites.org/handcart-exhibit/.

84. "Iowa City: Birthplace of Handcart Venture," *LDS Church News*, June 15, 2006, http://www.ldschurchnewsarchive.com/articles/49085/Iowa-City-birthplace-of-handcart-venture.html.

85. R. Scott Lloyd, "'Eyes Westward' Tells Prophetic Vision," *LDS Church News*, July 25, 2008, http://www.ldschurchnewsarchive.com/articles/53020/Eyes-Westward-tells-prophetic-vision.html.

86. R. Scott Lloyd, "Honoring Handcart Pioneers," *LDS Church News*, July 31, 1999, http://www.ldschurchnewsarchive.com/articles/32187/Honoring-handcart-pioneers.html. See also Lisa Riley Roche, "Old Deseret Village," *Deseret News* (Salt Lake City), June 27, 1996, http://www.deseretnews.com/article/498359/OLD-DESERET-VILLAGE.html?pg=all; "Old Deseret Village," *Ensign*, July 1998, https://www.lds.org/ensign/1998/07/old-deseret-village?lang=eng.

87. Lloyd, "Honoring Handcart Pioneers."

88. Ibid.

CHAPTER 7. INCLUSIVITY AND THE LIMITS OF PIONEER MEMORY

1. Brian Black and Bryn Varley, "Contesting the Sacred: Preservation and Meaning on Richmond's Monument Avenue," in Mills and Simpson, *Monuments to the Lost Cause*, 234–50, quotation on 235.

2. Alfredo González-Ruibal, "Time to Destroy: An Archaeology of Supermodernity," *Current Anthropology* 49, no. 2 (2008): 247–79; Connerton, *How Modernity Forgets*, 99. See also Connerton, *How Societies Remember*; Trouillot, *Silencing the Past*.

3. Hamilakis and Labanyi, "Time, Materiality, and the Work of Memory," 5. See also Mills and Walker, *Memory Work*.

4. Reynolds, *Masters of American Sculpture*, 220.

5. "Gloss," *Pioneer Mother, Center of the West Online Collections*, https://collections.centerofthewest.org/treasures/view/pioneer_mother3 (accessed June 23, 2017).

6. Tracie Mauriella, "Lady in Distress," *Springfield (Ohio) News-Sun Press*, April 12, 1999, *Inventories of American Painting and Sculpture*, Smithsonian American Art Museum.

7. Andrew McGinn, "Downtown Springfield Is Making a Comeback: The Tide of Migration to Springfield's Center Seems Irreversible," *Dayton (Ohio) Daily News*, September 26, 2011, sec. Local; "Madonna of the Trail," *Historical Marker Database*, last revised September 19, 2017, http://www.hmdb.org/marker.asp?marker=45529.

8. Cameron W. Barr, "Listing Madonna Rescued in Bethesda: Sinkhole Had Statue Tilting to Its Left," *Washington Post*, December 11, 2004.

9. Jason A. Bezis, "70-Year Reign of Bethesda's Pioneer Mother," *Washington Times*, May 2, 1999.

10. "Cumberland Covets Bethesda's 'Madonna,'" *Charleston (W.Va.) Gazette*, April 20, 2001, sec. News.

11. Helen Peters, "Madonna of the Trail," *New Mexico Magazine*, December 1993; Reed, "How Sacagawea Became a Pioneer Mother," 38–39.

12. U.S. Census Bureau, "American FactFinder—Community Facts," http://factfinder.census.gov/faces/nav/jsf/pages/community_facts.xhtml (accessed May 24, 2016).

13. "Madonna of the Trail—Albuquerque," *Envision* (blog), December 12, 2011, https://beheld.wordpress.com/2011/12/12/madonna-of-the-trail-albuquerque/.

14. "Upland History," *MooseRoots*, http://places.mooseroots.com/1/316638/Upland-CA (accessed May 30, 2017).

15. U.S. Census Bureau, "2010 Census Interactive Population Map: Ontario, California," *Census.gov*, https://www.census.gov/2010census/popmap/ipmtext.php?fl=06:0653896 (accessed May 30, 2017).

16. David Allen, "In Upland, the Hits Just Keep on Coming," *Inland Valley Daily Bulletin* (Ontario, Calif.), April 12, 2011, sec. News.

17. "John Weeks: To Be or Not to Be Squeamish," *San Bernardino (Calif.) Sun*, May 12, 2011, sec. News.

18. Steve Brandt, "Pioneers Are on the Move in Northeast," *Minneapolis (Minn.) Star Tribune*, September 15, 2010.

19. Steve Brandt, "Pioneer Statue Will Head to New Frontier," *Minneapolis (Minn.) Star Tribune*, July 30, 2008, sec. News; Eric Roper, "Streetscapes: Minneapolis' 'Park for Posterity' Never Materialized," *Minneapolis (Minn.) Star Tribune*, November 20, 2015, http://www.startribune.com/streetscapes-a-park-for-posterity-that-never-materialized/352257081/; "Visions of Grandeur: A Civic Center for Minneapolis," *The Historyapolis Project*, May 21, 2014, http://historyapolis.com/blog/2014/05/21/visions-of-grandeur-a-civic-center-for-minneapolis/; John K. Daniels, Pioneers' Monument sculpture file, *Inventories of American Painting and Sculpture*, Smithsonian American Art Museum.

20. Sherri Nee, "Esther Short Park Develops New Image," *Vancouver (Wash.) Columbian*, April 15, 1997; Brett Oppegard, "Taken Back: The Story of Esther Short Park's Rebirth Begins with a Transient Ramming the Mayor with a Shopping Cart," *Vancouver (Wash.) Columbian*, November 11, 2001.

21. "Public Art Has Its Fans, Critics," *Vancouver (Wash.) Columbian*, September 9, 2012.

22. Chris Shull, "Vandals Assault Bronze Sculpture a Second Time," *Wichita (Kans.) Eagle*, January 5, 2007; Amy Renee Leiker, "Sculpture Vandalized in Downtown Wichita Park," *Wichita (Kans.) Eagle*, January 9, 2013, http://www.kansas.com/news/local/crime/article1106235.html; Angela Cato, "Sculpture Vandalized in Heritage Park," *City of Wichita, Kansas, News*, January 9, 2013, http://www.wichita.gov/Government/News/Pages/2013-01-09d.aspx (accessed August 19, 2016).

23. "Bronze Statue Is Stolen from Jefferson Memorial," *St. Louis Globe-Democrat*, September 17, 1969; "Statue Stolen From Park," *St. Louis Post-Dispatch*, September 16, 1969; "Stolen Statue Recovered," *St. Louis Post-Dispatch*, September 18, 1969; Nancy Coonsman Hahn sculptor file, Missouri History Museum, St. Louis,

Missouri; Katharine T. Corbett, *In Her Place: A Guide to St. Louis Women's History* (St. Louis: Missouri History Museum, 1999).

24. "Theft of Pioneer Museum Statue Spurs Action," *Joplin (Mo.) Globe*, July 15, 2013; Kerri Stowell and Kasey Babbitt, "Museum Chooses Replacement for Original Statue Destroyed by Vandals in Independence," *Fox4 News*, February 24, 2015, http://fox4kc.com/2015/02/24/museum-chooses-replacement-for-original-statue-destroyed-by-vandals-in-independence/; "New Statue Chosen to Replace One Stolen from Independence Museum," *KMBC News*, February 24, 2015, http://www.kmbc.com/news/new-statue-chosen-to-replace-one-stolen-from-independence-museum/31444800.

25. "Monumental Tom Otterness Sculpture Rides into DUMBO," *Art Daily*, April 12, 2008, http://www.artdaily.com/index.asp?int_new=23857&int_sec=2#.Ufg4FG3DKvQ.

26. Kate Taylor, "A Covered Wagon Will Roll into DUMBO," *New York Sun*, March 27, 2008.

27. Sandy Moss, "'Not-So-Gentle-Tamer' Commemorates Arizona's 100 Years of Statehood," *Prescott Woman*, November 2010.

28. Bob Boze Bell, "Not-So-Gentle Comments," *True West Magazine Blog*, May 26, 2013, http://blog.truewestmagazine.com/2013/05/not-so-gentle-comments.html.

29. Philip Haldiman, "Prescott Valley Statue a Tribute to Pioneer Women," *Arizona Republic* (Phoenix), July 28, 2013.

30. "Yavapai County Installing a 10-Foot Tall Bronze Sculpture—'Not So Gentle Tamer,'" *Prescott (Ariz.) Business Pages*, September 7, 2012.

31. Karen Despain, "The Story Behind 'Not-So-Gentle Tamer' Statue Coming to Prescott Valley," *Prescott (Ariz.) Daily Courier*, November 3, 2012.

32. Pierce, *Making the White Man's West*.

33. "Plans Monument to Texas Germans," *Mattoon (Ill.) Commercial Star*, July 21, 1914.

34. Scott Wyman, "Panel Split on Statue Coloring: Bonnet, Dress Have Blue Cast," *Independence (Mo.) Examiner*, February 20, 1990, 1.

35. Blake Ursch, "Carving out a Place for Themselves: Black Settlers' Pursuit of Dream in Late 1800s Nebraska Gets New Attention," *Omaha (Neb.) World-Herald*, March 21, 2016, http://www.omaha.com/living/carving-out-a-place-for-themselves-black-settlers-pursuit-of/article_4658f6ec-eddf-11e5-842f-df85a963c447.html.

36. "*The Guardian* by Enoch Kelly Haney," *Oklahoma Arts Council*, April 4, 2011, http://arts.ok.gov/Art_at_the_Capitol/Capitol_Collection/Haney/The_Guardian.html; "'The Guardian' by Enoch Kelly Haney," *Seminole State College*, https://www.sscok.edu/HLC/Story_GuardianPg.htm (accessed March 2, 2017); Jim Campbell, "Indian Statue Placed atop Okla. Capitol," *UPI*, June 7, 2002, http://www.upi.com/Indian-statue-placed-atop-Okla-capitol/84551023484200/; Brian Ford, "'The Guardian' Now Watches over Oklahoma," *Tulsa World*, June 8, 2002, http://www.tulsaworld.com/archives/the-guardian-now-watches-over-oklahoma/article_8cd62517-e848-51c0-b08a-06f79da88e24.html; Michael

McNutt, "Oklahoma Capitol Statue 'The Guardian' to Be Cleaned, Inspected," *NewsOK*, July 21, 2013, http://newsok.com/oklahoma-capitol-statue-the-guardian-to-be-cleaned-inspected/article/3864317.

37. "Essay Winner Says 'The Guardian' Is Not Just a Symbol for Natives," *Indian Country* (Verona, N.Y.), March 1, 2015, https://indiancountrymedianetwork.com/education/native-education/essay-winner-says-the-guardian-is-not-just-a-symbol-for-natives/.

38. Jamie Wickliffe-Ary, "Land Run," *Native American Times* (Tulsa, Okla.), August 1, 2001; "Indian Statue Placed atop Okla. Capitol"; Jaclyn Houghton, "Oklahoma Capitol Dome Nears Pay-off Date," *Norman Transcript*, January 21, 2007, http://www.normantranscript.com/news/local_news/oklahoma-capitol-dome-nears-pay-off-date/article_b774c257-8b9b-52a9-b8bf-08123fd636ea.html.

39. Quoted in Swain, "Claims to History," 107.

40. Ibid., 106–9; Carey, "Celebrating Memory and Space," chap. 3; William Crum, "Statues Added to Oklahoma City's Centennial Land Run Monument," *NewsOK*, July 28, 2015, http://newsok.com/article/5436618.

41. All quoted in Wickliffe-Ary, "Land Run."

42. All quoted in Kyle Schwab, "Artistic Skulls Draw Attention at Oklahoma City's Centennial Land Run Monument," *NewsOK*, June 25, 2013, http://newsok.comarticle/3855887/artistic-skulls-draw-attention-at-oklahoma-citys-centennial-land-run-monument.

43. "Oklahoma City, OK Population: Census 2010 and 2000 Interactive Map, Demographics, Statistics, Quick Facts," *CensusViewer*, http://censusviewer.com/city/OK/Oklahoma%20City (accessed March 6, 2017).

44. City of Colorado Springs, "New Sculpture Installed at Colorado Springs Pioneers Musem [*sic*]," http://permits.springsgov.com/Page.asp?NavID=2684 (accessed July 5, 2013).

45. Tanya Bell, "Board Wants New Name for Pioneers Museum," *Colorado Springs Gazette-Telegraph*, January 20, 1996; Tanya Bell, "Attempt to Change Name of Pioneers Museum Fails Again: Petition Campaign Helps Panel Put Longstanding Issue to Rest," *Colorado Springs Gazette-Telegraph*, June 7, 1996; Tanya Bell, "Historical Group Angry over Plan to Change Museum's Name," *Colorado Springs Gazette-Telegraph*, March 16, 1996; Raquel Rutledge, "Changing Name of Museum Is Touchy Subject for Springs," *Colorado Springs Gazette*, August 8, 1998.

46. City of Colorado Springs, "New Sculpture Installed"; Mark Arnest, "Putting the 'Public' in Public Art: Private-Sector Contributions Put Sculpture on the Streets," *Colorado Springs Gazette-Telegraph*, November 17, 2002, sec. Life.

47. Dennis Huspeni, "Past, Future Meet in New Sculpture; Pyramid Going Up This Week at the Pioneers Museum," *Colorado Springs Gazette*, April 18, 2005.

48. "Forward to the Past: Westside Artist's Contemporary/Historic Sculpture to Be Erected Outside Pioneers' Museum," *Westside Pioneer*, September 30, 2004, http://www.westsidepioneer.com/Articles/093004/PioneersMuseum.html.

49. Arnest, "Putting the 'Public' in Public Art."

50. Leah Witherow, personal communication, October 21, 2015.

51. "'The Barnards of the Brazos' Dedication Ceremony in Glen Rose, Texas—Speeches," *Somervell County (Tex.) Salon*, September 16, 2007, http://salon.glenrose.net/default.asp?view=plink&id=4704; John Watson, "Barnards of the Brazos Statue Unveiled in Glen Rose," *Cleburne (Tex.) Times-Review*, September 24, 2007.

CONCLUSION

1. Michael J. Ybarra, "San Francisco Journal: A Monument Caught in the Middle," *New York Times*, May 7, 1996, sec. U.S., http://www.nytimes.com/1996/05/07/us/san-francisco-journal-a-monument-caught-in-the-middle.html.

2. Quoted in Art Peterson, *Why Is That Bridge Orange? San Francisco for the Curious* (San Francisco: Inquiring Minds Productions, 2013), 83. See also Diana Scott, "Public Art: Whose Version of History?," *Albion Monitor*, May 5, 1996, http://www.albionmonitor.com/free/whosehistory.html; Diana Scott, "SF 'Pioneer' Plaque Changed, New Calls for Library Statue Removal," *Albion Monitor*, May 27, 1996, http://www.albionmonitor.com/free/whosehistoryII.html.

3. Sara Gaiser, "Process Begins to Remove San Francisco Statue," *San Mateo Daily Journal*, October 2, 2017.

4. Savage, *Standing Soldiers, Kneeling Slaves*; Shackel, *Memory in Black and White.*

5. Justin Worland, "New Orleans Will Remove Confederate Monuments," *Time*, December 17, 2015, http://time.com/4154117/new-orleans-confederate-flag/; Tegan Wendland, "With Lee Statue's Removal, Another Battle of New Orleans Comes to a Close," *NPR*, May 20, 2017, http://www.npr.org/2017/05/20/529232823/with-lee-statues-removal-another-battle-of-new-orleans-comes-to-a-close.

6. Joe Sterling, "A New Alabama Law Makes Sure Confederate Monuments Are Here to Stay," *CNN*, May 26, 2017, http://www.cnn.com/2017/05/26/us/alabama-confederate-monuments-bill-trnd/index.html.

7. John Savage, "Where the Confederacy Is Rising Again," *Politico Magazine*, August 10, 2016, http://www.politico.com/magazine/story/2016/08/texas-confederacy-rising-again-214159.

8. John S. Marshall, "Bunch Says the Woodlands Could Be Home—in a Museum—for Removed Statues," *Houston Chronicle*, September 20, 2017.

9. Mills, "Gratitude and Gender Wars," 183–200.

10. The classic work on this topic is Juanita Brooks, *The Mountain Meadows Massacre* (Norman: University of Oklahoma Press, 1963). For an examination of public memory of the event, see Seefeldt, "Constructing Western Pasts," chap. 6.

11. Seefeldt, "Constructing Western Pasts," 303–4.

12. Quoted ibid., 308.

13. Ibid., 315–18.

14. Ibid., chap. 6.

15. "Statue of Utah Massacre Figure Fails to Find Home," *Washington Times*, June 14, 2014.

16. Mori Kessler, "City Council Votes against Displaying John D. Lee Statue," *St. George (Utah) News,* June 12, 2014.

17. Shaun D. Stahle, "Monument Pays Tribute to Pioneer Women," *Deseret News* (Salt Lake City), May 10, 2001; Joanne Rideout, "Statue Pays Tribute to Pioneer Women," *Deseret News* (Salt Lake City), May 5, 2001.

18. Family and Friends of Dakota Uprising Victims, "Monument Narratives," *1862 U.S.-Dakota War in Minnesota,* http://www.dakotavictims1862.com/monuments/index.html (accessed June 15, 2017).

19. LeMay, "Minnesota Works on Forgiving"; "Mankato: Dakota Men Hanged in 1862 Are Honored with Memorial," *St. Paul Pioneer Press,* December 25, 2012, http://www.twincities.com/2012/12/25/mankato-dakota-men-hanged-in-1862-are-honored-with-memorial/.

20. LeMay, "Minnesota Works on Forgiving."

21. Sam Durant, "A Statement from Sam Durant (05.29.17)," *Walker News,* May 29, 2017, Walker Art Center, https://walkerart.org/magazine/a-statement-from-sam-durant-05-29-17.

22. Olga Viso, "Learning in Public: An Open Letter on Sam Durant's *Scaffold,*" *Walker News,* May 26, 2017, Walker Art Center, https://walkerart.org/magazine/learning-in-public-an-open-letter-on-sam-durants-scaffold.

23. "Minneapolis Sculpture Garden," Walker Art Center, https://walkerart.org/visit/garden/ (accessed June 26, 2017).

24. LeMay, "'Scaffold' Sculpture"; LeMay, "Dakota Elders Will Oversee Dismantling"; Tim Nelson, "Walker Director Says 'Scaffold' Should Be Dismantled," *MPRNews,* May 27, 2017, https://www.mprnews.org/story/2017/05/27/sioux-community-wants-walker-sculpture-taken-down-more-discussion; Liz Sawyer, "After Outcry and Protests, Walker Art Center Will Remove 'Scaffold' Sculpture," *Minneapolis Star Tribune,* May 28, 2017, http://www.startribune.com/walker-will-take-down-controversial-sculpture-after-protests/424820003/.

25. Caitlin Swieca, "DU Pioneers Mascot Committee Recommends against Adopting a New Mascot," *Denver Post,* August 9, 2013, http://www.denverpost.com/2013/08/09/du-pioneers-mascot-committee-recommends-against-adopting-a-new-mascot/; Bradford Richardson "Whitman College Drops 'Imperialistic' Missionary Mascot," *Washington Times,* April 14, 2016, http://www.washingtontimes.com/news/2016/apr/14/whitman-college-drops-imperialistic-missionary-mas/; "'Pio' Joins the Lewis & Clark Campus as Latest Sculpture from the Expedition to Be Unveiled," *Lewis and Clark Pioneers,* October 5, 2010, http://www.lcpioneers.com/sports/general/2010-11/Pio_unveiling.

26. Percy Bryant Baker v. The Petroleum Publishing Co. and National Bank of Tulsa, Civil Action No. 4522, 1958, in Bryant Baker, Pioneer Woman sculpture file, *Inventories of American Painting and Sculpture,* Smithsonian American Art Museum.

27. E. W. Marland, "Marland in High Tribute to Pioneers," *Ponca City (Okla.) News,* April 22, 1930.

28. Angel Riggs, "Missing Book Provokes Questions: Why Is the Pioneer Woman's Bible Not on the Quarter? Mint May Have Decided It Was 'Inappropriate,'" *Tulsa (Okla.) World*, April 26, 2007.

29. Tracy Mumford, "Where the Wilder Things Are: The Laura Ingalls Wilder Road Trip," *MPRNews*, August 12, 2015, http://www.mprnews.org/story/2015/08/12/bcst-thread-books-laura-ingalls-wilder-road-trip; Sunshine Flint, "A Little Drive on the Prairie," *Travel and Leisure*, May 14, 2009, http://www.travelandleisure.com/articles/a-little-drive-on-the-prairie; "The Wilder Trail," *Travellerspoint*, last edited February 13, 2018, http://www.travellerspoint.com/guide/The_Wilder_Trail/; "Explore the Laura Ingalls Wilder Historic Highway," *Walnut Grove, MN*, http://www.walnutgrove.org/hhwy04.pdf (accessed August 3, 2016); Anna Bahney, "Trading Tiaras for Calico on the Prairie," *New York Times*, August 7, 2011.

30. Melissa Locker, "You Can Now Play *Oregon Trail* Online for Free," *Time*, January 6, 2015, http://time.com/3656635/play-oregon-trail-ms-dos-games-free/; Macy Cate Williams, "Play All Your Favorite '80s and '90s Video Games Online for Free," *Popsugar*, May 10, 2018, http://www.popsugar.com/tech/Oregon-Trail-Available-Online-36470459; "Watch Out for Dysentery: 'Oregon Trail' Computer Game Returns as a Card Game," *Los Angeles Times*, August 1, 2016, http://www.latimes.com/entertainment/herocomplex/la-et-hc-oregon-trail-card-game-20160801-snap-story.html.

31. "Malone University Introduces New Pioneer Mascot," *Akron (Ohio) Suburbanite*, October 13, 2011.

32. Daniel Fandino, "Latest Oregon Uniforms Reference Lewis and Clark and the Oregon Trail," H-PCAACA, *H-Net*, October 5, 2015, https://networks.h-net.org/node/13784/discussions/87138/article-latest-oregon-uniforms-reference-lewis-and-clark-and-oregon; Kyle Newport, "Nike Unveils New 'Pioneers' Uniforms for Oregon, Pays Tribute to Lewis and Clark," *Bleacher Report*, October 5, 2015, http://bleacherreport.com/articles/2575913-nike-unveils-new-pioneers-uniforms-for-oregon-pays-tribute-to-lewis-and-clark.

33. Richard Guy Wilson, "Monument Avenue, Richmond: A Unique American Boulevard," in Mills and Simpson, *Monuments to the Lost Cause*, 100–15.

34. "History of Wall Drug," *Wall Drug Store*, http://www.walldrug.com/about-us (accessed April 29, 2018); "Wall Drug, South Dakota's Most Famous Road Trip Pit Stop, Loves Billboards," photos, *Huffington Post*, December 14, 2012, http://www.huffingtonpost.com/2012/12/14/wall-drug-south-dakota-billboard-photos_n_2296122.html; "Wall Drug Store, Inc.," *Travel South Dakota*, August 3, 2015, South Dakota Department of Tourism, https://www.travelsouthdakota.com/business-detail/wall-drug-store-inc.

35. "Photos: Coming Out Together—A Community Celebrates," *Eugene Daily Emerald* (University of Oregon), October 17, 2011, Emerald Media, https://www.dailyemerald.com/2011/10/17/photo-essay-coming-out-together-a-community-celebrates/.

36. Karl Zinke, “Woman Gets Probation in Pioneer Woman Statue Theft,” *Independence (Mo.) Examiner*, June 17, 2014, http://www.examiner.net/article/20140617/News/140619100.

37. Bezis, “70-Year Reign of Bethesda’s Pioneer Mother”; Barr, “Listing Madonna Rescued in Bethesda”; “Cumberland Covets Bethesda’s ‘Madonna.’”

BIBLIOGRAPHY

PRIMARY SOURCES

Archives and Manuscript Collections

Allred, James V., Records of Texas Governor, Archives and Information Services Division, Texas State Library and Archives Commission, Austin, Texas

Archives of American Art, Smithsonian Institution, Washington, D.C.
Fairbanks, Avard T., Papers Concerning, 1944–2008
Gage, Robert Merrell, Papers, 1911–1982
MacMonnies, Frederick William, Papers
Proctor, Alexander Phimister, Papers Concerning *The Pioneer Mother*, 1924–1950

Brown County Historical Society Archives, New Ulm, Minnesota
Defenders Monument vertical file
Dingman Brick Sculpture vertical file

City of Portland Archives and Records Center, Portland, Oregon (PARC)
Metropolitan Arts Commission Special Arts Project Files
Oregon Trail Coordinating Council (OTCC) Papers

Capitol Reconstruction Commission (CRC) Papers. Oregon State Archives, Salem, Oregon

Fairbanks, Avard T., Papers, J. Williard Marriott Library, University of Utah, Salt Lake City, Utah

Kansas State Historical Society, Topeka, Kansas

Kansas City Parks and Recreation Department Archives, Kansas City, Missouri

Missouri Valley Special Collections, Kansas City Public Library, Kansas City, Missouri.
Baker, Bryant, *Pioneer Woman* art file 1927
Pioneer Park Committee Records
Statues—*Madonna of the Trail* vertical file
Statues—*Pioneer Mother* vertical file

Oregon Historical Society Research Library, Portland Oregon
Oregon Artists vertical file
Portland Sculpture vertical file

Smithsonian American Art Museum, Washington, D.C.
Inventories of American Painting and Sculpture [online catalog], http://siris-artinventories.si.edu

Starcher, George, Papers, 1927–1979. Elwyn B. Robinson Department of Special Collections, Chester Fritz Library, University of North Dakota, Grand Forks.

Texas Woman's University, Denton, Texas

Tom Perry Special Collections, Harold B. Lee Library, Brigham Young University, Provo, Utah.
Fairbanks, Avard T., Papers
Young, Mahonri M., Papers

Wichita State University Special Collections, Wichita State University Libraries, Wichita, Kansas
Grafly, Charles, Papers

Books and Articles

"Art in Denver." *Art and Progress* 2, no. 10 (August 1, 1911): 306.

"The Brigham Young Memorial." *Contributor*, June 1892.

Cottman, George Streiby, Christopher Bush Coleman, and Logan Esarey. "The Memorial to the Pioneer Mother of Indiana." Reviews and Notes. *Indiana Magazine of History* 12, no. 1 (March 1916): 285.

Daughters of the American Revolution. *Twenty-Second Report of the National Society of the Daughters of the American Revolution: March 1, 1918, to March 1, 1919.* Washington, D.C.: U.S. Government Printing Office, 1921.

Gordon, Elizabeth. *What We Saw at Madame World's Fair: A Series of Letters from the Twins at the Panama-Pacific International Exposition to Their Cousins at Home.* San Francisco: Levinson, 1915.

Greer, H. H. "Frederick MacMonnies, Sculptor." *Brush and Pencil* 10, no. 1 (April 1, 1902): 1–15.

Hill, W. Lair. "Annual Address." In *Transactions of the Eleventh Annual Re-union of the Oregon Pioneer Association for 1883*, 21. Salem, Ore.: E. M. Waite, 1884.

"Historical News." *Indiana Magazine of History* 17, no. 3 (September 1921): 298–309.

Holman, Frederick V. "Qualities of the Oregon Pioneers." *Quarterly of the Oregon Historical Society* 20, no. 3 (September 1919): 235–42.

Indiana Historical Commission. *The Indiana Centennial, 1916: A Record of the Celebration of the One Hundredth Anniversary of Indiana's Admission to Statehood.* Edited by Harlow Lindley. Indianapolis: Indiana Historical Commission, 1919.

James, Juliet Helena Lumbard. *Sculpture of the Exposition Palaces and Courts: Descriptive Notes on the Art of the Statuary at the Panama-Pacific International Exposition, San Francisco.* San Francisco: H. S. Crocker, 1915.

"The Kansas Pioneer Woman's Memorial Association." *Kansas Womans Journal: The Western Womans Forum* [*sic*], May 1927, 8.

Mighels, Ella Sterling. *Literary California: Poetry, Prose and Portraits.* San Francisco: Harr Wagner, 1918.

Morton, Jennie C., A. C. Quisenberry, and Howard Pyle. "Memorial to 'Kit' Carson." *Register of Kentucky State Historical Society* 9, no. 25 (January 1, 1911): 83–84.

"Motherhood Monument." *Journal of Education* 80, no. 9 (1914): 240.

Patrick, Mae C. "Kansas Pioneer Woman's Memorial." *Jayhawk: The Magazine of Kansas,* February 1929, n.p.

Phimister Proctor, Alexander. *Sculptor in Buckskin: The Autobiography of Alexander Phimister Proctor.* Edited by Katharine C. Ebner. 2nd ed. Norman: University of Oklahoma Press, 2009.

Porter, Elizabeth Cannon. "A Monument to the Handcart Pioneers." *Improvement Era,* July 1925, 834–37.

Ralston, Mrs. Samuel M., ed. *The Memorial to the Pioneer Mother of Indiana.* Indianapolis: Hollenbeck Press, 1916.

Ring, Elizabeth Clendenning. *San Francisco: Glimpses of the Fairy Palaces of the Great Panama-Pacific International Exposition.* Philadelphia: Book News Monthly, 1915.

"Some Recent Public Memorials." *Monumental News: Devoted to Monumental and Kindred Interests* 34, no. 1 (January 1922): 164–67.

"To Be No Change in Kansas Pioneer Woman's Memorial Monument." *Jayhawk: The Magazine of Kansas,* September 1929, 272.

Todd, Frank Morton. *The Story of the Exposition: Being the Official History of the International Celebration Held at San Francisco in 1915 to Commemorate the Discovery of the Pacific Ocean and the Construction of the Panama Canal.* Vol. 2. New York: Putnam, for the Panama-Pacific International Exposition Company, 1921.

U.S. Commission of Fine Arts. *Annual Report.* Washington, D.C.: U.S. Government Printing Office, 1920.

Westport Improvement Association. *Westport, 1812–1912.* Kansas City, Mo.: Franklin Hudson, 1912.

Wilder, Laura Ingalls. *Pioneer Girl: The Annotated Autobiography.* Edited by Pamela Smith Hill. Pierre: South Dakota Historical Society Press, 2014.

Wingert, Paul S. *The Sculpture of William Zorach.* New York: Pitman, 1938.

Zorach, William. *Art Is My Life: The Autobiography of William Zorach.* Cleveland, Ohio: World, 1967.

Newspapers and Magazines

Akron (Ohio) Suburbanite
Albion Monitor
Albuquerque (N.Mex.) Journal
Amarillo (Tex.) Daily News
Arizona Republic (Phoenix)
Arlington (Tex.) Daily News
Ashland (Ore.) Daily Tidings
Atlanta Journal-Constitution
Austin (Tex.) American Statesman
Bakersfield Californian
Baltimore Sun
Big Basin Herald (Muldrow, Okla.)
Big Spring (Tex.) Daily Herald
Bigfork (Mont.) Eagle
Billings (Mont.) Gazette
Bismarck (N.Dak.) Capitol Journal
Bismarck (N.Dak.) Tribune
Black Hills Pioneer (Spearfish, S.Dak.)
Bloomington (Ill.) Pantagraph
Bloomington (Ind.) Herald Times
Brooklyn (N.Y.) Daily Eagle
Brooklyn (N.Y.) Life
Brownsville (Tex.) Herald
Cameron (Tex.) Herald
Canonsburg (Pa.) Daily Notes
Carroll (Iowa) Daily Herald
Charleston (W.Va.) Daily Mail
Charleston (W.Va.) Gazette
Chicago Daily Herald
Chicago Tribune
Chronicle of Higher Education (Washington, D.C.)
Cincinnati Enquirer
Cincinnati Post
Clare County (Mich.) Review
Cleburne (Tex.) Times-Review
Cleveland (Ohio) Plain Dealer
Colby (Kans.) Free Press
Colorado Springs Gazette
Colorado Springs Gazette-Telegraph
Corsicana (Tex.) Daily Sun
Council Bluffs (Iowa) Nonpareil
Daily Ardmoreite (Ardmore, Okla.)

Daily Deadwood Pioneer-Times
Daily Gate City (Keokuk, Iowa)
Daily Herald Suburban Chicago
Daily Oklahoman (Oklahoma City)
Dakota Student (University of North Dakota, Grand Forks)
Dallas News
Danville (Ky.) Advocate-Messenger
Daughters of the American Revolution Magazine (New York)
Dayton (Ohio) Daily News
Decatur (Ill.) Herald
Denison (Tex.) Herald
Denton (Tex.) Record-Chronicle
Denver Post
Deseret News (Salt Lake City)
East Bay News (Walnut Creek, Calif.)
Elgin (Ill.) Neighbor Newsletter
Emporia (Kans.) Gazette
Enid (Okla.) News and Eagle
Ensign (Salt Lake City)
Escanaba (Mich.) Daily Press
Eugene Daily Emerald (University of Oregon)
Eugene (Ore.) Guard
Eugene (Ore.) Register-Guard
Fairfield-Suisun (Calif.) Daily Republic
Fayette County (Iowa) Leader
Fort Worth (Tex.) Star-Telegram
Franklin (Ind.) Evening Star
Fredericksburg (Tex.) Standard
Freeport (Ill.) Journal-Standard
Garden City (Kans.) Telegram
Gary (Ind.) Post-Tribune
Gladwin County (Mich.) Record and Beaverton Clarion
Gloucester (Mass.) Daily Times
Gold Coast Chronicle (Biscayne Park, Fla.)
Goodwin's Weekly (Salt Lake City)
Grand Rapids (Mich.) Press
Great Bend (Kans.) Tribune
Grizzly Bear (Los Angeles, Calif.)
Harper's Weekly (New York City)
Harrisburg (Pa.) Daily Independent
Hays (Kans.) Daily News
Houston Chronicle
Humboldt (Iowa) Republican

Hutchinson (Kans.) News
Independence (Mo.) Examiner
Indian Country (Verona, N.Y.)
Indianapolis News
Inland Valley Daily Bulletin (Ontario, Calif.)
Inside Higher Ed (Washington, D.C.)
Iron County Record (Cedar City, Utah)
Joplin (Mo.) Globe
Kalispell (Mont.) Daily Inter Lake
Kansas City Star
Kansas City Times
Kenosha (Wisc.) News
Kerrville (Tex.) Mountain Sun
Kingsport (Tenn.) Times
Kingston (N.Y.) Daily Freeman
Klamath Falls (Ore.) Herald and News
Laker Current (Lake Michigan Catholic Middle High School)
Lamar (Colo.) Ledger
Las Cruces (N.Mex.) Sun-News
Latter Day Saints' Millennial Star (Salt Lake City)
Lawrence (Kans.) Daily Journal World
Lawton (Okla.) Constitution-Morning Press
LDS Church News (Salt Lake City)
Leavenworth (Kans.) Times
Lincoln (Neb.) Journal Star
Llano (Tex.) News
London Financial Times
Long Island (N.Y.) Newsday
Los Angeles Herald
Los Angeles Times
Mankato (Minn.) Free Press
Mason City (Iowa) Globe-Gazette
Mattoon (Ill.) Commercial Star
Mattoon (Ill.) Daily Journal-Gazette
McCook (Neb.) Daily Gazette
Medford (Ore.) Mail Tribune
Miami (Okla.) Daily News-Record
Minneapolis (Minn.) Morning Tribune
Minneapolis (Minn.) Star Tribune
Minnesota Public Radio News
Morgan County (Utah) News
Murray (Utah) Eagle
Nashville Post

Native American Times (Tulsa, Okla.)
Nebraska State Journal (Lincoln)
Nevada State Journal (Reno)
New Mexico Magazine
New Ulm (Minn.) Journal
New York Art Digest
New York Evening Post
New York Sun
New York Times
Norman (Okla.) Transcript
Northwest Magazine
Norton (Okla.) Telegram
Oakland (Calif.) Tribune
Oberlin (Kans.) Herald
Ogden (Utah) Standard-Examiner
Oklahoma City Journal Record
Olathe (Kans.) News
Omaha Magazine
Omaha (Neb.) World-Herald
Oregon Daily Journal (Portland)
Oregon Statesman (Salem)
Oregonian (Portland)
Pampa (Tex.) Daily News
Pittsburgh (Pa.) Post-Gazette
Politico Magazine (Washington, D.C.)
Ponca City (Okla.) News
Portland (Ore.) Business Journal
Postville (Iowa) Herald
Prescott (Ariz.) Business Pages
Prescott (Ariz.) Daily Courier
Provo (Utah) Daily Herald
Provo (Utah) Herald
Provo (Utah) Sunday Herald
Pueblo (Colo.) Chieftain
Relief Society Magazine (Salt Lake City)
Riverside (Calif.) Press-Enterprise
Rocky Mountain News (Denver)
Rogue River Courier (Grants Pass, Ore.)
Rushville (Ind.) Republican
Sacramento Bee
Salem (Ore.) Daily Capital Journal (later *Salem (Ore.) Capital Journal*)
Salina (Kans.) Journal
Salt Lake Telegram

Salt Lake Tribune
San Bernardino (Calif.) Sun
San Francisco Call
San Francisco Chronicle
San Francisco Examiner
San Mateo (Calif.) Daily Journal
Santa Cruz (Calif.) Evening News
Santa Cruz (Calif.) Sentinel
Santa Fe New Mexican
Seattle Times
Shawnee (Kans.) Dispatch
Sit News (Ketchikan, Alas.)
Sophian (Northampton, Mass.)
Southeast Missourian (Cape Girardeau, Mo.)
Southport (N.C.) Leader
Spanish Fork (Utah) Press
Springfield (Ohio) News-Sun Press
St. George (Utah) News
St. Joseph (Mo.) News-Press
St. Louis Daily Globe-Democrat
St. Louis Globe-Democrat
St. Louis Post-Dispatch
St. Paul (Minn.) Pioneer Press
Stillwater (Okla.) News Press
Stilwell (Okla.) Democrat-Journal
Storm Lake (Iowa) Times
Terre Haute (Ind.) Tribune
Texas Tribune (Austin)*Time* (New York City)
Tipton (Ind.) Daily Tribune
Topeka (Kans.) Capital Journal
Tulsa (Okla.) World
UPI NewsTrack (Washington, D.C.)
Vancouver (Wash.) Columbian
Visalia (Calif.) Times-Delta
Waikato Times (Hamilton, New Zealand)
Washington Post
Washington Times
Waterloo (Ind.) Press
Weekly Westport (Mo.) Reporter
Weekly Wisconsin (Milwaukee)
Westside Pioneer (Colorado Springs)
Wichita (Kans.) Eagle

SECONDARY SOURCES

Books and Articles

Ahmad, Aijaz. "Jameson's Rhetoric of Otherness and the 'National Allegory.'" *Social Text* 17 (Autumn 1987): 3–25.

Ahrens, Kent. "Avard T. Fairbanks and the Winter Quarters Monument." *Nebraska History* 95, no. 3 (Fall 2014): 176–85.

Alexander, Thomas G. *Mormonism in Transition: A History of the Latter-Day Saints, 1890–1930.* Urbana: University of Illinois Press, 1996.

Alvarez, Elizabeth Hayes. *The Valiant Woman: The Virgin Mary in Nineteenth-Century American Culture.* Chapel Hill: University of North Carolina Press, 2016.

Amley, Ted. "The Visual Politics of the Myth of the Frontier." *Midwest Review* 14 (1992): 71–90.

Antolini, Katharine Lane. *Memorializing Motherhood: Anna Jarvis and the Struggle for Control of Mother's Day.* Morgantown: West Virginia University Press, 2014.

Aron, Stephen. *How the West Was Lost: The Transformation of Kentucky from Daniel Boone to Henry Clay.* Baltimore, Md.: Johns Hopkins University Press, 1999.

Barraclough, Laura. "The Western Spirit of '76: The American Bicentennial and the Making of Conservative Multiculturalism in the Mountain West." *Western Historical Quarterly* 47, no. 2 (Summer 2016): 161–81.

Basso, Matthew, Laura McCall, and Dee Garceau, eds. *Across the Great Divide: Cultures of Manhood in the American West.* New York: Routledge, 2001.

Baur, John I. H. *William Zorach.* New York: Praeger, 1959.

Bederman, Gail. *Manliness and Civilization: A Cultural History of Gender and Race in the United States, 1880–1917.* Women in Culture and Society. Chicago: University of Chicago Press, 1996.

Benedict, Burton. *The Anthropology of World's Fairs: San Francisco's Panama Pacific International Exposition of 1915.* Berkeley: Scolar Press, 1983.

Berglund, Barbara. *Making San Francisco American: Cultural Frontiers in the Urban West, 1846–1906.* Lawrence: University Press of Kansas, 2007.

Bergman, Teresa. *Exhibiting Patriotism: Creating and Contesting Interpretations of American Historic Sites.* Walnut Creek, Calif.: Left Coast Press, 2013.

Bigler, David L. *Forgotten Kingdom: The Mormon Theocracy in the American West, 1847–1896.* Logan: Utah State University Press, 1998.

Bishir, Catherine W. "Landmarks of Power: Building a Southern Past, 1885–1915." *Southern Cultures,* December 2, 1993, 5–45.

Blee, Lisa. "Completing Lewis and Clark's Westward March." *Oregon Historical Quarterly* 106, no. 2 (Summer 2005): 232–53.

Bodnar, John E. *Remaking America: Public Memory, Commemoration, and Patriotism in the Twentieth Century.* Princeton, N.J.: Princeton University Press, 1991.

Boisseau, T. J., and Abigail M. Markwyn, eds. *Gendering the Fair: Histories of Women and Gender at World's Fairs.* Urbana: University of Illinois Press, 2010.

Bradley, Martha Sonntag. *Pedestals and Podiums: Utah Women, Religious Authority, and Equal Rights.* Salt Lake City: Signature Books, 2005.

Brekus, Catherine A. "Mormon Women and the Problem of Historical Agency." *Journal of Mormon History* 37, no. 2 (Spring 2011): 58–87.

Broder, Patricia Janis. *Bronzes of the American West.* New York: Abrams, 1975.

———. "The Pioneer Woman, Image in Bronze." *American Art Review* 2, no. 5 (1975): 127–34.

Brokaw, Tom. *The Greatest Generation.* New York: Random House, 2001.

Brooks, Juanita. *The Mountain Meadows Massacre.* Norman: University of Oklahoma Press, 1963.

Brosnan, Kathleen A., and Amy Louise Scott, eds. *City Dreams, Country Schemes: Community and Identity in the American West.* Reno: University of Nevada Press, 2011.

Bryan, Jimmy L., Jr. "The Weary West." In *Branding the American West: Paintings and Films, 1900–1950,* edited by Marian Wardle and Sarah E. Boehme, 88–113. Norman: University of Oklahoma Press, 2016.

Butler, Anne M. "Selling the Popular Myth." In *The Oxford History of the American West,* edited by Clyde A. Milner II, Carol A. O'Connor, and Martha A. Sandweiss, 771–801. New York: Oxford University Press, 1994.

Carley, Kenneth. *The Dakota War of 1862: Minnesota's Other Civil War.* 2nd ed. St. Paul: Minnesota Historical Society Press, 2001.

Carter, Lyndia McDowell. "The Mormon Handcart Companies." *Overland Journal* 13, no. 1 (1995): 2–18.

Casey, Janet Galligani. "The American Pioneer Woman circa 1930: Cultural Debates and the Role of Public Art." *American Studies* 51, no. 3 (2010): 85–107.

———. *A New Heartland: Women, Modernity, and the Agrarian Ideal in America.* New York: Oxford University Press, 2009.

Cikovsky, Nicolai, Jr. "'Ravages of the Axe': The Meaning of the Tree Stump in Nineteenth-Century American Art." *Art Bulletin* 61 (December 1979): 611–26.

Cocks, Catherine. *Doing the Town: The Rise of Urban Tourism in the United States, 1850–1915.* Berkeley: University of California Press, 2001.

Cohen, Lizabeth. *A Consumers' Republic: The Politics of Mass Consumption in Postwar America.* New York: Knopf, 2003.

Connerton, Paul. *How Modernity Forgets.* New York: Cambridge University Press, 2009.

———. *How Societies Remember.* Themes in the Social Sciences. New York: Cambridge University Press, 1989.

Coontz, Stephanie. *Marriage, a History: From Obedience to Intimacy, or How Love Conquered Marriage.* New York: Viking, 2005.

———. *A Strange Stirring: The Feminine Mystique and American Women at the Dawn of the 1960s.* New York: Basic Books, 2011.

———. *The Way We Never Were: American Families and the Nostalgia Trap.* New York: Basic Books, 1993.

Corbett, Katharine T. *In Her Place: A Guide to St. Louis Women's History.* St. Louis: Missouri History Museum, 1999.

Corcoran, Brent. *Multiply and Replenish: Mormon Essays on Sex and Family*. Salt Lake City: Signature Books, 1994.

Corn, Wanda M. *Women Building History: Public Art at the 1893 Columbian Exposition*. Berkeley: University of California Press, 2011.

Cornwall, Marie, Tim B. Heaton, and Lawrence A. Young, eds. *Contemporary Mormonism: Social Science Perspectives*. Urbana: University of Illinois Press, 2001.

Cox, Karen L. *Dixie's Daughters: The United Daughters of the Confederacy and the Preservation of Confederate Culture*. Gainesville: University Press of Florida, 2003.

Critchlow, Donald T. *Phyllis Schlafly and Grassroots Conservatism: A Woman's Crusade*. Princeton, N.J.: Princeton University Press, 2005.

Cronon, William, George A. Miles, and Jay Gitlin. *Under an Open Sky: Rethinking America's Western Past*. New York: Norton, 1992.

Crouch, David, and Nina Lübbren. *Visual Culture and Tourism*. New York: Berg, 2003.

Dawson, Jan C. "Sacagawea: Pilot or Pioneer Mother?" *Pacific Northwest Quarterly* 83, no. 1 (Spring 1992): 22–28.

Daynes, Kathryn M. *More Wives than One: Transformation of the Mormon Marriage System, 1840–1910*. Urbana: University of Illinois Press, 2001.

Delegard, Kirsten. *Battling Miss Bolsheviki: The Origins of Female Conservatism in the United States*. Philadelphia: University of Pennsylvania Press, 2012.

Deloria, Philip J. *Playing Indian*. New Haven, Conn.: Yale University Press, 1998.

Deverell, William. *Whitewashed Adobe: The Rise of Los Angeles and the Remaking of Its Mexican Past*. Berkeley: University of California Press, 2004.

Dimmick, Lauretta, and Donna J. Hassler. *American Sculpture in the Metropolitan Museum of Art: A Catalogue of Works by Artists Born between 1865 and 1885*. New York: Metropolitan Museum of Art, 1999.

Doezema, Marianne, and June Ellen Hargrove. *The Public Monument and Its Audience*. Cleveland, Ohio: Cleveland Museum of Art, 1977.

Dorius, Guy L. "Crossroads in the West: The Intersections of the Donner Party and the Mormons." *Nauvoo Journal* 9, no. 1 (1997): 17–27.

Doss, Erika. *Twentieth-Century American Art*. New York: Oxford University Press, 2002.

Douglas, Susan J. *Where the Girls Are: Growing up Female with the Mass Media*. New York: Times Books, 1995.

DuVal, Kathleen. *The Native Ground: Indians and Colonists in the Heart of the Continent*. Philadelphia: University of Pennsylvania Press, 2007.

Eliason, Eric A. "The Cultural Dynamics of Historical Self-Fashioning: Mormon Pioneer Nostalgia, American Culture, and the International Church." *Journal of Mormon History* 28, no. 2 (April 2002): 139–73.

Esplin, Scott C., and E. Vance Randall. "Living in Two Worlds: The Development and Transition of Mormon Education in American Society." *History of Education* 43, no. 1 (2014): 3–30.

Esser, Greg. "Hazardous Trail to a Lasting Legacy." *Public Art Review* 13, no. 1 (Fall/Winter 2001): 29–33.

Fairbanks, Eugene F. *A Sculptor's Testimony in Bronze and Stone: The Sacred Sculpture of Avard T. Fairbanks*. Salt Lake City: Publishers Press, 1972.

Faragher, John Mack. "Americans, Mexicans, Métis: A Community Approach to the Comparative Study of North American Frontiers." In *Under an Open Sky: Rethinking America's Western Past*, edited by William Cronon, George A. Miles, and Jay Gitlin, 90–109. New York: Norton, 1992.

Farmer, Jared. *On Zion's Mount: Mormons, Indians, and the American Landscape*. Cambridge, Mass.: Harvard University Press, 2010.

Fass, Paula S. *The Damned and the Beautiful*. New York: Oxford University Press, 1977.

Fields, Alison. "Memory, Reenactment, and Oklahoma's Pioneer Woman Statue." *Journal of the West* 52, no. 1 (Winter 2013): 25–32.

Filene, Peter G. *Him/Her/Self: Sex Roles in Modern America*. Baltimore, Md.: Johns Hopkins University Press, 1986.

Findlay, John M. *Magic Lands: Western Cityscapes and American Culture after 1940*. Berkeley: University of California Press, 1993.

Findling, John E. *Chicago's Great World's Fairs*. New York: Manchester University Press, 1994.

Flake, Kathleen. "Re-Placing Memory: Latter-Day Saint Use of Historical Monuments and Narrative in the Early Twentieth Century." *Religion and American Culture* 13, no. 1 (Winter 2003): 69.

Fleming, David. *City of Rhetoric: Revitalizing the Public Sphere in Metropolitan America*. Albany: SUNY Press, 2008.

Foley, Doris. *The Pioneer (Donner) Monument: The Origin of a Statue*. Nevada City, Calif.: Nevada County Historical Society, 2000.

Forty, Adrian, and Susanne Küchler, eds. *The Art of Forgetting*. New York: Berg, 1999.

Frink, Brenda D. "San Francisco's Pioneer Mother Monument: Maternalism, Racial Order, and the Politics of Memorialization, 1907–1915." *American Quarterly* 64, no. 1 (2012): 85–113.

Gable, Eric, and Richard Handler. "After Authenticity at an American Heritage Site." *American Anthropologist* 98, no. 3 (1996): 568–78.

———. *The New History in an Old Museum: Creating the Past at Colonial Williamsburg*. Durham, N.C.: Duke University Press, 1997.

Ganz, Cheryl. *The 1933 Chicago World's Fair: A Century of Progress*. Urbana: University of Illinois Press, 2008.

Givens, Terryl. *People of Paradox: A History of Mormon Culture*. New York: Oxford University Press, 2007.

Glassberg, David. *Sense of History: The Place of the Past in American Life*. Amherst: University of Massachusetts Press, 2001.

Glazer, Nathan. "'Subverting the Context': Public Space and Public Design." *Public Interest*, no. 109 (Fall 1992): 3–20.

———. "What Happened to the Social Agenda? Leading Modernist Architects Once Wanted to Improve the Lives of Everyday People: Now They Hope to

Astonish and Amuse Their Elite Clients." *American Scholar* 76, no. 2 (Spring 2007): 108–13.

Goetzmann, William H., and William N. Goetzmann. *The West of the Imagination.* Norman: University of Oklahoma Press, 2009.

Goffman, Erving. *Gender Advertisements.* Cambridge, Mass.: Harvard University Press, 1979.

Goggin, Maureen Daly, and Beth Fowkes Tobin. *Women and the Material Culture of Needlework and Textiles, 1750–1950.* Burlington, Vt.: Ashgate, 2009.

González-Ruibal, Alfredo. "Time to Destroy: An Archaeology of Supermodernity." *Current Anthropology* 49, no. 2 (April 1, 2008): 247–79.

Gordon, Linda. *Pitied but Not Entitled: Single Mothers and the History of Welfare, 1890–1935.* New York: Free Press, 1994.

Gordon, Sarah Barringer. "'The Liberty of Self-Degradation': Polygamy, Woman Suffrage, and Consent in Nineteenth-Century America." *Journal of American History* 83, no. 3 (1996): 815–47.

Green, Rayna D. "The Pocahontas Perplex: The Image of Indian Women in American Culture." *Massachusetts Review* 16, no. 4 (Winter 1975): 698–714.

Haarsager, Sandra. *Organized Womanhood: Cultural Politics in the Pacific Northwest, 1840–1920.* Norman: University of Oklahoma Press, 1997.

Hajdik, Anna Thompson. "'You Really Ought to Give Iowa a Try': Tourism, Community Identity, and the Impact of Popular Culture in Iowa." *Online Journal of Rural Research and Policy* 4, no. 1 (2009): 1–20.

Hall, David. "New Identities for a New Century: Shifting Gender Roles for Mormon Women in the Early Twentieth Century." Paper presented at the Western History Association Annual Conference, St. Paul, Minnesota, October 20–23, 2016.

Hamilakis, Yannis, and Jo Labanyi. "Time, Materiality, and the Work of Memory." *History and Memory: Studies in Representation of the Past* 20, no. 2 (2008): 5–17.

Hartley, William G. "The Place of Mormon Handcart Companies in America's Westward Migration Story." *Annals of Iowa* 65 (Spring/Summer 2006): 101–23.

Hartman, Andrew. *A War for the Soul of America: A History of the Culture Wars.* Chicago: University of Chicago Press, 2015.

Haseltine, James L. "Mormons and the Visual Arts." *Dialogue: A Journal of Mormon Thought* 1, no. 2 (Summer 1966): 17–29.

Hassrick, Peter H. "The Oregon Art of Alexander Phimister Proctor." *Oregon Historical Quarterly* 104, no. 3 (Fall 2003): 394–413.

———. *Wildlife and Western Heroes: Alexander Phimister Proctor, Sculptor.* Fort Worth, Tex.: Amon Carter Museum, 2003.

Hayden, Dolores. *Building Suburbia: Green Fields and Urban Growth, 1820–2000.* New York: Vintage Books, 2003.

Hinton, Wayne K. "Mahonri Young and the Church: A View of Mormonism and Art." *Dialogue: A Journal of Mormon Thought* 7, no. 4 (1972): 35–43.

Hirsch, Marianne, and Valerie Smith. "Feminism and Cultural Memory: An Introduction." *Signs*, 28, no. 1 (Autumn 2002): 1–19.

Hochschild, Arlie Russell. *The Second Shift: Working Parents and the Revolution at Home*. New York: Avon Books, 1990.

Holt, Marilyn Irvin. *Cold War Kids: Politics and Childhood in Postwar America, 1945–1960*. Lawrence: University Press of Kansas, 2014.

Hufbauer, Benjamin. *Presidential Temples: How Memorials and Libraries Shape Public Memory*. Lawrence: University Press of Kansas, 2005.

Huhndorf, Shari M. *Going Native: Indians in the American Cultural Imagination*. Ithaca, N.Y.: Cornell University Press, 2001.

Hunter, Jane. *How Young Ladies Became Girls: The Victorian Origins of American Girlhood*. New Haven, Conn.: Yale University Press, 2002.

Hunter, J. Michael. "The Monument to Brigham Young and the Pioneers: One Hundred Years of Controversy." *Utah Historical Quarterly* 68, no. 4 (Fall 2000): 332–50.

Hurtado, Albert L. *Intimate Frontiers: Sex, Gender, and Culture in Old California*. Albuquerque: University of New Mexico Press, 1999.

Hutchinson, W. H. *The World, The Work, and the West of W. H. D. Koerner*. Norman: University of Oklahoma Press, 1978.

Irwin, Mary Ann, and James F. Brooks, eds. *Women and Gender in the American West*. Albuquerque: University of New Mexico Press, 2004.

Jackson, Kenneth T. *Crabgrass Frontier: The Suburbanization of the United States*. New York: Oxford University Press, 1987.

Jameson, Fredric. "Third-World Literature in the Era of Multinational Capital." *Social Text* 15 (Autumn 1986): 65–88.

Janicke, Tim J. *City of Art: Kansas City's Public Art*. Kansas City, Mo.: Kansas City Star Books, 2001.

Johnson, Susan Lee. *Roaring Camp: The Social World of the California Gold Rush*. Reprint ed. New York: Norton, 2000.

Johnson, Wendell, B. Wheeler, and Rell G. Francis. *Frontier to Fame: Cyrus E. Dallin, Sculptor*. Edited by Denice Dallin Wheeler. [Mass.]: self-pub., 2005.

Kammen, Michael. *Mystic Chords of Memory: The Transformation of Tradition in American Culture*. New York: Knopf, 1991.

———. *Visual Shock: A History of Art Controversies in American Culture*. New York: Vintage Books, 2006.

Kaye, Harvey J. "The Making of American Memory." *American Quarterly* 46, no. 2 (June 1, 1994): 251–59.

Kimball, Stanley Buchholz. *Historic Sites and Markers Along the Mormon and Other Great Western Trails*. Urbana: University of Illinois Press, 1988.

———. *Mormon Pioneer National Historic Trail: Historic Resource Study*. Washington, D.C.: National Park Service, 1991.

Kimmel, Michael S. *Manhood in America: A Cultural History*. New York: Oxford University Press, 2006.

Kirshenblatt-Gimblett, Barbara. *Destination Culture: Tourism, Museums, and Heritage*. Berkeley: University of California Press, 1998.

Kogan, Nathaniel Smith. "The Mormon Pavilion: Mainstreaming the Saints at the New York World's Fair, 1964–65." *Journal of Mormon History* 35, no. 4 (Fall 2009): 1–52.

Kotkin, Joel. *The New Suburbanism: A Realist's Guide to the American Future.* Costa Mesa, Calif.: Planning Center, 2005.

Koven, Seth, and Sonya Michel. "Womanly Duties: Maternalist Politics and the Origins of Welfare States in France, Germany, Great Britain, and the United States, 1880–1920." *American Historical Review* 95, no. 4 (October 1, 1990): 1076–1108.

Kovinick, Phil. "South Dakota's 'Other' Borglum." *South Dakota History* 1, no. 3 (1971): 207–30.

Kropp, Phoebe S. *California Vieja: Culture and Memory in a Modern American Place.* Berkeley: University of California Press, 2006.

Kushner, Howard I. "The Persistence of the 'Frontier Thesis' in America: Gender, Myth, and Self-Destruction." *Canadian Review of American Studies* 23, no. 1 (1992): 53–82.

Laga, Barry. "In Lieu of History: Mormon Monuments and the Shaping of Memory." *Dialogue: A Journal of Mormon Thought* 43, no. 4 (Winter 2010): 131–53.

———. "Making the Absent Visible: The Real, Ideal, and the Abstract in Mormon Art." *Dialogue: A Journal of Mormon Thought* 40, no. 2 (June 1, 2007): 47–77.

Lajimodiere, Denise K. "American Indian Females and Stereotypes: Warriors, Leaders, Healers, Feminists, Not Drudges, Princesses, Prostitutes." *Multicultural Perspectives* 15, no. 2 (2013): 104–9.

Landsman, Gail H. "The 'Other' as Political Symbol: Images of Indians in the Woman Suffrage Movement." *Ethnohistory* 39, no. 3 (1992): 247–84.

LaRossa, Ralph. *The Modernization of Fatherhood: A Social and Political History.* Chicago: University of Chicago Press, 1997.

Lasansky, D. Medina, and Brian McLaren, eds. *Architecture and Tourism: Perception, Performance and Place.* Oxford: Berg, 2004.

Levinson, Sanford. *Written in Stone: Public Monuments in Changing Societies.* Durham, N.C.: Duke University Press, 1998.

Limerick, Patricia Nelson. "The Adventures of the Frontier in the Twentieth Century." In *Frontier in American Culture,* edited by James R. Grossman, 66–102. Berkeley: University of California Press, 1994.

———. *The Legacy of Conquest: The Unbroken Past of the American West.* New York: Norton, 1987.

Lovett, Laura L. *Conceiving the Future: Pronatalism, Reproduction, and the Family in the United States, 1890–1938.* Chapel Hill: University of North Carolina Press, 2007.

Markwyn, Abigail M. *Empress San Francisco: The Pacific Rim, the Great West, and California at the Panama-Pacific International Exposition.* Lincoln: University of Nebraska Press, 2014.

Marschall, Sabine. "Transforming the Landscape of Memory: The South African Commemorative Effort in International Perspective." *South African Historical Journal* 55 (2006): 165–85.

Marter, Joan M. *The Grove Encyclopedia of American Art.* New York: Oxford University Press, 2011.

Mathews, John Joseph. *Life and Death of an Oilman: The Career of E. W. Marland.* Norman: University of Oklahoma Press, 1951.

Mauss, Armand L. *The Angel and the Beehive: The Mormon Struggle with Assimilation.* Urbana: University of Illinois Press, 1994.

———. "Assimilation and Ambivalence: The Mormon Reaction to Americanization." *Dialogue: A Journal of Mormon Thought* 22, no. 1 (Spring 1989): 30–67.

———. "The Mormon Struggle with Assimilation and Identity: Trends and Developments Since Midcentury." *Dialogue: A Journal of Mormon Thought* 27, no. 1 (Spring 1994): 129–49.

———. "Rethinking Retrenchment: Course Corrections in the Ongoing Campaign for Respectability." *Dialogue: A Journal of Mormon Thought* 44, no. 4 (Winter 2011): 1–42.

May, Elaine Tyler. *Homeward Bound: American Families in the Cold War Era.* New York: Basic Books, 1988.

McClintock, Anne. "Family Feuds: Gender, Nationalism and the Family." *Feminist Review* 44 (Summer 1993): 61–80.

———. *Imperial Leather: Race, Gender, and Sexuality in the Colonial Contest.* New York: Routledge, 1995.

McElya, Mick. "Commemorating the Color Line: The National Mammy Monument Controversy of the 1920s." In *Monuments to the Lost Cause: Women, Art, and the Landscapes of Southern Memory,* edited by Cynthia J. Mills and Pamela H. Simpson, 203–18. Knoxville: University of Tennessee Press, 2003.

McGirr, Lisa. *Suburban Warriors: The Origins of the New American Right.* Princeton, N.J.: Princeton University Press, 2001.

Mead, Rebecca. *How the Vote Was Won: Woman Suffrage in the Western United States, 1868–1914.* New York: NYU Press, 2006.

Medlicott, Carol, and Michael Heffernan. "'Autograph of a Nation': The Daughters of the American Revolution and the National Old Trails Road, 1910–1927." *National Identities* 6, no. 3 (2004): 233–60.

Menlove, Frances Lee. "A Forty-Year View: Dialogue and the Sober Lessons of History." *Dialogue: A Journal of Mormon Thought* 39, no. 3 (Fall 2006): 88–97.

Meyerowitz, Joanne. "Beyond the Feminine Mystique: A Reassessment of Postwar Mass Culture, 1946–1958." *Journal of American History* 79, no. 4 (March 1993): 1455–82.

Meyerowitz, Joanne J., ed. *Not June Cleaver: Women and Gender in Postwar America, 1945–1960.* Philadelphia: Temple University Press, 1994.

Michalski, Sergiusz. *Public Monuments: Art in Political Bondage, 1870–1997.* London: Reaktion Books, 1998.

Miller, Steven P. *The Age of Evangelicalism: America's Born-Again Years*. New York: Oxford University Press, 2014.

Mills, Barbara J., and William H. Walker. *Memory Work: Archaeologies of Material Practices*. School for Advanced Research Advanced Seminar Series. Santa Fe, N.Mex.: School for Advanced Research Press, 2008.

Mills, Cynthia J. "Gratitude and Gender Wars: Monuments to the Women of the Sixties." In *Monuments to the Lost Cause: Women, Art, and the Landscapes of Southern Memory*, edited by Cynthia J. Mills and Pamela H. Simpson, 183–200. Knoxville: University of Tennessee Press, 2003.

Mills, Cynthia J., and Pamela H. Simpson, eds. *Monuments to the Lost Cause: Women, Art, and the Landscapes of Southern Memory*. Knoxville: University of Tennessee Press, 2003.

Milner, Clyde A., II, Carol A. O'Connor, and Martha A. Sandweiss, eds. *The Oxford History of the American West*. New York: Oxford University Press, 1994.

Mintz, Steven. *Huck's Raft: A History of American Childhood*. Cambridge, Mass.: Belknap Press of Harvard University Press, 2004.

Mintz, Steven, and Susan Kellogg. *Domestic Revolutions: A Social History of American Family Life*. New York: Free Press, 1988.

Mitchell, Lee Clark. "Whose West Is It Anyway? Or, What's Myth Got to Do with It? The Role of 'America' in the Creation of the Myth of the West." *American Review of Canadian Studies* 33, no. 4 (December 2003): 497–508.

Moore, Sarah J. *Empire on Display: San Francisco's Panama-Pacific International Exposition of 1915*. Norman: University of Oklahoma Press, 2013.

Moore, William D. "'United We Commemorate': The Kentucky Pioneer Memorial Association, James Isenberg, and Early Twentieth-Century Heritage Tourism." *Public Historian* 30, no. 3 (2008): 51–81.

Moss, Sandy. "'Not-So-Gentle-Tamer' Commemorates Arizona's 100 Years of Statehood." *Prescott Woman*, November 2010.

Mould, Tom, ed. *Still, the Small Voice: Narrative, Personal Revelation, and the Mormon Folk Tradition*. Logan: Utah State University Press, 2011.

Murphy, Carl. "The Marriage Metaphor in Nineteenth-Century English Canadian Fiction." *Studies in Canadian Literature / Études En Littérature Canadienne* 13, no. 1 (January 1, 1988).

Nora, Pierre. "Between Memory and History: Les Lieux de Mémoire." *Representations*, no. 26 (April 1, 1989): 7–24.

Norkunas, Martha K. *Monuments and Memory: History and Representation in Lowell, Massachusetts*. Washington, D.C.: Smithsonian Institution Press, 2002.

Olsen, Deborah M. "Fair Connections: Women's Separatism and the Lewis and Clark Exposition of 1905." *Oregon Historical Quarterly* 109, no. 2 (2008): 174–203.

"Other Matter." *Dialogue: A Journal of Mormon Thought* 1, no. 2 (June 1, 1966).

Patterson, Sara M. "The Plymouth Rock of the American West: Remembering, Forgetting, and Becoming American in Utah." *Material Religion: The Journal of Objects, Art and Belief* 11, no. 3 (2015): 329–53.

Peterson, Art. *Why Is That Bridge Orange? San Francisco for the Curious.* San Francisco: Inquiring Minds Productions, 2013.

Peterson del Mar, David. *The American Family: From Obligation to Freedom.* New York: Palgrave Macmillan, 2011.

Phillips, Richard. "Settler Colonialism and the Nuclear Family." *Canadian Geographer* 53, no. 2 (Summer 2009): 239–53.

Philpott, William. *Vacationland: Tourism and Environment in the Colorado High Country.* Seattle: University of Washington Press, 2014.

Pierce, Jason E. *Making the White Man's West: Whiteness and the Creation of the American West.* Boulder: University Press of Colorado, 2016.

Plant, Rebecca Jo. *Mom: The Transformation of Motherhood in Modern America.* Chicago: University of Chicago Press, 2010.

Prescott, Cynthia Culver. "The All-American Eternal Family: Sacred and Secular Values in Western Pioneer Monuments." In *We Are What We Remember: The American Past through Commemoration,* edited by Jeffrey Meriwether and Laura D'Amore, 334–58. Cambridge: Cambridge Scholars Publishing, 2012.

———. *Gender and Generation on the Far Western Frontier.* Tucson: University of Arizona Press, 2007.

———. "Pioneer Mothers for the New Millennium." In *Excavating Memory: Material Culture Approaches to Sites of Remembering and Forgetting,* edited by Maria Theresia Starzmann and John R. Roby, 172–98. University Press of Florida, 2016.

———. "Representing the Ideal American Family." *Pacific Historical Review* 85, no. 1 (February 2016): 110–42.

Prince, Gregory A., and William Robert Wright. *David O. McKay and the Rise of Modern Mormonism.* Salt Lake City: University of Utah Press, 2005.

Prothero, Stephen. *Why Liberals Win (Even When They Lose Elections): How America's Raucous, Nasty, and Mean "Culture Wars" Make for a More Inclusive Nation.* New York: HarperCollins, 2016.

"Public History and Memory (Bibliography)." *Journal of American History* 83, no. 4 (1997): 1549.

Quinn, D. Michael. "LDS 'Headquarters Culture' and the Rest of Mormonism: Past and Present." *Dialogue: A Journal of Mormon Thought* 34, nos. 3–4 (Fall 2001): 135–64.

Quinn, D. Michael, ed. *The New Mormon History: Revisionist Essays on the Past.* Salt Lake City: Signature Books, 1992.

Radke-Moss, Andrea G. "Mormon Women, Suffrage, and Citizenship at the 1893 Chicago World's Fair." In *Gendering the Fair: Histories of Women and Gender at World's Fairs,* edited by T. J. Boisseau and Abigail M. Markwyn, 97–112. Urbana: University of Illinois Press, 2010.

Reed, Maureen. "How Sacagawea Became a Pioneer Mother: Statues, Ethnicity, and Controversy in Portland and Santa Fe." In *Public Memory, Race, and Ethnicity,* edited by G. Mitchell Reyes, 33–49. Cambridge: Cambridge Scholars Publishing, 2010.

Reed, Walt. *Harvey Dunn: Illustrator and Painter of the Pioneer West.* Santa Cruz, Calif.: Flesk, 2010.

Reeve, W. Paul. *Religion of a Different Color: Race and the Mormon Struggle for Whiteness.* New York: Oxford University Press, 2015.

Reynolds, Donald Martin. *Masters of American Sculpture: The Figurative Tradition from the American Renaissance to the Millennium.* New York: Abbeville Press, 1994.

Reynolds, Donald Martin, ed. *Remove Not the Ancient Landmark: Public Monuments and Moral Values.* London: Routledge, 1996.

Rohrbough, Malcolm J. *Days of Gold: The California Gold Rush and the American Nation.* Berkeley: University of California Press, 1997.

Rosaldo, Renato. "Imperialist Nostalgia." *Representations,* no. 26 (April 1, 1989): 107–22.

Rothman, Hal. *Devil's Bargains: Tourism in the Twentieth-Century American West.* Lawrence: University Press of Kansas, 1998.

Rowlands, Michael. "Remembering to Forget: Sublimation as Sacrifice in War Memorials." In *The Art of Forgetting,* edited by Adrian Forty and Susanne Küchler, 129–45. New York: Berg, 1999.

Rugh, Susan Sessions. *Are We There Yet? The Golden Age of American Family Vacations.* Lawrence: University Press of Kansas, 2008.

Rydell, Robert W. *World of Fairs: The Century-of-Progress Expositions.* Chicago: University of Chicago Press, 1993.

Rymph, Catherine E. *Republican Women: Feminism and Conservatism from Suffrage through the Rise of the New Right.* Chapel Hill: University of North Carolina Press, 2006.

Saab, A. Joan. *For the Millions: American Art and Culture Between the Wars.* Philadelphia: University of Pennsylvania Press, 2004.

Sackman, Douglas Cazaux. *Wild Men: Ishi and Kroeber in the Wilderness of Modern America.* New Narratives in American History. New York: Oxford University Press, 2010.

Sanders, Jeffrey. "Public Art, Memory, and Mobility in 1920s New Mexico." In *City Dreams, Country Schemes: Community and Identity in the American West,* edited by Kathleen A. Brosnan and Amy Louise Scott, 178–95. Reno: University of Nevada Press, 2011.

Sarna, Jonathan D. *Minority Faiths and the American Protestant Mainstream.* Urbana: University of Illinois Press, 1998.

Savage, Kirk. *Monument Wars: Washington, D.C., the National Mall, and the Transformation of the Memorial Landscape.* Berkeley: University of California Press, 2009.

———. *Standing Soldiers, Kneeling Slaves: Race, War, and Monument in Nineteenth-Century America.* Princeton, N.J.: Princeton University Press, 1997.

Scheer, Brenda Case, and Mintcho Petkov. "Edge City Morphology: A Comparison of Commercial Centers." *Journal of the American Planning Association* 64, no. 3 (September 30, 1998): 298–310.

Schimmel, Julie. "Inventing 'the Indian.'" In *The West as America: Reinterpreting Images of the Frontier, 1820–1920*, edited by William H. Truettner, 172–74. Washington, D.C.: Smithsonian Institution Press, 1991.

Shackel, Paul A. *Memory in Black and White: Race, Commemoration, and the Post-Bellum Landscape.* Walnut Creek, Calif.: Altamira Press, 2003.

Shaffer, Marguerite S. *See America First: Tourism and National Identity, 1880–1940.* Washington, D.C.: Smithsonian Institution Press, 2001.

Shipps, Jan. "Difference and Otherness: Mormonism and the American Religious Mainstream." In *Minority Faiths and the American Protestant Mainstream*, edited by Jonathan D. Sarna, 81–109. Urbana: University of Illinois Press, 1998.

———. "From Peoplehood to Church Membership: Mormonism's Trajectory since World War II." *Church History* 76, no. 2 (June 2007): 241–61.

———. "The Mormons' Progress." *Wilson Quarterly* 15 (Spring 1991): 48–50.

Simpson, Pamela H. "Pioneer Mother Monuments, 1914–1930: Images of Western Expansion." *Southeastern College Art Conference Review* 13, no. 5 (2000): 435–43.

Skarstein, Karl Jakob, Richard Rothaus, and Dakota Goodhouse. *The War with the Sioux: Norwegians against Indians 1862–1863.* Translated by Melissa Gjellstad and Danielle Mead Skjelver. Grand Forks: University of North Dakota Digital Press, 2015.

Smith, Don H. "Leadership, Planning, and Management of the 1856 Mormon Handcart Emigration." *Annals of Iowa* 65 (Spring/Summer 2006): 124–61.

Smith, George D. *Nauvoo Polygamy: ". . . but We Called It Celestial Marriage."* Salt Lake City: Signature Books, 2008.

Smith, Sherry L. *Reimagining Indians: Native Americans through Anglo Eyes, 1880–1940.* Oxford: Oxford University Press, 2000.

Solnit, Rebecca. "The Struggle of Dawning Intelligence: Creating, Revising, and Recognizing Native American Monuments." In *Storming the Gates of Paradise: Landscapes for Politics*, 40–50. Berkeley: University of California Press, 2007.

Spirou, Costas, and Dennis R. Judd. "The Changing Geography of Urban Tourism: Will the Center Hold?" *disP—The Planning Review* 50, no. 2 (April 3, 2014): 38–47.

Springhall, John. "Have Gun, Will Travel: The Myth of the Frontier in the Hollywood Western." *Historian* 112 (Winter 2011): 20–24.

Stanley, David. "Cowboy Poetry Then and Now: An Overview." In *Cowboy Poets and Cowboy Poetry*, edited by David Stanley and Elaine Thatcher, 1–18. Urbana: University of Illinois Press, 2000.

Starr, Kevin. *Americans and the California Dream, 1850–1915.* New York: Oxford University Press, 1986.

Starrs, Paul F. "Meetinghouses in the Mormon Mind: Ideology, Architecture, and Turbulent Streams of an Expanding Church." *Geographical Review* 99, no. 3 (July 2009): 323–55.

Stauffer, Suzanne M. "A Good Social Work: Women's Clubs, Libraries, and the Construction of a Secular Society in Utah, 1890–1920." *Libraries and the Cultural Record* 46, no. 2 (2011): 135–55.

Steenkamp, Alta. "Apartheid to Democracy: Representation and Politics in the Voortrekker Monument and Red Location Museum." *Architectural Research Quarterly* 10, nos. 3–4 (2006): 249–54.

Stock, Catherine McNicol. *Main Street in Crisis: The Great Depression and the Old Middle Class on the Northern Plains.* Chapel Hill: University of North Carolina Press, 1992.

Stoeltje, Beverly J. "Making the Frontier Myth: Folklore Process in a Modern Nation." *Western Folklore* 46, no. 4 (Fall 1987): 235–54.

Stott, Annette. "Prairie Madonnas and Pioneer Women: Images of Emigrant Women in the Art of the Old West." *Prospects* 21 (October 1996): 299–325.

Sturken, Marita. *Tourists of History: Memory, Kitsch, and Consumerism from Oklahoma City to Ground Zero.* Durham, N.C.: Duke University Press, 2007.

Swigger, Jessie. *"History Is Bunk": Assembling the Past at Henry Ford's Greenfield Village.* Amherst: University of Massachusetts Press, 2014.

Tetrault, Lisa. *The Myth of Seneca Falls: Memory and the Women's Suffrage Movement, 1848–1898.* Chapel Hill: The University of North Carolina Press, 2014.

Thall, Bob. *The New American Village.* Baltimore, Md.: Johns Hopkins University Press, 1999.

Tolles, Thayer, Peter H. Hassrick, Andrew Walker, and Sarah E. Boehme. *Shaping the West: American Sculptors of the 19th Century.* Denver: Denver Art Museum, 2011.

Trachtenberg, Alan. *Shades of Hiawatha: Staging Indians, Making Americans, 1880–1930.* New York: Hill and Wang, 2004.

Trouillot, Michel-Rolph. *Silencing the Past: Power and the Production of History.* Boston: Beacon Press, 1995.

Truettner, William H., ed. *The West as America: Reinterpreting Images of the Frontier, 1820–1920.* Washington, D.C.: Smithsonian Institution Press, 1991.

Turner, Frederick Jackson, and John Mack Faragher. *Rereading Frederick Jackson Turner: The Significance of the Frontier in American History, and Other Essays.* New York: Holt, 1994.

Ulrich, Laurel Thatcher. *The Age of Homespun: Objects and Stories in the Creation of an American Myth.* New York: Vintage, 2002.

———. "Mormon Women in the History of Second-Wave Feminism." *Dialogue: A Journal of Mormon Thought* 43, no. 2 (Summer 2010): 45–63.

Umbach, Greg (Fritz). "Learning to Shop in Zion: The Consumer Revolution in Great Basin Mormon Culture, 1847–1910." *Journal of Social History* 38, no. 1 (Fall 2004): 29–61.

Upward, Geoffrey C. *A Home for Our Heritage: The Building and Growth of Greenfield Village and Henry Ford Museum, 1929–1979.* Dearborn, Mich.: Henry Ford Museum Press, 1979.

Veracini, Lorenzo. "Introducing." *Settler Colonial Studies* 1, no. 1 (January 1, 2011): 1–12.

———. *The Settler Colonial Present.* New York: Palgrave Macmillan, 2015.

———. *Settler Colonialism: A Theoretical Overview.* New York: Palgrave Macmillan, 2010.

———. "Suburbia, Settler Colonialism and the World Turned Inside Out." *Housing, Theory and Society* 29, no. 4 (December 1, 2012): 339–57.

Vettel-Becker, Patricia. "Sacagawea and Son: The Visual Construction of America's Maternal Feminine." *American Studies* 50, no. 1 (2011): 27–50.

Vivian, Bradford. *Public Forgetting: The Rhetoric and Politics of Beginning Again.* University Park: Pennsylvania State University Press, 2010.

Wardle, Marian, and Sarah E. Boehme. *Branding the American West: Paintings and Films, 1900–1950.* Norman: University of Oklahoma Press, 2016.

Warren, Louis S. "Cody's Last Stand: Masculine Anxiety, the Custer Myth, and the Frontier of Domesticity in Buffalo Bill's Wild West." *Western Historical Quarterly* 34, no. 1 (April 1, 2003): 49–69.

Weaver-Hightower, Rebecca. "'Before God This Was Their Country': History and Guilt in Stuart Cloete's Turning Wheels and the Voortrekker Monument, Pretoria." *English in Africa* 40, no. 2 (October 2013): 101–20.

———. "Frontier Fictions: Settler Stories and the Origins of White Guilt." Unpublished manuscript, in Weaver-Hightower's possession, n.d.

———. "The Frontier Landscape and Guilty Settler in Nineteenth Century Colonial Literature." In *Geocritical Explorations: Space, Place, and Mapping in Literary and Cultural Studies,* edited by Robert Tally, 123–38. New York: Palgrave Macmillan, 2011.

———. "'Do We Reverse the Medal?': Settler Guilt, the Indian Speech, and the Untold Side of the Story." *Journal of Settler Colonial Studies* 52, no. 1 (2017): 25–53.

Weeks, Jim. *Gettysburg: Memory, Market, and an American Shrine.* Princeton, N.J.: Princeton University Press, 2003.

Weiss, Jessica. *To Have and to Hold: Marriage, the Baby Boom, and Social Change.* Chicago: University of Chicago Press, 2000.

White, O. Kendall, and Daryl White. "Polygamy and Mormon Identity." *Journal of American Culture* 28, no. 2 (June 2005): 165–77.

White, Richard. *"It's Your Misfortune and None of My Own": A History of the American West.* Norman: University of Oklahoma Press, 1991.

White, Richard, and Patricia Nelson Limerick. *The Frontier in American Culture: An Exhibition at the Newberry Library, August 26, 1994–January 7, 1995.* Edited by James R. Grossman. Berkeley: University of California Press, 1994.

Wilson, Chris. *The Myth of Santa Fe: Creating a Modern Regional Tradition.* Albuquerque: University of New Mexico Press, 1997.

Wilson, Richard Guy. In *Monuments to the Lost Cause: Women, Art, and the Landscapes of Southern Memory,* edited by Cynthia J. Mills and Pamela H. Simpson, 100–15. Knoxville: University of Tennessee Press, 2003.

Wolfe, Patrick. "Settler Colonialism and the Elimination of the Native." *Journal of Genocide Research* 8, no. 4 (December 2006): 387–409.

Worster, Donald. *Under Western Skies: Nature and History in the American West*. New York: Oxford University Press, 1992.

Wright, Helen. *James Lick's Monument: The Saga of Captain Richard Floyd and the Building of the Lick Observatory*. New York: Cambridge University Press, 1987.

Wrobel, David M., and Long, Patrick T. *Seeing and Being Seen: Tourism in the American West*. Lawrence: University Press of Kansas, 2001.

Yorgason, Ethan R. *Transformation of the Mormon Culture Region*. Urbana: University of Illinois Press, 2010.

Young, Neil J. "'The ERA Is a Moral Issue': The Mormon Church, LDS Women, and the Defeat of the Equal Rights Amendment." *American Quarterly* 59, no. 3 (September 2007): 623–44.

Yuhl, Stephanie E. *A Golden Haze of Memory: The Making of Historic Charleston*. Chapel Hill: University of North Carolina Press, 2005.

Zaretsky, Natasha. *No Direction Home: The American Family and the Fear of National Decline, 1968–1980*. Chapel Hill: University of North Carolina Press, 2007.

Zelizer, Viviana A. Rotman. *Pricing the Priceless Child: The Changing Social Value of Children*. New York: Basic Books, 1985.

Theses and Dissertations

Andersen, Jeffrey D. "Portrait of the 1890–1892 LDS Paris Art Mission: An Andragogical Perspective." PhD diss., University of Idaho, Moscow, 2006.

Barber, Alicia Marie. "Living It Up, Living It Down: Civic Reputation, Tourism and Urban Development in Reno, Nevada." PhD diss., University of Texas at Austin, 2003.

Bohl, Charles C. "The Social, Civic and Symbolic Functions of the Public Realm: A Comparative Analysis of New Urbanist Town Centers and Conventional Shopping Centers." PhD diss., University of North Carolina at Chapel Hill, 2004.

Branam, Easton L. "Spanning the Rural Urban Divide: Toward an Expanded Theory of Landscape Architecture." Master's thesis, University of Washington, Seattle, 2012.

Carey, Jeremy Adam. "Celebrating Memory and Space: Three Case Studies of Centennial Projects to Commemorate Oklahoma's History." Master's thesis, University of Central Oklahoma, Edmond, 2013.

Hajdik, Anna Thompson. "Agricultural Romance: Constructing and Consuming Rural Life in Modern America." PhD diss., University of Texas at Austin, 2011.

Harris, Jenny Lynn Mcgee. "The Silent Majority: Conservative Perception, Mobilization, and Rhetoric at the Utah State International Women's Year Conference." Master's thesis, Brigham Young University, Provo, Utah, 2005.

Marsh, Meredith. "Striking the Balance: Finding a Place for New Urbanism on Main Street." Master's thesis, University of Pennsylvania, Philadelphia, 2009.

Mayer, Justin J. "Historical Memory of Mount Rushmore." Master's thesis, University of North Dakota, Grand Forks, 2010.

Reeder, Jennifer. "'To Do Something Extraordinary': Mormon Women and the Creation of a Usable Past." PhD diss., George Mason University, Fairfax, Virginia, 2013.

Ryan, John Michael. "Easton: A 21st Century (R)evolution in Consumption, Community, Urbanism, and Space." Master's thesis, University of Maryland, College Park, 2005.

Scolari, Paul. "Indian Warriors and Pioneer Mothers: American Identity and the Closing of the Frontier in Public Monuments, 1890–1930." PhD diss., University of Pittsburgh, Pennsylvania, 2005.

Seefeldt, W. Douglas. "Constructing Western Pasts: Place and Public Memory in the Twentieth-Century American West." PhD diss., Arizona State University, Tempe, 2001.

Swain, Joseph Benjamin Norris. "Claims to History: Commemorating Progress in Oklahoma Territory, 1989–2007." PhD diss., University of Oklahoma, Norman, 2008.

INDEX

References to illustrations appear in italic type.